Call Center
Operations Management
Handbook and Study Guide
Version 2.1

Brad Cleveland and Debbie Harne
Editors

Part of ICMI's Handbook/Study Guide Series

Published by:

Call Center Press

A Division of ICMI, Inc.

Post Office Box 6177

Annapolis, Maryland 21401 USA

Copyright 2003, 2004 by ICMI, Inc.

Printed in the United States of America

ISBN 0-9709507-5-6

Call Center
Operations Management
Handbook and Study Guide
Version 2.1

Brad Cleveland and Debbie Harne
Editors

Part of ICMI's Handbook/Study Guide Series

Call Center Press
A Division of ICMI, Inc.

Acknowledgements

The publications in this series are the result of a lot of hard work on the part of many people. We would like to thank the following individuals for their contributions:

Gerry Barber
Jean Bave-Kerwin
Michael Blair
Lori Bocklund
Henry Dortmans
Mike Dunne
Rebecca Gibson
John Goodman
Cindy Grimm
Linda Harden
Susan Hash
Cheryl Helm
Ellen Herndon
Ted Hopton
Betty Layfield
Jill Leigh
Greg Levin
Don McCain
Teresa Metzler
Jay Minnucci
Tim Montgomery
Rose Polchin
Paul Pope
Laurie Solomon
Wanda Sitzer

Without their hard work, dedication and talents, this project would not have been possible!

Brad Cleveland and Debbie Harne
Editors

To Sophia, may the little things in life continue to bring you joy.

Debbie Harne

To Kirsten, thank you for your unfailing love and support.
And to Grace Elizabeth Cleveland (born August 2002); Grace means God's love, and you truly are!

Brad Cleveland

Call Center
Operations Management
Handbook and Study Guide
Version 2.1

Brad Cleveland and Debbie Harne
Editors

Part of ICMI's Handbook/Study Guide Series

Contents

Introduction

Operations Management

Thank you for purchasing this publication – we hope it provides you with solid information that helps you advance your organization and your career! Although designed to stand alone, it is one of an integrated, four-part series, which includes:

- Call Center People Management Handbook and Study Guide
- Call Center Operations Management Handbook and Study Guide
- Call Center Customer Relationship Management Handbook and Study Guide
- Call Center Leadership and Business Management Handbook and Study Guide

The series was originally developed to prepare call center professionals for CIAC Certification assessments (and it follows the CIAC competency model and format, providing 100 percent coverage of CIAC competencies for both strategic and operational levels). However, many people have told us they are using the guides for internal training programs, team meetings and general reference. Content is sliced into digestible servings of information that lend themselves to these uses.

If you have received training from ICMI in the past, you will see some familiar diagrams and explanations. We have compiled information from ICMI courses, books and *Call Center Management Review* to develop an effective resource. We encourage you to be creative so you get the most out of this material.

However you plan to use the series, we hope it will also serve as an introduction (or re-introduction) to Incoming Calls Management Institute (ICMI) and the many content areas in which we can provide training and consulting services. We've included a summary of ICMI's products and services, but be sure to visit www.incoming.com for the latest offerings.

If we can assist you in any way, please let us know. We welcome your comments, feedback and questions, so let us know how we can help you.

Best wishes,

Brad Cleveland
President and CEO
ICMI, Inc.
bradc@incoming.com

Debbie Harne
Director, Educational Services
ICMI, Inc.
debbieh@incoming.com

If You Are Pursuing Certification

Operations Management

If you are pursuing CIAC certification, congratulations on your decision to increase your skills and knowledge in the area of Operations Management. As you prepare for CIAC assessments, you will learn valuable information to help you succeed in your profession.

We have worked hard to provide you with a handbook/study guide that is clear, concise and complete. Since each of us has a different set of past experiences and training, there will be some topics that you know well and others with which you may be unfamiliar. This guide is intended to meet a variety of needs by providing summary review information, as well as reference lists for further study. We encourage you to use it in whatever way works best for you. (Please remember that all material is either owned and copyrighted to ICMI or has been used with permission and noted as such; any reproduction of this material by any means is strictly prohibited.)

The remainder of this section includes the following:

ICMI's Role with the Call Center Industry Advisory Council (CIAC)

Incoming Calls Management Institute (ICMI) is an independent think tank and membership organization that specializes in call center management research, education, publications and consulting. While ICMI co-founded the CIAC in 1997, the CIAC is now a nonprofit organization consisting of an elected body to represent the industry in certification matters. ICMI is independent of the CIAC and does not control the quality or administration of the CIAC certification process.

CIAC Certification Options – Strategic vs. Operational

The CIAC certification assessments are delivered at both the operational and strategic levels:

- Managers with tactical, day-to-day operational responsibilities will generally choose to take the operational level exams, and are certified with the CIAC Certified Operations Manager (CCOM) designation. The operational role competencies are also applicable to individuals pursuing certification as a CIAC Certified Management Apprentice (CCMA).

- Managers with higher-level, strategic responsibilities will generally choose to take the strategic level exams, and are certified with the CIAC Certified Strategic Leader (CCSL) designation. The strategic role competencies are also applicable to individuals pursuing certification as a CIAC Certified Management Consultant (CCMC).

This handbook/study guide is designed to prepare you for either the operational (CCOM or CCMA) or strategic (CCSL or CCMC) level of certification. If you are pursuing operational level certification, you can skip over the topics labeled strategic. If you are pursuing strategic level certification, you will need to be knowledgeable in all areas of the study guide. For each certification level, we have included an outline of the competencies and the contents of this guide. The strategic outline begins on page 5; the operational outline begins on page 9.

Note: In many call centers, the line between what is strategic and what is operational is becoming increasingly blurry as distinctions between job roles fade. In short, we encourage managers in operational roles to also acquire an understanding of strategic issues.

How to Get the Most From Your Handbook/Study Guide

To get the most out of this guide, we'd like to explain how it works. In the pages that follow, you will find the CIAC Operations Management competency outlines, as well as information on ICMI services. We hope these assist you in understanding CIAC certification and the ways in which ICMI can support you in achieving your certification goals.

The CIAC Operations Management competency outlines provide the competencies and where they are covered in this study guide. We have carefully structured each section to cover the required material in the most logical manner. The material is presented in a building-block fashion for review purposes, and does not always flow in the same order as the competency model.

Sections three through seven include the content for the assessment. Each section is divided into topics that are organized as follows:

- Subject
- Key Points
- Explanation
- Exercise (in the back of each section)
- References for further study (in the back of each section)

This structure is designed to give you the flexibility to spend as much or as little time studying each topic as you require. The boxes on the top right of each topic are available for you to perform a self-assessment. Read through the key points to determine if your understanding of the material is:

1 unfamiliar territory, more time is needed here
2 pretty good, but worth reviewing
3 excellent

You can then review your self-assessment to focus your study time in the areas that need it the most. To complete a self-assessment of all topics at once, see page 11 of this introduction.

We've provided article reprints and other materials including a comprehensive glossary in sections eight and nine. Each section provides references for further study. These are intended to give you more detailed information on areas that you may have limited knowledge. We hope you'll continue to use this material for ongoing self-development.

The goals of the *Call Center Operations Management Handbook and Study Guide* are:

- Increase learners' knowledge and skills regarding operations management in call centers

- Prepare candidates to pass the CIAC certification knowledge assessment for Module Two, Operations Management

The learning objectives of the *Call Center Operations Management Handbook and Study Guide* include the ability of the learner to:

1. Recognize, identify, discuss, and/or list key operations management concepts, principles, and processes related to:
   - Service level/response time
   - Key performance indicators
   - Forecasting and scheduling
   - Call center technology
   - Facilities and disaster recovery

2. Apply key operations management concepts, principles, and processes to call center situations

Assessment Information

CIAC certification exams assess knowledge, skills and abilities in each competency domain. Candidates demonstrate role-specific knowledge and skills, and the application of these on the job through an objective assessment and work products.

This guide is intended to prepare you for the objective assessment. The objective assessment is composed entirely of multiple-choice questions. Some questions simply involve selecting from a list of possibilities to determine the correct answer, to the stated question. Other questions may require you to select the choice that is not true or the exception, select the choice that is the best or least correct answer, or select all of the correct answers from a list of choices. Multiple-choice questions also are included that require the interpretation of tables, charts or scenarios to determine the correct answer.

Your handbook/study guide includes exercises in many different formats, such as fill in the blank, multiple choice, and matching, with the answers to the exercises included in Section 10. These exercises are intended to help you determine your readiness to take the CIAC exam.

The specific questions on the CIAC assessments have been developed and validated by a diverse team of industry professionals. As an independent organization, ICMI provides educational services for the assessments, but is not responsible for the quality of the test questions.

For more information:

- See the CIAC Certification Handbook in Section 11
- See www.ciac-cert.org
- See www.incoming.com

The CIAC Operations Management Competency Outline – Strategic Level

This document maps the content of this study guide with CIAC operations management competencies. In order to produce a study guide that is easy to use and understand, we have presented the contents of each section in building-block fashion. Therefore, contents may be presented in a different order than in the competency list. We have taken care to ensure that all content is covered in each section, so that you can be confident in your preparation for the test at the strategic level.

This guide covers requirements for certification at both the strategic and operational levels. If you are studying for certification at the strategic level, you will need to be knowledgeable in all areas of the guide. The "Strategic" designation of some topics within each content section of the guide indicates that managers pursuing certification at the operational level do not need to be familiar with this material.

Study Guide Contents	Operations Management Competencies – Strategic Level
	A. Establish, Achieve, and Maintain Service Level and Quality Goals

Service Level/Response Time
Section 3
	1. Negotiate, establish, and maintain internal and external service level agreements with business units and service providers that have an impact on the center's performance
	  • Develop and implement a plan to meet service level agreements
	  • Create a service provider assessment instrument to manage service level agreements
	  • Utilize a service provider assessment instrument to manage vendors
	2. Establish service level, response time, and quality goals
	  • Create a plan to meet service level, response time, and quality goals
	  • Maintain agreed service level and quality standards

Key Performance Indicators
Section 4
	3. Establish key performance indicators that enable the center to meet customer requirements
	  • Demonstrate working knowledge of key performance indicators (not all inclusive):
	    Average Call Value
	    Customer Satisfaction
	    Service Level
	    Percent Abandoned
	    Cost Per Call
	    Errors and Rework/First Call Resolution
	    Forecasted Call Load vs. Actual
	    Scheduled Staff to Actual
	    Adherence to Schedule

Section 2

Key Performance Indicators Section 4 *(continued)*	*Average Handling Time* *Productive vs. Non-Productive* *Average Speed of Answer (ASA)* *Occupancy* • Develop and utilize a mechanism to track and report key performance indicators data • Manage the center in adherence with established key performance indicators • Identify obstacles to meeting key performance indicator targets; enact a resolution that meets customer requirements and supports the center's business objectives
Forecasting and Scheduling Section 5	4. Forecast workload using statistical techniques • Optimize staff and schedule requirements • Create and implement a plan to ensure the center's contact activities meet requirements 5. Schedule staff to forecasted workload • Assure adherence to schedule 6. Identify and apply principles that enable continuous quality assurance and process improvement
	B. Align Technologies and Processes to Maximize Service Delivery
Call Center Technology Section 6	1. Align technology with business objectives, application need(s), and financial considerations • Maximize the center's investment in technology • Manage the implementation of technology • Ensure technology is implemented with minimal negative impact 2. Identify and address issues related to single versus virtual-site environments (multi-site, remote agents, etc.) 3. Identify and manage key customer related processes 4. Align technology, processes and customer requirements to enhance service and reduce cost 5. Evaluate the applicability of new and emerging technology to enable enhanced customer service and better support business objectives • Develop a business case to evaluate new and emerging technology • Ensure successful integration of new technology with legacy systems • Leverage system integration opportunities to maximize service delivery 6. Formulate and execute a call distribution strategy • Develop a call distribution rationale

	C. Select and Design Site; Manage the Center Work Environment

Facilities and Disaster Recovery
 	
Section 7
	1. Apply the principles of site selection and design
	  • Develop site selection criteria based on the organization's business objectives
	2. Select a site based on agreed selection criteria and approved business case
	  • Develop a site selection business case that aligns with strategic objectives
	3. Assess floor plan design options
	  • Select an optimal floor plan design
	4. Develop a disaster recovery strategy and contingency plan
	  • Test and execute a disaster recovery strategy
	  • Implement a contingency plan
	5. Maintain a healthy, safe, and secure work environment
	  • Assess and address workplace ergonomic issues and considerations
	  • Assure adherence to ergonomic requirements
	  • Monitor the safety and security of the work environment
	  • Assure staff adherence to applicable health and safety policy and regulations
	6. Assure adherence to applicable disability policy and regulations

The CIAC Operations Management Competency Outline – Operational Level

This document maps the content of this study guide with CIAC operations management competencies at the operational level. In order to produce a study guide that is easy to use and understand, we have presented the contents of each section in building-block fashion. Therefore, contents may be presented in a different order than in the competency list. We have taken care to ensure that all content is covered in each section, so that you can be confident in your preparation for the test.

This guide covers requirements for certification at both the strategic and operational levels. If you are studying for certification at the operational level, you will need to be knowledgeable in the areas of the guide that are NOT designated as "Strategic."

Study Guide Contents	Operations Management Competencies – Operational Level
	A. Establish, Achieve, and Maintain Service Level and Quality Objectives
Service Level/Response Time Section 3	1. Develop and implement a plan to meet service level agreements • Utilize a service provider assessment instrument to manage vendors 2. Create and manage a plan to meet service level, response time, and quality goals • Maintain service to agreed performance levels and quality standards
Key Performance Indicators Section 4	3. Demonstrate working knowledge of key performance indicators (not all inclusive): *Average Call Value* *Customer Satisfaction* *Service Level* *Percent Abandoned* *Cost Per Call* *Errors and Rework/First Call Resolution* *Forecasted Call Load vs. Actual* *Scheduled Staff to Actual* *Adherence to Schedule* *Average Handling Time* *Productive vs. Non-Productive* *Average Speed of Answer (ASA)* *Occupancy* 4. Develop and utilize a mechanism to track and report key performance indicator data • Manage the center in adherence with established key performance indicators • Identify obstacles to meeting key performance indicator targets; enact a resolution that meets customer requirements and supports the center's business objectives

Forecasting and Scheduling Section 5	5. Forecast workload using statistical techniques • Optimize staff and schedule requirements • Create and implement a plan to ensure the center's contact activities meet requirements 6. Schedule staff to forecasted workload • Assure adherence to schedule 7. Identify and apply principles that enable continuous quality assurance and process improvement
	B. Align Technologies and Processes to Maximize Service Delivery
Call Center Technology Section 6	1. Maximize the center's investment in technology • Implement technology with minimal negative impact • Ensure successful integration of new technology with legacy systems • Leverage system integration opportunities to enhance service delivery 2. Identify and manage key customer-related processes 3. Execute a call distribution strategy • Develop a call distribution rationale
	C. Manage the Center Work Environment
Facilities and Disaster Recovery Section 7	1. Test and execute a disaster recovery strategy • Implement a contingency plan 2. Maintain a healthy, safe, and secure work environment • Assess and address workplace ergonomic issues • Assure adherence to ergonomic requirements • Monitor the safety and security of the work environment • Assure staff adherence to applicable health and safety policy and regulations 3. Assure adherence to applicable disability policy and regulations

Pre/Post Self-Assessment for Call Center Operations Management Study Guide

The purpose of this self-assessment tool is to provide you with an opportunity to identify areas where you are confident in your knowledge and experience, and areas where you may need to do some additional study or receive additional training.

First, go through the pre-assessment and circle your perceived level of knowledge for each area. As you study the guide, focus on the areas where you are not satisfied with your current knowledge level.

Following your study, conduct a post-assessment. For each area, note the shift in your ratings. Place a check (√) by the content areas you in which want to pursue more in-depth training. ICMI offers training and further resources on most of these topics. For further information, on ICMI's Operations Management training, see page 19.

Use the following scale to indicate your level of knowledge in the areas described.

1 = Unfamiliar territory, more time is needed here

2 = Pretty good, but worth reviewing

3 = Excellent

	Pre-Assessment			Post Assessment			√ Training
Service Level/Response Time, Section 3							
Establishing and Using Service Level and Response Time Objectives							
1. Establishing a Customer Access Strategy [Strategic]	①￪	2	3	1	2	3	
2. Definitions and Use of Service Level, Response Time and Quality	1	2	3	1	2	3	
3. Alternative Service Level Calculations	①	2	3	1	2	3	
4. Variations of Response Time	①	2	3	1	2	3	
5. Typical Timeframes for Service Level and Response Time Planning	①	2	3	1	2	3	
6. Choosing Service Level and Response Time Objectives	①	2	3	1	2	3	
Planning and Managing Service Level and Quality							
7. Traffic Arrival Types: Random, Smooth and Peaked	①	2	3	1	2	3	
8. Visible vs. Invisible Queue	①	2	3	1	2	3	
9. Factors Affecting Caller Tolerance	①	2	3	1	2	3	
10. The Planning and Management Process	①	2	3	1	2	3	
11. Quality in the Call Center Environment	1	②	3	1	2	3	

	Pre-Assessment				Post Assessment				√ Training
Real-Time Management									
12. Interpreting Real-Time Information	①	2	3		1	2	3		
13. Alternatives for Providing Real-Time Information	①	2	3		1	2	3		
14. Setting Real-Time Thresholds	1	②	3		1	2	3		
15. Informational and Delay Announcements	①	2	3		1	2	3		
16. Establishing and Using Real-Time Tactics	①	2	3		1	2	3		
Establishing and Managing Service Level Agreements									
17. Definition and Use of Service Level Agreements	①	2	3		1	2	3		
18. Establishing and Managing Service Level Agreements	①	2	3		1	2	3		
Key Performance Indicators, Section 4									
Managing and Reporting Key Performance Indicators									
1. Identifying Key Performance Indicators	①	2	3		1	2	3		
2. Call (Contact) Quality	1	②	3		1	2	3		
3. First-Call Resolution/Errors and Rework	①	2	3		1	2	3		
4. Service Level and Response Time	1	②	3		1	2	3		
5. Average Speed of Answer	1	②	3		1	2	3		
6. Abandoned and Blocked Calls	①	2	3		1	2	3		
7. Forecasted Call Load vs. Actual	1	②	3		1	2	3		
8. Scheduled Staff to Actual	1	②	3		1	2	3		
9. Adherence to Schedule	1	②	3		1	2	3		
10. Average Handling Time (AHT)	①	2	3		1	2	3		
11. Occupancy and Productive/Nonproductive	①	2	3		1	2	3		
12. Cost per Call (Cost per Contact)	①	2	3		1	2	3		
13. Average Call Value	①	2	3		1	2	3		
14. Revenue	①	2	3		1	2	3		
15. Budget/Cost Objectives	①	2	3		1	2	3		
16. Objectives for Outbound	①	2	3		1	2	3		
17. Customer Satisfaction	1	②	3		1	2	3		
18. Employee Satisfaction	1	②	3		1	2	3		
19. Turnover	1	②	3		1	2	3		
20. Overall Call Center ROI	①	2	3		1	2	3		

	Pre-Assessment			Post-Assessment			√ Training
Resolving Problems in Meeting Key Performance Indicators							
21. KPIs as Interrelated Outcomes [Strategic]	(1)	2	3	1	2	3	
22. How KPIs Relate to Customer Expectations [Strategic]	(1)	2	3	1	2	3	
Forecasting and Scheduling, Section 5							
Forecasting Definitions, Principles and Methodologies							
1. Key Forecasting Definitions	(1)	2	3	1	2	3	
2. Forecasting Principles and Methodologies	(1)	2	3	1	2	3	
3. Dominant Call Patterns	(1)	2	3	1	2	3	
4. Breaking Down a Time Series Forecast	(1)	2	3	1	2	3	
5. Incorporating Average Handling Time	(1)	2	3	1	2	3	
6. Blending in Judgment	(1)	2	3	1	2	3	
Staffing Calculations and Queue Dynamics							
7. Queuing Formulas and Simulation	(1)	2	3	1	2	3	
8. Calculating Base Staff for Service Level Contacts	(1)	2	3	1	2	3	
9. The Impact of Service Level on Longest Wait	(1)	2	3	1	2	3	
10. Calculating Trunks	(1)	2	3	1	2	3	
11. Immutable Laws of Call Centers	(1)	2	3	1	2	3	
12. The Implications of Agent Group Structure	(1)	2	3	1	2	3	
13. The Cost of Delay	(1)	2	3	1	2	3	
14. Long Calls	(1)	2	3	1	2	3	
15. Skills-Based Routing	(1)	2	3	1	2	3	
16. Peaked Traffic	(1)	2	3	1	2	3	
17. Calculating Base Staff for Response Time Contacts	(1)	2	3	1	2	3	
18. Outbound Contacts	(1)	2	3	1	2	3	
Scheduling Principles and Methodologies							
19. Rostered Staff Factor (Shrinkage)	(1)	2	3	1	2	3	
20. Scheduling Considerations and Applications	(1)	2	3	1	2	3	
21. Full-Time Equivalents (FTEs)	(1)	2	3	1	2	3	
22. Managing Schedule Adherence	(1)	2	3	1	2	3	

	Pre-Assessment				Post Assessment				√ Training
Managing and Improving Quality									
23. The Components of a Quality Contact/Costs of Poor Quality	1	2	3		1	2	3		
24. A Process for Root-Cause Analysis	1	2	3		1	2	3		
Call Center Technology, Section 6									
Understanding Today's Environment									
1. Today's Business Drivers	1	2	3		1	2	3		
2. Key Technology Trends	1	2	3		1	2	3		
Identifying, Aligning and Leveraging Existing and Emerging Technologies and Applications									
3. ACD Systems	1	2	3		1	2	3		
4. Networks	1	2	3		1	2	3		
5. IVR/Voice Processing Capabilities	1	2	3		1	2	3		
6. Workforce Management Systems	1	2	3		1	2	3		
7. Quality Monitoring/Recording Systems	1	2	3		1	2	3		
8. Desktop/Agent System Interface	1	2	3		1	2	3		
9. Dialers	1	2	3		1	2	3		
10. Fax Servers	1	2	3		1	2	3		
11. Telecommuting Technologies	1	2	3		1	2	3		
12. CTI Capabilities	1	2	3		1	2	3		
13. Email Response Management Systems	1	2	3		1	2	3		
14. Web Communication Channels	1	2	3		1	2	3		
15. Voice over IP	1	2	3		1	2	3		
16. Multimedia Routing and Queuing	1	2	3		1	2	3		
17. CRM Capabilities	1	2	3		1	2	3		
18. Technology Infrastructure Components	1	2	3		1	2	3		
Building a Technology Strategy and Managing New Implementations									
19. Creating an Enabling Technology Strategy [Strategic]	1	2	3		1	2	3		
20. Developing the Business Case	1	2	3		1	2	3		
21. Financial Methodologies	1	2	3		1	2	3		
22. Basic Project Management Principles	1	2	3		1	2	3		
23. Managing New Technology Implementations	1	2	3		1	2	3		

Facilities and Disaster Recovery, Section 7	Pre-Assessment			Post Assessment			√ Training
Site Selection Issues							
1. Site Selection Considerations [Strategic]	1	2	3	1	2	3	
2. Legislation Factors [Strategic]	1	2	3	1	2	3	
Floor Plan Design							
3. The Phases of Design [Strategic]	1	2	3	1	2	3	
4. Determining Space and Workstation Requirements [Strategic]	1	2	3	1	2	3	
5. Floor Plan Design [Strategic]	1	2	3	1	2	3	
Health, Safety and Security							
6. Identifying Health, Safety and Security Issues	1	2	3	1	2	3	
7. Lighting and Noise Considerations [Strategic]	1	2	3	1	2	3	
8. Individual Comfort and Protection	1	2	3	1	2	3	
Regulatory Requirements							
9. Primary OSHA Requirements (U.S.)	1	2	3	1	2	3	
10. Primary ADA Requirements (U.S.)	1	2	3	1	2	3	
11. Canadian Regulations	1	2	3	1	2	3	
Disaster Recovery							
12. Elements of Protection and Recovery	1	2	3	1	2	3	
13. What Disaster Plans Cover	1	2	3	1	2	3	
14. Calculating the Cost of Being Out of Business [Strategic]	1	2	3	1	2	3	

Frequently Asked Questions

What is CIAC certification?

The Call Center Industry Advisory Council (CIAC) is a nonprofit and independent organization established and funded to develop competencies and provide industry-standard certification for call center managers. Successful completion of CIAC certification means formal recognition of the individual's mastery of specified competencies and commitment to staying abreast of new developments in the profession.

CIAC Certification requires successful completion of the CIAC certification assessment process. There are four modules; each has its own test:

- People Management
- Operations Management
- Customer Relationship Management
- Leadership and Business Management

Tests are provided at regularly scheduled times and locations. See www.ciac-cert.org for a complete listing.

Why does ICMI support CIAC certification?

In recent years, a number of call center vendors have promoted their own versions of certification programs. Some of these programs have since come and gone, but ICMI has maintained from the beginning that there can be no valid certification program without a broadly-representative and recognized body overseeing the process. The CIAC is a nonprofit organization established by the industry to develop, administer and govern professional certification for the call center profession. It has broad support from end-users, consultants and suppliers, and will likely remain in favor with the industry as long as it remains unbiased, representative, open and tuned in to industry needs.

Are certain training classes required?

No. The CIAC does not provide educational services, but is instead committed to an "open-systems" approach whereby managers can acquire required competence through the combination of on-the-job experience, training courses and published materials they choose. This ensures that call center professionals are free to choose the best training programs and publications available as they build their knowledge and skills. And it enables experienced managers to avoid the expense and time involved in the prescribed training classes that are often necessary in other programs.

Do these handbooks/study guides replace ICMI seminars?

That depends on your objectives. The handbook/study guide series is designed to cover CIAC certification competencies. Each guide covers a significant range of material in a review fashion but does not replace the need for job experiences nor the formal training other ICMI courses provide. However, through a step-by-step review process, the guides enable managers with sufficient experiences or management training to identify areas that require further study, and they provide the essential information needed to fill in any gaps.

How else can ICMI help?

ICMI has developed innovative review courses and self-study resources for those who want an efficient review of the content areas addressed by CIAC competencies. In addition, ICMI's full range of call center management training and publications support specific content areas included in the CIAC competencies. See information on additional ICMI services, next page.

Where can I find more information?

- See the CIAC Certification Handbook in Section 11
- See www.ciac-cert.org
- See www.incoming.com

Additional ICMI Services

If you have chosen to pursue certification through the CIAC, ICMI is the authoritative source for the information and training you need for success. The CIAC is a nonprofit organization that administers certification but, by design, does not provide certification training. That enables you to choose the training alternatives you need and prefer.

That's where ICMI comes in. ICMI offers many choices, including:

Handbook/Study Guide Series

The ICMI handbook/study guide series, which this book is part of, includes four publications:

- *Call Center People Management Handbook and Study Guide*
- *Call Center Operations Management Handbook and Study Guide*
- *Call Center Customer Relationship Management Handbook and Study Guide*
- *Call Center Leadership and Business Management Handbook and Study Guide*

These guides provide a 100 percent comprehensive review of each module along with self-study tools to ensure you are prepared.

Foundational Seminars

ICMI's powerful instructor-led seminars are designed to provide a practical working knowledge of core call center management disciplines. As over 50,000 ICMI alumni from around the world will attest, these two-day courses offer an unmatched combination of content, support materials, expert facilitation and interaction. Current offerings include:

- *Essential Skills and Knowledge for Effective Incoming Call Center Management*
- *Results-Oriented Monitoring and Coaching for Improved Call Center Performance*
- *Understanding and Applying Today's Call Center Technologies*
- *Effective Leadership and Strategy for Senior Call Center Managers*
- *Workforce Management: The Basics and Beyond*

Web-Based or In-Person Study Courses

Perhaps you'd like to combine the power of self-study with personal guidance from call center experts. ICMI's CIAC study courses enable your entire management team to successfully prepare for certification. Through expert facilitation and focused study, your team will prepare for the assessment, and acquire the skills and knowledge you need to advance your call center's services. These courses can be delivered in traditional classroom style or, for organizations with geographically dispersed centers, over the Internet. Public seminars (Web-based and in-person) are also available. ICMI's handbook/study guide series is included with these courses.

Combination

Those who need preparation only in specific content areas can choose from ICMI's full range of Web seminars, books, papers, studies and other services. Consistency, quality and usability are trademarks of these services.

For more information, or help with planning your approach, contact us at icmi@incoming.com or 410-267-0700.

Service Level/Response Time

Operations Management

Section 3: Service Level/Response Time

Contents

[handwritten: 50% of questions 3, 4, 5]
[handwritten: 3 Q's Section 7]
[handwritten: 2 Q's Section 6]

1. Establishing a Customer Access Strategy
[Strategic] *[handwritten: Not Needed for Management Apprentice]*

Ready? | 1 | 2 | 3 |

Key Points

- A customer access strategy is a framework – a set of standards, guidelines and processes – defining the means by which customers are connected with resources capable of delivering the desired information and services.

- An effective customer access strategy includes the following components:

    - Customer segmentation
    - Major call types
    - Access channels
    - Service level and response time objectives
    - Hours of operation
    - Routing methodology
    - Person/technology resources required by contact
    - Knowledge bases
    - Tracking and integration

- As call center responsibilities increase, the meaning of what a call center is and does is expanding.

Explanation

A customer access strategy is a framework – a set of standards, guidelines and processes – defining the means by which customers are connected with resources capable of delivering the desired information and services. Establishing a customer access strategy is an important prerequisite to creating and managing service level and quality standards, and service level agreements. There are various terms that sometimes are used interchangeably with customer access strategy, including channel strategy, contact strategy and call center strategy.

Components of a Customer Access Strategy

An effective customer access strategy includes the following components:

- **Customer segmentation:** How customers and prospective customers are segmented, e.g., by geography, volume of business, or unique requirements.

Customer segmentation generally comes from the organization's marketing strategy.

- **Major call types:** This is not the channels used, but, instead, is the reasons for contacts between the organization and customers. General categories include placing orders, changing orders, checking account status and problem resolution.

- **Access channels:** This is a major area of development in call centers. Access channels include telephone, Web, fax, email, IVR, kiosk, handhelds, face-to-face service, and postal mail, as well as corresponding telephone numbers, Web URLs, email addresses, fax numbers and postal addresses.

- **Service level and response time objectives:** Essentially, how fast the organization intends to respond to customer contacts. (See Definitions and Use of Service Level, Response Time and Quality, this section.)

- **Hours of operation:** The days and hours the call center will be open for business.

- **Routing methodology:** How, by customer, type of contact and access channel, each contact will be routed and distributed. (Note, while these terms have inbound connotations they also apply to outbound; e.g., specifying the agent group or system through which contacts will be made.)

- **Person/technology resources required by contact:** The resources, including people, technologies and databases, required to provide callers with the information and assistance they need and the organization with the information it needs to track and manage customers and services. This aspect of strategy helps to guide hiring, training, technology deployment, database development and many other aspects of operations.

- **Knowledge bases:** The information systems used to capture, store and process information on customers, products and services.

- **Tracking and integration:** The methods/systems required to capture information on each customer interaction, and define how that data will be used to strengthen customer profiles, identify trends and improve products and services.

Drivers of Customer Access Strategy

The need for a cohesive, up-to-date customer access strategy is driven by a number of factors:

- Multiple access methods are evolving.

- Caller tolerance is evolving rapidly, and customers are increasingly savvy and well-informed. Being "easy to do business with" is a primary driver of

customer satisfaction.

- Services are becoming more complicated from both the customer's and organization's perspective.

- With multiple technology and process "owners" across the organization, ensuring a common customer focus is critical.

From a customer's perspective, an effective customer access strategy will result in simplified access, consistent services, ease of use and a high degree of convenience and satisfaction. From the organization's perspective, the benefits translate into lower overall costs, increased capacity, higher customer retention, and a workable framework that guides ongoing developments.

Developing a sound customer access strategy requires leadership, persistence, participation from across the organization, and cross-functional collaboration and cooperation. It is not something that can be developed in a vacuum; call center strategy cannot develop independent of broader corporate strategy.

What Is a Call Center?

Given the growing responsibilities of call centers, along with proliferating channels of contact, a fundamental and frequently asked question today is: What is a call center? Incoming Calls Management Institute defines a call center (a.k.a. contact center, interaction center) as:

> *A coordinated system of people, processes, technologies and strategies that effectively integrates organizational resources and multiple channels of communication to enable customer interactions that create value for customers and the organization.*

Call centers exist in a "demand-chasing" environment. At virtually any moment in time, there are either more contacts to be handled than there are resources to handle them, or there are more resources than there are contacts to be handled. Demand must be "chased" with the supply of call center resources.

Call centers don't exist simply because telephones, toll-free service, ACDs or email servers were invented. They exist because there is ongoing, variable demand for services and they are extremely effective at meeting those demands. In other words, call centers aren't just about handling telephone calls, email messages or Internet transactions. Rather, *they are focused on aligning and matching organizational resources with customer demands through any channel of communication.*

(For a complete discussion of strategy, see ICMI's *Call Center Leadership and Business Management Handbook and Study Guide*.)

2. Definitions and Use of Service Level, Response Time and Quality

Ready? | 1 | 2 | 3 |

Key Points

- Service level and response time objectives are concrete targets for planning and budgeting.

- For planning and management purposes, all contacts must be categorized into either service level or response time buckets:

  1. Contacts that must be handled when they arrive are measured by service level. Service level is "X percent of contacts answered in Y seconds."

  2. Contacts that can be handled at a later time are measured by response time. Response time is "100 percent of contacts handled within N days/hours/minutes."

- Service level/response time and quality work together, and are not at odds.

Explanation

The principle of service level (sometimes generally referred to as "accessibility") is at the heart of effective call center management. Without service level objectives, answers to many important questions would be left to chance, e.g., How accessible is the call center? How many staff do you need? How do you compare to the competition? Are you prepared to handle the response to marketing campaigns? How busy are your agents going to be? What are your costs going to be?

Service level and response time objectives tie the resources you need to the results you want to achieve. They measure how well you are getting the transactions "in the door" and to agents so that you can get on with the business at hand, and they are stable, concrete targets for planning and budgeting.

Definition of Service Level

Service level is defined specifically as: "X percent of contacts answered in Y seconds," e.g., 90 percent answered in 20 seconds.

Service level is NOT:

Service level is the most possible measurement

- Average speed of answer, although average speed of answer is a related measure that is derived from the same set of data. (See Average Speed of Answer, Section 4.)

- X percent of all calls answered, which is the inverse of abandonment. For example, a 97 percent answer rate would inherently mean a 3 percent abandonment rate. (See Abandoned and Blocked Calls, Section 4.)

- Longest delayed call. (See The Impact of Service Level on Longest Wait, Section 5.)

Definition of Response Time

Response time is the equivalent of service level for transactions that don't have to be handled the moment they arrive. Response time is defined as "100 percent of contacts handled within N days/hours/minutes," e.g., all email will be handled within four hours or all faxes will be responded to within 24 hours.

Categorization of Contacts

Contacts that must be handled when they arrive require a service level objective, and those that can be handled at a later time require a response time objective:

	Use Service Level	Use Response Time
Inbound calls	X	
Outbound calls		X
Email		X
Text chat	X	
Web "call me back now"	X	
Web "call me back later"		X
Web call through	X	
Fax		X
Postal Mail		X

The Differences Between Service Level and Response Time

In application and function, service level and response time are similar. Both provide the necessary linkage between base staff required and the results you would like to achieve. However, there are important differences between service level and response time. Most notably, base staff calculations are different. Service level is used in situations with randomly arriving traffic, and requires Erlang C or computer simulation. (See Calculating Base Staff for Service Level

Section 3

Contacts, Section 5.) Response time contacts can be held for later processing, and thus can rely on more traditional methods of industrial planning. (See Calculating Base Staff for Response Time Contacts, Section 5.)

When Response Time Becomes Service Level

There is a point at which response time objectives are so quick that they belong in the service level category. For example, to raise the bar of customer service, an organization may decide to improve response time objectives for customer email from same-day or next-day response to, say, within 15 minutes. Most queuing experts agree that with an objective of less than an hour, base staff requirements should be calculated using either Erlang C or computer simulation programs that account for random contact arrival.

Some assumptions and definitions must also change. Service level, when applied to telephone calls, is based on when the calls reach agents and the conversations begin. But in the case of email, customer perceptions are geared around when they receive the responses. If you want to respond to email messages within 15 minutes and they require an average five minutes of handling time, they must reach agents 10 minutes after customers send them. That becomes the threshold for which staffing requirements must be calculated.

Example Objectives

Example service level objectives:

General Comparisons	Service Levels (X percent/Y seconds)*
Emergency Services (e.g., 911 call centers)	100/0
SL objectives that are comparatively "high"	90/20, 85/15
SL objectives that are comparatively "moderate"	80/20, 90/60
SL objectives that are comparatively "modest"	90/120, 80/300

* from industry surveys

Example response time objectives:

Type of Transaction	Low end of range*	High end of range*
Customer email	48 to 72 hours	Less than one hour
Fax	Three days	Three hours
Voicemail	Next day	Within one hour
Letter by mail	One week	Same day

* from industry surveys

Section 3
Service Level/Response Time

must know

Incoming Calls
Management Institute
Advancing the Call Center Profession Worldwide

Section 3

When establishing and assessing either service level or response time objectives, remember that it's not just how high your overall stated objectives are, but how consistently you hit them throughout the day.

Service Level and Quality Work Together

Obviously, you can achieve your service level objectives, and still be creating waste, extra work and low quality. But long term, service level and quality work together. Accessibility is an enabler – it means that contacts are getting in and being answered/handled so that the call center can accomplish its mission. When quality is poor, things such as repeat calls, unnecessary service calls, escalation of calls and complaints to higher management, and callbacks will drive service level down even more. Service level and quality are complementary – an important theme that will be covered in more detail later in this section, and in Section 5.

Why Service Level?

Why service level and not percent answered, percent abandoned, average speed of answer or other alternatives? The answer is "X percent answered in Y seconds" gives the clearest indication of what callers experience when they attempt to reach the call center. You know exactly what happens to the percentage of callers you define. Service level is the most stable measurement of the queue.

Average speed of answer (ASA) is a close cousin of service level and is derived from the same set of data. But a big problem with ASA is that it is often misinterpreted. Most of us assume that the average lies somewhere in the middle of a set of data, or that average represents a "typical experience." Not so with ASA! It is mathematically correct, but does not represent what happens to individual callers.

Most callers get connected to a rep much quicker than the average, but some wait far beyond the average. For example, with an average speed of answer at 15 seconds, about 70 percent of callers get answered immediately, but a small percent of callers will wait three or four minutes in queue. Many people forget that reality when they look at ASA. ASA has its uses (e.g., in calculating trunk load), so don't throw it out the window. But service level is a more reliable and more telling measure of what callers experience.

What about abandoned calls? Looking solely at abandonment rates as a measure of whether staffing levels were appropriate can be highly misleading. We aren't suggesting that you ignore abandonment. A high abandonment is probably a symptom of staffing problems. But a low abandonment doesn't necessarily mean everything is fine.

Further, if abandonment is beyond acceptable, what are you going to do? You are going to look at when it's out of whack, and why. You will likely run smack into a low service level. When service level is appropriate, abandonment tends to take care of itself.

A good question to ask for any service level is, "What happens to the calls that don't get answered in Y seconds?" Most Erlang C and computer simulation software programs will

---

(continued, next page)

calculate the answers to that and other questions. For a service level of 80 percent answered in 20 seconds, you will discover that about 30 percent of your callers end up in queue, that the longest wait will be around three minutes, and that average speed of answer will be around 10 to 15 seconds.

All of this brings up an important point: Different callers have different experiences with your call center, even if they are part of the same set of data measured by service level, ASA and other reports. Why? Random call arrival! Because of this reality, you will need an understanding of what happens to different callers. At a high level, service level is the single best measure of these experiences.

Excerpt from *Call Center Management on Fast Forward: Succeeding In Today's Dynamic Inbound Environment* by Brad Cleveland and Julia Mayben, Call Center Press, 1999.

3. Alternative Service Level Calculations

Ready? | 1 | 2 | 3 |

Key Points

There are a number of alternative methods your call center technology may use to calculate service level. Four of the most common include:

1. (Calls answered in Y seconds + calls abandoned in Y seconds) ÷ (total calls answered + total calls abandoned) $201+5 \div 243+11 = 206 \div 254$ 8190

2. Calls answered in Y seconds ÷ total calls answered 82.7 8390 $201 \div 243$

3. Calls answered in Y seconds ÷ (total calls answered + total calls abandoned) $201 \div (243+11 = 201 \div 254 = 7990$

4. Calls answered in Y seconds ÷ (total calls answered + calls abandoned after Y seconds)

$201 \div 243 + 6 = 201 \div 249 = 8190$

Explanation

There are a number of alternative methods your call center technology may use to calculate service level. With some systems, you can specify the calculation you prefer. In any case, you need to know which calculation is being used since each one handles abandoned calls differently. Here are the most common formulas for calculating service level:

1. (Calls answered in Y seconds + calls abandoned in Y seconds) ÷ (total calls answered + total calls abandoned): For most situations, we prefer this alternative because the calculation includes all of the traffic received by the automatic call distributor (ACD). Calls that abandon before the objective positively affect service level. This calculation provides a complete picture of what is happening since it takes all calls into consideration. (See ACD Systems, Section 6.)

2. Calls answered in Y seconds ÷ total calls answered: This alternative only considers answered calls, and therefore is not a good reflection of all activity. Abandonment is entirely ignored. We do not recommend this calculation.

3. Calls answered in Y seconds ÷ (total calls answered + total calls abandoned): This alternative tends to be the least popular among call center managers because all calls that abandon negatively affect service level, even those that abandon before the objective. Canada-based consultant Cheryl Odee

Helm, who has made call center reporting a focus of her practice, recommends that this measure may be appropriate in situations where calls enter a queue after they hear a delay announcement. She does not recommend this calculation in settings where callers enter a queue before they hear the announcement.

4. Calls answered in Y seconds ÷ (total calls answered + calls abandoned after Y seconds): With this calculation, abandoned calls only impact service level negatively if they happen after the Y seconds specified. Calls that abandon before the objective do not affect service level. Consequently, this is a way to avoid getting "penalized" by callers who abandon quickly without ignoring abandoned calls altogether. This is an acceptable approach.

Blocked Calls

When calls are blocked (receive busy signals), they are generally not included in service level reports. Since those calls would have increased workload had they been handled, busies have the effect of making service level reports look better than they should. (See Abandoned and Blocked Calls, Section 4.)

4. Variations of Response Time

Ready? | 1 | 2 | 3 |

Key Points

- There are three types of "response" including:
  - Reply
  - Response — *Staffing to this number*
  - Resolution

- There are two types of response time objectives:
  - Scheduled
  - Rolling

Explanation

Three Types of "Response"

The three types of response include:

- **Automated reply:** This is a system-generated response that automatically sends a reply to the customer acknowledging that the email they sent was received and informing them of when to expect a response. This establishes appropriate expectations and minimizes telephone calls or other additional contacts inquiring about the status of the original message.

- **Response:** This refers to the response the customer receives when the transaction is actually handled by the call center. The time that elapses between the customer's original message and the call center's response is measured as "response time."

- **Resolution:** This is a measure of when the problem or issue is actually resolved and is used in environments where the call center's initial response may not fully resolve the issue. For example, in a technical support environment additional research may be necessary; the problem is "resolved" when the matter is handled to completion and the "trouble ticket" is closed.

Two Types of Response Time

There are two types of response time, scheduled and rolling.

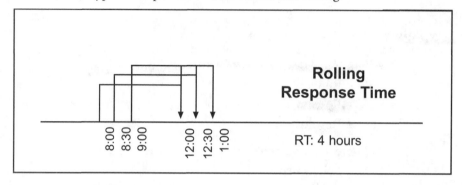

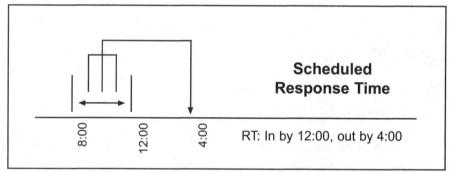

Scheduled response time, like a dry-cleaning service, is geared around blocks of time. For example, you may commit to handle all messages received up to noon by 5 p.m., and to respond to messages received between noon and 5 p.m. by 10 a.m. the next morning.

Rolling response time is hinged on the specific times each message arrives. For example, if you establish a four-hour response time, a customer who sends a message at 9:03 a.m. should get a response by 1:03 p.m., and one who sends a message at 9:12 a.m. should receive a response by 1:12 p.m.

Today, many call centers are establishing straightforward, 24-hour scheduled response time objectives, but some in more competitive environments are targeting rolling response times of four hours or even one hour or less. A small but growing number of call centers are handling email messages like telephone calls, handling them as they arrive or soon thereafter, in which case, service level rather than response time objectives apply.

Section 3
Service Level/Response Time

5. Typical Timeframes for Service Level and Response Time Planning

Ready? 1 | 2 | 3

Key Points

- A prerequisite to accurate forecasting and staffing is to establish planning timeframes that are best-suited to the environment.

- Long-term forecasts of one year or more are used for creating annual budgets and long-term hiring plans.

- Shorter term forecasts are used for organizing schedules and adjusting plans based on current conditions.

- For most inbound call centers, staffing calculations in half-hour increments are appropriate. However, hour increments may be more appropriate for environments handling long calls, and five-to-10-minute increments are necessary for peaked traffic.

Explanation

Forecasting and staffing timeframes should be established to best reflect the environment in which the call center operates, and to find a balance between planning that is too general vs. planning that is so specific it becomes overly detailed and time-consuming.

Forecasting Timeframes

Forecasting timeframes are generally differentiated as follows:

- **Long-term forecasts:** One year and beyond. Long-term forecasts are used for estimating future annual budgets, long-term hiring plans and future system needs.

- **Short-term forecasts:** Up to three months. Short-term forecasts are used for organizing and adjusting schedules, anticipating seasonal staffing needs, planning for holidays and determining short-term hiring requirements.

- **Weekly, daily, intraday forecasts:** Short-term tactical forecasts are used to tighten schedules and adjust priorities around current conditions.

There is also a distinction made around the smallest unit of time reflected in the forecast. For example, 30-minute units provide an adequate level of detail

Section 3

and accuracy for most inbound call centers. However, large call centers may forecast down to 15-minute increments in order to gain more efficiencies. Call centers that have predominantly long calls (approaching 30 minutes) may need to forecast for hour increments vs. half-hour increments. (See Long Calls, Section 5.) And centers with planned peaked call arrival will need to forecast down to 10- or even five-minute increments for these events. (See Peaked Traffic, Section 5.)

Staffing Timeframes

One of the most common misconceptions among new call center managers is that base staff requirements can be calculated or averaged for an entire day or week. However, given the variation in workload throughout the day, staff requirements must be calculated at more specific increments (which are generally the smallest units of time reflected in the forecast):

- Thirty-minute reporting periods, which, in turn, become the basis for forecasts and staff calculations, provide an adequate level of detail and accuracy for most inbound call centers.

- Call centers that handle long calls (approaching 30 minutes) generally establish report increments and staff calculations around hours.

- Peaked traffic, which is a surge beyond random variation within a half-hour, requires reports and staffing calculations at five- or 10-minute increments.

6. Choosing Service Level and Response Time Objectives

Ready? | 1 | 2 | 3

Key Points

- There is no such thing as an "industry standard" service level because the optimum service level is affected by:
  - The value of a call
  - Labor costs
  - Network costs
  - The seven factors of caller tolerance
  - The organization's desire to differentiate products or services by the level of service provided in the call center

- Alternatives for choosing service level and response time objectives include:
  - Follow the crowd
  - Relate to the competition
  - Ask: "How low can we go without losing customers?"
  - Conduct a customer survey
  - Meet regulatory or contractual obligations
  - Align with enterprise goals

Explanation

There is generally no "industry standard" service level on which you can hang your hat. (There are some exceptions, e.g., some utilities have regulatory requirements that mandate certain service level results.) The optimum service level is affected by a myriad of factors including the value of the call, fully loaded labor costs, trunk costs, caller tolerances and the organization's service objectives. An industry standard would have to be based on all call centers having the same values for these things. Overall, customer expectations and the organization's goals must be predominant considerations when choosing objectives.

The appropriate objective for a given situation will:

- Meet callers' needs and expectations
- Keep abandonment at acceptable levels
- Minimize agent burnout and errors

• Minimize expenses
• Maximize revenue
• Be supported by senior management

Approaches for Choosing Objectives

• **Follow the crowd:** There are a number of alternative approaches you can use to determine your service level and response time objectives, though all require some subjectivity and judgment. One alternative is to choose "middle-of-the-road" objectives. For example, a service level of 80 percent answered in 20 seconds is fairly common across the call center industry. The 80/20 objective was once published in ACD manuals as an "industry standard." In reality, it never was a universal standard although many early call centers used this target. 80/20 is still fairly common because, for many call centers, it is a reasonable balance between callers' expectations and the practicality of having enough staff to meet the objective. But 80/20 may or may not be right for you.

• **Relate to the competition:** Another popular method for choosing objectives is to benchmark competitors or organizations similar to yours, and use that input as a starting point. Determining what others are doing can be as informal as simply asking for the information, or as involved as undertaking a full-blown benchmarking study.

• **Ask: "How low can we go without losing customers?":** A third approach is, essentially, to determine how low you can go without losing callers. Of course, a major flaw with this approach is it assumes that as long as callers don't abandon, service is acceptable. It also assumes that a higher level of service means lower abandonment and vice versa, which is not always the case. (See Abandoned and Blocked Calls, Section 4.)

• **Conduct a customer survey:** A fourth method for choosing objectives is to conduct a customer survey. However, remember, that while it's always a good idea to know what callers expect, random call arrival means that different callers have different experiences with your call center. Even for a modest service level, such as 80 percent answered in 60 seconds, more than half the callers will get an immediate answer while some will wait in queue for three to five minutes (assuming no overflow or other contingency). As a result, many in that set of callers would say that your service level is great, while a handful would tell you that it is not good. (See The Impact of Service Level on Longest Wait, Section 5.)

• **Meet regulatory or contractual obligations:** A fifth method, when applicable, is to choose objectives that meet regulatory or contractual

obligations. Some companies, e.g., regulated utilities and credit reporting bureaus, must meet regulatory requirements for service level and/or response time. Others, especially service bureaus, have service level agreements with clients that specify service level and response time objectives.

- **Align with organizational goals:** Generally, the overall best approach to choosing objectives is an iterative process that combines the best of these methods in order to align with organizational goals (which, in turn, should be in alignment with customer requirements).

Section 3

7. Traffic Arrival Types: Random, Smooth and Peaked

Ready? | 1 | 2 | 3 |

Key Points

- There are three types of traffic arrival that represent how contacts arrive moment by moment:

  - *Random traffic* represents the moment-by-moment ebb and flow of calls typical in inbound call centers.

  - *Smooth traffic* is when calls arrive in an even flow, which is virtually nonexistent in incoming call centers, but can apply in outbound environments.

  - *Peaked traffic* is a surge of calls beyond random variation within a half-hour.

- The traffic arrival type determines the formulas used for staffing calculations, impacts performance standards and dictates which real-time strategies make the most sense.

Explanation

To correctly calculate staffing needs, you need to know whether traffic arrival will be random, smooth or peaked. An understanding of call arrival is also essential to setting the right performance standards and managing effectively in real-time. Telecommunications traffic engineers have assigned statistical "variance-to-mean" ratios to designate each type of traffic, but, essentially, the patterns look like this:

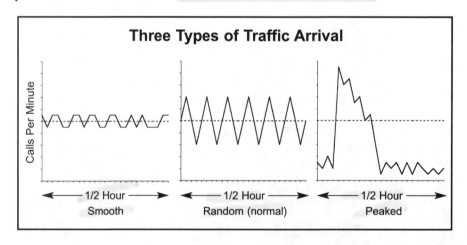

Three Types of Traffic Arrival

Random (Normal) Call Arrival

Calls arrive randomly most of the time in the vast majority of inbound call centers. Exactly when calls arrive from moment to moment is the result of decisions made by callers who are motivated by a myriad of individual needs and conditions. Put another way, calls "bunch up!"

There is an important distinction between random call arrival and predictable call arrival patterns. Virtually all inbound call centers – even those of the more volatile type, such as emergency services centers – have distinctive calling patterns that are usually detectable down to at least half-hour increments. You can predict that you will get around 175 calls next Tuesday between 11 a.m. and 11:30 a.m. What you can't predict with any precision is how many of those calls are going to arrive in the first minute, the second minute and so forth; that is random. There are several important implications to random call arrival:

- First, staffing must be calculated by using either a queuing formula that takes random call arrival into account (generally Erlang C) or a computer simulation program that accurately models this phenomenon. Other approaches almost always lead to inaccurate staffing calculations. And because staffing impacts the load the network and systems must carry, miscalculated staff inherently leads to miscalculated system and network resources. (See Queuing Formulas and Simulation, Section 5.)

- Second, inbound call centers operate in a demand-chasing environment. At any given time, there are either more calls than staff to handle them or more staff than calls. That means call centers must augment good forecasting and staff-planning with real-time management. A solid understanding of random arrival is necessary to avoid overreacting to normal variation in traffic arrival or underreacting to bona fide trends. (See Interpreting Real-Time Information, this section.)

- Third, performance objectives and standards must take random call arrival into account. For example, a standard of "N widgets per day" may make sense in a traditional assembly-line setting, but it doesn't work in an environment where the workload arrives randomly. Unless the queue is always backed up and service levels are chronically low, agents will spend a portion of their day just waiting for calls to arrive. (See Occupancy and Productive/Nonproductive, Section 4.)

Smooth Traffic

Smooth traffic is virtually nonexistent in incoming call centers, but can apply in outbound environments. For example, a group of people may be assigned to make outbound calls, one after another, for the duration of their shift. In that case, the number of circuits required is equal to the number of agents placing the calls.

Peaked Traffic

Peaked traffic is a surge of calls beyond random variation, e.g., calls prompted by television or radio ads. Many of us use the term "peak" in a general sense when referring to call traffic, e.g., What's your peak time of year? Peak day of the week? Peak time of day? But the term "peaked traffic" specifically refers to a surge of traffic beyond random variation. It is a spike within a short period of time.

It is important to correctly distinguish between random and peaked traffic. When a catalog company sends out thousands of new catalogs, they begin receiving calls within a day or two after the mail drop. But that's not peaked call arrival. It's random arrival, but at a much higher level than recent history. Similarly, a utility that has a power outage will get a lot of calls until the problem is fixed. But other than the few minutes following the outage, calls will arrive randomly, albeit at a much higher level than usual.

The key question is this: Is there a surge of calls that comes and goes within less than a half-hour? If the surge lasts longer than a half-hour, it's probably random call arrival.

The implications of peaked call arrival on resource requirements include:

- Staffing must be calculated at a smaller interval than half-hour, such as 10 minutes or even five minutes.

- For a given service level, peaked traffic requires more staff than random traffic.

- How concentrated peaked traffic is within a brief period of time will dramatically impact service level.

(See Peaked Traffic, Section 5.)

8. Visible vs. Invisible Queue

Ready? | 1 | 2 | 3 |

Section 3

Key Points

- How much callers know about their place and progress in a queue impacts their perceptions and behaviors.

- Callers who wait longer than they feel is appropriate often voice their complaints to agents; this takes time, drives up average handling time and further backs up the queue.

- Many ACDs can now be programmed to predict and announce expected wait times to individual callers. These predictions are generally accurate in straightforward queues, especially large agent groups.

- Callers who abandon a visible queue usually do so immediately after hearing the prediction; those who decide to remain generally do not abandon before reaching an agent.

Explanation

Queue means "line of waiting people." Queues are a fact of life in most incoming call centers because, to answer every call immediately, would require as many agents as callers who need service at any given time. That is impractical for most organizations (although emergency services centers do staff at levels that enable immediate answer much of the time).

The difference between an incoming call center and the lines at the grocery store is that callers often don't know where they are in queue and the progress they are making. The queue is "invisible" to them.

The top row of faces in the illustration on the next page represents the psychology of customers when they can "see" the queue. Few would choose to wait in line, so as they enter the queue they are represented by the first face. As they move forward, the subsequent faces illustrate their progress.

The second row of faces represents a setting where customers are ignorant of the queue they are entering. Expectations are initially high, but as time passes, they become frustrated.

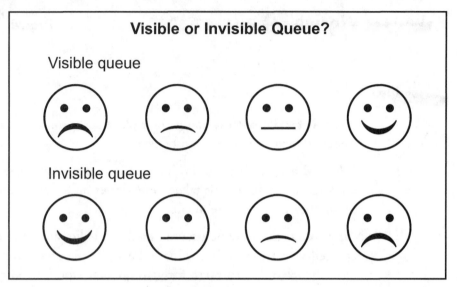

Many ACD systems now have the ability to announce expected wait times to callers, by using predictive wait messaging. With this feature, the ACD is programmed to analyze real-time variables, make predictions and announce expected wait times to callers as they arrive. These systems provide fairly accurate predictions in reasonably straightforward environments, especially in large agent groups. They are far less accurate when complex, contingency-based routing is in place or in small, volatile agent groups.

Providing estimated wait times may cause some callers to hang up soon after reaching the center, if wait times are long. But those who stay in queue are more likely to remain until they get an answer.

Many call center managers keep a diligent eye on *how many* callers abandon. But *when* callers abandon is an important consideration as well. If they are abandoning early because they are making an informed choice, that's a very different scenario than waiting for a lengthy period only to abandon in frustration.

9. Factors Affecting Caller Tolerance

Ready? | 1 | 2 | 3 |

Key Points

- There are seven primary factors that affect caller tolerance:
    1. Degree of motivation
    2. Availability of substitutes
    3. Competition's service level
    4. Level of expectations
    5. Time available
    6. Who's paying for the call
    7. Human behavior

- These factors influence such things as:
    - How long callers will wait in queue
    - How many callers will abandon
    - How many will retry when they get busy signals
    - How they will react to automation, such as IVR or Web services
    - How they perceive the service the call center is providing

Explanation

The seven factors of caller tolerance include:

1. **Degree of motivation**: How motivated are callers? For example, those experiencing a power outage will usually wait longer to reach their utility than catalog customers placing an order for merchandise.

2. **Availability of substitutes**: Are there substitutes callers can use (e.g., Web or IVR services) if they can't get through to the initial number? If they are highly motivated and have no substitutes, they will retry many times if they get busies and generally will wait a long time in queue, if necessary.

3. **Competition's service level**: If it's easier for callers to use competitive services, they may go elsewhere.

4. **Level of expectations**: An organization or industry's reputation for service – or the level of service being promoted – has a bearing on caller tolerance.

5. **Time available**: The time callers have when attempting to reach the center can have a large impact on tolerance. For example, doctors who call insurance

providers are infamous for being intolerant of even modest queues; retirees, on the other hand, may be more forgiving.

6. Who's paying for the call: In general, callers are more tolerant of a queue when toll-free service is available. They are less tolerant of a queue when they are paying toll charges.

7. Human behavior: The weather, the caller's mood, the time of day and other human behavior factors all have a bearing on caller tolerance.

The factors that influence tolerance are constantly changing, which make predicting abandonment extremely difficult. (See Abandoned and Blocked Calls, Section 4.) Even so, it is important to have a general understanding of the factors affecting callers' tolerance. Important questions to consider include:

- How motivated are callers?
- What type of caller is least motivated? Why?
- What type of caller is most motivated? Why?
- What substitutes to calling do they have?
- Which substitutes would you want them to use?
- Which substitutes would you not want them to use?
- What are their expectations?
- What level of service are others in the industry providing?
- Who pays for the calls?
- How might callers' lifestyles influence their tolerance?
- All things considered, how high is their tolerance level?

The answers to these questions will enable you to better understand caller behavior and establish services that meet their needs and expectations.

10. The Planning and Management Process

Ready? | 1 | 2 | 3 |

Section 3

Key Points

- In the evolving multichannel call center, accurate planning is essential.

- An effective planning and management process includes these basic steps:
    1. Choose service level and response time objectives
    2. Collect data
    3. Forecast the call load
    4. Calculate base staff
    5. Calculate trunks (and related system resources)
    6. Calculate rostered staff factor (shrinkage)
    7. Organize schedules
    8. Calculate costs
    9. Repeat for higher and lower levels of service

- A collaborative effort among call center personnel and managers in other departments is necessary to ensure accurate planning.

Explanation

As call centers have grown in importance, call center managers are facing significant new challenges. Perhaps most notably, the call center is becoming a multichannel "connected" environment that handles telephone, email, Web, fax and other types of contacts.

ICMI defines incoming call center management as:

> *The art of having the right number of skilled people and supporting resources in place at the right times to handle an accurately forecasted workload, at service level and with quality.*

This definition can be boiled down to two major objectives: 1) Get the right people and supporting resources in the right places at the right times, and 2) do the right things. Or, in other words, provide accessibility with quality.

To accomplish these objectives, a systematic planning and management process is required.

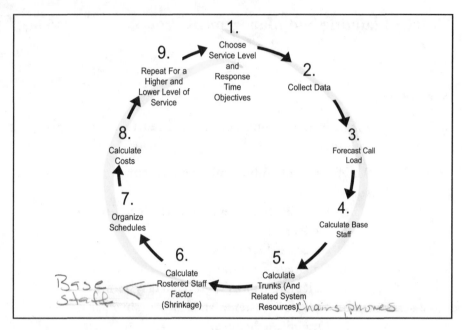

Step 1: Establish Service Level and Response Time Objectives

As discussed, service level and response time objectives (accessibility objectives) are at the heart of effective incoming call center management. These objectives are essential in defining staffing and network requirements, and associated costs. (See Choosing Service Level and Response Time Objectives, this section.)

Step 2: Collect Data

This benign-sounding step is one of the most involved, politically charged and outwardly focused aspects of managing a call center. In fact, a major driver behind the development of customer relationship management (CRM) software is the need to collect previously fragmented data located throughout the enterprise and unify the information into a shared, customer-focused knowledge base, available on a real-time and historical basis.

Step 3: Forecast the Call Load

Forecasting in today's call center must include all of the choices customers have for interacting with the organization. A good forecast predicts all three components of call load – talk time, after-call work and volume – for future time periods, usually down to half-hours.

(See forecasting topics, Section 5.)

Step 4: Calculate Base Staff

Because of random call arrival, base staffing for service level transactions must be calculated using either a queuing formula that takes random call arrival into account (e.g., Erlang C) or computer simulation. (See Calculating Base Staff for Service Level Contacts, Section 5.)

To calculate the staff required for response time transactions, you can generally use traditional "units of output" methods of planning. (See Calculating Base Staff for Response Time Contacts, Section 5.)

Step 5: Calculate Trunks (and Related System Resources)

Staffing and trunking needs are inextricably associated and must be considered together. The more staff you have handling a given call load, the less the load on the telecommunications network. (See Calculating Trunks, Section 5.)

Steps 6 and 7: Calculate Rostered Staff Factor (Shrinkage) and Organize Schedules

Schedules need to realistically reflect the many things that can keep agents from actually being at their desks, handling the workload. Consequently, you will need to account for these activities in a way that reflects their variation. Rostered staff factor, alternatively called shrink factor, is a representation of the additional staff you need on schedule by specific time of day, over and above base staff requirements, to meet your accessibility objectives. (See Rostered Staff Factor, Section 5.)

Schedules are essentially forecasts of who needs to be where and when, and plans of action for agents and supervisors. They should lead to getting the right people in the right places at the right times. (See Scheduling Considerations and Applications, Section 5.)

Steps 8 and 9: Calculate Costs, and Repeat for Higher and Lower Levels of Service

These final steps in the process involve projecting costs for the resources required and preparing budgets. Organizing three budgets around different accessibility objectives provides an invaluable illustration of cost tradeoffs to financial decision makers. (For more information on budgeting, see ICMI's *Call Center Leadership and Business Management Handbook and Study Guide*.)

11. Quality in the Call Center Environment

Ready? ☐ 1 ☐ 2 ☐ 3

Key Points

- Service level and quality are complementary, and are not at odds.

- A poor service level contributes to poor quality as it puts workload pressure on agents and creates impatient and unhappy callers.

- By causing repeat calls, unnecessary service calls, escalation of calls and complaints to higher management, and other forms of waste and rework, poor quality contributes to poor service levels.

Explanation

The conventional wisdom that quality and service level (or response time) are at odds and must therefore be "balanced" is one of the most fundamentally damaging misconceptions in the industry. Remember the two objectives that flow out of the definition of call center management: Get the right people and supporting resources in the right places at the right times, and do the right things. They are complementary. (See The Planning and Management Process, this section.)

On the surface, it *does* appear that accessibility and quality are at odds. After all, you can have an excellent service level, but your agents can still:

- Misunderstand callers' requests
- Enter the wrong information
- Relay the wrong information to callers
- Make callers mad
- Fail to accomplish the primary purpose (sell or service)
- Unnecessarily cause repeat contacts
- Miss opportunities to capture valuable feedback

But it is important to put this issue in context. Poor accessibility will rob the call center of productivity. For example, as service level deteriorates, more and more callers are likely to verbalize their criticisms when their calls are finally answered. Agents will spend valuable time apologizing to callers. Call handling time goes up and occupancy increases. If this condition continues, employee morale will sink. Turnover and burnout go up, as will recruitment and training costs.

When you consider the specific results of poor quality, the complementary relationship between accessibility and quality becomes more clear. For example, what if data are not entered correctly? What if the caller doesn't have confidence the call was handled correctly? What if the agent didn't capture needed and useful information about the transaction? These problems contribute to repeat calls, escalation of calls and complaints to higher management, and callbacks, all of which further drive down service level. Or, if a customer doesn't receive a reply to an email as quickly as expected, he or she may send another; this can be the start of a similar cycle.

In short, there is no such thing as quality vs. service level or response time. These objectives work hand-in-hand. (See Call (Contact) Quality, Section 4 and The Components of a Quality Contact/Costs of Poor Quality, Section 5.)

12. Interpreting Real-Time Information

Ready? | 1 | 2 | 3 |

Key Points

• Random call arrival makes real-time management challenging, but important.

• Monitoring and responding to real-time reports should generally flow as follows:
1. Assess number of calls in queue
2. Assess longest current wait (oldest call)
3. Assess service level/average speed of answer
4. Assess agent status
5. Implement escalation plan as required

Explanation

The key to effective real-time management is to react appropriately to evolving conditions. Consequently, it is important to monitor developments and identify trends as early as possible. Random call arrival means that, at times, it will *appear* as though you are falling behind even though you are staffed appropriately. But if you *are* experiencing a genuine trend, you will need to move quickly to prevent further degradation of service.

Interpreting Reports

Service level is "rolling" history. The ACD has to look at what happened to the last N calls (e.g., 20 calls), or what occurred in the last N minutes (e.g., five minutes) in order to make calculations. That suggests, even though service level is a primary focus in call center planning, it is not an especially time-sensitive real-time report. Service level will tell you what has already happened, given recent unique call volume, random arrival, average handling time and staff availability patterns. But it's important to realize that what is being reported is not necessarily an indication of what is about to happen.

On the other hand, the number of calls presently in queue is a real-time report, as is longest current wait and current agent status. Understanding the distinction between reports that are genuinely real-time vs. those that must incorporate some history explains apparent contradictions.

For example, service level may indicate 65 percent answered in 20 seconds, even though there are no calls in queue at the moment. Keep watching the monitor, though, and service level will begin to climb. Alternatively, service level may look high at the moment, even though a large number of calls recently entered the queue. Give it a few minutes and, unless circumstances change, it will drop significantly.

There will be at least several minutes of delay before service level reflects the magnitude of a trend. As a result, for service level to have meaning, it must be interpreted in light of the recent past, calls in queue and current longest wait. If you focus only on service level, you could misread the situation.

Since the number of calls in queue foretells where service level is about to go (unless conditions change), it should be a primary focus, along with longest current wait. As circumstances dictate, you would then assess the state agents are in – signed off, auxiliary, handling calls, etc. – and make appropriate adjustments.

In sum, focus on reports in this order when managing in real-time:

1. Number of calls in queue: This is the real-time report most sensitive to changes and trends. Look at this first.

2. Longest current wait (oldest call): This is a real-time report, but behaves like a historical report (e.g., many calls can come into the queue, but longest current wait will take some time to reflect the problem). This report gives context to number of calls in queue. For example, if there are far more calls in queue than normal, but longest current wait is modest, you are at the beginning of a downward trend. Now is the time to react.

3. Service level, average speed of answer, average time to abandonment and other measures of the queue and caller behavior: These reports of rolling history provide additional context to number of calls in queue and longest current wait. For example, if service level is low, but there are few or no calls in queue, then the problem is clearing and service level will begin to climb.

4. Agent status: This real-time report indicates how many agents are available and what modes they are in.

Some call center managers suggest that agent status should be at the top of the list. However, agent status ideally comes after other reports because it can be difficult to interpret unless you know something about the queue. So what if few agents are taking calls, if few calls are coming in? In that case, you would want agents to be working on other tasks. In the end, the debate on the order of reports doesn't matter much, because you should monitor and interpret them

together. With the right training on what real-time information means and the activity it is reporting, experienced agents and supervisors can scan and decipher these reports quickly.

13. Alternatives for Providing Real-Time Information

Ready? | 1 | 2 | 3 |

Key Points

- **Agents should have access to information on the queue and be trained to interpret it correctly.**

- **There are a number of alternatives for providing real-time information, including:**
  - **Agent workstations**
  - **Agent telephone sets**
  - **Wall- or ceiling-mounted readerboards**
  - **Supervisor monitors**
  - **Low-tech alternatives, e.g., updated white boards**

Explanation

Everyone in your call center needs to be aware of the impact each agent has on the queue. Each person makes a big difference. (See Immutable Laws of Call Centers, Section 5.)

This issue sheds light on the importance of training agents on how a queue behaves (e.g., how fast it can spin out of control) and providing them with real-time information so they can adjust priorities as necessary. Real-time information can be delivered via:

- Graphically displayed queue information in a window on each person's workstation

- Displays on the telephones

- Wall- or ceiling-mounted readerboards

- Supervisor monitors

- Low-tech alternatives, e.g., regularly updated results on easels or white boards throughout the center (not an ideal solution, but better than nothing)

Queue information must be complemented with appropriate training so agents know what to look for and how to react.

14. Setting Real-Time Thresholds

Ready? | 1 | 2 | 3 |

Key Points

- The size of samples ACDs use to generate real-time reports can often be defined by users, and should be set to provide usable, current data.

- ACDs, desktops and wall display systems allow you to establish a variety of display thresholds.

- Overflow thresholds established in the ACD and network should reflect real-time circumstances.

Explanation

There are a number of thresholds related to real-time reporting and management with which you need to be familiar.

Report Thresholds

With many ACDs, you can define the sample size the ACD uses to provide reports, e.g., the last N calls or the last N minutes. You may need to experiment some to settle on a sample size that works best. Set them high enough that the reports aren't jumpy, but low enough that they provide information that is as current as possible. "From the beginning of the half-hour" or "150 calls" is too much history, and the reports will have little real-time value. But the last 60 seconds or five calls is too little history, and reporting will be volatile. Also, note that screen refresh does not correlate to the timeframe used for calculations. Your monitors may display updated information every five to 10 seconds, but that has nothing to do with how much data your ACD uses for the calculations that require rolling history.

Display Thresholds

Many ACD, desktop and wall display systems allow you to establish various priority thresholds. For example, you can color-code information yellow when the queue begins to back up, and red when it's in bad shape. Alternatively, some ACDs, particularly older models, do not have queue displays on phones, but, instead, provide blinking lights. The lights can be programmed to blink more rapidly as the queue builds.

These thresholds are often set arbitrarily. Further, agents often do not understand what is expected from them at different levels. If that's the case, real-time information will raise everybody's stress level. And agents might feel like it's their fault that they can't clear up the queue. Proper programming and training are necessary:

- **First threshold**: Generally the first threshold should be set for one call in queue. Agents should proceed normally, and no tactical adjustments are required.

- **Second threshold**: The second threshold should indicate that there are more calls in queue than the average expected for the desired service level. (See the discussion on Q2 in Calculating Base Staff for Service Level Contacts, Section 5.) Routine adjustments should be made (e.g., postpone flexible work) to get the calls answered.

- **Third Threshold**: The next threshold should indicate that there are more calls in queue than the agents can handle. In this case, more involved real-time tactics are required (e.g., calling in reinforcements).

You can program some systems to adjust thresholds as calling loads change (10 calls in queue may be no problem during a fully staffed shift, but would be a big problem for two people handling calls at 3 a.m.).

Overflow Thresholds

You can often improve service by changing call-routing thresholds between groups or sites. A common strategy is to overflow to agents who are assigned to work that is not as time-sensitive as service level contacts.

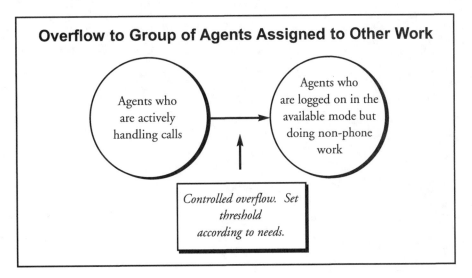

Overflow to Group of Agents Assigned to Other Work

Agents who are actively handling calls

Agents who are logged on in the available mode but doing non-phone work

Controlled overflow. Set threshold according to needs.

Most modern ACDs are capable of if-then programming logic to automate this process. But there are cases that may require some adjustments. There are several things to keep in mind when setting overflow thresholds:

• Secondary or tertiary groups must be sufficiently equipped and trained to handle the contacts.

• Management must determine in advance that calls to the primary group should take precedence over the work secondary groups otherwise would be handling.

• Thresholds should reflect these tradeoffs, and should be established with an understanding of how queues behave. (See The Impact of Service Level on Longest Wait, Section 5.)

15. Informational and Delay Announcements

Ready? | 1 | 2 | 3 |

Key Points

• Delay announcements are adjustable, and should reflect real-time circumstances.

• The first delay announcement recognizes callers, explains the delay and promises that the calls will be answered.

• The second delay announcement is designed to give callers assurance that they haven't been forgotten.

Explanation

Most inbound call centers provide delay announcements to callers who wait in queue, e.g., "All of our representatives are currently assisting other callers. Your call is important to us..." The first announcement recognizes callers, explains the delay and promises that the calls will be answered. This announcement should also advise them of what to have ready for the call (e.g., account number), and provide alternative contact methods (e.g., "visit our Web site at www...").

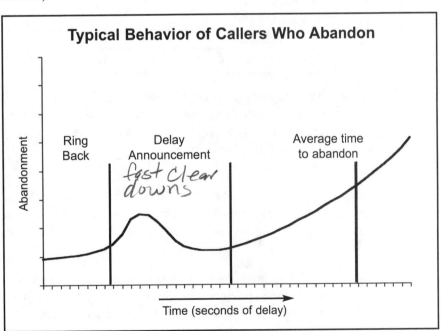

Typical Behavior of Callers Who Abandon

Abandonment

Ring Back

Delay Announcement

fast clear downs

Average time to abandon

Time (seconds of delay)

The typical behavior of callers who abandon can provide insight into the use of delay announcements. Callers who hang up when they hear the first delay announcement are called "fast clear-downs." They may have dialed the wrong number or they may just be the type to hang up when it's confirmed that they are in a queue.

Sometimes, repositioning the first delay announcement will lower the rate of abandonment. For example, if the delay announcement is normally set to play after 10 seconds of ringing, moving the threshold to 20 or 25 seconds will give your agents more time to get to callers before they become fast clear-downs.

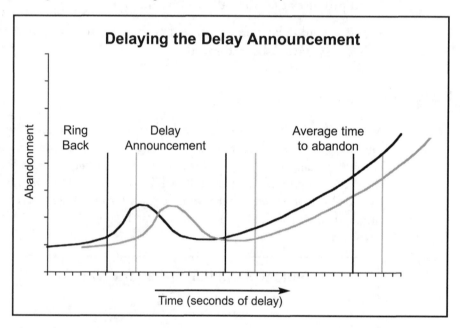

Further, because many callers don't mentally register that they are in a queue until they hear the announcement, they may wait longer. Keep in mind, this technique will actually increase average speed of answer and reduce service level. But you have a higher value in mind: get to as many callers as possible before they give up and hang up.

You also may be able to reduce abandonment by adjusting the position of the second delay announcement. For example, if average time to abandonment is 55 seconds and the second delay announcement is set for 60 seconds, you might hang on to more callers by programming it to play earlier.

The purpose of the second delay announcement is to give callers who are about to abandon renewed assurance that you will get to them: "We haven't forgotten you. One of our representatives will be with you momentarily."

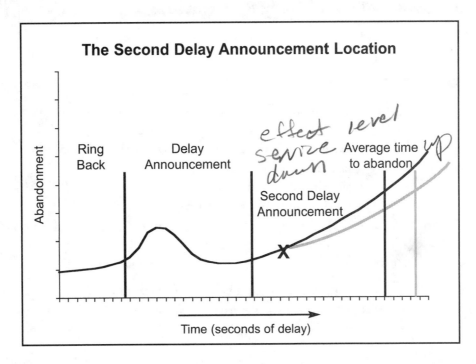

The first and second delay announcements are valuable, but repeating delay announcements of the same message tends to make things worse.

Section 3

16. Establishing and Using Real-Time Tactics

Ready? | 1 | 2 | 3 |

Key Points

- Establishing an effective real-time escalation plan involves:
  - Identifying feasible real-time tactics
  - Determining the conditions for which each should be implemented
  - Monitoring conditions
  - Deciding on adjustments necessary
  - Coordinating and communicating changes to all involved
  - Implementing the tactics
  - Assessing how well the escalation plan worked

- Most call centers used a tiered approach to categorize appropriate tactics based on the severity of the situation.

Explanation

To achieve your service level and response time objectives in real-time, you will need to make appropriate tactical adjustments as conditions change. An important principle in effective real-time management is to outline a workable escalation plan that is understood *before* a crisis occurs.

Most call centers use a tiered approach.

Level 1 Tactics

The first level of action involves routine, commonsense adjustments that enable you to get the calls answered.

- **Focus on agent status:** Many use a variation of the time-honored phrase: "Everybody take a call!" This is generally directed toward people on the floor who are not currently handling calls. It also can be for agents stuck in after-call work.

- **Postpone flexible work:** At this level, agents make routine adjustments to work priorities. Flexible tasks are postponed. If you have a secondary group handling correspondence, outbound calls or data entry, they can be temporarily assigned to the inbound traffic. You might also overflow calls to agents in other groups (who are trained to handle the calls).

Section 3
Service Level/Response Time

Level 2 and Beyond

If the workload still outpaces the staff required to handle it, the ca.
move on to more involved real-time alternatives:

- **Reassign agents to groups that need help**: For example, it may be feasible
  to reassign agents from one group to another.

- **Situation-specific messages**: Another possible Level 2 activity is to change
  system announcements so that they off-load what otherwise would be
  routine calls. Utilities use messages such as: "We are aware of the power
  outage in the southwest area caused by nearby construction. We hope to
  have power restored by 2 p.m. We apologize for the inconvenience. If you
  need further assistance, please stay on the line, one of our representatives
  will be with you momentarily..."

- **Redirection messages**: More routinely, calls can be directed elsewhere:
  "Thank you for calling ABC airline. If you would like to use our
  automated flight arrival and departure system, please press... or visit our
  Web site at www..." Some call centers also give callers the ability to check
  the status of an order, listen to specific product information or hear answers
  to commonly asked questions while they wait and without losing their
  place in the queue.

- **Adjust call routing priorities**: You might also be able to improve
  circumstances by changing call-routing thresholds between groups or sites.
  Most modern ACDs are capable of if-then programming logic to automate
  this process. But there are cases that may require some adjustments. And
  if you have a network that sends fixed percentages of calls to various sites,
  you may need to adjust these thresholds.

- **Use supervisors to help handle calls**: It may make sense for supervisors and
  managers to help handle calls. However, this approach must be well-
  thoughtout because, if they are unavailable when agents need help, the
  situation could further deteriorate. Some union agreements restrict
  supervisors and managers from taking calls, but if allowed, this can be an
  effective tactic.

- **Take messages for callback**: Some call centers take messages for later
  callback. However, this approach doesn't work well for most. (Consider
  the new challenges created: How do you ensure that the callbacks are
  timely? What do you do when you reach Junior, who informs you that
  Mom or Dad is gone? What is your policy when you reach the caller's
  voicemail? Or secretary?) This strategy can work in call centers that
  handle complex calls and have defined customers who are easy to reach –

but you may have to experiment with it to find out whether it's workable in your environment.

- **Mobilize the swat team:** Other Level 2 tactics include calling in a swat team, bringing in agents who are on reserve, routing some calls to established outsourcers, adjusting the placement of delay announcements and generating controlled busy signals.

Post-Analysis Improvement Process

An important but sometimes neglected aspect of real-time management is to analyze what happened, once the crisis has passed. How well did your escalation plan work? Were the right tactics deployed? This analysis will help you fine-tune your escalation plan and improve the planning process.

Real-Time Recovery Planning

An effective real-time queue management program is essential to running an efficient inbound call center, but it's often the piece that's left out of the planning process. Let's look at a few considerations for establishing or updating a real-time recovery program.

Continually Update the Plan

Your ability to institute a successful real-time recovery program starts with an effective planning and scheduling process. This process must include the ability to look ahead to the coming week and identify the intervals that lack the minimum number of phone agents required to meet your service level objective. This capability is a common component of most workforce management systems, or it can be manually tracked via a spreadsheet or database application. If you do not have a process in place that allows you to look ahead and review staffing gaps by interval, you should implement one before moving forward with a real-time recovery plan.

Once you have a process that allows for ongoing staffing gap analysis by interval, it is important to keep it updated. If you create schedules several weeks in advance, they need to be continuously updated with all changes that will affect the number of employees planned for incoming calls. This includes changes to the volume forecasts, last-minute agent training sessions and/or meetings, short-term disability leave, etc.

Last, and most important, your plan must be updated with the last-minute changes first thing in the morning (e.g., sick leave, broken-down cars, sick children, etc.). This will give you an accurate picture of the workforce availability and will provide you with ample time to review alternatives for any intervals that look hopeless. Keep in mind that your current day planning does not end after your initial morning update. Additional unexpected events will influence your workforce throughout the day and the plan must be adjusted accordingly.

Communicate Expectations to the Front Line

The key to a successful real-time recovery program is the communication of expectations.

The first step is to develop a process of communicating the expected workforce variances and any last-minute changes to the plan. This can be accomplished by consolidating the expected workforce variances by interval for an entire week on one spreadsheet. The spreadsheet, along with the ongoing updates, could then be emailed to your staff or posted on an intranet site.

Providing this continual "snapshot" of the workforce and workload distribution by interval will eliminate many of the queue surprises that tend to catch everyone off guard. If the snapshot shows fewer people staffed than needed to meet the minimum service level, the odds are you're going to have calls in queue and everyone should be aware and prepared.

Once the plan is communicated to the front line, expectations should be clear as to what actions are to be taken. For instance, if you have cross-trained agents who can handle response time activities (e.g., email, fax, etc), you may have them log onto the phones once your queue threshold has been exceeded. Better yet, in the intervals when the plan is at a significant deficit, you could have them log onto the phones in advance, which will help to avoid the painfully long process of driving down the queue. You'll need to recover the time lost against the response time activities and move phone agents into non-inbound modes during intervals when the plan illustrates excess capacity.

Don't Set a Reaction Based on a Static Number

Once you've defined and communicated the actions to be taken, you will need to determine when the program should be implemented and when to escalate to the next level. Using static indicators as criteria for implementation will result in over- or under-reacting in many cases.

For example, let's say the first phase of your plan is to begin when your expected interval-staffing shortfall is at negative five. A staffing deficit of negative five will result in significantly longer hold times when the required staffing is 20 than it will when the required staffing is 40. Using a single number as your threshold tends to mask the urgency in your lower volume intervals. A good method for setting your proactive adjustment threshold is to use a percentage approach — plan to invoke different phases based on the deficit percentage and not a static number.

This same approach should be used for those intervals when the calls don't arrive as planned and you need immediate help. You'll first have to work with an Erlang program to get a feel for the "planned" number of calls in queue based on the expected volume for the time of day. Next, determine how long the threshold can be exceeded before enacting the plan. It'll take a few attempts to get this right but, once established, it will definitely reduce the number of "hair-on-fire" events.

Excerpt from "Real-Time Recovery Should Be the Exception, Not the Rule" by Tim Montgomery, *Call Center Management Review*, September 2001.

17. Definition and Use of Service Level Agreements   Ready? | 1 | 2 | 3 |

Key Points

- Service level agreements define the performance expectations between a service bureau and client company or between two departments within an organization.

- Service level agreements go well beyond service level and response time standards.

- Well-defined service level agreements help clarify expectations, meet enterprise goals and open communication between the organizations.

Explanation

Service Level Agreements (SLAs) define performance objectives and expectations, and typically are established between a client organization and an outsourcer (although they sometimes exist between departments within an organization).

Confusion exists surrounding SLAs and the term "service level." Service level refers to the specific call center objective of "X percent of calls answered in Y seconds." (See Definitions and Use of Service Level, Response Time and Quality, this section.) Usually, a service level objective is one element of an SLA, but does not comprise the entire agreement. SLAs are broader in nature and touch on all significant areas of performance.

Common components of a service level agreement include:

- Service level and response time objectives
- Hours of operation
- Forecasted workload
- Abandoned call objectives
- First-call resolution
- Services provided
- Products supported
- Quality procedures and standards
- Reporting requirements, methodology and timelines
- Disaster recovery expectations and procedures
- Escalation procedures

The establishment of SLAs helps client organizations overcome concerns about the quality of work that will be handled by the outsourcer or other department. In addition, written SLAs:

- Provide objectives and timeframes by which to measure performance
- Eliminate confusion regarding expectations (e.g., clearly outline forecasted workloads, establish first-call resolution goals)
- Put both organizations on the "same page" regarding objectives
- Establish a formal process for communicating expectations

Section 3

18. Establishing and Managing Service Level Agreements

Ready? | 1 | 2 | 3 |

Key Points

- Both parties must understand and agree to the financial ramifications of SLA criteria.

- Problems with SLAs are often the result of assumptions that are not clarified or a lack of understanding of call center principles.

- A lack of attention to details can cause a service level agreement to provide little or no value to either organization.

Explanation

In establishing the proper criteria for the SLA, care must be taken to ensure that the objectives are fully defined. For instance, telephone service levels can almost always be met by "busying out" enough trunks so that queue size will always remain small. To help clarify the objective, it may be best to put another in place – in this case, a percent-busy objective.

It is important for the outsourcer to communicate the financial implications of the SLAs to the client. An abandon rate objective of one percent sounds impressive, but the client needs to understand that aggressive goals result in higher costs. The cost may be well worth it, but this needs to be understood by all parties. One-time costs, such as custom reporting packages, are likely to be less expensive than requirements that create ongoing costs.

While SLAs offer great potential for clarifying and understanding performance expectations, they can also backfire. More often than not, problems with the SLAs are the result of assumptions that are not clarified or a lack of understanding of call center principles. Examples include:

- **Objectives in contention:** Quite often, both service level and abandon rates are included in SLAs, but, they are rarely in sync. A service level of 90 percent in 10 seconds is aggressive, but, in most environments, it will never be met if the organization is managing to an abandon rate objective of 5 percent.

- **No definition around calculations:** Some managers assume calculations are the same, but they are not. For instance, the top ACD manufacturers use four different calculations for service level – and many organizations

customize the calculation. To avoid these problems, SLAs should include calculation definitions where appropriate. (See Alternative Service Level Calculations, this section.)

- **No "teeth" in the SLAs:** What happens if objectives are not met – or if objectives are exceeded? The SLAs should clearly spell out any penalties and incentives.

- **Agreements that are one-sided:** Client organizations want outsourcers to take responsibility for performance, but it's rare that an outsourcer can take complete responsibility. What happens when a marketing program is not communicated effectively and volume is 25 percent over projections? Exceptions should be noted in the SLAs for those situations that "nullify" certain objectives for a given period of time.

Actual results should be reported regularly, and compared to objectives. But written reports should not be the only form of communication. The organizations also should have regular planning and review meetings to discuss performance, ensure that expectations and results are in sync, and identify improvement opportunities. Some items that should be discussed include:

- Product changes
- Level of service changes
- Disruptions in service
- Training issues

With the right amount of attention to detail, the SLAs will drive performance activities that will meet client goals.

Clients that gather data and understand performance gaps through careful analysis (such as monitoring calls and reviewing productivity information) will better understand and manage the performance of the provider.

(For a complete discussion of service level agreements, see ICMI's *Call Center Leadership and Business Management Handbook and Study Guide*.)

Section 3

Service Level/Response Time

Exercises

Definitions and Use of Service Level, Response Time and Quality

1. Place an X under the appropriate column for each contact type to indicate if a service level or response time objective should be used.

	Use Service Level	Use Response Time
Inbound calls	X	
Outbound calls		X
Email		X
Text chat	X	
Web "call me back now"	X	
Web "call me back later"		X
Web call-through	X	
Fax		X
Postal mail		X

Alternative Service Level Calculations

2. Use the following table below to determine the service level for this queue using each of the four alternative service level calculations. Assume Y=20 seconds and express answers as percentages rounded to the nearest whole number.

	Seconds	Calls Answered	Calls Abandoned
	0	174	0
	5	8	3
	10	7	0
	15	6	2
Threshold	20	6	0
	30	9	2
	40	8	0
	50	6	2
	60	5	0
	90	9	1
	120	4	1
	180	1	0
	240	0	0
	TOTAL	243	11

Note: Include the numbers up to and including Y seconds in the calculations. E.g., for calls answered in 20 seconds, use the value 201.

a. (Calls answered in Y seconds + calls abandoned in Y seconds) ÷ (total calls answered + total calls abandoned)

$174 + 0 = 174$ $201 + 5 = 206 = 81\%$
$243 + 11 = 254$

b. Calls answered in Y seconds ÷ total calls answered

$206 ÷ \frac{254}{243} = 83\%$

c. Calls answered in Y seconds ÷ (total calls answered + total calls abandoned)

$201 ÷ 254 = 79\%$

d. Calls answered in Y seconds ÷ (total calls answered + calls abandoned after Y seconds)

$201 ÷ 243 + 5 = 248$ 81% ✓

Variations of Response Time

3. What are the three types of responses?

Reply, response, resolution

4. What are the two types of response time objectives?

Scheduled, Rolling

Typical Timeframes for Service Level and Response Time Planning

5. Match each timeframe with the most appropriate scenario.

a. 5 or 10 minutes   _C_ Most typical timeframe

b. 15 minutes   _D_ Center with long troubleshooting calls

c. half-hour   _A_ Catalog center whose television campaigns create peaked traffic

d. hour   _B_ Large center with over 200 agents

Choosing Service Level and Response Time Objectives

6. What is the industry standard service level? _80/av nrd_

Traffic Arrival Types: Random, Smooth and Peaked

7. True or false

_B/T_ Random call arrival requires the use of a queuing formula or computer simulation for calculating staff.

_F_ Smooth call arrival is typical in inbound centers.

_F_ Billing statements to customers delivered via postal mail generate peaked traffic on the days that follow.

The Planning and Management Process

8. Put the following planning and management steps in order by placing a number (1-9) in the blank beside each one.

_7_ Organize schedules

_9_ Repeat for higher and lower levels of service

_4_ Calculate base staff

_7_ Calculate costs

_6_ Calculate rostered staff factor (shrinkage)

_5_ Calculate trunks (and related system resources)

_2_ Collect data

_1_ Choose service level and response time objectives

_3_ Forecast call load

Quality in the Call Center Environment

9. True or false

_F_ Service level and quality tend to contradict each other, long term.

_F_ A satisfied caller naturally means you had a quality call.

Section 3

Interpreting Real-Time Information

10. Place an X in the appropriate column for each report to indicate if it is an historical or real-time report.

	Historical	Real-time
Service level	X	
Agent status		X
Longest current wait	~~X~~	X
Average speed of answer	X	~~X~~
Abandonment rate	X	

Definition and Use of Service Level Agreements

11. True or false

F___ Service level agreements are synonymous with service level objectives.

F___ Service level agreements guarantee success.

Answers to these exercises are in Section 10.

Note: These exercises are intended to help you retain the material learned. While not the exact questions as on the CIAC Certification assessment, the material in this handbook/study guide fully addresses the content on which you will be assessed. For a formal practice test, please contact the CIAC directly by visiting www.ciac-cert.org.

Section 3

Service Level/Response Time
Reference Bibliography

Related Articles from *Call Center Management Review* (See Section 9)

A Primer on Developing Effective Call Center Strategy (2 parts)

How Incoming Call Centers Behave: Back to the Basics (3 parts)

Real-Time Management...Without the Hangover

For Further Study

Books

Call Center Forecasting and Scheduling: The Best of Call Center Management Review. Call Center Press, 2000.

Cleveland, Brad and Julia Mayben. *Call Center Management on Fast Forward: Succeeding in Today's Dynamic Inbound Environment.* Call Center Press, 1999.

Dawson, Keith. *Call Center Savvy: How to Position Your Call Center for the Business Challenges of the 21st Century.* CMP Books, 1999.

LaBounty, Char. *How to Establish and Maintain Service Level Agreements.* Help Desk Institute, 1994.

Articles

Montgomery, Tim. "Real-Time Recovery Should Be the Exception Not the Rule." *Call Center Management Review*, September 2001.

Seminars

Essential Skills and Knowledge for Effective Incoming Call Center Management public seminar, presented by Incoming Calls Management Institute.

Workforce Management: The Basics and Beyond public seminar, presented by Incoming Calls Management Institute.

Achieving Better Service Levels When Adding Staff Isn't an Option Web-based seminar, presented by Incoming Calls Management Institute.

Getting Real Results from Real-Time Management Web seminar, presented by Incoming Calls Management Institute.

An Introduction to the Call Center Environment Web seminar, presented by Incoming Calls Management Institute.

Understanding ACD Data: What You Need to Know and Why Web seminar, presented by Incoming Calls Management Institute.

Section 3

Key Performance Indicators

Operations Management

Section 4: Key Performance Indicators

Contents

Managing and Reporting Key Performance Indicators

Resolving Problems in Meeting Key Performance Indicators

1. Identifying Key Performance Indicators

Ready? | 1 | 2 | 3 |

Key Points

- Key performance indicators (KPIs) are high-level measures of call center performance.

- KPIs generally include:
  - Call (Contact) Quality
  - First-Call Resolution/Errors and Rework
  - Service Level and Response Time
  - Average Speed of Answer
  - Abandoned and Blocked Calls
  - Forecasted Call Load vs. Actual
  - Scheduled Staff vs. Actual
  - Adherence to Schedule
  - Average Handling Time (AHT)
  - Occupancy and Productive/Nonproductive
  - Cost per Call (Cost per Contact)
  - Average Call Value
  - Revenue
  - Budget/Cost Objectives
  - Objectives for Outbound
  - Customer Satisfaction
  - Employee Satisfaction
  - Turnover
  - Overall Call Center ROI

Explanation

A significant amount of information is required to effectively manage a call center. You need, for example, data on caller needs and expectations, the queue and caller tolerance, the load on the system, agent satisfaction and performance, call patterns, cost components, the activities of other parts of the organization, and conditions in the external environment. But you also must be able to climb above the detail and assess overall performance without having to review dozens of reports.

Acquiring the data required to track some key performance indicators is

straightforward and comes directly from system reports; other KPIs require many more data sources and much more assembly. Given the variety of systems, reports and statistics available, the emerging solution is to use CTI/middleware to pull disparate sources of information into consolidated reports. (See CTI Capabilities, Section 6.)

The question, then, is, "What measures adequately summarize the numerous activities of a call center?" While any measure by itself has the potential to mislead, the following key performance indicators typically provide a good picture of the call center's performance when they are interpreted together.

The following table summarizes:

- Common call center performance objectives

- The formula or approach for measuring each objective

- Sources of data and tracking methodologies

- A summary of suggested applications and relevant roles

Objectives Related to Quality:	
Call (Contact) Quality Approach: Assigns a value to the quality of individual contacts. Data typically comes from samples via monitoring and/or recording contacts; however, some criteria may also be generated from ACD-based call coding or reports from customer information systems. Either supervisors or quality assurance specialists review monitored/recorded contacts for initial data capture.	Application: Appropriate in all environments as both a high-level objective (overall summary of the results of individual contacts), which is generally tracked monthly, and as the basis for specific objectives for agents and supervisors, contact by contact. Notes: The quality of each contact is essential to successful call center performance. Quality should be defined to reflect the needs and objectives of both the organization and customers. Criteria generally include such things as interpreting customer requirements correctly, entering data accurately, providing the correct information, accurate call coding, capturing needed and useful information, etc. These criteria should be an inherent part of monitoring and coaching processes.
First-Call Resolution Formula: Calls resolved upon initial contact ÷ total calls. First-call resolution is generally tracked through a database system (customer infor-	Application: Appropriate in all environments as a high-level objective, which is generally tracked monthly (however, with the right systems, can be viewed at any time). Components that lead to first-call resolution should also be built into specific

mation system) or by ACD call coding. How first-call resolution is defined drives tracking – e.g., does it refer to a call not being transferred or to an issue that is resolved even if it must be escalated or transferred? Ideally, first-call resolution should be defined as an issue resolved on first contact (the caller doesn't have to contact the center again or vice versa), even if escalated or transferred during the contact; transferred/escalated calls can be tracked as supporting data.

quality objectives for agents (however, because not all aspects are within their control, these components must be selected carefully).

Notes: Studies indicate that organizations incur many types of additional expenses (some hidden and difficult to track) when callers' issues are not fully resolved with the first contact. There is significant value in analyzing relative increases and decreases in first-call resolution, in response to changes in call center processes, systems and customer requirements.

Errors and Rework

Approach: The percent (and types) of errors and rework that are occurring.

Data generally comes from a database system (customer information system) and/or by ACD call coding.

Application: Appropriate in all environments as high-level objective, reported monthly or (with the right systems) as often as the manager chooses. Specific components of errors and rework are often built into quality objectives for agents (however, because not all errors are within their control, variables must be selected carefully).

Notes: Errors lead to rework, unreliable data and potential interpretation problems downstream. As with first-call resolution, there is significant value in analyzing increases and decreases in errors and rework, in response to changes in processes, systems and other factors.

Objectives Related to Accessibility:

Service Level and Response Time

Formula, service level: X percent of contacts answered in Y seconds.

Formula, response time: 100% of contacts handled within N days/hours/minutes.

Service level is available directly from ACD reports. Response time reports may come from additional systems, e.g., email response management systems (ERMS), Web servers, workforce management systems (WFMS).

Application: Service level and response time are key accessibility measures and are appropriate high-level objectives. They should be reported by "reporting intervals" (e.g., the number of half-hours within, above and below objectives) NOT as averages across days, weeks or months. Managers should be able to identify recurring problematic intervals. These objectives are also key planning targets, used for base staff calculations.

Notes: Establishing concrete service level and response time objectives is a prerequisite to the solid planning necessary to ensure that the organization is accessible through whatever channel customers use.

(continued, next page)

Average Speed of Answer (ASA) Formula: Total delay ÷ total number of calls. Available directly from ACD reports and the WFMS.	Application: ASA comes from the same set of data as service level. It is not necessary to have both service level and ASA objectives. ASA has important operational applications, e.g., it is a component of trunk load. Notes: ASA is often misinterpreted as a "typical" experience, but the average is skewed by many callers who get answered before ASA and some who wait far longer than ASA.
Abandoned and Blocked Calls Formula, abandoned calls: Calls abandoned ÷ calls received. Formula, busy signals: Number or percent of attempts that received busy signals. Abandoned calls are available directly from ACD reports. Reports on busy signals may come from the ACD (if using ACD controlled busies), the local telephone company and the interexchange (long distance) company (IXC).	Application: Abandoned and blocked calls are caused by insufficient staffing or trunking resources. They should be supporting information to service level and response time reports, not primary objectives. Notes: Abandonment rate is not a concrete measure of call center performance, because it is driven by caller behavior that the center cannot directly control; it should be of secondary importance to service level. Busy signals may be due to insufficient trunks, but are often the result of inadequate staffing and the resulting queues of waiting callers.

Objectives Related to Efficiency:

Forecasted Call Load vs. Actual Approach: The percent variance between the call load forecasted and the call load actually received. Forecasted call load is available from the system used for forecasting, e.g., workforce management system or spreadsheets. Actual call load is tracked by the WFMS, ACD, ERMS, fax servers, Web servers, etc.	Application: Appropriate in all environments as a high-level objective, reported by interval; it is also used for ongoing tactical adjustments. Notes: Forecasting the workload is a high-leverage activity that is fundamental to managing a call center effectively. Underestimating demand will mask and defeat all other efforts to provide good service. And overestimating demand results in waste. As a high level objective, forecasting accuracy should NOT be reported as a summary of forecasted versus actual calls across a day, week or month, but an illustration of accuracy for each reporting interval (typically, half-hours).

Scheduled Staff vs. Actual Approach: A comparison of the number of agents scheduled versus the number actually in the center. Scheduled staff is available from the system used for scheduling, e.g., WFMS or spreadsheets. Actual staff available is reported primarily by the ACD. It may also be tracked by the WFMS, with some components available from ERMS and other systems.	Application: Appropriate in all environments as a high-level objective for a center and for teams. As with forecasts, reports should show each interval. Notes: The purpose of the objective is to understand and improve staff adherence and schedules.
Adherence to Schedule Approach: A measure of how much time and when, during the agents' scheduled log-in time, they are taking or available to take calls. Data comes from the WFMS and/or ACD reports.	Application: Appropriate in all environments as a high-level objective. Is also a common and recommended objective for individuals and teams. Notes: Adherence consists of time spent in talk time, after-call work, waiting for calls to arrive, and placing necessary outbound calls. The two terms most often associated with adherence include availability (how much time agents were available) and compliance (when agents were available to take calls). In today's environment, it is more important than ever for agents to be "in the right places at the right times, doing the right things." The measure is independent of whether the call center actually has the staff necessary to achieve a targeted service level and/or response time; it is simply a comparison of how closely agents adhere to schedules.
Average Handling Time (AHT) Formula: The sum of average talk time + average after-call work. Available from ACD reports for incoming calls, and from ERMS and Web servers for those contacts. May also be available from a WFMS.	Application: Appropriate in all environments for high-level purposes and for ongoing tactical planning; it is generally not recommended as a strict agent standard. Notes: In many centers, AHT is increasing as contacts become more complex and as objectives focus on building relationships and capturing needed and useful information. However, all things equal, reductions in AHT through better processes, technologies and training will create significant efficiencies. Creating strict AHT targets at the individual level often backfires, resulting in repeat calls, lower quality or in agents using work modes incorrectly (which skews reports).

(continued, next page)

Occupancy and Productive/Nonproductive	**Application:** These figures are not appropriate objectives, other than as a part of high-level analysis, because occupancy and contacts handled are driven by random call arrival, call type, caller communication skills and many other variables outside the control of agents. It is important that the manager understand and account for the influence of occupancy in these measures.
Approach, occupancy: The percentage of actual log-in time agents spend handling calls. The rest of the time agents are waiting for calls to arrive. The inverse of occupancy is often referred to as available time or availability.	
Approach, productive and nonproductive: Generally measures the volume of work (e.g., number of contacts) that agents produce.	**Notes:** When adherence to schedule improves (goes up), occupancy – as well as average contacts handled per person – goes down. Adherence to schedule is within the control of individuals, whereas occupancy is determined by the laws of nature, which are outside of an individual's control.
Reports on occupancy and contacts handled come directly from the ACD and ERMS, as well as the WFMS.	

Objectives Related to Cost Performance:

Cost Per Call (Cost Per Contact)	**Application:** Appropriate in all environments as a high-level objective, but must be interpreted carefully, e.g., a climbing cost per call can be a good sign (process improvements may result in fewer calls, spreading fixed costs over fewer calls and driving up cost per call).
Formula: Total costs ÷ total calls.	
Volume of contacts requires ACD reports, and potentially other systems that track contacts, e.g., the ERMS, fax servers, and Web servers.	
Cost data comes from several reports/sources; e.g., payroll for staffing costs; budget for equipment and building depreciation; telecommunications reports for toll and line usage costs.	**Notes:** Cost per call should ideally be differentiated by each channel or combination of channels of contact (i.e., inbound call, IVR only, IVR to agent, Web only, Web to agent, etc.).
Average Call Value	**Application:** Appropriate for revenue-generating environments, such as reservation centers and catalog companies, where calls have a measurable value.
Formula: Total revenue ÷ total number of calls.	
Revenue information requires data from several reports/sources; e.g., sales reports, total orders, CRM system reports, etc. In other words, any report that indicates revenue generated by the call center. Volume of contacts requires ACD reports, and potentially other systems that track contacts; e.g., the email ERMS, fax servers, Web servers, etc.	**Notes:** Average call value is tough to apply (and generally not recommended) in call centers where the value of calls is difficult to measure; i.e., customer service centers and help desks.
Revenue	**Application:** As with average call value, it is appropriate for revenue-generating environments.
Approach: Tracks revenues attributed to call center services.	

Revenue information requires data from several reports/sources; e.g., sales reports, total orders, CRM system reports, etc. In other words, any report that indicates revenue generated by the call center.	Notes: Results are often correlated with other variables such as call center costs, market conditions and revenues through other channels of contact (e.g., retail or direct sales force) to gauge the call center's impact on the organization's profits.
Budget/Cost Objectives Approach: The difference between projected and actual expenditures, for various budget categories. Budget vs. actual information can be formulated from corporate accounting systems, or developed in a spreadsheet.	Application: Appropriate in all environments as a high-level objective, assuming it is considered within the context of changing workload variables and call center responsibilities. Notes: Generally produced both quarterly and annually, and is available monthly in some environments.
Objectives for Outbound [1] Approach: Many objectives including the number or percentage of attempted calls, connected calls, contacts, abandoned calls, contacts per hour, contact rate, cost per contact, cost per minute and penetration rate.	Application: These objectives are appropriate and necessary in outbound environments. Notes: Call blending literally combines inbound and outbound work, making integrated KPI measures for inbound and outbound work a necessity.
Objectives Related to Strategic Impact:	
Customer Satisfaction Approach: Measures the percentage of customers who felt satisfied with the service they received. Data can come from a variety of sources, e.g., customer satisfaction surveys, mystery shopping, automated IVR surveys, and focus groups.	Application: Appropriate in all environments as an overall objective. Customer satisfaction data is often presented quarterly or monthly, broken down by channel of contact and customer segment. Notes: Studies have linked customer satisfaction to customer loyalty, repeat purchases and word-of-mouth advertising. If customer satisfaction drops, both customers and agents are great sources of information on how to improve results. Customer satisfaction has greatest value as a relative measure and in conjunction with other objectives (e.g., when policies, service level performance, system enhancements and other changes take place, what happens to customer satisfaction).
Employee Satisfaction Approach: Measures how satisfied call center employees are with their jobs. Data is captured via surveys, focus groups or one-on-one interviews.	Application: Appropriate in all environments as a high-level objective. Generally produced once or twice per year. Notes: Studies have demonstrated that customer satisfaction increases as agent job satisfaction increases. Further, retention, pro-

(continued, next page)

	ductivity and quality often have a definable, positive correlation to agent satisfaction. Results of surveys to gauge agent satisfaction should be compared to job satisfaction levels in other parts of the organization. Results are typically provided in summarized hard copy, and are often compiled by parties outside of the call center.
Turnover Formula: (number of agents exiting the job ÷ avg. actual number of agents during the period) x (12 ÷ number of mos. in the period). Data is captured via entries into HR records and/or a WFMS, and retrieval is typically a manual calculation or a report from the WFMS.	Application: Appropriate in all environments as a high-level objective. Turnover reports are often produced monthly (calculated on an annualized basis), and should be categorized as voluntary (natural) or involuntary (unnatural). Notes: Retention is an increasingly important objective as call centers become more complex, and agent and management skill requirements escalate. Reductions in turnover can typically be translated into financial savings for the organization, and overall improvements in quality and productivity.
Overall Call Center ROI Approach: Objectives related to the call center's overall return on investment (ROI) seek to identify, measure, track, improve and communicate the call center's impact on the organization. These objectives include: • Customer satisfaction • Improved quality and innovation • Innovative products and services • Highly leveraged marketing and CRM initiatives • Efficient delivery of services • Supporting self-service systems • Revenue/sales (in commercial organizations) These measures are a synthesis of samples and analysis, and data comes from a variety of sources.	Application: ROI-related objectives are appropriate in all environments as high-level objectives. Notes: Revenue- and profit-related measures will not apply to noncommercial organizations (e.g., government, nonprofits) but the call center's impact on things like innovation, quality, etc. can and should be measured through samples and analysis.

(1) Outbound is categorized with cost performance, but can feasibly fall in any other area depending on the reasons for and effectiveness of outbound.

2. Call (Contact) Quality

Ready? | 1 | 2 | 3 |

Key Points

- Quality should be defined to reflect the needs and objectives of both the organization and customers.

- Call (or contact) quality is appropriate as both a high-level objective and an individual performance measurement.

- If qualitative measurements are refined enough to ensure that agents are spending the appropriate amount of time handling calls, then adherence to schedule and qualitative measurements make a powerful pair of key performance objectives for individuals.

Explanation

The quality of each contact is essential to successful call center performance. Quality should be defined to reflect the needs and objectives of both the organization and customers. Criteria generally include such things as interpreting customer requirements correctly, entering data accurately, providing the correct information, accurate call coding, and capturing needed and useful information.

Call (or contact) quality is appropriate as both a high-level objective and an individual performance measurement. Call center-wide quality data can be used to assess the effectiveness of call center programs and processes (e.g., if training and coaching programs are effective, and if data entry systems support accurate data capture). Individual quality assessment is typically done through some form of monitoring (i.e., silent, with a beep tone, side-by-side, or record and review) to evaluate individual performance and identify individual training and coaching needs. (See Quality Monitoring/Recording Systems, Section 6.)

An important and developing aspect of quality is that agents take the necessary time to do the job right – no more, no less. This means not rushing calls, but also not spending excess time on calls over and above what is necessary to satisfy callers and handle them completely and correctly. If qualitative measurements are refined enough to ensure that agents are spending the appropriate amount of time handling calls, then adherence to schedule and call quality make a powerful pair of key performance objectives for individuals. (See

Adherence to Schedule, this section.)

This is easier said than done in environments where qualitative measurements are vague and indeterminate. And many managers still believe that tracking production outputs, such as calls per hour or average handling time, is necessary. But the trend is clear: well-defined qualitative measurements are beginning to erode reliance on measurements that are after-the-fact outputs. (See The Components of a Quality Contact/Costs of Poor Quality, Section 5.)

Identifying Call Quality Standards

The right quality measurements create a reasonable and valid set of standards that can be fairly applied to all interactions and to all agents.

Articulating standards that define a minimum level of acceptable performance while encouraging agents to continually evolve and improve their performance is a challenge. Also, to inspire new-hires and veteran agents alike, you will need a combination of objective and subjective measurements.

There are two basic standards that encourage accuracy and consistency, while allowing for individual styles and variations in performance. These measurements – called foundation and finesse standards – provide your monitors with the means to accurately and realistically measure the quality of interactions. Following is a description of each standard (see box, below, for examples).

• Foundation standards. Foundation or cornerstone standards are exactly what the name implies. These are the basic skills we expect agents to demonstrate during every customer interaction – regardless of their experience or level.

Foundation standards are easy to observe – they are measured by whether or not an agent demonstrated a particular skill (e.g., "agent stated his name during the greeting"). Foundation standards often address those skills that contribute to consistency and procedure completion, such as providing accurate information to the caller, or following the correct opening and closing steps. Typically, these are the skills that can be measured using black-and-white, quantitative standards ("skill was achieved" or "skill was not achieved").

Foundation standards are often preferred by managers and agents because they're so simple to measure and leave no room for judgments, which can be challenged. Disputes are easily resolved by listening to call recordings (either the agent completed the task or didn't).

However, this approach can be problematic because it doesn't allow for variations in skill level or incremental performance improvements. Although foundation standards can encourage performance consistency and efficiency, they don't inspire agents to use the more subjective skills that have a more positive effect on the overall interaction. Agents who skillfully handle interactions with "finesse" can create a "wow" experience for customers.

• Finesse standards. These standards address the human interaction element of customer service. They're typically referred to as "soft skills" (i.e., listening skills, handling difficult callers, demonstrating empathy).

Unlike foundation standards, which measure whether or not a skill was demonstrated, finesse standards measure the quality of the skill or how it was demonstrated. It uses performance ranges to encourage continual and incremental performance improvement.

Finesse skills are measured using a graduated scoring method, which reflects the range of acceptable performance (e.g., 1 = needs improvement, 2 = achieves skill satisfactorily, 3 = exceeds skill expectation). With proper coaching, agents can see improvements in specific skills (moving through the range from 1 to 3), which motivates them toward continued performance improvement. On the other hand, if soft skills were measured using a yes/no scale, agents would be rated by whether or not they attempted the skill, not how well they performed it. That would also restrict opportunities to offer ongoing coaching to achieve higher levels of skills.

When trying to find the right mix of foundation and finesse standards for your particular call center, try not to emphasize one over over the other. A balanced combination of standards clearly defines and models the desired behaviors while leaving breathing room for agents to reveal their personalities and provide a meaningful human interaction. While foundation skills provide the basis for consistency and accuracy, finesse skills allow for a customer experience that goes beyond the basic expectations and provide agents with the opportunity to stretch and improve.

Excerpt from "A Five-Step Performance Development Plan for Revving Up Call Quality" by Rebecca Gibson, *Call Center Management Review*, July 2002.

(For a complete discussion of monitoring, coaching and call/contact quality, see ICMI's *Call Center People Management Handbook and Study Guide*.)

3. First-Call Resolution/Errors and Rework

Ready? | 1 | 2 | 3 |

Key Points

- First-call resolution is the percentage of calls that do not require any further contacts to address the customer's reason for calling (calls resolved upon initial contact divided by total calls).

- Defining and measuring "resolved" and "total calls" in the formula is difficult.

- Despite the challenges and costs of measuring first-call resolution, it has great value as a relative measure over time.

Explanation

First-call resolution (first-contact resolution) is the percentage of calls that do not require any further contacts to address the customer's reason for calling. The customer does not need to contact the call center again to seek resolution, nor does anyone within the organization need to follow up.

First-call resolution and the related measure of "errors and rework" are a lasting outgrowth of the quality movement. Studies indicate that companies incur all sorts of additional expenses (many hidden and difficult to track) when callers' issues are not fully resolved with the first call. First-call resolution can be used as a management indicator to drive down costs and improve operational efficiency.

However, as with any objective, there is always a point of diminishing returns. Few call centers, for example, would find 100 percent first-call resolution to be a cost-effective way to operate. Analysis of each call center's particular data, cost-structure, other KPI's and competitive environment will be required to set an appropriate first-call resolution target. Often, first-call resolution measures can indicate the need for targeted training programs, e.g., training may be needed for certain types of contacts that have high transfer rates.

The Issues of "Resolved" and "Total Calls"

There is wide variation in the call center industry on how first-call resolution is actually calculated. The basic concept is simple (calls resolved upon initial contact divided by total calls), but the definition of "resolved" or "total calls"

can change the results significantly. Because the definition of "resolved on the first call" will vary from call center to call center, benchmarking data on first-call resolution present interpretation challenges for call center managers.

Some of the definitions of resolved include:

- Caller states, upon being asked, that his/her reason for calling was resolved.

- Agent has no followup work to do as a result of the call.

- Agent does not need to transfer the call.

- Agent resolves all of the caller's concerns that fall within the call center's defined responsibility.

- One of the call tracking codes designated to count as "resolved" is associated with the call.

There are also differences in ways of measuring total calls, including:

- Calls answered.

- Calls answered plus calls abandoned.

- Calls offered.

- Calls answered that meet certain criteria, e.g., omit wrong numbers, calls with invalid data from a call tracking system, calls handled entirely by the IVR or calls that the call center is not authorized to resolve.

Worth the Effort

Although it may seem there are more questions than answers when it comes to setting up a first-call resolution calculation, this KPI's greatest value is likely to be as a relative measure over time.

4. Service Level and Response Time

Ready? | 1 | 2 | 3 |

Note: Service level and response time are the best overall measures of call center accessibility and are covered in detail in Section 3.

5. Average Speed of Answer

Ready? | 1 | 2 | 3 |

Section 4

Key Points

- Average speed of answer (ASA) is total delay divided by total number of calls.

- Average speed of answer is a close cousin of service level and is derived from the same set of data.

- It makes little sense to have both service level and average speed of answer objectives.

Explanation

Average speed of answer reflects the average delay of all calls, including those that receive an immediate answer. ASA is often compared to an objective or goal established by the call center, such as 10, 20 or 30 seconds.

Some call centers set targets for both ASA and service level (e.g., a service level goal of 80 percent answered within 20 seconds and an ASA goal of 15 seconds). However, for an 80/20 service level (or any other service level objective), ASA will *be what it will be*. Further, it does not reflect a "typical caller's experience,"

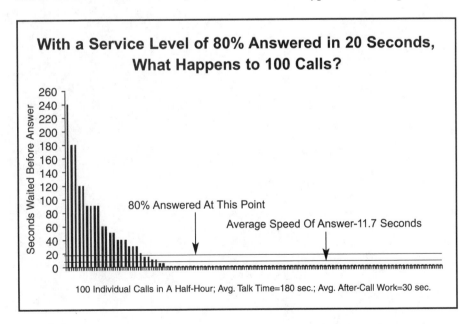

With a Service Level of 80% Answered in 20 Seconds, What Happens to 100 Calls?

80% Answered At This Point

Average Speed Of Answer-11.7 Seconds

100 Individual Calls in A Half-Hour; Avg. Talk Time=180 sec.; Avg. After-Call Work=30 sec.

as some incorrectly assume. Most calls get answered more quickly than ASA, and some wait far beyond ASA.

Average speed of answer is calculated by taking the total time all answered calls have waited and dividing it by the number of answered calls. This calculation is usually made over a specific timeframe. For example, if your reports can be generated for every half-hour of the day, the ASA would be for a specific half-hour. Since it is an average, the average speed of answer for the whole day is not a very meaningful measurement.

The timing of ASA by the ACD generally should begin as soon as the call has queued and is waiting to be answered. With some ACD systems, a message may be played prior to queuing the call, but this time should not be part of the ASA measurement. If your ACD is using overflow, the ASA should reflect the caller's point of view, that is, timing should begin as soon as the call has queued, not at the time the call overflowed.

6. Abandoned and Blocked Calls

Ready? | 1 | 2 | 3 |

Key Points

- Abandoned calls are calculated as percent abandonment rates using one of the following two formulas:
  - All calls abandoned ÷ (all calls abandoned + all calls answered)
  - Calls abandoned after objective ÷ (calls abandoned after objective + all calls answered)

- Abandoned calls and blocked calls (busy signals) are components of offered calls, which are all of the attempts callers made to reach the call center.

- Abandoned calls and blocked calls are often symptoms of other problems, e.g., insufficient staffing and system resources.

- Abandonment rate is not a concrete measure of call center performance.

Explanation

Abandoned and blocked calls are components of offered calls. Offered calls are all of the attempts callers make to reach the call center. There are three possibilities for offered calls:

1. They can get busy signals.

2. They can be answered by the system, but hang up before reaching an agent.

3. They can be answered by an agent.

Forecasting Data

Offered calls are the foundation for the planning process, so if you ignore abandoned and busy calls, you will underestimate demand. Offered calls become the basis for forecasting future demand. Busy signals should be discounted for retries so that the forecast accurately reflects the actual number of individuals who attempted to reach you.

Section 4

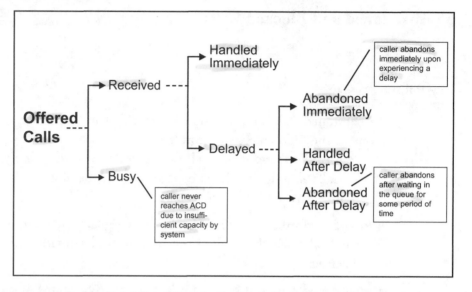

In principle, blocked calls will result when you don't have enough physical capacity to handle the call load or when you've programmed your ACD system to reject calls from entering the queue if the wait backs up beyond a threshold you define. Consequently, data on busy signals may come from your ACD, local telephone company and long-distance provider. (See Calculating Trunks, Section 5.)

In reality, call load balloons when service level drops, so adding staff can eliminate busy signals. (See Immutable Laws of Call Centers, Section 5.)

Calculating Abandonment Rate

Abandoned calls are calculated as percent abandonment rates using one of the following two formulas:

on acd report

1. All calls abandoned ÷ (all calls abandoned + all calls answered)

2. Calls abandoned after objective ÷ (calls abandoned after objective + all calls answered)

The second formula does not include any calls that abandoned before your service level objective, so you are not penalized by those callers. Deciding which formula is best for your center to use will depend on many factors including your service level objective and how important it is for you to answer every call. For example, most sales environments would want to use the first formula since lost calls may result in callers choosing to use a competitor's services.

Calculating abandonment rate is fairly straightforward. The following table illustrates an example using the first abandonment rate calculation.

	Calls Answered	Abandoned Calls	Abandonment Rate
Monday	1551	149	8.7%
Tuesday	1429	93	6.1%
Wednesday	1364	28	2.0%
Thursday	1300	57	4.2%
Friday	1363	183	11.8%
Total for the Week	7007	510	6.8%

You will notice that the abandonment rate for the week is not calculated by averaging averages (which would incorrectly add the five abandoned rates together and divide by five). Instead, totals for calls answered and calls abandoned are first determined, and then the abandonment rate for the week is calculated.

Considerations of Abandoned Calls as a KPI

In quite a few call centers, abandonment rate is viewed as a key measure of how adequately the call center is staffed. The usual assumptions are: a) There must be industry "standards" for abandonment, and b) abandonment is a good indicator of call center performance. But neither is true.

For one thing, abandonment is tough to forecast, at least, with any consistent level of accuracy. That would mean you would be able to accurately predict the seven factors that affect caller tolerance. This is very difficult given that conditions are constantly changing and there are an almost unlimited number of variables than can impact abandonment. (See Factors Affecting Caller Tolerance, Section 3.)

Further, abandonment can be a misleading measure of call center performance. The conventional wisdom is that longer queues translate into higher abandonment. But the factors of tolerance can help explain apparent paradoxes.

For example, when the stock market swings significantly, financial organizations get a flood of calls. Even though service level may drop, abandonment also goes down because callers have a higher degree of motivation – and are willing to wait longer, if necessary.

In the final analysis, you can control how accessible you are through: 1) How many trunks you have, and 2) how many skilled agents are plugged in. But you can't control how callers will react or the myriad circumstances that influence their behavior. Too many call center managers are being held accountable for abandonment, which is something they cannot directly control. It is much more equitable and productive to hold them accountable for things they can control, such as service level.

7. Forecasted Call Load vs. Actual

Ready? | 1 | 2 | 3 |

Key Points

- Forecasted call load vs. actual call load is the percent variance between the call load forecasted and the call load actually received.

- Forecasts that are off by more than 3 percent to 5 percent for large centers and 10 percent for small centers generally point to problems with the forecasting process.

Explanation

Forecasting the workload is a high-leverage activity that is fundamental to managing a call center effectively. Underestimating demand will mask and defeat all other efforts to provide good service. And overestimating demand results in waste. Good forecasting comes from constantly tracking results and making improvements to the forecasting process.

Common practice is to blend quantitative "time series" forecasting with judgmental forecasting, e.g., what is the expected impact of a new marketing campaign? (See discussions of forecasting, Section 5.) If your forecasts are routinely off by more than 3 percent or 5 percent for large centers and 10 percent for small centers, you will need to identify the variables causing the inaccuracies and work on better anticipating or resolving them.

Call centers that produce accurate forecasts are not necessarily those that have the most stable environments; rather, they have a group of people (or an individual) who have made accurate forecasting a priority. They have taken responsibility, established good ties with other departments, pulled in the data required and established a forecasting process they are continually improving. They set accuracy goals and monitor progress. They consider accurate forecasting to be mission-critical.

8. Scheduled Staff vs. Actual

Ready? | 1 | 2 | 3 |

Key Points

- Scheduled staff to actual is a comparison of the number of agents scheduled vs. the number actually in the center.

- This measure is independent of whether or not you actually have the staff necessary to achieve a targeted service level and/or response time.

Explanation

Scheduled staff to actual is a comparison of the number of agents scheduled vs. the number actually in the center involved in the activities specified by the schedule. This measure is independent of whether or not you actually have the staff necessary to achieve a targeted service level and/or response time; it is simply a comparison of how closely reality aligned with the schedules you established.

If this measurement indicates a problem, root-cause analysis may point to one or more areas, such as:

- Adherence to schedule. (See Adherence to Schedule, this section.)

- Inaccurate or unrealistic schedules (e.g., nonphone work is greater than accounted for).

- Conflicting priorities, e.g., supervisors encourage their groups to deviate from schedules as circumstances unfold. (Either schedules need to better reflect workload realities or supervisors need training/coaching on adhering to planned schedules.)

- Inaccurate workload and shrinkage forecasts. If these forecasts are off the mark, schedules will be improvised by groups and individuals.

9. Adherence to Schedule

Ready? | 1 | 2 | 3 |

Key Points

- In today's environment, it is more important than ever for agents to be "in the right places at the right times, doing the right things."

- Adherence to schedule is a measure of how much time and when, during the agents' scheduled log-in time, they are taking or available to take calls. For example, if adherence is expected to be 85 percent, agents should be available to take calls 51 minutes (.85 x 60 minutes) per scheduled hour – at the right times.

- The two terms most often associated with adherence include availability (how much time agents were available) and compliance (when agents were available to take calls).

Explanation

Adherence to schedule is a measure of how much time and when, during the agents' scheduled log-in time, they are taking or available to take calls. It generally consists of all plugged-in time, including the time spent waiting for transactions to arrive. More specifically, adherence consists of time spent in talk time, after-call work, waiting for calls to arrive, and placing necessary outbound calls.

Adherence should incorporate the issue of timing – when a person was available to take calls. This is sometimes called "schedule compliance." The idea is to ensure that agents are plugged in for the amount of time required, as well as when required. The two terms most often associated with adherence include:

- Availability – *How much time* agents were available.

- Compliance – *When* they were available to take calls.

Because of the need to have the right number of staff available at the right times, it is important that agents know adherence to schedule is a matter of not just how much time they are plugged in, but also when they are available. For example, staying 15 minutes longer to make up for getting started 15 minutes late is not a viable solution in a call center environment.

Adherence to schedule should be established at levels that are reasonable and reflect the many things that legitimately keep agents from the phones. It should also be flexible (i.e., adjustable downward) when the workload is light.

Adherence vs. Occupancy

Adherence to schedule and occupancy are two different things. In fact, when adherence to schedule goes up, service level will go up, which drives occupancy down. (See Occupancy and Productive/Nonproductive, this section.)

A primary advantage of adherence to schedule is that it is a reasonably objective measurement. Agents cannot control how many calls are coming in, the mood of callers, the types of calls they will handle, how accurate resource planning is, and so on. But they can be in the right places at the right times.

Growing Importance

Today, with multiple channels of contact and growing responsibilities, it is more important than ever for agents to be "in the right places at the right times, doing the right things." Not all systems provide seamless reports across all channels of contact, so some piecing together of data may be necessary.

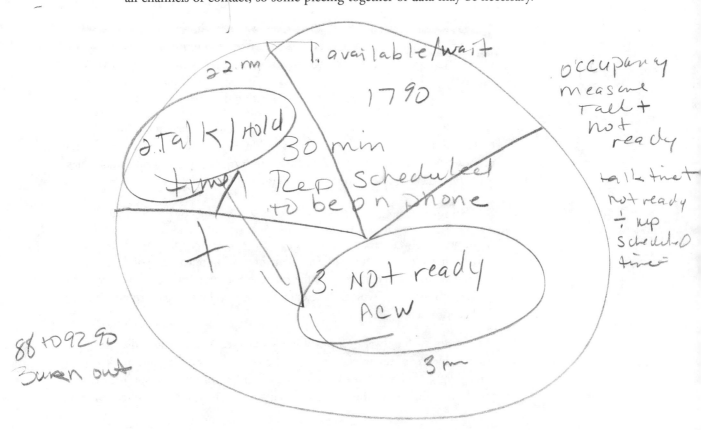

10. Average Handling Time (AHT)

Ready? | 1 | 2 | 3 |

Key Points

- Average handling time (AHT) is the sum of average talk time plus average after-call work.

- Like volume, average handling time for a group must be forecasted for specific times of day; daily averages do not work.

- In many centers, AHT is increasing as contacts become more complex and as objectives focus on building relationships and capturing needed and useful information.

- All things equal, reductions in AHT through better processes, technologies and training will create significant efficiencies.

Explanation

Average handling time (AHT), the sum of average talk time plus average after-call work (wrapup), is as important as call volume in terms of establishing the workload in a call center. Average handling time, when coupled with volume, makes up call load, and call load is what matters; volume alone is insufficient for planning and management. (See forecasting discussions, Section 5.)

Average handling time, like call volume, is generally incorporated into planning by half-hour. Assuming the same average handling time all day for forecasting purposes will not accurately reflect the environment. (See Typical Timeframes for Service Level and Response Time Planning, Section 3.)

Repeating Patterns

As with call volume, average talk time and average after-call work usually fall into predictable, repeating patterns. For forecasting purposes, you begin by looking at the average handling time for a recent week, broken down by half-hour. If the week is "typical," the data represented by this pattern are what will likely continue.

Patterns for each answer group will likely emerge. You may also discover patterns by day of the week, season of the year, billing cycles and marketing campaigns. AHT is often useful for identifying improvement opportunities, trends, training needs, the impact of changes in call type mix, group structure,

billing dates, etc.

Resource Requirements

AHT has a direct relationship to the resources required to meet service level and response time objectives. All other things equal, reducing either call volume or the handling time will decrease costs and increase profitability. However, reductions should not come at the expense of quality. In fact, AHT in many centers continues to increase as contacts become more complex, and as objectives focus on taking the time to build relationships and capture needed and useful information. Effective reductions in average handling time can be achieved by making real improvements in people, processes and technology.

It is essential that for staffing purposes the "real or true" average handling time be utilized not the "goal." Using the goal, if it is lower than the true AHT, will lead to understaffing, low service level and high occupancy. If the goal is higher than reality, the reverse will be true. In either case, the objective of utilizing resources efficiently and effectively will not be met.

11. Occupancy and Productive/Nonproductive

Ready? | 1 | 2 | 3 |

Key Points

- Occupancy is the percentage of time agents spend handling calls vs. waiting for calls to arrive.

- When service level goes up, occupancy goes down; when adherence to schedule goes up, occupancy goes down.

- Occupancy is a result of random call arrival and cannot be directly controlled by agents.

- High occupancy can negatively affect quality, since agents may be stressed without sufficient breaks between calls; low occupancy can lead to agent boredom.

- Raw calls per agent can be converted to true (normalized) calls per agent for a more fair productivity assessment.

Explanation

Occupancy is the percentage of time agents spend handling calls vs. waiting for calls to arrive. More specifically, occupancy for a given half-hour is (call volume x average handling time in seconds) ÷ (number of agents x 1800 seconds). The 1800 seconds is the number of seconds in a half-hour. The inverse of occupancy is the time agents spend waiting for contacts, plugged in and available. It is important to remember that occupancy is a result of service level and random call arrival and is not a driver of service level or budgets. The service level that you are achieving at any given time will dictate the resulting occupancy rate.

As the example illustrates, a service level at 82 percent of calls answered in 20 seconds at the given call load equates to an occupancy of 86 percent. If service level drops to 24 percent answer in 20 seconds, occupancy goes up to 97 percent.

Erlang C Module

Avg. Talk Time: 180 sec; Avg. Work Time: 30 sec; Calls: 250		
Agents	SL% in 20 Sec.	Occ.
30	24%	97%
31	45%	94%
32	61%	91%
33	73%	88%
34	82%	86%
35	88%	83%
36	92%	81%
37	95%	79%
38	97%	77%
39	98%	75%
40	99%	73%
41	99%	71%
42	100%	69%

In most call centers, agents handle various nonphone tasks when the inbound call load slows down. In fact, blended environments make a lot of sense because no one has a perfect forecast all of the time, and schedules don't always perfectly match staff to the call load. (See Dialers, Section 6.) But don't be misled. When nonphone work is getting done, there are either: a) more agents on the phones than the base line staff necessary to handle the call load at service level, at that time, or b) the service level objective is sacrificed. In other words, don't try to force occupancy higher than what base staffing calculations predict it should be. (See Immutable Laws of Call Centers, Section 5.)

Anyone in a call center knows extended periods of high occupancy are stressful. Studies suggest that from 88 percent to 92 percent occupancy is where agents begin to burn out, if the condition lasts for an extended time (i.e., several half-hours in a row). Most call center managers agree, but unfortunately, a high occupancy tends to feed on itself. Taking breaks is a natural reaction to high occupancy, and this tends to compound the problem.

WWW.incomming.com
Staffing Calculator

Occupancy vs. Adherence To Schedule

The terms adherence to schedule and occupancy are often incorrectly used interchangeably. They not only mean different things, they move in opposite directions. When adherence to schedule improves (goes up), occupancy goes down. Further, adherence to schedule is within the control of individuals, whereas occupancy is determined by the laws of nature, which are outside of an individual's control. (See Adherence to Schedule, this section.)

Calls per Agent

Traditionally, calls per agent has been an almost universal productivity measurement. There always have been concerns about sacrificing quality for quantity, but in practice, calls per hour has been the preferred benchmark for establishing productivity standards, comparing performance among agents and groups, and assessing the impact of changes to call center processes. However, calls per hour has always been problematic. In any inbound environment, there are mathematical realities at work that are not within the control of an individual. For example, smaller groups are less efficient, meaning they have lower occupancy at a given service level than larger groups, as illustrated by the table.

Calls in 1/2 Hour	Service Level	Agents Required	Occupancy	Avg. Calls Per Agent	True Calls Per Agent
50	80/20	9	65%	5.6	8.6
100	80/20	15	78%	6.7	8.6
500	80/20	65	90%	7.7	8.6
1000	80/20	124	94%	8.1	8.6
Assumption: Calls last an average 3.5 minutes.					

Since the number of calls is changing throughout the day, so does average calls per hour or half-hour for a group or individuals in a group.

True Calls (Normalized Calls) per Agent

Although occupancy is not within the control of an individual or group of agents, it can be "neutralized" by dividing calls handled by percent occupancy. For example, using the numbers in the table, 5.6 average calls per agent divided by 65 percent is 8.6 normalized calls, as is 6.7 calls divided by 78 percent, 7.7 calls divided by 90 percent and 8.1 calls divided by 94 percent. The result is essentially a measurement of average handling time and is relatively more fair

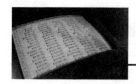

and meaningful than calls per hour.

However, as a productivity standard, some age-old problems remain. Type of calls, knowledge and communication ability of callers, call routing, distribution and other factors lead to inherent variability in call handling time. In the end, normalized calls per hour is an improvement on raw calls per hour, but is not an infallible productivity standard. As the next-generation call centers take shape, marked by growing complexity and a greater variety of transactions, call center managers will increasingly focus on: a) Getting the right people in the right places at the right times, and b) providing the tools, training and environment that enable them to handle workload with quality.

Section 4

12. Cost per Call (Cost per Contact)

Ready? | 1 | 2 | 3 |

Key Points

- Cost per call is total costs divided by total calls for a given period of time.

- You will need to agree on assumptions related to assigning costs (e.g., how to allocate equipment and facilities).

- A rising cost per call may be a good sign.

Explanation

There are various ways to calculate cost per call (i.e., determining which factors to include in staff costs, how to allocate equipment, how to value the building), but the basic formula is to divide total costs by total calls received for a given period of time, usually a month. The potential in following cost per call is to identify the variables that are driving it upward or downward, and the impact they have.

A climbing cost per call can be a good sign, depending on the variables driving it up. For example, process improvements may result in fewer calls than would otherwise be necessary (e.g., eliminating the need for customer callbacks, improving the IVR and coordinating with other departments to eliminate problems that generate calls). As a result, the fixed costs (in the numerator) get spread over fewer calls (in the denominator), driving up cost per call. But, of course, total costs will drop over time, because the elimination of waste and rework will drive down variable costs. Similarly, cost per call usually goes down during the busy times of the year, and up during the slower times of year.

Cost per call should be differentiated by each channel of contact. Figures should also be broken out by types of services provided (e.g., placing orders, changing orders, checking account status, problem resolution).

13. Average Call Value

Ready? | 1 | 2 | 3 |

Key Points

- Average call value is total revenue divided by total number of calls.

- Average call value has been traditionally applied in revenue-generating environments (such as reservation centers and catalog companies) where calls have a measurable value.

- Average call value is much tougher to use in call centers where the value of calls is difficult to measure, such as customer service centers and help desks.

Explanation

At a basic level, average call value can be used effectively as a KPI to put the value of a revenue-generating call center on a unit basis. However, any metric based on volume of calls, rather than the workload required to handle the calls, presents a trade-off between ease of understanding and depth of understanding. Changes in average talk time or average after-call work affect call center costs, but will not be reflected in an average call value calculation. An alternative would be to measure average value per minute of handle time:

Total Revenue ÷ [Number of calls x (Average Talk Time + Average After-Call Work)]

Variations on the average call value calculation may be applicable in different call centers, depending on the data available. For example, average call value could be calculated for new customers separately from repeat customers, or for customers of different product lines.

14. Revenue

Ready? | 1 | 2 | 3 |

Key Points

- Revenue is an appropriate key performance indicator in revenue-generating centers. These centers may be primarily sales centers or they may be customer service centers with sales objectives.

- The indirect impact of customer satisfaction and customer retention can also be included as part of the revenue impact of the call center.

Explanation

Revenue is an appropriate key performance indicator in revenue-generating centers. These centers may be primarily sales centers or they may be customer service centers with sales objectives. Results are often correlated with other variables such as call center costs, market conditions and revenues through other channels of contact (e.g., retail or direct sales force) to gauge the call center's impact on the organization's profits.

The indirect impact of customer satisfaction and customer retention can also be included as part of the revenue impact of the call center. Studies continue to show the power of customer loyalty as a way to boost long-term profits. The call center's role in achieving these objectives should not be ignored.

(For more information on the call center's role in revenue goals, see ICMI's *Call Center Leadership and Business Management Handbook and Study Guide*.)

15. Budget/Cost Objectives

Ready? | 1 | 2 | 3 |

Key Points

- Budget/cost objectives look at the difference between projected and actual expenditures, for various budget categories.

- The variances between budgeted and actual expenditures can be expressed as percentages or in actual currency and are typically broken down into subcategories such as labor expenses, telecom costs, technology charges, and rent and utilities.

Explanation

Budget/cost objectives look at the difference between projected and actual expenditures, for various budget categories. Often called variance reports, these measures are appropriate in all environments as high-level objectives, assuming they are considered within the context of changing workload variables and call center responsibilities.

The variances between budgeted and actual expenditures can be expressed as percentages or in actual currency and are typically broken down into subcategories such as labor expenses, telecom costs, technology charges, and rent and utilities. A typical budget variance report may run many pages. The following illustrates a typical format for these reports.

(continued, next page)

	Month				Year to Date			
	Budget	Actual	$ Variance	% Variance	Budget	Actual	$ Variance	% Variance
Salary								
Team 1	36,434	33,079	-3,355	-9.21%	101,497	94,331	-7,166	-7.06%
Team 2	39,502	41,441	1,939	4.91%	116,595	120,037	3,442	2.95%
Team 3	31,117	34,508	3,391	10.90%	95,021	102,595	7,574	7.97%
Team 4	34,049	35,089	1,040	3.05%	101,314	101,010	-304	-0.30%
Salary Subtotal	141,102	144,117	3,015	2.14%	414,427	417,973	3,546	0.86%
Building Expenses								
Rent	9,000	9,000	0	0.00%	27,000	27,000	0	0.00%
Utilities	3,988	4,161	173	4.34%	12,131	12,337	206	1.70%
Security	11,150	13,000	1,850	16.59%	33,450	37,150	3,700	11.06%
Building Subtotal	24,138	26,161	2,023	8.38%	72,581	76,487	3,906	5.38%
Total	165,240	170,278	5,038	3.05%	487,008	494,460	7,452	1.53%

(For more information on call center budgeting, see ICMI's *Call Center Leadership and Business Management Handbook and Study Guide.*)

16. Objectives for Outbound

Ready? | 1 | 2 | 3 |

Key Points

- Many terms and concepts are similar for inbound and outbound environments. However, there are important differences.

- Key objectives/measures in the outbound environment include:
  - Abandon rate
  - Attempted calls
  - Connected (completed) calls
  - Contacts
  - Contacts per hour
  - Contact rate
  - Cost per contact
  - Cost per minute
  - Penetration rate
  - Time of day effectiveness *driver on Staffing*

- It is important to understand the context of a term, because ACD vendors and dialer vendors sometimes use the same terms to mean different things.

Explanation

KPIs for the outbound environment build upon many of the same KPIs that apply to the inbound environment. Work is work, agents are agents, and getting more work done with fewer resources while maintaining quality remains the goal in both environments. Call blending literally combines inbound and outbound work, making integrated KPI measures for inbound and outbound work a necessity.

Unique Terms/Objectives

Despite overlap with inbound terms and concepts, there are KPIs unique to the outbound environment. (Note: Different outbound dialing systems may use different terminology for these concepts and may differ in the way that they track or calculate them.) Key terms and objectives include:

- **Abandon Rate:** In predictive dialing mode, this is the percentage of calls connected to a live person that are never delivered to an agent. If no agent is available when the phone is answered, the person called hears silence (or the outbound version of a "please hold" message) and either hangs up or is disconnected by the dialer after a set amount of time if no agent becomes available.

- **Attempted Calls:** Calls made, regardless of results.

- **Connected (Completed) Calls:** Calls that reached a live person (or answering machine, if leaving a message is acceptable).

- **Contacts:** Calls that reached the intended person (e.g., Mrs. Smith, not her five-year-old).

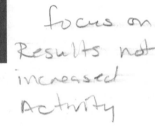

- **Contacts per Hour:** The number of contacts divided by agent hours on the dialer.

- **Contact Rate:** The percentage of attempts that result in a contact (contacts divided by attempts).

- **Cost per Contact:** Total expenses divided by contacts.

- **Cost per Minute:** Total expenses divided by agent workload minutes (talk time plus after-call work).

- **Penetration Rate:** The percentage of the call list that has been called.

- **Time of Day Effectiveness:** The periods of the day when the most contacts are made. This is the most important driver of optimum staffing in an outbound environment.

Improvement Drivers

Automating the outbound dialing process is often the best way to improve productivity in the outbound environment. However, predictive dialing is just what it sounds like (guessing), so, inevitably, the dialer guesses wrong at times and calls will be answered for which no agent is available. The more aggressively the pacing is set on the dialer, the more often this will happen. However, aggressive pacing will result in less staff idle time, so that is the trade-off. (See Dialers, Section 6.)

The quality of the list being called can have a significant impact on outbound efficiency. In contrast to inbound environments, even relatively straightforward KPIs can be affected. For example, lists with many invalid phone numbers will result in a low contact rate. Contacts per hour can also be depressed by a poor

quality list.

Unlike the inbound environment, where callers call whenever they wish, the call center manager can control when calls are made in the outbound environment. The interval-level analysis that helps inbound call center managers determine when to have staff ready applies a bit differently. In the outbound environment, the most productive intervals of the day are sought so that schedules ensure as many staff as possible available to place calls when they will yield the greatest results.

Unit Cost Measures

Due to the additional complexities presented by outbound dialing, unit cost measures offer particular appeal as high-level KPIs. Cost per contact gets right to the point and is simple to communicate, but cannot be compared across different types of outbound campaigns because valid differences in call length (e.g., a brief "welcome" call compared to an intricate "retention" call) directly affect cost per contact. Using cost per minute allows efficiency comparisons across programs, as well as overall for the organization, and provides an urgent warning to investigate further when there are significant changes.

17. Customer Satisfaction

Ready? | 1 | 2 | 3 |

Key Points

- Customer satisfaction, simply stated, measures the percentage of all customers who felt satisfied.

- Customer satisfaction has greatest value as a relative measure (significant increases or decreases serve as a barometer) and in conjunction with other KPIs (e.g., when service level performance decreases, what happens to customer satisfaction?).

- Studies have linked customer satisfaction to customer loyalty, repeat purchase behavior and word-of-mouth advertising.

Explanation

Customer satisfaction long has been a priority of well-run call centers. However, there is a trend today to go beyond satisfaction, to measure and improve customer loyalty.

A prerequisite to accurately assessing satisfaction/loyalty is to collect data on a representative sample of customer experiences and perceptions across the full range of contact channels and issues. Accordingly, many firms conduct ongoing customer satisfaction surveys via outbound calls, mail and fax even as they add email, Web and automated IVR-based samples.

Assessing loyalty – a burgeoning art and science that, by nature, involves predictions of consumer behavior – is more difficult than gauging customer satisfaction. However, a growing number of organizations are providing resources related to defining and measuring loyalty.

There is often a conflict within organizations between the desire for an organization (and those who run it) to look good and the need to learn what is going wrong. Designing a customer satisfaction measure that consistently yields 99 percent satisfaction ratings may make the organization feel good, but likely will fail to provide information that could be valuable to the organization.

No Industry Standard

There is no industry standard method for calculating customer satisfaction. The great variety of customers served by different call centers, for many different reasons, makes it unlikely that there ever will be one standard. However, a variety of industry studies have detailed the behavior of dissatisfied customers. By collecting appropriate data and modeling the impact that changes in the call center could make upon dissatisfied customers, call center managers can cost-justify investments that improve service.

Some organizations outsource the measurement of customer satisfaction because:

- Employing an outside organization avoids internal conflicts of interest in tallying results.

- The expert statistical and survey resources usually required may be less expensive to hire than to set up in-house.

(For a complete discussion of customer satisfaction and loyalty, see ICMI's *Call Center Customer Relationship Management Handbook and Study Guide*.)

18. Employee Satisfaction

Ready? | 1 | 2 | 3 |

Key Points

- How employees feel about their jobs can have a significant impact on:
    - Absenteeism
    - Turnover
    - Customer satisfaction
    - Productivity
    - Overall call center performance
- Employee satisfaction is typically measured through surveys or focus groups.

Explanation

Optimizing employee satisfaction is an important success factor in any call center. How employees feel about their jobs can have a significant impact on:

- Absenteeism

- Turnover

- Customer satisfaction

- Productivity

- Overall call center performance

Employee satisfaction surveys are typically conducted once or twice a year and are good ways to gather feedback quickly and, if desired, anonymously. It is advisable to ask quantitative questions that are easily summarized as well as qualitative questions that may help explain some of the quantitative results.

Conducting focus groups can also be an effective way to get feedback on employee satisfaction. However, it may be best to bring in an unbiased, outside firm to conduct the feedback sessions since employees may be less than candid in front of call center management.

Before surveys or focus groups take place, employees should be aware of how the results will be communicated and whether or not actions to improve problems will be taken. Collecting this type of feedback from employees

typically produces an expectation that management will take action to improve job satisfaction.

(Employee satisfaction is discussed in detail in ICMI's *Call Center People Management Handbook and Study Guide*.)

Section 4

19. Turnover

Ready? | 1 | 2 | 3 |

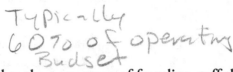

Typically 60% of operating Budget

Key Points

- Turnover is typically defined as the percentage of frontline staff that leave their positions. This may include voluntary turnover (e.g., internal promotions, employee resignations, retirement) or involuntary turnover (e.g., dismissals and layoffs).

- Call center managers should calculate an annualized turnover rate using the following formula:
  Turnover = (number of agents exiting the job ÷ avg. actual number of agents during the period) x (12 ÷ number of mos. in the period)

Explanation

Since the largest call center expense is usually labor costs, the impact of turnover as a key performance indicator is significant. For example, high turnover can drive down quality, drive up cost per call, drive up errors and rework, and drive up average handling time. The list could go on. Traditionally, however, moderate to high turnover has been the norm in many call centers because frontline agent positions often involve repetitive work, may offer little room for career advancement and require strict adherence to schedules. As call centers have become more sophisticated and more central to effective strategy, the nature of call center work is changing, which has had a positive impact on recruitment and retention. (Retention strategies are discussed in ICMI's *Call Center People Management Handbook and Study Guide*.)

Turnover is typically defined as the percentage of frontline staff that leave their positions. This may include voluntary turnover (e.g., internal promotions, employee resignations, retirement) or involuntary turnover (e.g., dismissals and layoffs).

To measure turnover in a way that provides a consistent basis for comparison and trending, call center managers should calculate an annualized turnover rate. An annualized number does not require 12 months worth of data. The calculation is as follows:

Turnover = (number of agents exiting the job ÷ avg. actual number of agents during the period) x (12 ÷ number of mos. in the period)

Input for Turnover Calculation

	# of agents exiting the job during month	Avg. # of agents on staff during month*
January	2	104
February	1	103
March	4	101
April	0	101
May	3	109
June	5	106
July	2	105
August	3	103
Total/Average	20	104

*The average number of agents on staff during the month is often calculated by taking an average of the counts at the end of each week of the month. Alternatively, an average can be taken of the trained staff count at the beginning and end of the month.

Using the data from the table above, the calculation yields the following result:

(20 ÷ 104) x (12 ÷ 8) = 28.8%

Consequently, the call center has an annualized turnover rate of about 29 percent.

20. Overall Call Center ROI

Ready? ☐1 ☐2 ☐3

Key Points

- Determining the call center's overall return on investment (ROI) begins with recognizing the center's value proposition, or the set of specific benefits it provides to the organization and customers.

- The call center's overall ROI seeks to summarize the benefits to both the organization and customers.

Explanation

Determining the call center's overall return on investment (ROI) begins with recognizing the center's value proposition, or the set of specific benefits it provides to the organization and customers. There are many viable call center value propositions, but most comprise contributions to one or more of the following:

- Business unit strategies

- Customer satisfaction and loyalty

- Improved quality and innovation

- Highly leveraged marketing and CRM initiatives

- Innovative products and services

- Efficient delivery of services

- Support of self-service systems

- Revenue/sales (in commercial organizations)

The call center's overall ROI seeks to summarize the benefits to both the organization and customers. Typically, these areas can be measured through data sampling and analysis of a variety of sources.

Call center managers need to be aware of the totality of benefits a call center can provide to customers and the organization. (For models and discussions of the call center's value proposition and impact, see ICMI's *Call Center Customer Relationship Management Handbook and Study Guide* and ICMI's *Call Center Leadership and Business Management Handbook and Study Guide*.)

21. KPIs as Interrelated Outcomes
[Strategic]

Ready? | 1 | 2 | 3

Key Points

- There are three important things to keep in mind about key performance indicators:

  1. As with any measure, you must ensure that they are as accurate, complete and unbiased as possible.

  2. These reports should be interpreted in light of how they relate to each other. By themselves, any can lead to erroneous conclusions, but together they paint a fairly complete, high-level picture of call center performance.

  3. Tracking high-level measurements won't inherently improve them. To make improvements, you have to work on the factors that cause these outputs to be what they are.

Explanation

An incoming call center is a process or system of causes. Taking a larger view, the call center is part of a larger process, the organization. In a lesser view, each agent group in a call center is a system of causes unto itself, as are individual agents in a group.

The central focus of the process can be any KPI or virtually any other measure or objective. Note that just about everything is interrelated, so the causes of performance problems are often difficult to isolate and measure.

(continued, next page)

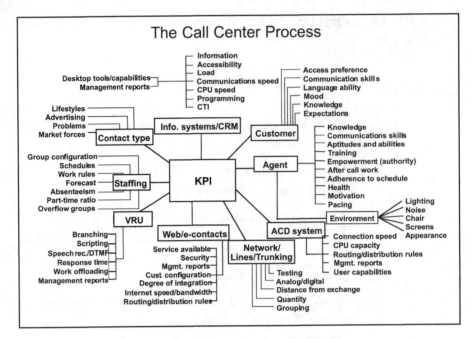

Tracking high-level measurements won't inherently improve them. To make improvements, you have to work on the factors that cause these outputs to be what they are. In other words, you have to work at a deeper level, the root causes. (See A Process for Root-Cause Analysis, Section 5.)

The Interrelated Nature of KPIs

KPIs should not be viewed in isolation. Consider a few examples:

- Cost per call going down may be a bad sign. Viewed alone, a dropping cost per call may seem like a positive indication. However, if call volume, errors and rework are going up, cost per call will naturally decrease as fixed costs are spread over more calls. This is not a good sign.

- Average handling time going up may be a positive indication. Viewed alone, an increasing AHT may seem to indicate inefficiencies. However, agents may be improving on cross-selling and upselling opportunities, and improving average call value.

- A high service level is not necessarily all positive. In isolation, a great service level may seem very positive. However, if schedules are assigning too many agents to service level contacts while short-changing response time work, adjustments need to be made to forecasting and scheduling processes.

In sum, KPIs are interrelated and viewing them as a whole is a prerequisite to understanding the environment.

22. How KPIs Relate to Customer Expectations [Stategic]

Ready? | 1 | 2 | 3 |

Key Points

- There are 10 primary customer expectations:
    1. Be accessible
    2. Treat me courteously
    3. Be responsive to what I need and want
    4. Do what I ask promptly
    5. Provide well-trained and informed employees
    6. Tell me what to expect
    7. Meet your commitments; keep your promises
    8. Do it right the first time
    9. Be socially responsible and ethical
    10. Follow up

- An important strategic responsibility is to understand and manage the connections between KPIs and customer expectations.

Explanation

One of the most critical – and difficult – aspects of managing a call center is to provide services that satisfy changing consumer demands. Those who fall behind will pay a brutal price: dissatisfied customers, insufficient support from the organization and low morale in the call center. But those who stay ahead of the curve will enjoy strong customer loyalty and the many of benefits that come with it.

Ten key customer expectations include:

1. Be accessible
2. Treat me courteously
3. Be responsive to what I need and want
4. Do what I ask promptly
5. Provide well-trained and informed employees
6. Tell me what to expect
7. Meet your commitments; keep your promises
8. Do it right the first time
9. Be socially responsible and ethical
10. Follow up

Section 4

Category/KPI	Customer Expectation
Customer Perception Measures • Customer Satisfaction • Errors and Rework/First Call Resolution	• Be accessible • Treat me courteously • Do it right the first time • Do what I ask promptly • Be responsive to what I need and want • Tell me what to expect • Provide well-trained and informed employees • Meet your commitments; keep your promises • Be socially responsible and ethical • Follow up
Call Center Accessibility Measures • Service Level • Average Speed of Answer • Abandoned and Blocked Calls	• Be accessible • Be responsive to what I need and want • Meet your commitments; keep your promises
Efficiency/Planning Measures • Forecasted Call Load vs. Actual • Scheduled Staff to Actual • Average Handling Time • Occupancy and Productive/Nonproductive	• Be responsive to what I need and want • Ensure that I deal with trained and equipped employees • Meet your commitments; keep your promises • Be accessible
Agent Performance Measures • Adherence to Schedule • Quality (Errors and Rework/First-Call Resolution)	• Be accessible • Treat me courteously • Do it right the first time • Meet your commitments; keep your promises • Follow up

The table above represents one way to categorize KPIs, and suggests the customer expectations impacted by category. Note, some KPIs and some expectations appear in more than one category.

An important strategic responsibility is to understand and manage the connections between KPIs and customer expectations. This involves:

• Tracking and comparing both KPIs and customer expectation trends.

• Educating all levels of call center staff on how KPIs and customer expectations are interrelated.

• Ensuring that specific objectives, systems, processes and technologies support and enable the call center to meet customer expectations and continuously improve KPIs.

(Customer expectations are covered in greater detail in ICMI's *Call Center Customer Relationship Management Handbook and Study Guide*.)

Key Performance Indicators

Exercises

Calculate the following KPIs based on the scenario below. Round your answers to the nearest whole number.

We collected the following data for Agent Group A from 9:00 to 9:30 on Tuesday, May 15:

Forecast:

Call volume: 270

Average talk time: 192 seconds

Average after-call work: 35 seconds

Number of agents scheduled: 38

Service Level Goal: 80 percent answered in 30 seconds

Actual results:

Total calls offered: 253

Total calls answered: 225

Calls answered within 30 seconds: 156

Total calls abandoned: 28

Calls abandoned within 30 seconds: 9

Average talk time: 185 seconds

Average after-call work: 39 seconds

Total delay: 4,495 seconds

Number of agents: 35

Calls resolved on initial contact: 197

Total revenue: $7,875

Total costs: $1,124

1. Average Call Value (use calls answered):

$$7875 \div 225 = 35$$

2. Service Level (using the calculation below):

   Calls answered in Y seconds ÷ (total calls answered + total calls abandoned)

   $$156 \div 253 = 6290$$

3. Average Speed of Answer (use calls answered):

   $$4495 \div 225 = 20 \text{ seconds}$$

4. Percent Abandoned (using the calculation below):

   Calls abandoned after objective ÷ (calls abandoned after objective + all calls answered)

   $$9 \div 9 + 225 = 234$$

5. Cost per Call (use calls answered):

   $$1124 \div 225 = 5.$$

6. First-Call Resolution (use calls answered):

   $$197 \div 225 = 88$$

7. Average Handling Time:

   $$185 + 39 = 224 \text{ sec}$$

8. Occupancy (use calls answered):

   $$225 \times 224 \div 35 \times 1800 =$$

9. Forecasted to Actual Call Load (use calls offered):

10. Scheduled to Actual Staff:

Answers to these exercises are in Section 10.

Note: These exercises are intended to help you retain the material learned. While not the exact questions as on the CIAC Certification assessment, the material in this handbook/study guide fully addresses the content on which you will be assessed. For a formal practice test, please contact the CIAC directly by visiting www.ciac-cert.org.

Key Performance Indicators
Reference Bibliography

Related Articles from *Call Center Management Review* (See Section 9)

Measuring Individual Agent Performance

How Key Performance Indicators Are Evolving

For Further Study

Books

Cleveland, Brad and Julia Mayben. *Call Center Management on Fast Forward: Succeeding in Today's Dynamic Inbound Environment.* Call Center Press, 1999.

Elliott, Susan, ed. *Call Center Operations.* American Productivity & Quality Center, 2000.

Articles

Gibson, Rebecca. "A Five-Step Performance Development Plan for Revving Up Call Quality." *Call Center Management Review*, July 2000.

Seminars

Essential Skills and Knowledge for Effective Incoming Call Center Management public seminar, presented by Incoming Calls Management Institute.

Workforce Management: The Basics and Beyond public seminar, presented by Incoming Calls Management Institute.

Understanding ACD Data: What You Need to Know and Why Web Seminar, presented by Incoming Calls Management Institute.

Forecasting and Scheduling

Operations Management

Section 5: Forecasting and Scheduling

Contents

(continued, next page)

Section 5

Section 5: Forecasting and Scheduling

1. Key Forecasting Definitions

Ready? | 1 | 2 | 3 |

Key Points

- Key terms related to forecasting include:
  - Talk Time
  - After-Call Work
  - Average Handling Time
  - Offered Calls
  - Answered Calls
  - Call Load

Explanation

The basic historical data you need for forecasting includes how many inbound transactions you have received in the past, when they arrived and how long they took to handle. A number of important terms reflect this activity:

1. **Talk Time**: Everything from "hello" to "goodbye." In other words, it's the time callers are connected with agents. Anything that happens during talk time, such as outbound calls or conferring with supervisors, should be included in this measurement.

2. **After-Call Work**: Also referred to as wrapup or not ready, after-call work is the time agents spend completing transactions after saying goodbye to callers. Legitimate after-call work should immediately follow inbound transactions.

3. **Average Handling Time:** The sum of average talk time plus average after-call work. (See Average Handling Time (AHT), Section 4.)

4. **Offered Calls**: All of the attempts callers make to reach the call center. There are three possibilities for offered calls: 1) They can get busy signals; 2) they can be answered by the system, but hang up before reaching an agent; or 3) they can be answered by an agent (with or without waiting in queue). The forecast should reflect offered calls discounted for multiple attempts from individual callers. (See Abandoned and Blocked Calls, Section 4.)

5. **Answered Calls**: When referring to an agent group, a call is counted as answered when it reaches an agent.

6. **Call Load:** Also called workload, call load is volume multiplied by average handling time, for a given period of time. Although the process of forecasting may initially project volume and average handling time separately, the forecast must ultimately bring these components together into an overall forecast of call load.

2. Forecasting Principles and Methodologies Ready? 1 2 3

Key Points

- Forecasting methodologies are broadly categorized into quantitative and judgmental approaches.

- Quantitative forecasts include:
  - Time series forecasts, which assume past data will reflect trends that continue into the future. Time series approaches are common in workforce management software.
  - Explanatory forecasting methods (e.g., regression analysis, econometric models and multivariate methods), which attempt to reveal a linkage between two or more variables.

- Judgmental forecasts go beyond purely statistical techniques. They involve intuition, interdepartmental committees, market research and executive opinion.

- Call center forecasts require both quantitative and judgmental approaches.

Explanation

Forecasting is a mix of art and science. It begins with predicting how many contacts you are going to get in a future period, usually a year. To do that, you look at historical data to determine patterns that reflect when people call, and you consider possible trends that will affect call patterns. You then take that information and break it into the contacts that will be coming to you in different months, weeks of the month, days of the week and half-hours of the day – or even five minutes of the half-hour, if you are forecasting peaked traffic. Next, you factor in the handling times of the transactions. Finally, you modify results based on conditions not reflected in historical data.

In the call center environment, long-term forecasts look out a year and beyond. They are used to estimate future annual budgets, establish long-term hiring plans and define future system needs. Short-term forecasts project workload out to three months. They are necessary for organizing and adjusting scheduling requirements, anticipating seasonal staffing needs, planning for holidays, and determining imminent hiring requirements. Weekly, daily and

intraday forecasts are short-term tactical forecasts used to tighten schedules and adjust priorities around current conditions and near-term events.

The major categories of quantitative forecasting include time series and explanatory approaches. Time series forecasting methods include simple or "naive" rules (e.g., the forecast equals last year's call load during the same month, plus 12 percent), decomposition, simple time series and advanced time series methods. The governing assumption behind time series forecasting is that past data will reflect trends that will continue into the future. Time series methodologies are common in workforce management software.

Explanatory forecasting methods include simple regression analysis, multiple regression analysis, econometric models and multivariate methods. Explanatory forecasting essentially attempts to reveal a linkage between two or more variables. For example, if you manage an ice cream shop, you could statistically correlate the weather (e.g., outside temperature) to ice cream sales. In a call center, you might correlate a price increase to the impact on calling volumes.

The examples in this guide and in the CIAC exam are basic time series scenarios. If you would like more information on advanced issues, *The Handbook of Forecasting: A Manager's Guide*, edited by Syros Makridakis and Steven C. Wheelright, is an excellent place to begin.

3. Dominant Call Patterns

Ready? | 1 | 2 | 3 |

Key Points

- Dominant call arrival patterns include:
  - Month of year (seasonality)
  - Day of week
  - Half-hour of day

- Other patterns may exist, e.g., the call center may see traffic increase when statements or notices are sent to customers.

- Patterns form the basis of time series forecasting.

Explanation

Virtually all incoming call centers notice that contacts arrive in at least three dominant patterns:

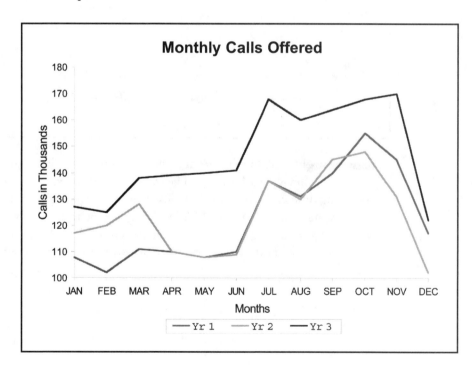

• **Month of year or seasonality:** This graph illustrates data from a financial company. Notice that the most recent year is at a higher plane, but looks similar to the patterns in previous years. Even if your organization is going through dramatic changes, you usually will detect seasonality in your call arrival patterns. Three years of data will provide a good reading on these patterns.

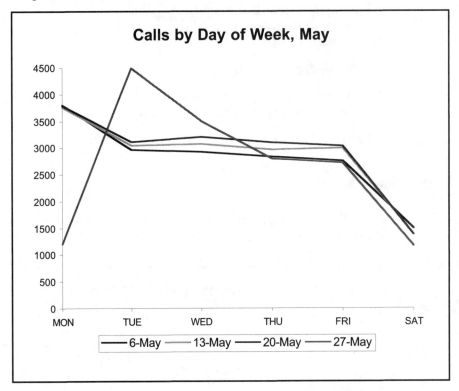

• **Day of week:** This graph is from a telephone company. The last week reflects a holiday on a Monday. The call center was open, but callers were behaving differently than usual. Consequently, the following Tuesday received more calls than normal, illustrating the "pent-up demand" that is common after holidays. Otherwise, the pattern is highly predictable from one week to the next. Four or five weeks-worth of history can reveal this pattern.

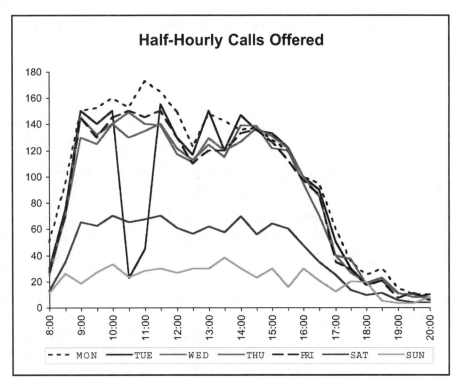

- **Half-hour of day:** This graph is from a bank. A system outage is evident in Tuesday's pattern. Exceptions such as the system outage should be removed from historical data before it is used for forecasting. A week or two worth of data will often be enough to identify this pattern.

These patterns form the basis of time series forecasting, and accurate projections depend on understanding them. You may have other patterns, as well. For example, if you send statements to your customers on the fifth and 20th of each month, you'll notice day-of-month patterns. And marketing campaigns will create their own traffic patterns.

4. Breaking Down a Time Series Forecast

Ready? | 1 | 2 | 3 |

Key Points

- Breaking down a time series forecast involves using historical patterns and proportions to project volume for a future period of time.

- The process begins with long-term patterns (e.g., month of year), and works down to specific half-hour increments.

- To the degree that patterns are a good indicator of future activity, these forecasts will be a good base on which to then blend in judgment.

Explanation

The following illustrates a basic approach for breaking down a time series forecast. This example starts with long-term patterns, and works its way down to specific half-hour increments.

Breaking Down a Forecast

720,000	Current year's calls
x 1.12	To add 12% (add after month prop.?)
806,400	Estimated calls in forecast year
x .071	January proportion
57,254	January calls
/ 31	Operation days-January
1,847	Average calls per day
x 1.469	Monday index factor
2,713	Monday's calls
x .055	10:00 to 10:30 proportion
149	Forecasted calls 10:00 to 10:30

Notes:

1) To determine operations days, count the days call center will be open.

2) To calculate day-of-week index factor, divide day-of-week proportion by average day-of-week proportion.

Example January

S	M	T	W	T	F	S
		1	2	3	4	5
6	7	8	9	10	11	12
13	14	15	16	17	18	19
20	21	22	23	24	25	26
27	28	29	30	31		

Example:	Prop.		Avg. Prop.		Index Factor
Monday	.210	÷	.143	=	1.469
Tuesday	.170	÷	.143	=	1.189
Wednesday	.165	÷	.143	=	1.154
Thursday	.165	÷	.143	=	1.154
Friday	.150	÷	.143	=	1.049
Saturday	.095	÷	.143	=	0.664
Sunday	.045	÷	.143	=	0.315

The steps include:

1. Obtain the number of calls received in the past 12 months, 720,000 in this example.

2. Multiply the year's calls by 1.12 to reflect 12 percent expected growth. Factoring in growth at this level assumes that transactions will increase proportionally to the previous year's patterns. (If growth instead will be concentrated around marketing campaigns or other events that don't necessarily happen at the same time from year to year, you should factor it in at a more specific level, such as monthly or weekly.)

3. Multiply the estimated calls in the year you are forecasting by January's proportion, 7.1 percent. This percentage comes from history and is the typical proportion of the year's calls that January receives.

4. Divide the number of operation days in the month into the estimated monthly calls. This yields average calls per day. In this example, the center is open every day of the month.

5. Adjust average calls per day, using the appropriate daily index factor. The first column in the index factor calculation gives the proportion of the week's contacts that typically arrive each day. For example, Monday normally gets 21 percent of the week's traffic, Tuesday gets 17 percent and so forth.

   The next column reflects the proportion of a week that an operation day represents. For example, if you are open seven days a week, each day is one-seventh or 14.3 percent of a week. If your center is open five days, each day is one-fifth, or 20 percent of a week. A day in a six-day work week is 16.7 percent of the week.

   The final column is the result of dividing the first column by the second column. These index factors are then multiplied against the average calls per day to estimate traffic by the specific day of week. In this example, Monday's index factor, 1.469, is multiplied against 1,847.

6. The final step is to multiply the predicted calls for each day of the week by each half-hour's proportion. In this example, the half-hour from 10:00 to 10:30 is projected to receive 149 calls.

Intraday or Intraweek Forecasts

Intraday or intraweek forecasts are easy to produce and are often quite accurate. Typically, short-term forecasts are more accurate than long-term forecasts.

Intraday Forecasting

402	Calls received by 10:30 a.m.
÷ .18	Usual proportion of calls by 10:30 a.m.
2,233	Revised forecast for day
x .066	3:30 - 4:00 p.m. proportion
147	Intraday forecast for 3:30 - 4:00 p.m.

The approach works like this: At some point in the morning, say just after 10:30 a.m., your reports indicate you have received 402 calls so far. Divide the usual proportion of the day's calls that you would expect by 10:30, 18 percent in this case, into 402. (Eighteen percent came from looking at traffic patterns on previous days and calculating half-hourly proportions.) You now know that, if the trend continues, you can expect to receive 2,233 calls for the day.

Next, you can break the revised daily forecast down into the remaining half-hours by multiplying historical half-hourly proportions by 2,233. For example, since you would normally expect to get 6.6 percent of a day's calls between 3:30 and 4:00 p.m., you can expect 147 calls during that half-hour.

Intraweek Forecasting

3,050	Calls received on Monday
÷ .23	Usual proportion of calls by Monday
13,261	Revised calls forecast for week
x .17	Friday's proportion
2,254	Intraweek forecast for Friday

You would use the same methodology for intraweek forecasting based on the percentage of contacts received up to that point in the week.

5. Incorporating Average Handling Time

Ready? | 1 | 2 | 3 |

Key Points

- Average handling time, when coupled with volume, makes up call load.

- Volume alone is relatively meaningless. Forecasts must project call load.

Explanation

Many managers have a tendency to refer to call volume as if it's the only criteria in the workload: "How many calls did you get last year? Yesterday? This morning?" Equally important, though, is average handling time that, when coupled with volume, makes up call load. It is call load that matters; volume alone is relatively meaningless.

As with call volume, average talk time and average after-call work usually fall into predictable, repeating patterns. Similarly, the basic forecasting approach involves utilizing historical reports along with a measure of judgment. You begin by looking at the average handling time for a recent week, broken down by half-hour. If the week is typical, the data represented by the pattern are what will likely continue. This then becomes the data you use for staff calculations and schedule requirements. (See Average Handling Time (AHT), Section 4.)

6. Blending in Judgment

Ready? | 1 | 2 | 3 |

Key Points

- Judgmental forecasting is in the realm of intuition, market research and executive opinion.

- Some judgment is inherent in virtually all forms of forecasting.

- Accurate judgmental forecasting requires an ongoing process that brings the right people and information into the approach.

Explanation

Judgmental forecasting goes beyond purely statistical techniques and encompasses what people think is going to happen. It is in the realm of intuition, interdepartmental committees, market research and executive opinion.

Some judgment is inherent in virtually all forms of forecasting, and good judgment can significantly improve accuracy. The key is to combine quantitative and judgmental approaches effectively, and to be aware of the limitations of each.

Blending in Judgment – Customer Service Example

	Mar 5	Mar 12	Mar 19	Mar 26	Apr 2
A. Projected Customers	5,000	5,000	5,100	5,100	5,150
B. Calls per Customer	1.5	1.5	1.5	1.5	2
C. Base Calls (A x B)	7,500	7,500	7,650	7,650	10,300
D. Specific Changes*					
1. New Customers	100	0	400	0	100
2. Media Attention	0	250	0	0	0
3. Advertising	200	300	0	0	0
4. New Rate Structure	300	200	150	75	75
5. New Terms and Cond.	150	150	150	150	150
6. New Service Procedures	0	0	(-50)	(-50)	(-75)
7. New Info Required	0	0	0	0	0
8. New Product Intro	0	0	0	0	0
9. Customer Activity Level	0	0	0	0	0
10. Product Performance	0	0	0	0	0
11. Competitors Actions	0	500	0	200	100
12. Other	(-100)	(-75)	(-50)	(-50)	(-50)
*Total (add 1 thru 12)	650	1,325	600	325	200
E. Projected Calls (C + D)	8,150	8,825	8,250	7,975	10,500

This worksheet illustrates an example of applying common sense to forecasting. In a customer service environment, the number of contacts is often primarily a function of the total number of customers or constituents in the organization's universe. It is possible to project calls based on historical data, utilizing the relationships between calling volume and total customers (calls per customer). To the degree that the future repeats the past, this forecast will be accurate.

Part D of the form is where judgment plays a significant role. In this section, you customize the forecast by adding or reducing calls, based on information you develop from your own and others' input. For some of these factors, you may have some hard data that you can use. For others, you'll be making more of an educated guess.

The factors in Part D are only examples, and you will need to create a list specific to your environment. For example, if you are a support center for broken-down or stranded vehicles, weather would be a key influence on call load.

An Ongoing Process

You will need a routine process for blending judgment into the forecast. A fairly common approach in incoming call centers is a weekly forecasting meeting. These meetings typically include members of the scheduling department and a representation of supervisors and managers from the call center and other departments. The meeting will typically last only 30 or 45 minutes. It often works like this:

- The person in charge of the meeting prepares an agenda of items to be discussed.

- The scheduling person (or team) prepares the quantitative forecast before the meeting.

- During the meeting, the attendees discuss issues that may influence the forecast, such as those in Part D of the worksheet. Each participant brings a unique perspective to the process.

- As each issue is discussed, the forecast is adjusted up or down, based on what the group believes will happen.

This collaborative approach is especially effective when key team members who are accountable for staffing take an active role in forecasting (in large call centers, they can be rotated through this process). The forecast not only improves as a result of their perspective, but they gain an understanding of the factors that contribute to staffing. As a result, they more effectively supervise their teams.

7. Queuing Formulas and Simulation

Ready? | 1 | 2 | 3 |

Key Points

- Erlang C is a formula commonly used for calculating base staff; in software form, it is easy to use and widely available.

- Computer simulation is more difficult to use than Erlang C, but can more accurately model complex environments.

- Erlang B, Poisson and Retrial Tables are alternatives used for calculating trunks and IVR ports.

- No calculation or methodology is perfect, and it is important to understand the assumptions each makes and to apply common sense.

Explanation

The following table summarizes the use and assumptions of alternatives for calculating staff and system resources.

Formula	Generally Used For	Assumptions
Erlang C	Calculating base staff and predicting occupancy, trunk load, delay times, etc.	Assumes no abandoned calls or busy signals. Assumes "steady state" arrival or that traffic does not increase or decrease beyond random fluctuation within the time period. Assumes you have a fixed number of staff handling calls throughout the time period. ½ hr. Assumes that all agents within a group can handle the calls presented to the group.
Computer Simulation	Simulates what happens in terms of service level, delay, busies, overflow, etc., for the set of variables you assume.	Can be programmed to assume a wide variety of variables, such as overflow, overlapping groups and skills-based routing.

Formula	Generally Used For	Assumptions
Erlang B	Calculating trunks and IVR ports required.	Assumes that if callers get busy signals, they go away forever, never to retry. Since some callers retry, Erlang B can underestimate trunks required.
Poisson	Calculating trunks and IVR ports required.	Assumes that if callers get busy signals, they keep trying until they successfully get through. Since some callers won't keep retrying, Poisson can overestimate trunks required.
Retrial Tables	Calculating trunks and IVR ports required.	Are used less frequently by traffic engineers, but correctly assume that some callers retry and others will go away.

In its "raw form," the widely used Erlang C is as follows:

Erlang C

$$P(>0) = \cfrac{\cfrac{A^N}{N!} \cdot \cfrac{N}{N-A}}{\displaystyle\sum_{x=0}^{N-1} \cfrac{A^X}{x!} + \cfrac{A^N}{N!} \cdot \cfrac{N}{N-A}}$$

Where

A = total traffic offered in erlangs

N = number of servers in a full availability group

P(>0) = probability of delay greater than 0

P = probability of loss – Poisson formula

Obviously, Erlang C would not be so popular without the help of software, nor would the other formulas used for traffic engineering. Further, simulation of an environment would be virtually impossible without the help of computers. (Note: CIAC Certification exams do not require manual application of any of these formulas – just a general understanding of what they are and how they are applied!)

Fortunately, software programs for modeling call center environments and calculating required resources are widely available today, ranging from free programs to workforce management software costing hundreds of thousands of dollars for large installations. For a list of available resources, visit the links in the resource section of www.incoming.com.

8. Calculating Base Staff for Service Level Contacts

Ready? | 1 | 2 | 3 |

Key Points

- Four input variables are required to calculate base staff requirements for service level contacts:
    - Average talk time
    - Average after-call work
    - Call volume
    - Service level objective

- In addition to calculating base staff requirements, you can predict many important queue dynamics, including average speed of answer, occupancy, trunk load and other variables.

- These calculations reveal many call center dynamics, such as:
    - With more staff handling contacts, service level will be higher.
    - The higher service level is, the better average speed of answer is.
    - With more staff handling contacts, occupancy will be lower.

Explanation

Erlang C requires four variables:

- **Average talk time, in seconds:** Input the projected average for the future half-hour you are analyzing.

- **Average after-call work, in seconds:** Input the projected average for the future half-hour you are analyzing.

- **Number of calls:** Input the projected volume for the future half-hour you are analyzing.

- **Service level objective in seconds:** If your service level objective is to answer 90 percent of calls in 20 seconds, input 20 seconds. If it's 80 percent in 15 seconds, plug in 15 seconds. In other words, the formula needs the Y seconds in the service level definition "X percent of calls answered in Y seconds."

QueueView: A Staffing Calculator

Incoming Calls Management Institute
Annapolis, Maryland

Average talk time in seconds: 180   Average after-call work in seconds: 30
Calls per half-hour: 250   Service level in seconds: 20

Agents	P(0)	ASA	DLYDLY	Q1	Q2	SL	OCC	TKLD
30	83%	209	252	29	35	24%	97%	54.0
31	65%	75	115	10	16	45%	94%	35.4
32	51%	38	74	5	10	61%	91%	30.2
33	39%	21	55	3	8	73%	88%	28.0
34	29%	13	43	2	6	82%	86%	26.8
35	22%	8	36	1	5	88%	83%	26.1
36	16%	5	31	1	4	92%	81%	25.7
37	11%	3	27	0	4	95%	79%	25.4
38	8%	2	24	0	3	97%	77%	25.3
39	6%	1	21	0	3	98%	75%	25.2
40	4%	1	19	0	3	99%	73%	25.1
41	3%	1	18	0	2	99%	71%	25.1
42	2%	0	16	0	2	100%	69%	25.0

Here's what the column headings stand for:

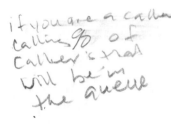

if you are a caller calling % of Callers that will be in the queue

- **Agents:** Number of agents required to be on the phones, plugged in and available to handle calls. In this case, 34 agents will achieve a service level of 82 percent answered in 20 seconds.

- **P(0):** Probability of a delay greater than zero seconds. In other words, the probability of not getting an immediate answer. In the example, 29 percent of calls will be delayed. That means that 71 percent won't be delayed, but instead will go right to an agent.

- **ASA (average speed of answer):** With 34 agents handling calls, ASA will be 13 seconds. ASA is the average delay of all calls, including the ones that aren't delayed at all. Note, while 13 seconds is the correct mathematical average, it's anything but a "typical experience" as most callers get through quicker than that, and some wait far longer. For that reason, ASA is often misinterpreted without further knowledge of what goes into the average. (See Average Speed of Answer, Section 4.)

- **DLYDLY (average delay of delayed calls):** This is the average delay only of those calls that are delayed – 43 seconds in this example.

- **Q1:** Average number of calls in queue at any time, including times when there is no queue. The label is somewhat of a misnomer, because Q1 incorporates all calls into the calculation, including those that don't end up

in queue.

- **Q2:** Average number of calls in queue when all agents are busy or when there is a queue. In the example, an average of six calls are in queue, when there is a queue. Again, this is an average, and some of the time there will be more than six calls in queue, some of the time less. But this figure can provide useful guidance for what to look for when monitoring real-time information, and can also be useful for determining overflow parameters.

- **SL (service level):** The percentage of calls that will be answered in the number of seconds you specify.

- **OCC (percent agent occupancy):** The percentage of time agents will spend handling calls, including talk time and after-call work. The balance of time, they are available and waiting for calls. In the example, occupancy will be 86 percent. Notice the trade-off: When service level goes up, occupancy goes down. (See Occupancy and Productive/Nonproductive, Section 4.)

- **TKLD:** This column is the hours (erlangs) of trunk traffic, which is the product of (talk time plus average speed of answer) multiplied by number of calls in an hour. Since Erlang B and other alternatives used for calculating trunks often require input in hours, these numbers can be readily used as is. The actual traffic carried by trunks in a half-hour will, in each row, be half of what is given.

Note, you will need to calculate base staff for each half-hour of the day and for every unique group of agents – sales, customer service and other types of groups you have. Obviously, a workforce management system that runs the calculations for many half-hours is a great time-saver. (See Workforce Management Systems, Section 6.)

Notice some of the dynamics that become evident from these calculations:

- The more agents you have handling calls, the higher service level will be.

- The more agents you have handling calls, the lower trunk load will be.

- The more agents you have handling calls, the lower occupancy will be.

These dynamics are summed up in Immutable Laws of Call Centers, this section.

(Note, in this example, we are using an Erlang C program provided by Incoming Calls Management Institute. Similar Erlang C calculators are available from ACD vendors and software companies.)

9. The Impact of Service Level on Longest Wait

Ready? | 1 | 2 | 3 |

Key Points

- Because of random call arrival, different callers may experience very different queue times, even though they may call during the same half-hour.

- Setting two service levels for the same queue, e.g., to answer 80 percent of calls in 20 seconds and the rest in 60 seconds, is impossible.

- Average speed of answer is not a "typical experience," but a simple mathematical average based on very different experiences. Consequently, it is often misinterpreted by managers.

Explanation

Different callers can experience very different queue times, even if they are part of the same set of data measured by service level, ASA and other reports. Why? Random call arrival!

A good question to ask for any service level is, "What happens to the calls that don't get answered in Y seconds?" Most Erlang C and computer simulation software programs will calculate the answers to that and other questions. For a service level of 80 percent answered in 20 seconds, about 30 percent of callers end up in queue, the longest wait will be around three minutes, and average speed of answer will be around 10 to 15 seconds.

As illustrated in the table, with 34 agents service level will be 82 percent of calls answered in 20 seconds. Sixty-five callers will wait five seconds or longer. In the next five seconds, seven of those callers reach agents, so only 58 callers are waiting 10 seconds or longer. In the next five seconds, six more callers will reach agents, leaving only 52 callers waiting 15 seconds or more. At this service level, one caller is still waiting at three minutes.

Delay Module

ERLANG C FOR INCOMING CALL CENTERS BY ICMI, INC.
TALK TIME IN SECONDS = **180**
AFTER-CALL WORK IN SECONDS = **30**
CALLS PER HALF-HOUR = **250**
SERVICE LEVEL OBJECTIVE IN SECONDS = **20**

|<========= Number of callers waiting longer than x seconds =========>|

Agents	SL%	5	10	15	20	30	40	50	60	90	120	180	240
30	24	203	199	195	191	184	177	170	163	145	129	101	80
31	45	156	149	143	137	126	115	105	97	74	57	34	20
32	61	118	111	104	97	85	74	65	56	38	25	11	5
33	73	89	81	74	67	56	47	39	32	19	11	4	1
34	82	65	58	52	46	37	29	23	18	9	5	1	0
35	88	47	41	36	31	24	18	14	10	4	2	0	0
36	92	34	29	24	21	15	11	8	6	2	1	0	0
37	95	24	20	16	14	9	6	4	3	1	0	0	0
38	97	16	13	11	9	6	4	2	2	0	0	0	0
39	98	11	9	7	5	3	2	1	1	0	0	0	0
40	99	7	6	4	3	2	1	1	0	0	0	0	0
41	99	5	4	3	2	1	1	0	0	0	0	0	0
42	100	3	2	2	1	1	0	0	0	0	0	0	0

Note two important implications of the principle of delay:

1. Because of random call arrival, different callers have different experiences even though they called during the same half-hour, and even though the call center may be hitting its target service level.

2. Some call centers attempt to set two service levels for the same queue, e.g., to handle 80 percent of calls in 20 seconds and the rest within 60 seconds. Obviously, that is not possible; 80/20 and 100/60 are distinctly different service levels.

Section 5

10. Calculating Trunks

Ready? | 1 | 2 | 3 |

Key Points

- The number of trunks you will need is determined by the delay callers experience and the conversation time for the period you are analyzing.

- The general method for calculating trunks is as follows:

  1. Forecast the call load (workload) to be handled for the busiest half-hour in the foreseeable future.

  2. Compute the number of agents required to handle the forecasted call load at your service level objective.

  3. Determine the trunk load, according to the call load you will be handling and the service level you can realistically achieve.

  4. Determine the number of trunks required to handle the calculated trunk load, using an appropriate formula.

- Two important considerations when calculating staff and trunks are:

  - Staff should be calculated in conjunction with trunks.

  - There is no single staff-to-trunk ratio you can count on.

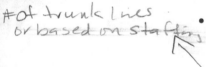
# of trunk lines or based on staffing

Explanation

The number of trunks you will need is determined by the delay callers experience (the time from the moment calls arrive at the telephone system until agents say "hello") and the conversation time (talk time), for the period you are analyzing. The general method for calculating trunks is as follows:

1. Forecast the call load (workload) to be handled for the busiest half-hour in the foreseeable future. (See discussions on forecasting, this section.)

2. Compute the number of agents required to handle the forecasted call load at your service level objective. (See Calculating Base Staff for Service Level Contacts, this section.)

3. Determine the trunk load, according to the call load you will be handling and the service level you can realistically achieve. The trunk load represents

how much time in hours callers are in queue or connected to agents over an hour.

4. Determine the number of trunks required to handle the calculated trunk load, using an appropriate formula. Erlang B is widely used, but there are other alternatives you can choose from. Each has built-in assumptions. With any of the formulas used for calculating trunks, you will need to specify the probability of busy signals you can live with, because if you specify none, you'll need as many trunks as there are calls! But if you can tolerate even a small probability of busy signals, (e.g., 1 percent) then the number of trunks required becomes much more realistic.

You may have an IVR system that callers go through before they reach an agent. If so, the time callers spend in the IVR will have to be factored into the calculations. And if trunks are shared among different agent groups, that would also be a consideration. Regardless, the basic concept holds true: staffing impacts trunking requirements. Delay is key – the fewer people you have for a given call load, the more trunks you'll need.

The Relationship Between Staff and Trunks

To understand the association between staff and trunks, you need to know some key definitions. When interpreting the following diagram, assume a "straight-in" environment, where callers dial a number and are routed directly to the agent group handling the calls. (This example assumes no IVR involvement.)

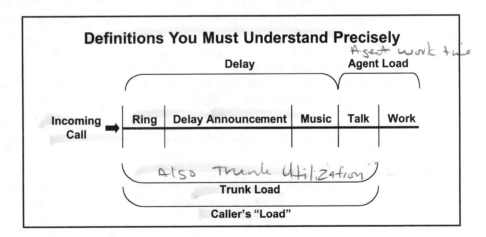

- **Delay:** Delay is everything from when the trunk is seized to the point at which the caller is connected to an agent.

- **Agent load:** Agent load includes the two components of handling time, talk time and after-call work.

- **Trunk load:** Trunk load includes all aspects of the transaction other than after-call work, which does not require a circuit. The caller's load is the same as the trunk load, other than the short time it takes for the network to route the call to the call center.

Notice that agent load and trunk load both include talk time. However, trunk load carries the delay, which is not a direct part of the agent load. And the agents handle after-call work, which is not carried by the trunks.

This realization leads to two important considerations when calculating staff and trunks:

1. Staff should be calculated in conjunction with trunks. The more staff handling a given call load, the less delay callers will experience. In other words, staffing impacts delay; therefore, it directly impacts how many trunks are required. There is no way to know base trunking needs without knowing how many staff will be handling the projected call load.

2. There is no single staff-to-trunk ratio you can count on. You may have heard the rule of thumb that you need 1.5 trunks per agent (e.g., 15 trunks for every 10 agents). If that's the ratio you end up needing, it's purely chance. There is no ratio that can be universally applied. The reasons? For one, after-call work, which occupies agents but doesn't require trunks, is different from one call center to the next.

Second, caller tolerances vary widely among organizations, as influenced by the seven factors affecting tolerance. (See Factors Affecting Caller Tolerance, Section 3.) If you have a high service level, the trunks will carry little delay. If your service level is low, the trunks will have to carry more delay and, consequently, you will need more trunks.

There's a better way to determine resources than to depend on ratios that may not work: calculate staff, then calculate trunks the right way. Whatever the staff-to-trunk ratio turns out to be, that is what will work for you.

Related Definitions

Other terms associated with trunking include:

- **All trunks busy (ATB):** When all trunks are busy in a specified trunk group. Generally, reports indicate how many times all trunks were busy (how many times the last trunk available was seized), and how much total time all trunks were busy. What they don't reveal is how many callers got busy signals when all trunks were busy. One telltale sign of ATB is call arrival patterns that flatten during peak times.

- **Blocked call:** A call that cannot be connected immediately because a) no trunk is available at the time the call arrives, or b) the ACD is programmed to block calls from entering the queue when the queue backs up beyond a desired threshold. (See Abandoned and Blocked Calls, Section 4.)

11. Immutable Laws of Call Centers

Ready? | 1 | 2 | 3 |

Key Points

- There are important immutable laws at work in inbound call centers:

  - For a given call load, when service level goes up, occupancy goes down.

  - Keep improving service level and you will reach a point of diminishing returns.

  - For a given service level, larger agent groups are more efficient than smaller groups.

  - All other things equal, pooled groups are more efficient than specialized groups.

  - For a given call load, add staff and average speed of answer will go down.

  - For a given call load, add staff and trunk load will go down.

- A good understanding of these principles is fundamental to a workable planning process, accurate budgets, fair standards and good strategy.

Explanation

Fundamental principles govern call centers. They are immutable in the sense that they are unchangeable. Understanding these dynamics is key to cultivating an effective planning process, setting fair standards, preparing accurate budgets and communicating call center activities to upper management and others.

When Service Level Goes Up, Occupancy Goes Down

Occupancy is the percent of time during a half-hour that those agents who are on the phones are in talk time and after-call work. The inverse of occupancy is the time agents spend waiting for inbound contacts, plugged in and available.

As the example illustrates, a service level at 82 percent of calls answered in 20 seconds equates to an occupancy of 86 percent. If service level drops to 24 percent answered in 20 seconds, occupancy goes up to 97 percent. (See Occupancy and Productive/Nonproductive, Section 4.)

Agents	SL% in 20 Sec.	ASA	Occ.	Trunk Load (in hours)
30	24%	208.7	97%	54.0
31	45%	74.7	94%	35.4
32	61%	37.6	91%	30.2
33	73%	21.3	88%	28.0
34	82%	12.7	86%	26.8
35	88%	7.8	83%	26.1
36	92%	4.9	81%	25.7
37	95%	3.1	79%	25.4
38	97%	1.9	77%	25.3
39	98%	1.2	75%	25.2
40	99%	0.7	73%	25.1
41	99%	0.5	71%	25.1
42	100%	0.3	69%	25.0

Avg. Talk Time: 180 sec.; Avg. Work Time: 30 sec.; Calls: 250

The Law of Diminishing Returns

The law of diminishing returns is a significant consideration in a queuing environment. It can be stated this way: When successive individual agents are assigned to a given call load, marginal improvements in service level that can be attributed to each additional agent will eventually decline.

As the table illustrates, 30 agents at the given call load will provide a service level of just over 24 percent in 20 seconds. With 31 agents, things improve dramatically. Service level jumps to 45 percent, a quantum improvement. Adding one more person yields another big improvement. In fact, adding only four or five people takes service level from the depths of poor service to something respectable. Each person has a significant positive impact on the queue when service level is low. Keep adding, though, and the improvements are less dramatic.

(continued, next page)

Calls in Half-hour	Service Level	Agents Required	Occupancy	Avg. Calls Per Agent
50	80/20	9	65%	5.6
100	80/20	15	78%	6.7
500	80/20	65	90%	7.7
1,000	80/20	124	94%	8.1

Assumption: Calls last an average 3.5 minutes.

Larger Groups Are More Efficient

As this table illustrates, mathematically, larger groups of agents are more efficient than smaller groups, at the same service level.

Consequently, average group "productivity" (transactions that a group handles) is not a constant factor. If you maintain a consistent service level by providing the correct number of staff to match fluctuating call loads throughout the day and week, you'll find that average productivity is relatively lower at lower call volumes and relatively higher at higher call volumes. As the number of calls is changing throughout the day, so is average group productivity. (See Occupancy and Productive/Nonproductive, Section 4.)

The Powerful Pooling Principle *Cross training*

The powerful pooling principle states: Any movement in the direction of consolidation of resources will result in improved traffic-carrying efficiency. Conversely, any movement away from consolidation of resources will result in reduced traffic-carrying efficiency. Put more simply, if you take several small, specialized agent groups, effectively cross train them and put them into a single group, you'll have a more efficient environment. (See The Implications of Agent Group Structure, this section.)

Add Staff and ASA Goes Down

When more agents are plugged in and handling inbound transactions, assuming they are proficient and equipped to do so, the queue on average will be shorter. Fewer agents mean a longer queue.

Add Staff and Trunk Load Goes Down

When more agents are assigned to a given call load, trunk load goes down. The converse is also true. When fewer agents are available to handle a given call load, trunk load goes up because delay increases. (See The Cost of Delay, this section.)

12. The Implications of Agent Group Structure

Ready? | 1 | 2 | 3 |

Key Points

- There is a continuum between pooled groups and specialized groups. There is no "formula" for finding the perfect balance between these opposite ends, so managers must look for symptoms of groups that are either too specialized or too generalized.

- Symptoms of agent groups that are too specialized:
  - Small groups with low occupancy and/or erratic service levels
  - An overly complicated planning process
  - Many calls not handled by the intended group (due to overflow)
  - Agents frustrated with narrow responsibilities

- Symptoms of agent groups that are too generalized:
  - Higher average handling time
  - Longer training time
  - Lower quality
  - Agents frustrated with "too much to know"

Explanation

As discussed in Immutable Laws of Call Centers, in this section, the powerful pooling principle works in favor of larger, combined agent groups. All other things equal, if you take several small, specialized agent groups, effectively cross train them and put them into a single group, you'll have a more efficient environment.

The pooling principle is a consideration from the highest levels of strategic planning (e.g., How many call centers should we have? How should existing call centers be networked?) down to moment-to-moment decisions about overflowing calls between groups.

A clear trend today, though, is the recognition that different types of callers often have different needs and expectations, and that different agents with a mix of aptitudes and skills are required. Capabilities in the intelligent network and in intelligent ACDs give call centers the means to pool resources as well as segment and prioritize their customer base. (See ACD Systems, and Networks, Section 6.) Skills-based routing is a notable example. (See Skills-Based

Section 5

Routing, this section.)

In short, as real and pervasive as the pooling principle is, it is not an all-or-nothing proposition. There is a continuum between pooling and specialization, and there is no perfect formula for deciding how pooled or specialized agent groups should be.

The symptoms of groups that are too pooled or too specialized are usually evident. For example, symptoms of agent groups that are too specialized include:

- You have small groups with low occupancy and/or erratic service level/response time results.

- The planning process is overly complicated.

- Many calls are not handled by the intended group (due to overflow).

- Agents are frustrated with narrow responsibilities.

Conversely, symptoms of agent groups that are too generalized include:

- Calls have a higher average handling time than necessary, as agents grapple with a broad range of issues.

- Training time is long.

- Quality suffers.

- Agents are frustrated with "too much to know."

Finding the right group structure requires being in tune with these issues, as well as ensuring that groups are structured to support the customer access strategy. (See Establishing a Customer Access Strategy, Section 3.)

(For more information on agent groups, see ICMI's *Call Center People Management Handbook and Study Guide*.)

13. The Cost of Delay

Ready? | 1 | 2 | 3 |

Key Points

- The cost of delay is the direct expense of putting callers in queue when you are paying for the calls.

- The cost of delay is typically represented as delay (expressed in minutes) multiplied by the cost of the service (expressed in minutes).

- The intent of determining cost of delay analysis is not to conduct a break-even analysis, but to be realistic and inclusive in assessing the real costs of staff and telecommunications services.

Explanation

As discussed in Immutable Laws of Call Centers, this section, when more agents are assigned to a given call load, trunk load goes down. The converse is also true. When fewer agents are available to handle a given call load, trunk load goes up because delay increases. The direct expense of putting callers in queue is called the cost of delay. It is expressed in terms of how much you pay for your network service each day just for callers to wait in queue until they reach a representative.

In an inbound call center, each person connected to your system requires a trunk, whether they are talking to an agent or waiting in queue. If you have toll-free service (or any other service that charges a usage fee), you are paying for this time. Telecommunications costs are inextricably wrapped in staffing issues. If service level is continually low, the cost of network services will be high.

In the following example, trunk load will be 26.8 erlangs (hours) at a service level of 82/20. To make this easy for comparison's sake, assume that you get the same call load two half-hours in a row so that you will need the number of agents shown for the entire hour. You can then easily compare hourly staffing costs to hourly network costs.

Assume that each agent costs $15 per hour and that your toll-free service costs $5 per hour. Using these costs, 34 agents will cost $510 per hour (34 x $15) and the toll-free service will cost $134 per hour (26.8 hours x $5 per hour) for a total of $644 per hour.

	Avg. Talk Time: 180 sec.; Avg. Work Time: 30 sec.; Calls: 250			
Agents	**SL% in 20 Sec.**	**ASA**	**Occ.**	**Trunk Load (in hours)**
30	24%	208.7	97%	54.0
31	45%	74.7	94%	35.4
32	61%	37.6	91%	30.2
33	73%	21.3	88%	28.0
34	82%	12.7	86%	26.8
35	88%	7.8	83%	26.1
36	92%	4.9	81%	25.7
37	95%	3.1	79%	25.4
38	97%	1.9	77%	25.3
39	98%	1.2	75%	25.2
40	99%	0.7	73%	25.1
41	99%	0.5	71%	25.1
42	100%	0.3	69%	25.0

Now, use the same approach to analyze any of the other service levels. For example, if you have 30 agents available to handle calls, total costs will be higher – $720 per hour, or $450 per hour for the staff and $270 per hour for the toll-free service.

The point is not to conduct a break-even analysis. Given relatively inexpensive toll costs today, break even may be below where service level should be to provide acceptable service. Rather, the objective is to get a handle on what both staff and telecommunications costs are for accurate budgeting purposes, and to illustrate that adding agents doesn't cost as much as it seems, given their impact on toll costs.

When cutting cost giving the best customer
, service
- forecast are the best
- schedules are the best

14. Long Calls

Ready? | 1 | 2 | 3 |

Key Points

- Long calls are when average handling time approaches or exceeds 30 minutes.

- If you regularly handle long calls, it usually makes sense to establish longer reporting intervals (typically hours instead of half-hours).

- Planning for long calls requires a balance of common sense and statistics.

- Two tiers of agents often make sense.

Explanation

Thirty-minute reporting periods provide an adequate level of detail and accuracy for most inbound call centers. However, some call centers, particularly those in help desk environments, handle calls that are complex enough that average handling time approaches or exceeds 30 minutes.

Since long calls are not distributed as Erlang C assumes, they may violate the assumptions of the formula. Compounding the problem is the fact that ACDs often count calls in the period in which they begin, but report handling times in the period in which they end. Consequently, reported averages can be skewed.

For planning and management purposes, report intervals may need to be adjusted upward, i.e., to hours. This minimizes the effects of skewed averages. It's also important to balance common sense with statistics. For example, if long calls are an anomaly, you might opt to adjust your statistics before using your reports to project staffing needs. And to avoid a low service level, you may need to force higher staffing in hours when long calls arrive.

Most Erlang C programs will allow you to define the interval you want to examine, e.g., hours instead of half-hours. Alternatively, you can program a simulator to model the mix of calls you are taking.

You will also need to consider how you manage long calls. For example, a second tier of staff may be an efficient way to handle complex calls. Calls to the initial group can be treated normally, all callers reach someone quickly, and

Section 5

those with simple questions don't have to wait for the second tier. Further, those with complex problems may be more willing to wait for service, and agents handling these calls can do so under less pressure. Be sure also to manage the service level of the second group or service in both tiers will suffer.

15. Skills-Based Routing

Ready? | 1 | 2 | 3

Key Points

- Skills-based routing matches a caller's specific needs with an agent who has the skills to handle that call on a real-time basis.

- Skills-based routing requires more sophisticated analysis than Erlang C can provide.

- Basic management steps of skills-based routing include:
  - Identify and define the skills required for each call type.
  - Identify and define individual agent skills.
  - Prioritize agent skills, based on individual competency levels.
  - Determine staff requirements and test assumptions; repeat as necessary.
  - Devise and program into the ACD an appropriate routing plan.
  - Develop ongoing management responsibilities.

Explanation

Skills-based routing matches a caller's specific needs with an agent who has the skills to handle that call on a real-time basis. In this environment, Erlang C's assumption of traditional ACD groups no longer fits. But computer simulation can help fill the gap. (See Queuing Formulas and Simulation, this section.)

The basic requirements to get started with skills-based routing include:

- Identify what differentiates caller needs and desires. This comes from the customer access strategy. (See Establishing a Customer Access Strategy, Section 3.)

- Identify and define the skills required for each call type.

- Identify and define individual agent skills.

- Prioritize agent skills, based on individual competency levels.

- Devise and program into the ACD an appropriate routing plan.

You will essentially create two "maps" when you program your ACD for skills-based routing. One will specify the types of calls to be handled and the other will identify the skills available by agent.

Consider a simple case that illustrates the basic steps in staffing for skills-based routing. Assume you have two languages to handle, English and Spanish. And let's say that you have four call types to handle, orders and technical support calls in each language. The chart on the following page may illustrate what your agent skills may look like.

Agent Skills									
Caller Types (Based upon IVR menu selections)	Agent Type 1	Agent Type 2	Agent Type 3	Agent Type 4	Agent Type 5	Agent Type 6	Agent Type 7	Agent Type 8	Agent Type 9
Orders - English	x	x						x	x
Orders - Spanish				x		x		x	x
Tech Support - English		x	x		x				x
Tech Support - Spanish			x			x	x		x

Next, let's assume that your plan is to route calls to the least-skilled agent who can handle the call because you want to preserve your more experienced or skilled agents for less common or more complex calls. Consequently, the routing plan would look like this.

Routing Plan				
Call Routing Hierarchy	Order-English	Order-Spanish	Tech Support-English	Tech Support-Spanish
Skill Choice 1	Agent Type 1	Agent Type 4	Agent Type 5	Agent Type 7
Skill Choice 2	Agent Type 2	Agent Type 8	Agent Type 2	Agent Type 6
Skill Choice 3	Agent Type 8	Agent Type 6	Agent Type 3	Agent Type 3
Skill Choice 4	Agent Type 9	Agent Type 9	Agent Type 9	Agent Type 9

You would set up the simulator the same way you would program the maps into your ACD. You program it for the types of calls you are going to get and the skills of your group. You will also plug in the same data required by Erlang C: volume of each transaction you expect, and corresponding talk-time and work-time estimates. Additionally, you can specify caller tolerance levels by type of call, trunking configurations and other conditions.

We used this information to run three different scenarios, all using the same call load and service level objective:

- Conventional ACD groups (one group for each call type)

- Skills-based routing

- Universal agents (a fully cross trained group)

Results of Each Scenario

Time Period	Separate Groups By Language and Call Type	Skills-Based Routing Scenario	Crossed-trained Universal Agents
09:00-9:30	30	27	24
09:30-10:00	43	41	39
10:00-10:30	64	62	59
10:30-11:00	58	56	52
11:00-11:30	44	41	40
11:30-12:00	31	28	27

As the results show, in this example skills-based routing is more efficient than separate, segmented groups. Also note that universal agents, where each agent is fully cross trained and speaks both languages, is the most efficient arrangement.

In general, skills-based routing works best in environments that have small groups where multiple skills are required. It can also help to quickly integrate new agents into call handling, by sending only simple calls to them. It also has the potential to improve efficiency by matching callers with "just the right agent."

Skills-based routing has some disadvantages. Getting people in the right place at the right times can be difficult, and small specialized groups are tough to manage. And they can eliminate the efficiencies of pooling, common to conventional ACD groups. (See The Implications of Agent Group Structure, in this section.)

Further, routing and resource planning become more complex. Be prepared to run enough simulations to learn what's workable in your environment. You also need to develop contingency plans, for when the call load of a specific call type is greater than expected or when you don't have the specialized staff for which you planned (e.g., because of sickness).

Skills-based routing is a powerful capability. But it must be managed well – which means going through the planning process diligently. You'll need a good

forecast and solid staff calculations.

Troubleshooting Skills-Based Routing

Skills-based routing is supposed to be the perfect answer to the challenge of getting the right call to the right place at the right time. But in many cases, skills-based routing also has created difficult new problems that have tempered or obviated the potential benefits: difficult forecasting challenges, complex staffing puzzles and volatile service levels. The top five problems that hamper good results and corresponding antidotes are summarized below:

Rostered staff factor (shrink factor) issues: There are many things that can keep agents from the phones. With necessary skills unavailable, calls end up with secondary and tertiary alternatives, sending a ripple effect through the process that can misappropriate available staff and send service level and quality plunging. If there are times in the day that service level is volatile for some types of contacts, this issue is a likely culprit. There's no substitute for realistically planning and budgeting for the things that keep agents from the phones.

Solution: Spend the time necessary to routinely and realistically anticipate and plan for the activities that keep agents from the phones, by time of day and by skill set. (See Rostered Staff Factor, this section.)

Not forecasting accurately at the skill level: The queuing formulas and simulation models available for calculating required staff are only as good as the accuracy of input they are analyzing. To anticipate staffing needs, you first need to know how many French-speaking callers you're going to get between 10:00 and 10:30. The inability to forecast accurately at the skill level is the Achilles' heel of the powerful simulation programs now available.

Solution: Invest the time necessary to forecast call load for each mix of calls requiring unique skill sets (e.g., French-speaking calls for service A, French-speaking calls for service B, etc.). Assess the accuracy of forecasted call load vs. actual; if it is routinely off by more than 5 percent to 10 percent by half-hour, consider combining skills to form more manageable groups. (See forecasting discussion, this section, and Forecasted Call Load vs. Actual, Section 4.)

Not calculating base-staff requirements accurately: Skills-based routing generally requires computer simulation, which can test a wide range of variables and assumptions before actually implementing changes.

Solution: Invest in a simulator, and spend the time necessary to run a wide range of scenarios to assess your current capacity capabilities and requirements. (See Queuing Formulas and Simulation, this section.)

Poor assumptions/rationale: In general, skills-based routing works best in environments that require many skills and have many possible combinations of skill sets. Help desks handling a wide variety of complex issues and call centers handling many languages are common examples. Skills-based routing can also help to quickly integrate new agents by initially routing only simple calls or calls of a predefined nature to them. What skills-based routing can't do is compensate for poor planning, inadequate training or poorly designed information systems. Remember, the core assumption of a call center is pooled groups, where crosstrained agents are equipped to share the work load. All things equal, pooled environments are more efficient than those with specialized groups.

Solution: Create an environment that is as pooled as possible. This requires an incessant effort to hire the right people, improve training, improve information systems and reduce staff turnover. In other words, go as far as you can toward obviating the need for skills-based routing. (See The Implications of Agent Group Structure, this section.)

No skills-based routing manager/coordinator: Even small call centers have learned through tough, practical experience that it takes a full-time person to keep skills-based routing running smoothly. Projecting requirements, assessing current capabilities, updating system programming and adjusting staffing plans and schedules to accommodate evolving circumstances are ongoing activities.

Solution: Create a position for managing skills-based routing. Equip this person or team with the tools, information and authority necessary to predict requirements, make necessary changes to system programming and staffing plans, and advise on future requirements.

Six Typical Errors

Used correctly, SBR can have powerful positive effects on contact center operations. However, there are a few common mistakes that can cause problems. Let's take a look at six typical errors and what you can do to avoid them.

- **Creating agent groups just because you can.** The ability to create separate queues for callers should first give rise to the question, "Does this make sense for us?" You should aim to have as large a pool of agents in each queue as makes sense for your application; the fewer skills groups you create, the better the system will work because you will be able to manage it. Sometimes it's just a matter of having the right support tools in place to avoid having to break down the more optimal, larger agent pools into smaller skills groups. Also, the process of creating skills should be controlled by the call center manager, not the telecom department or IT.

(continued, next page)

• **Failing to invest in a workable call-sorting system.** If you're experiencing high transfer rates between agent groups, the problem might be that customers don't understand how to make the choices they're offered in your sorting system (usually an IVR or other automated system). High transfer rates eat into your resources and frustrate your customers, who naturally prefer first-contact service.

• **Never or rarely revisiting your agent group setup after it's been programmed.** You will need to look at your call-flow scheme every time your business changes, the nature of your calls change, or when you add Web-based self-services. Also, typical call center attrition transforms agent skill groups. For instance, the number of agents who can handle a particular type of call may dwindle during attrition and you may end up with fewer agents in a particular skill group. That often results in a few agents being overwhelmed with calls while others sit idle. And customers who need the services of that specific highly skilled group have to wait, decreasing their satisfaction, driving up handle time and rendering those agents even more overloaded.

• **Failing to assign responsibility for workload balance and staffing each queue.** The task of managing multiple queues becomes more complex with the addition of each skills group. If you have centers that are virtually networked, it becomes even more complex. The absence or attrition of staff, particularly in small agent groups, can have a profound effect on service level. The decision to switch staff from one answer group to another, likewise, will have a substantial impact, especially if the group from which staff is being switched is small. If you're not prepared to handle this kind of contingency, you will be perpetually behind the curve. You need to have a predetermined plan to handle unforeseen staff shortages in any queue, and someone needs to be responsible for implementing that plan.

• **Failing to coordinate with other divisions.** Make sure HR knows what skills groups they will need to staff, and on what timetable. The training unit needs to be ready to train the appropriate skills at the right time. Telecom needs to understand that it must not make changes to call flow without consulting you. Marketing needs to give advance warning of new promotions or product changes that will affect how you allocate calls. IT needs to understand the effect of system changes on service level, and that you need to be included in the planning process.

• **Incompatibility between call-routing capabilities and workforce management systems.** If you're shopping for a workforce management system with SBR capabilities, be sure to request an explanation of the system's capabilities and a guarantee (with penalties for nonperformance) that the system will be compatible with the way your telecommunications system is able to route calls. If there isn't a close match, managing SBR will be further compounded.

Excerpt from "Six Common Skills-Based Routing Mistakes to Avoid" by Jean Bave-Kerwin, *Call Center Management Review*, May 2002.

16. Peaked Traffic

Ready? | 1 | 2 | 3 |

Section 5

Key Points

- There are two types of peaked traffic – the type you can plan for (e.g., television ads) and those incidents that are impossible to predict (e.g., a network outage in a sister call center).

- Peaked traffic requires shorter increments of time for planning and reporting (e.g., five or 10 minutes).

- Queuing principles are different for peaked traffic, and service level results are dramatically affected by how "peaked" the traffic is.

Explanation

Peaked traffic is a surge beyond random variation within a half-hour, which poses a unique staffing challenge. (See Traffic Arrival Types: Random, Smooth and Peaked, Section 3.) For the purposes of this discussion, there are two types of peaked traffic – the type you can plan for and incidents that are impossible to predict.

Unplanned Peaked Traffic

If a national news program unexpectedly provides your telephone number to the viewing audience as part of its story, you will get unannounced peaked traffic. The problem is, you can't predict these events, and you're probably not willing to staff up for them just in case they happen. So staffing for unexpected peaks falls more in the categories of real-time management or disaster recovery planning. (See Establishing and Using Real-Time Tactics, Section 3, and What Disaster Plans Cover, Section 7.)

Planned Peaked Traffic

Peaked traffic that you are expecting belongs squarely in the realm of fundamental call center planning. Forecasting, staffing and scheduling to meet a specified service level still apply. However, planning must happen at much more detailed periods of time, often in five- or 10-minute increments. For a given service level, peaked traffic requires more staff than random traffic, and agents will have a lower occupancy over a half-hour period.

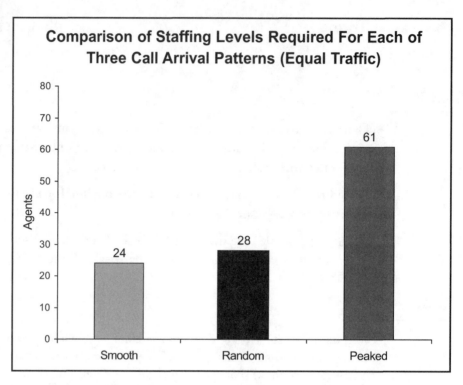

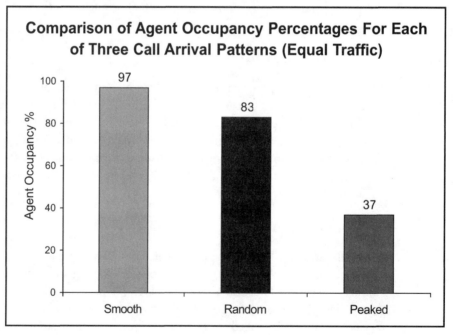

Most use Erlang C to calculate base staff for predicted peaks. If you expect 200 calls in a five-minute span, that's the equivalent of 1,200 calls in a half-hour. If you use an Erlang C program based on half-hour data, you will assume 1,200 calls for the calculations. Alternatively, some Erlang C software allows you to specify the timeframe you choose.

But common sense is required. If you have 75 people to handle the 200 calls, and the 200 calls come in virtually at the same time, you know that the first 75 calls are going to get immediate answer. The next 75 are going to have to wait, and the average wait will be similar to the average handling time of the first 75 calls. The last 50 calls will have to wait something like two times the average handling time of the calls.

The situation can be similar to a bus dropping people off in front of a stadium. Those reaching the gates first get quick service. For others, service levels can be dramatically different, depending on where they end up in the line. Consequently, how peaked the traffic is (how concentrated it is within a small period of time) will dramatically impact service level results.

17. Calculating Base Staff For
Response Time Contacts

Ready? | 1 | 2 | 3 |

Key Points

- Calculating staff to handle email and other response time contacts is generally based on a units-of-output approach.

- Since response time contacts do not have to be handled immediately, there are many ways to distribute the workload into staff schedules.

- An efficiency factor ensures that you are scheduling enough agents to prevent them from burnout, the result of handling one transaction after another for extended periods.

Explanation

Calculating staff requirements for a workload that does not have to be handled at the time it arrives is generally based on the centuries-old units-of-output approach. Here's the logic: If you get 60 messages that have an average handling time of four minutes, that's four hours of workload. One agent working nonstop could handle the load in four hours. If you need to complete the transactions within two hours, you will need a minimum of two agents working over a period of two hours. So, as with service level and inbound telephone calls, the email workload and response time objective dictate staff requirements. (See Definitions and Use of Service Level, Response Time and Quality, Section 3.) Accordingly, the basic formula for calculating the minimum staff required is:

Basic Formula

$$\frac{\text{Volume}}{(\text{RT} \div \text{AHT})} = \text{Agents}$$

Volume = Volume for forecast increment (e.g., volume per hour)
RT = Response time   *how much time do I have*
                      have I allowed
AHT = Average handling time

Volume is the quantity of transactions you must handle, AHT is the average amount of time it takes agents to handle the transactions (the equivalent of

average talk time and average after-call work for inbound telephone calls), and response time is the time you have to respond to customers after receiving their messages. Using the formula, you could handle the 60 messages previously mentioned in two hours with $60 \div (120 \div 4) = 2$ agents.

There are several things to keep in mind:

- There are many ways you can slice and dice base staff schedules to achieve your objectives. In fact, in the example, you could have 60 agents rush in and handle all 60 transactions just before the promised response time and still meet your objective. What you are really doing is looking for an efficient way to distribute the workload across your schedules within the promised response time.

- When response time objectives are less than an hour, traffic engineers generally recommend using Erlang C or computer simulation to calculate base staff. This would be a queuing and service level scenario, like inbound telephone calls. (See Calculating Base Staff for Service Level Objectives, this section.)

- Breaks, absenteeism and other activities that keep agents from the work need to be added to base staff calculations. (See Rostered Staff Factor, this section.)

- An efficiency factor acknowledges that agents cannot handle one transaction after another with no "breathing" time in between. For example, if you want to build in an efficiency factor with a ceiling of 90 percent, divide base staff calculations by .9 to calculate if additional agents are required.

Email-Handling Strategies

Call centers with successful records of handling customer email have developed a variety of tactics for dealing with the uncertainties they face. Following are a few recommendations.

- **Build a historical record.** Tracking email volume, subject matter and handling times eventually builds a database that can be used to improve forecasting.

- **Incorporate additional factors into the forecasting model.** In addition to historical data, companies are using other information to forecast email — for example, sales projections, plans for special marketing efforts and planned changes to the Web site.

- **Set standards for responding to email.** There is no one "right" standard. Mitch Johnson, president and CEO of Email Solutions, an outsourcing company, says his clients require response times "anywhere from 24 hours down to immediate, depending on the

---

(continued, next page)

www ciac-cert.org
-cert.org

application." Some companies set different standards for different types of customers (e.g., email from business customers may get faster turnaround time) or for different types of requests (e.g., a brochure promised during a phone call may be emailed immediately so the customer won't call back and repeat the request).

• **Use the forecasts and the response standards to staff the email center.** Call centers with service level objectives need models such as Erlang C to estimate the number of agents they need at any time. With a response time objective, the calculation is simpler.

While some contact centers use "universal agents," others find that combining the service-level-driven telephone group with the response-time-driven email group results in email being neglected. After trying the universal agent approach, Aaron Hunt, customer service manager for Xerox's Small Office/Home Office group (also known as Team Xerox), eventually took the agents with good writing skills and formed a dedicated email group.

• **Develop a backup plan.** Given the uncertainty about email volume and content, a backup plan is crucial. One tactic is to aim for a response time better than what you're promising the customer. Then customers will be delighted if your forecasts are correct, and if your forecasts are off they won't be unhappy.

Keeping a pool of trained agents in reserve is also useful. Contact center managers in large companies sometimes "borrow" agents from the phone queue or from another contact center in the same company. Outsourcers servicing multiple companies regularly crosstrain staff so they can assign them to different clients based on volume. Smaller companies handling their own email may contract with outsourcers to cover unexpected peaks. If all else fails, supervisors and managers may find themselves answering customer email.

• **Monitor the email queue as closely as you monitor the telephone queue.** Supervisors and managers need to watch the email queue to make sure the backlog doesn't threaten the response time target. (Email response management software generally allows real-time queue monitoring.)

Excerpt from "Plan Ahead for Erratic Workloads to Improve Email Response Times" by Masha Zager, *Call Center Management Review*, August 2001.

18. Outbound Contacts

See KPIs for Outbound, Section 4.

19. Rostered Staff Factor (Shrinkage)

Ready? | 1 | 2 | 3 |

Key Points

- Rostered staff factor (RSF) leads to the minimum staff needed on schedule over and above base staff required to achieve your service level and response time objectives. It is a form of forecasting for the things that typically keep agents from the phones.

- As with time series forecasting, the assumption behind rostered staff factor is that the past will help predict the future, or that the proportion of staff off the phones will be similar to what is happening now.

- In many call centers, rostered staff factor falls between 1.1 and 1.4 throughout the day, meaning that a minimum of 10 percent to 40 percent additional staff are required on schedule over base staff required. However, it can be much higher in some call centers.

always going to be greater than 1

Explanation

Rostered staff factor, alternatively called an overlay or shrink factor, is a numerical factor that leads to the minimum staff needed on schedule over and above base staff required to achieve your service level and response time objectives. It is calculated after base staffing is determined and before schedules are organized.

Calculating Rostered Staff Factor

Calculating RSF is a form of forecasting. The major assumption is that the proportion of staff off the phones will be similar to what is happening now. In other words, if one person is on break in a group of 10, 10 people will be on break in a group of 100.

An illustration of how to calculate RSF is shown in the following table.

The mechanics include five steps:

> 1. **Enter the base staff required by half-hour:** What base staff includes will depend on the structure of your groups. If you have separate agent groups for transactions that must be handled when they arrive and transactions

Rostered Staff Factor (Shrinkage) Calculations

	Base Staff Required		Absent	Break	Training	On Schedule	Rostered Staff Factor
	Phone	Email					
08:00-08:30	18 ✈	4 = 22	2	0	0	24	1.09
08:30-09:00	20	4	2	0	4	30	1.25
09:00-09:30	20	4	2	0	4	30	1.25
09:30-10:00	25	5	2	3	4	39	1.3
10:00-10:30	25	5	2	3	4	39	1.3
10:30-11:00	31	5	2	3	4	45	1.25

$$\text{Rostered Staff Factor} = \frac{\text{On Schedule}}{\text{Base Staff Required}}$$

that can be handled at a later time, the base staff entered represents one of those groups. You will need shrinkage calculations for each group. On the other hand, if you set up groups that handle both types of transactions, base staff is first calculated for both types of work separately and then added together. You would then calculate the shrink factor for the combined group.

2. **Identify the things that routinely keep agents from the workload**: The next three columns reflect the numbers of staff absent, on break and in training, as they now occur. These categories are just examples, and you can include research, outbound calls (those that are not part of talk time or after-call work) and other activities. You may also want to further subdivide the categories. For example, absenteeism can be divided into planned absenteeism, such as vacations, and unplanned absenteeism, such as sick leave.

3. **Add base staff to the number of agents who will be away from the workload, for each half-hour**: The "on-schedule" column is the sum of the entries in previous columns, by half-hour.

4. **Calculate RSF**: The last column is derived by dividing the staff required on schedule by base staff required, for each half-hour. The proportions are the mechanism you will use to project future shrinkage.

5. **Use the factors when organizing future schedules**: The result of these calculations is a set of factors reflecting expected shrinkage by half-hour. You multiply them against the base staff you will need when assembling future schedules. For example, if you are putting together a schedule for two weeks from now, and you need 32 base staff between 8:30 and 9:00, you will need to schedule 40 agents (32 x 1.25) for that half-hour – plus any staff required to be working on projects, in meetings or anything else not included in the shrinkage calculation.

Section 5

What to Include

While breaks and absenteeism should almost always be included in shrink factor calculations, other activities require some analysis and judgment. For example, should training be included? If training schedules frequently change and/or require differing proportions of staff, keep training information out of shrinkage calculations and, instead, factor it into schedules on a case-by-case basis. But if training happens in predictable proportion to the base staff required, include it.

Note: After-call work (also called wrap-up) is already included in base staff calculations (as part of average handling time) so it should not be included in shrink factor calculations. (See Incorporating Average Handling Time, this section.)

In many call centers, shrink factor falls between 1.1 and 1.4 throughout the day, meaning that a minimum of 10 percent to 40 percent additional staff are required on schedule over those handling the workload. But don't trust rules of thumb; you will need to produce your own calculations. If activities not related to the workload are significant, shrink factor can be as high as 2.0, meaning that you'll need to schedule two people for each agent required. This is fairly common in some help desks that have extensive off-line research.

We recommend that you initially produce a table of factors for each day of the week and for each agent group you will be scheduling. Then, adjust the calculations as circumstances dictate (i.e., for vacation season or major changes in training schedules).

20. Scheduling Considerations and Applications   Ready? | 1 | 2 | 3 |

Key Points

- Scheduling is inherently an iterative process, and involves a certain amount of trial and error. Important scheduling parameters include:
  - Schedule horizon
  - Union and legal requirements
  - Agent preferences
  - Alternatives available

- It is important to explore as many scheduling alternatives as possible. Look for those that enable you to match staff with customer demands while balancing the needs of agents and the organization.

Explanation

Scheduling is inherently an iterative process, meaning that it involves a certain amount of trial and error. As you identify scheduling alternatives, there are a number of other parameters to consider.

Schedule Horizon

For example, how far in advance will you determine schedules (the schedule horizon)? If you schedule further out, say for two or three months from now, your schedules will be less efficient. They will be locked in place, even if call load deviates from the forecast. But a big plus is that they will be more agreeable to your staff, who prefer to know their work schedules well in advance. On the other hand, if you use a shorter timeframe, the scheduling process will be less popular with some agents, but schedules will likely be more accurate. This issue is a balancing act.

Union and Legal Requirements

You will also need to carefully consider union and legal requirements. Restrictions on part-time staff, hours worked and overtime pay will impact the alternatives you can use. If you are in a union environment, union representatives should be involved in scheduling decisions up front.

Section 5

Agent Preferences

You will also need to be realistic about agent preferences. If you involve agents in identifying scheduling possibilities up front, they will often generate ideas you didn't consider and will better accept and adhere to the schedules that are produced.

Scheduling Alternatives

Considering that staffing needs fluctuate significantly throughout the day, month and year, it is important to explore scheduling alternatives that will enable you to match staff as closely as possible with customer demands. Some alternatives include:

- **Utilize conventional shifts:** Many call centers have a core group of agents who work traditional five-day-a-week shifts during "normal hours" (e.g., 9 a.m. to 5 p.m.).

- **Stagger shifts:** For example, one shift begins at 7 a.m., the next at 7:30 a.m., the next at 8 a.m., until the center is fully staffed for the busy mid-morning traffic.

- **Adjust breaks, lunch, meeting and training schedules:** Even slight changes to when these activities are scheduled can mean that a few more people are handling inbound transactions at just the right times.

- **Forecast and plan for regular collateral work:** If you can accurately forecast call loads, then you can forecast collateral work (various nonphone activities). Collateral work provides flexibility, if it is planned for and managed well. (See Rostered Staff Factor, this section.)

- **Schedule part-timers:** Some call centers are prevented from using part-time help by union agreements or logistics (e.g., complex call center services requiring extensive training). But when available and practical, this is a popular and common strategy.

- **Establish "internal" part-timers:** This approach is sometimes called the reinforcement method. When contact-handling duties are combined with other types of tasks, such as correspondence, outbound calling or data entry, the agents assigned to these collateral duties can act as reinforcements when the workload gets heavy.

- **Create a "swat team":** This takes the reinforcement method one step further. Some call centers bring in employees from other departments to help when the call volume soars. Training, scheduling, pay and cultural issues must be addressed.

- **Offer concentrated shifts:** Given the choice, some agents prefer to work fewer days, with more hours per day while others prefer to work fewer hours in a day, even if that means a six- or seven-day work week.

- **Offer overtime:** No additional training is required and many agents will volunteer for the extra work. However, overtime can be expensive as an ongoing strategy and there is a question of whether or not agents can remain effective in extended hours.

- **Give agents the option to go home without pay:** This is a popular strategy on slower days, and there are usually enough agents willing to take you up on it. It's referred to as LWOP (leave without pay, pronounced "el-wop").

- **Offer split shifts:** In split shifts, agents work a partial shift, take part of the day off, then return later to finish their shift.

- **Arrange for some agents to be "on call":** Although this strategy is impractical for many, it can work in situations where events cannot be precisely predicted (i.e., catalog companies during the initial days of a new promotion). Typically, agents must either live near the call center or be equipped to telecommute.

- **Set up a telecommuting program:** This is not a scheduling alternative, per se, but it can provide an environment in which unpopular shifts can be more palatable and enable agents to begin handling the workload on short notice. (See Telecommuting Technologies, Section 6.)

- **Use hiring to your advantage:** An important criteria when hiring new agents should be the hours they can (or can't) work.

- **Send calls to a service bureau:** Today, service bureaus of all types and capabilities are available. Some can handle calls of virtually any type or degree of complexity.

- **Collaborate with similar organizations:** Some call centers have partnered with other centers that have different seasonality patterns to share staff during busy seasons.

- **Sacrifice service level for a planned period of time:** It may be unrealistic for some customer service centers to meet service level objectives during the initial weeks of a new product introduction, or during the busiest season. Consequently, some plan to sacrifice service level for three to six weeks and rely on customers to understand. This must be carefully planned, and to be acceptable to callers, it must fall within the realm of their expectations.

Section 5

- **Use an envelope strategy:** With more types of work to handle in today's environment, many call centers are using an envelope strategy. This approach recognizes that some types of work have to be handled at specific times of the day, and other types of work allow more flexibility. The idea is to move in and out of the various types of work as circumstances dictate.

Troubleshooting the Scheduling Process

The list below provides questions designed to help you and your team identify the root cause(s) of your scheduling problem. Answer each question with either a "yes," "no" or "not applicable." Answering a question with a "no" response indicates that there is room for improvement and that the area represents a potential problem or root cause. (Remember, continuous scheduling improvement is an ongoing process, so even if you answer a question with a "yes," there may still be room for improvement in that area.)

1. Are you considering all feasible scheduling alternatives, such as:
   - using conventional, staggered, concentrated or split shifts?
   - adjusting breaks, lunches, training session times?
   - incorporating part-timers and/or flex-timers?
   - offering overtime or leave without pay?
   - establishing a telecommuting (work-at-home agent) program?
   - sharing staff with another call center with complementary scheduling needs?

2. Do you solicit input from everyone involved in scheduling (e.g., forecasters, supervisors and agents)?

3. When making adjustments to the schedule, do you make sure that all the newest agents are NOT assigned to the newest supervisors/managers?

4. Do you make sure that agents who exchange shifts have compatible skill sets?

5. Do you factor in inevitable "exceptions" that affect schedules, without allowing too many exceptions?

6. Do you have a real-time escalation process that is in writing and well-understood by staff?

7. Do you manage around each half-hour rather than around daily averages?

8. Do your supervisors provide coaching on adherence-to-schedule?

9. Do your agents "buy into" adherence, and do they understand the "Power of One" (the big impact that each of them has on the center's overall performance/service level)?

10. When examining adherence, do you measure how much and WHEN?

Excerpt from "Overcoming Common Scheduling Problems: Part 1" by Rose Polchin, *Call Center Management Review*, February 2000.

(For more information on scheduling, see ICMI's *Call Center People Management Handbook and Study Guide*.)

21. Full-Time Equivalents (FTEs)

Ready? | 1 | 2 | 3 |

Key Points

- Full-time equivalent (FTE) is a unit of measure representing the amount of paid hours contributed by a regular full-time employee.

- In the U.S., one FTE equals eight paid hours for one day, 40 paid hours for one week, or 2,080 paid hours for one year.

- Monthly FTEs are commonly estimated by dividing annual paid hours (2,080) by 12 months: 173.3 hours per month. Note that this calculation ignores the different number of paid hours in different months.

- Fractional FTEs are used to represent part-time staff (e.g., a half FTE can represent part-time staff working 20 hours per week).

- FTE units are used to map staffing calculations to actual staff available or required.

Explanation

Full-time equivalent (FTE) is a unit of measure representing the amount of paid hours contributed by a regular full-time employee, and should not be confused with:

- Headcount (the number of staff employed)

- Agent seats (the number of workstations available for agents)

- Full-time staff (full-time staff work 40 hours per week)

The 40 hours per week represented by one weekly FTE may be contributed by one person working 40 hours, two people working 20 hours, four people working 10 hours, 40 people working one hour, etc.

FTEs have normal mathematical properties within the time period for which they are calculated. For example, adding 10 new-hire weekly FTEs to a base staff of five weekly FTEs equals 15 weekly FTEs.

FTEs in multiple time periods have the same mathematical properties as any other averages. Calculations spanning time periods can be performed either by

Section 5

converting FTEs to paid hours or by using weighted averages. For example, 10 daily FTEs available for the next two days and five daily FTEs available for the following three days does not equal 15 weekly FTEs, but seven weekly FTEs. Converting to paid hours makes the math clear:

- (10 FTEs x 8 hours per day x 2 days) + (5 FTEs x 8 hours per day x 3 days) = 160 paid hours + 120 paid hours = 280 paid hours

- 280 ÷ (5 days x 8 hours per day) FTEs = 7 FTEs for the week

Recognizing that FTE units are implied weighted averages, the math is faster:

- 10 FTEs x 2 days + 5 FTEs x 3 days = 20 + 15 person-days = 35 person-days

- 35 person days ÷ 5 days = 7 FTEs for the week

(For more information on predicting FTEs, see ICMI's *Call Center People Management Handbook and Study Guide*.)

22. Managing Schedule Adherence

Ready? ☐1 ☐2 ☐3

See Adherence to Schedule, Section 4.

Section 5

23. The Components of a Quality Contact/ Costs of Poor Quality

Ready? | 1 | 2 | 3 |

Key Points

- The components of a quality call are typical from one call center to another.

- Good quality will have a direct and positive impact on service level. Quality service pays for itself because it helps to eliminate the many costs incurred when quality is lacking.

- Reducing errors and rework has a positive impact on service level, morale, customer satisfaction and costs.

Explanation

The components of a quality call include:

- Caller is satisfied.
- All data entry is correct.
- Contact is necessary in the first place.
- Agent provides correct response.
- Customer receives correct information.
- Agent captures all needed/useful information.
- Customer is not transferred around.
- Customer doesn't get rushed.
- Customer has confidence contact was effective.
- Call center's mission is accomplished.
- Unsolicited marketplace feedback is detected and documented.
- Customer doesn't feel it necessary to check up, verify or repeat.
- People down the line can correctly interpret the order.
- Agent has pride in workmanship.
- Customer does not get a busy signal when using telephone or no response from Web site.
- Customer is not placed in queue for too long.

These items apply almost universally. Using this framework, think about the possible repercussions if quality is lacking. For example, what happens if the caller is not satisfied? What happens if data is entered incorrectly? What happens if the agent does not provide the correct response? Things like repeat calls, unnecessary service calls and escalated calls probably come to mind.

Examples of costs when quality is lacking include:

- Escalation of contacts and complaints to higher management
- Repeat contacts from customers
- Callbacks to customers for missing or unclear information
- Cancellations
- Cost of closing accounts
- Handling product returns
- Unnecessary service contacts
- Wrong problems get fixed
- Contacts to customer relations
- Negative publicity from angry customers
- Diversion of agents to activities that should be unnecessary
- Agents "taking the heat" for mistakes made by others
- Bad moves, adds and changes
- Shipping expenses to reship, express mail
- Loss of referrals
- Cancellations causing inaccurate inventory status

Unlike the components of a quality call, not all of these items will apply in every situation. For example, if you are an insurance company, the cost of handling product returns won't apply. Similarly, tax collection agencies don't incur the cost of closing accounts. But repeat calls, escalated calls and diversion of agents to activities that should be unnecessary *do* apply.

Consider these issues within the context of service level and staffing. What portion of average talk time represents waste and rework? How about after-call work? What percent of calls were unnecessary in the first place? And what amount of time are agents spending on activities that should be unnecessary?

It becomes very clear that good quality will have a direct and positive impact on service level. Quality service pays for itself because it helps to eliminate the many costs incurred when quality is lacking. (See Quality in the Call Center Environment, Section 3 and Call (Contact) Quality, Section 4.)

24. A Process for Root-Cause Analysis

Ready? | 1 | 2 | 3 |

Section 5

Key Points

- Making improvements and leveraging opportunities requires a systematic approach for improving quality.

- Key Performance Indicators (KPIs) are necessary for tracking and measuring results (outcomes), but they usually do not provide the kind of detailed guidance necessary to work on root causes.

- Tools such as flow charts, cause-and-effect diagrams and control charts are necessary to understand processes and locate the root causes of problems.

- Because yesterday's best practices quickly become the norm today, quality improvement must be a continuous process.

Explanation

A call center is a process or system of causes. (See the diagram in KPIs as Interrelated Outcomes, Section 4.). Without the appropriate methodology and tools, identifying the root causes of quality problems in a call center is a significant challenge. Consider a recurring problem, such as providing incomplete information to callers. Maybe the cause is insufficient information in the database. Or a need for more training. Or maybe a lack of coordination with marketing. Or carelessness. Or agent stress from a chronically high occupancy rate. Or a combination of any of these factors, coupled with many other things.

To make improvements and leverage opportunities, you need to have a systematic approach for improving quality, such as illustrated in the graphic on the next page.

key Quality: If you have a problem what action should you take
what action should you take
look for answer that states
Root cause
gap analysis
analysis - the problem reason why it's happening

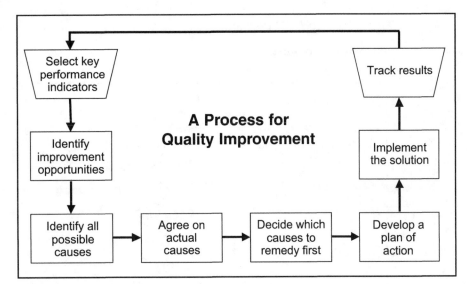

Key Performance Indicators (KPIs) are high-level measures of call center performance. Tracking these high-level measurements won't inherently improve results. To make improvements, you have to work on the factors that cause these outputs to be where they are. In other words, you have to work at a deeper level and resolve the root causes.

The tools the quality movement has produced over the years are necessary to understand processes and locate the root causes of problems. If you've had training on the subject of quality, you are probably well-versed in their use. The purpose here is to review how they can be applied in the call center environment.

Flow Chart

A flow chart is a map of a process that is used to analyze and standardize procedures, identify root causes of problems and plan new processes. Flow charts are also excellent communication tools, and can help you visualize and understand the flow of a process.

One of the most useful applications for a flow chart is to analyze the specific types of transactions you handle. Even a simple transaction consists of many steps. To really understand a transaction, especially the more complex variety, it is necessary to chart what happens, step by step.

Example applications:

- Transactions, step by step

- The planning and management process

Section 5

• IVR and ACD programming

• Key procedures

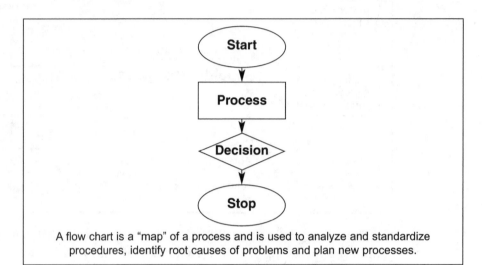

A flow chart is a "map" of a process and is used to analyze and standardize procedures, identify root causes of problems and plan new processes.

Cause-and-Effect Diagram

The cause-and-effect diagram, alternatively called a fishbone diagram because of its shape, was first developed by Dr. Kaoru Ishikawa of the University of Tokyo, in the mid-1900s. It has since become recognized and used worldwide. The chart illustrates the relationships between causes and a specific effect you want to study.

The traditional cause categories used in these diagrams are often referred to as the "4Ms," manpower, machines, methods and materials. A variation on these categories – people, technology, methods and materials/information – works better for call centers. However, these labels are only suggestions, and you can use any that help your group creatively focus on and think through the problem. Possible causes leading to the effect are drawn as branches off the main category. The final step is to prioritize the causes and work on the most prevalent problems first.

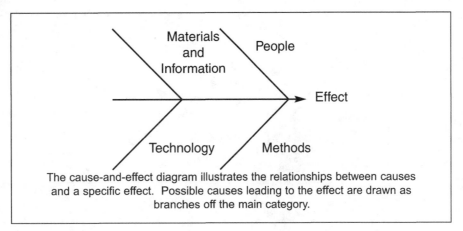

The cause-and-effect diagram illustrates the relationships between causes and a specific effect. Possible causes leading to the effect are drawn as branches off the main category.

Example applications:

- Long calls

- Repeat calls

- Poor adherence to schedule

- Inaccurate forecast

Scatter Diagram

A scatter diagram assesses the strength of the relationship between two variables and is used to test and document possible cause-and-effect. If there is positive correlation between the two variables, dots will appear as an upward slope. If there is a negative correlation, the dots will appear as a downward slope. The closer the pattern of dots is to a straight line, the stronger the correlation is between the two variables.

Example applications:

- Average handling time vs. experience level

- Average handling time vs. revenue generated

- Service level vs. error rate

- Experience level vs. quality scores

(continued, next page)

Section 5

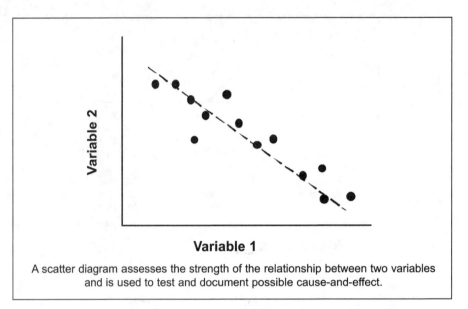

A scatter diagram assesses the strength of the relationship between two variables
and is used to test and document possible cause-and-effect.

Pareto Chart

Created by economist Vilfredo Pareto, a Pareto chart is simply a bar chart that
ranks events in order of importance or frequency.

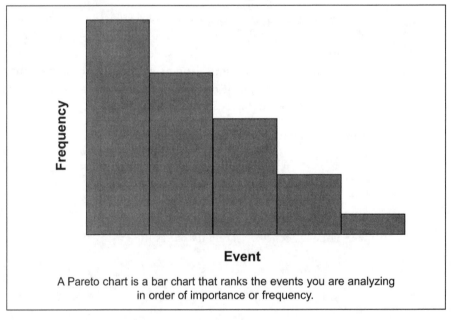

A Pareto chart is a bar chart that ranks the events you are analyzing
in order of importance or frequency.

For errors by type, an important measure in call centers, you can create two
more Pareto charts: cost to fix and time to fix. The Pareto principle dictates that

you should work first on the things that will yield the biggest improvements.

Example applications:

- Transactions by type

- Errors by type

- Transactions by customer demographics (e.g., age, region of country and how long they've been customers)

- Responses to customer surveys

Control Chart

One of the reasons that quality problems in the call center are challenging and often confusing is because they are a part of a complex process, and any process has variation from the ideal. A control chart is a tool that provides information on variation. There are two major types of variation: special causes and common causes. Special causes create erratic, unpredictable variation. For example, unusual calls from unexpected publicity or a computer terminal with intermittent problems are special causes. Common causes are the rhythmic, normal variations in the system.

A control chart enables you to bring a process under statistical control by eliminating the chaos of special causes. You can then work on the common causes by improving the system and, thus, the whole process. Special causes show up as points outside of the upper control or lower control limits, or as points with unnatural patterns within the limits.

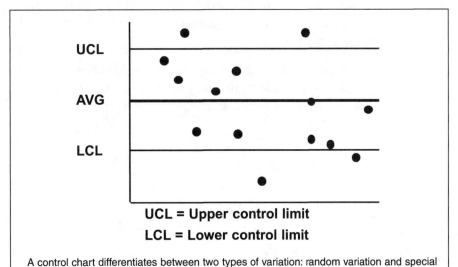

UCL = Upper control limit
LCL = Lower control limit

A control chart differentiates between two types of variation: random variation and special causes (nonrandom variation). Control charts are based on specific statistical calculations.

A control chart cannot reveal what the problems are. Instead, it reveals where and when special causes occur. Once special causes are eliminated, improving the system itself will have far more impact than focusing on individual causes. Improvements to the system will move the entire process in the right direction.

Example applications:

- Average handling time

- Percent adherence

- Errors and rework

- Requests for supervisory assistance

Benchmarking

While many of these tools focus on improvements from within, the idea behind benchmarking is that break-through ideas often come from the outside. Benchmarking is the process measuring your products, services and procedures against other organizations.

Keep some cautions in mind. Organizations are different, even within a given industry, so universally accepted standards usually are not defensible. Things like labor rates, caller demographics, caller tolerances, trunk and network configuration, hours of operation and the mix of part-timers and full-timers vary widely.

Further, organizations often interpret performance measures differently. For example, one may measure service level as a daily average, another as a monthly average, and another as the number of half-hours per day that met the objective within a specified range.

These cautions in mind, a disciplined, focused benchmarking effort can produce the information necessary to make significant improvements in areas such as forecasting, handling time, service level and customer satisfaction.

Ongoing Process

Quality improvement should be an ongoing effort. As your center and other centers improve, what were once cutting-edge practices become the norm. As best practices become generally accepted, they can no longer be considered "best practices."

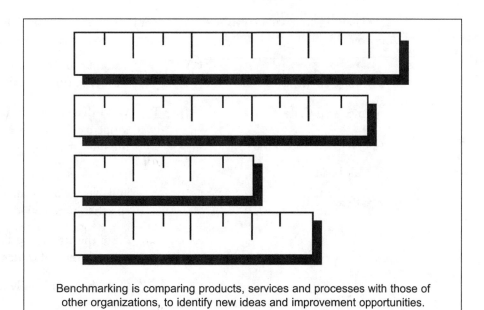

Benchmarking is comparing products, services and processes with those of other organizations, to identify new ideas and improvement opportunities.

Forecasting and Scheduling

Exercises

Key Forecasting Definitions

1. Match the following terms with their definitions. You will use each term only once.

a. After-Call Work

b. Answered Calls

c. Average Handling Tine

d. Call Load

e. Offered Calls

f. Talk Time

_F_ The time an agent spends with a caller during a transaction.

_A_ Work that is necessitated by and immediately follows an inbound transaction.

_C_ The sum of average talk time and average after-call work for a specified time period.

_E_ All of the attempts callers make to reach the call center.

_B_ Calls that successfully reach an agent.

_D_ The product of average handling time and call volume for a specified time period.

Breaking Down a Forecast

2. Break this forecast down for Mondays in May from 9:00 to 9:30, using the numbers below:

Current year's calls:	650,000
Growth for year:	14% _1.14_
Prop. of year's calls/May:	7% _×.07_
Operation days:	31
Open:	7 days/week
Prop. of week's calls/Monday:	.215 _×1.5_
Prop. of day's calls/9:00-9:30:	.04 _.04 =100_

(Hint: Monday's index factor, as a result of this proportion, is 1.5.)

Queuing Formulas and Simulation

3. Match the following terms to the statements (you may use a term more than once).

a. Erlang C

b. Computer Simulation

c. Erlang B

d. Poisson

e. Retrial Tables

_C_ , _D_ , _E_ Used for calculating trunks and IVR ports required (three alternative answers).

_A_ _B_ Used for calculating base staff, and predicting occupancy, trunk load, delay times, etc.

_B_ Simulates what happens in terms of service level, delay, busies, overflow, etc., for the set of variables you assume.

_D_ _E_ Assumes that, if callers get busy signals, they keep trying until they successfully get through.

_A_ Assumes no abandoned calls or busy signals.

_C_ Assumes that if callers get busy signals, they go away forever, never to retry.

_E_ Assumes that some callers retry and others will go away.

(continued, next page)

Calculating Base Staff for Service Level/Related Queue Dynamics

4. Answer the following questions using the Erlang C staffing table below.

   a. How many agents are required to meet a service level of 88 percent in 20 seconds? *35*

Erlang C For Incoming Call Centers

Incoming Calls Management Institute
Annapolis, Maryland

Average talk time in seconds: 180   Average after-call work in seconds: 30
Calls per half-hour: 250   Service level in seconds: 20

Agents	P(0)	ASA	DLYDLY	Q1	Q2	SL	OCC	TKLD
30	83%	209	252	29	35	24%	97%	54.0
31	65%	75	115	10	16	45%	94%	35.4
32	51%	38	74	5	10	61%	91%	30.2
33	39%	21	55	3	8	73%	88%	28.0
34	29%	13	43	2	6	82%	86%	26.8
35	22%	8	36	1	5	88%	83%	26.1
36	16%	5	31	1	4	92%	81%	25.7
37	11%	3	27	0	4	95%	79%	25.4
38	8%	2	24	0	3	97%	77%	25.3
39	6%	1	21	0	3	98%	75%	25.2
40	4%	1	19	0	3	99%	73%	25.1
41	3%	1	18	0	2	99%	71%	25.1
42	2%	0	16	0	2	100%	69%	25.0

   b. What is service level when average speed of answer is 75 seconds? *45%*

   c. As service level increases, what happens to occupancy? *occupancy decreases*

   d. As service level increases, what happens to trunk load? *trunk load decreases*

   e. With a service level of 95 percent in 20 seconds, what percentage of callers will be answered by an agent without any delay? *89%* *11% delayed*

   f. With a service level of 61 percent in 20 seconds, what is the average delay of delayed calls? *74 seconds*

   g. Is service level or average speed of answer a better indicator of the typical caller's experience? *SL*

   h. Can two different service levels be set for the same agent group? *no*

Section 5
Forecasting and Scheduling

The Impact of Service Level on Longest Wait

5. Answer the following questions using the Erlang C delay table below.

Delay Module

ERLANG C FOR INCOMING CALL CENTERS BY ICMI, INC.
TALK TIME IN SECONDS = **180**
AFTER-CALL WORK IN SECONDS = **30**
CALLS PER HALF-HOUR = **250**
SERVICE LEVEL OBJECTIVE IN SECONDS = **20**

|<========= Number of callers waiting longer than x seconds =========>|

Agents	SL%	5	10	15	20	30	40	50	60	90	120	180	240
30	24	203	199	195	191	184	177	170	163	145	129	101	80
31	45	156	149	143	137	126	115	105	97	74	57	34	20
32	61	118	111	104	97	85	74	65	56	38	25	11	5
33	73	89	81	74	67	56	47	39	32	19	11	4	1
34	82	65	58	52	46	37	29	23	18	9	5	1	0
35	88	47	41	36	31	24	18	14	10	4	2	0	0
36	92	34	29	24	21	15	11	8	6	2	1	0	0
37	95	24	20	16	14	9	6	4	3	1	0	0	0
38	97	16	13	11	9	6	4	2	2	0	0	0	0
39	98	11	9	7	5	3	2	1	1	0	0	0	0
40	99	7	6	4	3	2	1	1	0	0	0	0	0
41	99	5	4	3	2	1	1	0	0	0	0	0	0
42	100	3	2	2	1	1	0	0	0	0	0	0	0

a. When service level is 82 percent in 20 seconds, how many callers wait longer than 60 seconds?   18

b. What is the lowest service level that you can achieve without having any callers wait longer than 120 seconds?

95% in 20 seconds

(continued, next page)

Immutable Laws of Call Centers

6. Choose one of the words below each statement to correctly fill in the blanks.

   a. For a given call load, when service level goes up, occupancy goes
      down. (down | up)

   b. Keep improving service level and you will reach a point of
      ~~increasing~~ diminishing returns. (increasing | diminishing)

   c. For a given service level, _lrgs of smaller_ agent groups are more
      efficient than _smaller/larger_ groups. (larger/smaller | smaller/larger)

   d. All other things equal, _pool/specialized_ groups are more efficient than
      specialized/pooled groups. (specialized/pooled | pooled/specialized)

   e. For a given call load, add staff and average speed of answer will go
      down. (down | up)

   f. For a given call load, add staff and trunk load will go _down_.
      (down | up)

The Implications of Agent Group Structure

7. Beside each statement below, indicate whether it is a symptom of agent
groups that are too specialized (with an "s") or too generalized (with a "g").

   _g_ Agents frustrated with "too much to know"

   _S_ Agents frustrated with narrow responsibilities

   _S_ An overly complicated planning process

   _g_ Higher average handling time

   _S_ Longer training time

   _g_ Lower quality

   _S_ More calls not handled by intended group (due to overflow)

   _S_ Small groups with low occupancy and/or erratic service levels

Cost of Delay

8. If the cost of employing each agent is \$15/hour and trunkload costs are \$4/hour, complete the table below to determine at which service level total costs are lowest.

ERLANG C FOR INCOMING CALL CENTERS BY ICMI, INC.
TALK TIME IN SECONDS = **180**
AFTER-CALL WORK IN SECONDS = **30**
CALLS PER HALF-HOUR = **250**
SERVICE LEVEL OBJECTIVE IN SECONDS = **20**

Agents	COST	ASA	SL	TKLD	COST	TOTAL
30	450	208.7	23.5%	54.0	216.-	666.-
31	445	74.7	45.2%	35.4	141.6	606.60
32	480.	37.6	61.3%	30.2	120.80	600.80
33	495	21.3	73.0%	28.0	112.	607.00
34	510	12.7	81.5%	26.8	107.20	617.20

a. The cost of delay is lowest when service level is _61%_.

Skills-Based Routing

9. Fill in the routing plan based on the following agent skills. Route calls to the least skilled agent who can handle the call so that your more skilled agents are available for more complex calls.

Agent Skills

	Agent Type 1	Agent Type 2	Agent Type 3	Agent Type 4	Agent Type 5	Agent Type 6	Agent Type 7	Agent Type 8	Agent Type 9
Sales – Printers	X			X	X		X		
Sales – Computers		X	X	X			X		
Service – Printers			X		X		X		X
Service – Computers			X			X	X	X	

Routing Plan

Call Routing Hierarchy	Sales – Printers	Sales – Computers	Service – Printers	Service – Computers
Skill Choice 1	Type 1	Type 2	9	6 or 8
Skill Choice 2	4 or 5	4	5	8 0 6
Skill Choice 3	5 or 4	3	3	3
Skill Choice 4	7	7	7	7

Calculating Base Staff for Response Time

10. Call Center Y uses a scheduled response time. They expect to receive 450 email messages by 10 a.m. The average handling time is four minutes. To handle this workload by 5 p.m., what are the base staff requirements? (Do not assume any adjustment for efficiency factor.)

[handwritten: 7HRS×60 =]

[handwritten: 7HR = 420 ÷ 4mn = 105]
[handwritten: 450 emails ÷ 105 = 4.3 = 5 agents]

Rostered Staff Factor

11. You've determined the base staff requirements for email and inbound phone calls in the table below. In your call center, email and inbound phone calls are handled in blended groups, with all agents equipped to handle both channels of contact. You estimate three people will be absent throughout the morning and plan for two people to receive training from 8:00 to 9:30. Three people will be on break from 9:30 to 10:00 and four people from 10:00 to 11:00. Complete the table to determine the number of people you need to schedule during this time period to meet your service level and response time objectives.

Rostered Staff Factor Exercise

| | Base Staff Required | | | | | | |
	Phone	Email	Absent	Break	Training	On Schedule	RSF
8:00-8:30	20	4	3	0	2	*29*	*1.21*
8:30-9:00	22	4	3	0	2	*31*	*1.19*
9:00-9:30	22	4	3	0	2	*31*	*1.19*
9:30-10:00	28	5	3	3	0	*39*	*1.18*
10:00-10:30	28	5	3	4	0	*40*	*1.21*
10:30-11:00	34	5	3	4	0	*46*	*1.18*

Full-Time Equivalents (FTEs)

12. ABC call center employs five agents who work 40 hours per week and five agents who work 20 hours per week. Calculate the FTEs per week available at this call center.

(continued, next page)

7.5 FTE

5 × 40 = 200 = 40

5 employees × 8 Hr × 5 days

5 × 20 = 100   20

5 people × 5 days × 40 = 8 Hrs

5 people × 5 × 20 = 4 Hr

Section 5

Section 5
Forecasting and Scheduling

ICMI
Incoming Calls
Management Institute
Advancing the Call Center Profession Worldwide

Key Quality Improvement Tools

13. Write the name of the quality improvement tool in the blank below each one.

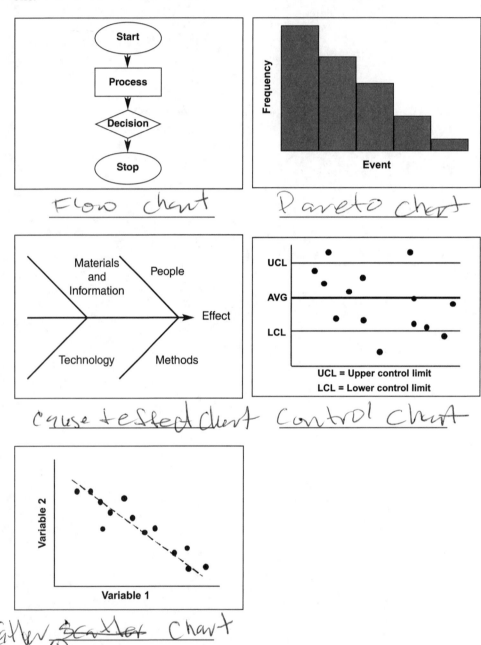

Flow chart

Pareto chart

cause + effect chart   Control chart

Scatter ~~Scatter~~ chart
~~Pareto~~

Answers to these exercises are in Section 10.

Note: These exercises are intended to help you retain the material learned. While not the exact questions as on the CIAC Certification assessment, the material in this handbook/study guide fully addresses the content on which you will be assessed. For a formal practice test, please contact the CIAC directly by visiting www.ciac-cert.org.

Section 5

Section 5

Forecasting and Scheduling
Reference Bibliography

Related Articles from *Call Center Management Review* (See Section 9)

How Incoming Call Centers Behave: Back to the Basics (3 parts)

Forecasting and Scheduling: Beyond the Basics

The Pain and Gain of Skills Based Routing

Calculating Staff Required to Meet E-Contact Response Time Objectives

Getting People in the Right Place at the Rights Times, Part 1: Rostered Staff Factor

Call Center Scheduling: Practical Tips for Today's Environment

For Further Study

Books

Call Center Forecasting and Scheduling: The Best of Call Center Management Review. Call Center Press, 2000.

Cleveland, Brad and Julia Mayben. *Call Center Management on Fast Forward: Succeeding in Today's Dynamic Inbound Environment.* Call Center Press, 1999.

Makridakis, Syros and Steven C. Wheelright, *Handbook of Forecasting: A Manager's Guide*, John Wiley & Sons, 1987.

Articles

Bave-Kerwin, Jean. "Common Skills-Based Routing Mistakes to Avoid." *Call Center Management Review*, May 2002.

Polchin, Rose. "Overcoming Common Scheduling Problems: Part 1." *Call Center Management Review*, February 2000.

Zager, Masha. "Plan Ahead for Erratic Workloads to Improve Email Response Times." *Call Center Management Review*, August 2001.

Seminars

Essential Skills and Knowledge for Effective Incoming Call Center Management, a public seminar presented by Incoming Calls Management Institute.

Workforce Management: The Basics and Beyond public seminar, presented by Incoming Calls Management Institute.

Effective Workforce Management, Step-by-Step Web Seminar Series, presented by Incoming Calls Management Institute.

Advanced Workforce Management Web Seminar Series, presented by Incoming Calls Management Institute.

Call Center Technology

Operations Management

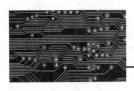

Section 6: Call Center Technology

Contents

(continued, next page)

Section 6

Note: Section 6 was developed with Vanguard Communications Corp., and is drawn from the seminar, *Understanding and Applying Today's Call Center Technologies* and related materials. Contents copyrighted to Vanguard Communications Corp. and/or ICMI, Inc., 2003

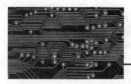

Section 6: Call Center Technology

Note: Section 6 was developed with Vanguard Communications Corp., and is drawn from the seminar, *Understanding and Applying Today's Call Center Technologies* and related materials. Contents copyrighted to Vanguard Communications Corp. and/or ICMI, Inc., 2003

1. Today's Business Drivers

Ready? | 1 | 2 | 3 |

Key Points

- Today's customers are becoming more informed and connected, and organizations must transition sales and customer service delivery systems to serve them better.

- The traditional telephone-centric center is becoming a multichannel environment with significantly expanded responsibilities.

Explanation

The convergence of Internet, telecommunications and computer technologies is creating vast new types of services and multiplying the connections between and among customers, organizations, suppliers, industry interest groups and government. Today's customers are informed and connected, and organizations must transition sales and customer service delivery systems to serve them better – or run the risk of dissatisfying, disillusioning, or, worst of all, driving them away.

Consequently, there is enormous pressure in call centers to:

- Handle more customers

- Retain customers

- Handle more volume

- Address more complex requests

- Provide more information

- Personalize service

- Accelerate service

- Lower costs

- Generate revenue

- Deliver "great" service

- Ensure closure and commitment

Section 6

Note: Section 6 was developed with Vanguard Communications Corp., and is drawn from the seminar, *Understanding and Applying Today's Call Center Technologies* and related materials. Contents copyrighted to Vanguard Communications Corp. and/or ICMI, Inc., 2003

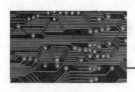

- Incorporate new technologies

- Be more available and accessible

- Give customers choice and control

Beyond these specific challenges, there is a fundamental development in the mission of call centers and how they operate. The table below depicts how traditional telephone-centric call centers are evolving.

From:	To:
Cost center	Revenue focus
Volume orientation	Customer relationships
Entry-level personnel	Professional personnel
High turnover	Career path
Rules oriented	Empowered teams
Uniform handling	Personalized handling
Generic campaigns	Targeted campaigns
Large, centralized centers	Also, decentralized and remote centers
Voice only	Multiple media
Traditional telephone center	Multichannel environment

These developments require that organizations upgrade the skills of their staff, improve processes and utilize technologies that enable them to meet the challenges.

(For more information on the call center's emerging role, see ICMI's *Call Center Leadership and Business Management Handbook and Study Guide*.)

Note: Section 6 was developed with Vanguard Communications Corp., and is drawn from the seminar, *Understanding and Applying Today's Call Center Technologies* and related materials. Contents copyrighted to Vanguard Communications Corp. and/or ICMI, Inc., 2003

2. Key Technology Trends

Ready? | 1 | 2 | 3 |

Key Points

- Call center technologies are evolving rapidly to accommodate changing customer requirements, increased competitive pressure and new business objectives. Being nimble is key.

- Call center technology trends that enable organizations to be nimble include: *Rep is the client*
    - Client-server environments
    - Standard open platforms and standard tools; middleware *intergrate* *Densable extract info them systems*
    - Packaged but configurable or customizable solutions
    - Adequate and appropriate data to service customer needs
    - Improved desktop tools
    - Multimedia queuing and transaction processing

- These developments are creating new management challenges. For example, managers must rethink planning and management methodologies and agents must handle increasingly complex transactions across a variety of contact channels.

Explanation

Call centers are evolving to accommodate rapidly changing customer requirements, increased competitive pressure and business imperatives to do more with less. Technology is a key enabler to meet these demands. Applying the appropriate technologies and clearly defining effective processes are keys to supporting and enabling rapid change. Companies must become nimble if they are to deal with change quickly and appropriately. On the technical front, being nimble requires:

- Client-server environments

- Standard open platforms and standard tools; middleware

- Packaged but configurable or customizable solutions

- Adequate and appropriate data to service customer needs

- Improved desktop tools

Note: Section 6 was developed with Vanguard Communications Corp., and is drawn from the seminar, *Understanding and Applying Today's Call Center Technologies* and related materials. Contents copyrighted to Vanguard Communications Corp. and/or ICMI, Inc., 2003

Section 6

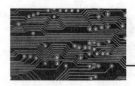

- Multimedia queuing and transaction processing

Client-Server Environments

The use of PCs, PC servers and client-server architectures has enabled rapid implementation of new applications and effective integration of applications and data sources; preserved legacy systems while avoiding the need for expensive mainframe programming; and created user-friendly tools at the desktop. (See Desktop/Agent System Interface, this section.)

Today, the data communications protocol of choice is TCP/IP, the transport protocol of the Internet. We will continue to see migration toward the browser (also referred to as a thin client) as the primary "front end" to all sorts of applications, with standards like HTML, ActiveX and Java being the primary tools for developing client-server applications.

Standard Open Platforms and Standard Tools; Middleware

In today's technology environment, systems must run on standard platforms with standard operating environments. They must be "open," that is, readily integrate with other systems and be extensible and scalable. While it is not likely that organizations will completely replace older, closed legacy systems, functionality can be migrated from these systems to newer client-server systems. The legacy systems become big database servers or back-end processors, with desktop computers running front-end applications to access these databases. (See Technology/Infrastructure Component, this section.)

As businesses evolve over time, important customer data can be spread over a multitude of legacy systems, database servers and data warehouses. In many cases, call center agents do not have access to all customer information, which restricts their ability to provide proper service. Middleware is evolving as an essential technology component. Serving as a buffer between the call center agent desktop and all current information databases, middleware applications are designed to retrieve all customer records, regardless of where they may reside.

Packaged But Customizable Solutions

While these standards provide for off-the-shelf packages, which can be purchased and integrated into any company's environment, most still require customization to meet the specific needs of the business. The advantages of packaged solutions include lower cost, faster ROI and more rapid implementation. Shortening time-to-market can be a critical factor in today's competitive environment. Future enhancements are easier, too, as suppliers are

Note: Section 6 was developed with Vanguard Communications Corp., and is drawn from the seminar, *Understanding and Applying Today's Call Center Technologies* and related materials. Contents copyrighted to Vanguard Communications Corp. and/or ICMI, Inc., 2003

constantly adding new capabilities in response to demands for new functions and new media. Finally, open architectures and standard interfaces allow companies to access powerful data analysis capabilities to tailor services.

Adequate and Appropriate Data to Service Customer Needs

Legacy systems, once called upon to provide all the facets of an organization's business applications, are becoming little more than repositories of a portion of the organization's data infrastructure in many companies. Real-time information is becoming increasingly important. Agents need the ability to update records for nearly simultaneous access by others in order to ensure continuity from contact to contact. Data must be common, up-to-date, updateable and accessible via many media options. (See Technology/Infrastructure Components, this section.)

Data gathering is becoming more structured to support business goals, processes and objectives. For example, companies are measuring what happened for the lifetime of a contact, regardless of media used or how many contact points were made. This approach is very different from the earlier focus, which was predominantly on agent and ACD statistics. Companies are also measuring their ability to meet commitments made to customers. Companies need to measure the *value* vs. the *cost* of a contact or customer. For example, a customer who calls frequently without generating revenue can be measured and assessed against a customer who calls once and generates a lot of revenue. This knowledge can then be used to differentiate service.

Many organizations are turning to increasingly sophisticated tools to gather data into "warehouses" and use these repositories for performing analytical queries and trend analysis. A related activity, data mining, is the growing use of analytical tools to uncover correlation between disparate sets of data. For instance, reports can be developed indicating which customers are more profitable and what products individual customers are most likely to buy. This information enables agents to better serve important customers, and facilitates cross-selling opportunities. (See CRM Capabilities, this section.)

Improved Desktop Tools

The agent desktop is changing, as well. In today's best-in-class centers, service agents have streamlined access to all the information they require, including support systems and multimedia tools through a user interface that is consistent in look and feel across applications.

Agent desktops are a single access point to all information and all media. They provide multimedia support to handle contacts ranging from voice, to IP

Note: Section 6 was developed with Vanguard Communications Corp., and is drawn from the seminar, *Understanding and Applying Today's Call Center Technologies* and related materials. Contents copyrighted to Vanguard Communications Corp. and/or ICMI, Inc., 2003

Section 6

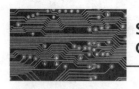

telephony, viewing image files, email and video. And, in line with the standard and open approach discussed earlier, browser-based interfaces are becoming the preferred desktop front end. (See Desktop/Agent System Interface, this section.)

Multimedia Queuing and Transaction Processing

Customers should have similar experiences, including processes, terminology and "look and feel," regardless of the media they choose. More importantly, response time and actions triggered by transactions need to be similar regardless of media type used by the customer. As different types of contacts and customers require different handling, business rules will increasingly define how any transaction, inquiry or problem is processed based on the customer's identity or purpose, current staffing conditions and other criteria. (See Multimedia Routing and Queuing, this section.)

New Management Challenges

Those who support and manage this new environment will require in-depth understanding of how these applications interact, and they must be aware of the implications of problems with one or more components from a business standpoint. In a new world where customers utilize a variety of channels, such as the call center, Internet, IVR and retail, emphasis will shift from the profitability of a given channel to the profitability of the customer relationship as a whole. Managers will have to determine new ways to measure performance as the evaluation of agents becomes more complex. In addition, scheduling and forecasting become more challenging in this type of environment.

Agents must be able to communicate in, and manage, a variety of media. This includes writing skills for responding to email, faxes, text-chat sessions or mail, selling and support skills, and the ability to serve as a "relationship manager" rather than just a representative or agent.

Note: Section 6 was developed with Vanguard Communications Corp., and is drawn from the seminar, *Understanding and Applying Today's Call Center Technologies* and related materials. Contents copyrighted to Vanguard Communications Corp. and/or ICMI, Inc., 2003

3. ACD Systems

Ready? | 1 | 2 | 3 |

Key Points

- Automatic call distributors (ACDs) are the systems that route, sequence and queue calls, and provide real-time and historical reports for planning and management purposes.

- ACDs offer numerous alternatives for routing calls, including:
  - Longest available agent routing
  - Specialized groups routing
  - Conditional routing
  - Skills-based routing
  - Data-directed routing

- Traditionally, ACDs have been the central nervous system of the call center. Today, they are becoming one of many systems required to deliver excellent service.

Explanation

An automatic call distributor is a software application that routes incoming calls and collects information associated with those calls. Following are basic ACD capabilities:

Primary function

- **Route calls:** Usually based on the trunk group of the call or the number the caller dialed, to the longest available agent in a group. ACDs can also route based on conditional parameters or agent skills.

- **Sequence calls:** Usually on a first-in/first-out basis. However, ACDs may also change sequence based on information gathered about the call or caller (e.g., from the number dialed or account information in the database).

- **Queue calls:** When there is no agent available, calls are queued.

- **Encourage callers to wait:** By playing delay announcements and, in some cases, predicting and announcing wait times.

- **Distribute calls among agents:** To balance workload as desired and give all agents a chance to excel.

Note: Section 6 was developed with Vanguard Communications Corp., and is drawn from the seminar, *Understanding and Applying Today's Call Center Technologies* and related materials. Contents copyrighted to Vanguard Communications Corp. and/or ICMI, Inc., 2003

Section 6

- **Capture planning and performance data both real-time and historical:** Most ACDs provide reporting capabilities as a part of the ACD software or as an add-on package.

- **Integrate with other systems:** The ACD has become just one of many systems in a comprehensive solution.

Types of ACDs

There are eight basic types of ACDs. Which ACD application you choose is a function of your organization's needs. The table below provides a more descriptive understanding of each approach:

Alternative	Key Strengths
PBX-based ACD (the ACD is a function on a PBX system)	• Single system to serve organizationwide needs • Suites of products and partners
Standalone ACD (ACD is the sole function)	• Call center focused development, sales and service • Suites of products and partners • Suitable for high-volume environments
Communications Server (all in one)	• Standards-based, open platform • Designed for multimedia, integrated solutions
Hybrid (CTI or add-on server)	• Leverage existing switching architecture • Enables extended services and capabilities
Key Systems	• Provides cost-effective, basic ACD capabilities for very small centers
Centrex (Central Office Based ACD)	• Provides ACD services across serving area • System maintained by telco
Third Party Managed/Hosted ACD Services	• Pay-as-you-go approach • System maintained by provider
IP Telephony (IP infrastructure with ACD functionality)	• Unlike traditional communications servers, uses the LAN to route calls

Note: Section 6 was developed with Vanguard Communications Corp., and is drawn from the seminar, *Understanding and Applying Today's Call Center Technologies* and related materials. Contents copyrighted to Vanguard Communications Corp. and/or ICMI, Inc., 2003

Information to Enable Call Routing

The ACD can route calls based on data from a number of sources, including:

- Caller input into an auto-attendant ("press one for this, two for that"). While some ACDs offer auto-attendant or prompt features, you can purchase an auto-attendant as a low-cost add-on. Prompting features can also be accomplished in IVR applications, but become considerably more expensive. (See IVR/Voice Processing Capabilities, this section.)

- DNIS (dialed number identification service), in which the network identifies the number the caller dialed.

- ANI (automatic number identification), in which the caller's number is relayed to the ACD.

- CTI-provided information collected from the Web or database systems.

Basic ACD Flow

In a basic ACD call flow, calls are directed to the appropriate queue based on programming in the switch software. The software either delivers the call to an available agent, or provides call treatment (e.g., messages, music) based on programmed parameters.

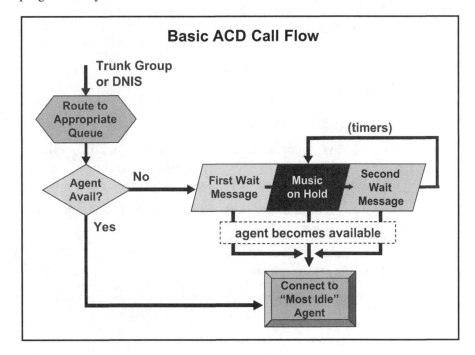

Note: Section 6 was developed with Vanguard Communications Corp., and is drawn from the seminar, *Understanding and Applying Today's Call Center Technologies* and related materials. Contents copyrighted to Vanguard Communications Corp. and/or ICMI, Inc., 2003

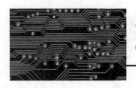

Alternative Methods for Routing Calls:

ACDs can also use alternative methods for routing calls, including:

- **Longest available agent routing**: The traditional approach.

- **Specialized groups routing**: The ACD routes calls based on DNIS or auto-attendant input to specialized groups of agents, e.g., sales, technical support.

- **Conditional routing**: The ACD is programmed to route calls based on current conditions, e.g., type of call, priority of call, agent availability, time of day.

- **Skills-based routing**: This is where specific types of calls are routed to the most suitable agents, based on call type and agent availability.

- **Data-directed routing**: This is an extended form of conditional routing tied to information in a database about the customer, call type or current situation. For example, a caller identified by the database as being overdue on his or her account may be automatically routed to collections. Or customers identified as being interested in a particular product via a Web interaction are routed to product specialists.

In addition to routing to agents, ACDs can also route to other systems, e.g., to an IVR to enable customers to leave messages for later callback. This approach should be used on a very limited basis since it can create workload problems if used too often.

Telephone Set Features

ACDs provide powerful, full-featured telephone sets that enable such capabilities as:

- Displays that offer information on calls (e.g., DNIS or caller identification), queue status (e.g., how many calls are in queue, current wait times), and call statistics (e.g., average talk time, after-call work).

- Buttons dedicated to work-states, such as talk time, after-call work or other work modes.

- Sign out with reason, whereby the agent can enter a code identifying the reason for signing off.

- Wrapup codes, whereby agents can identify the types of calls they are handling, enabling the ACD to generate reports on call types.

Note: Section 6 was developed with Vanguard Communications Corp., and is drawn from the seminar, *Understanding and Applying Today's Call Center Technologies* and related materials. Contents copyrighted to Vanguard Communications Corp. and/or ICMI, Inc., 2003

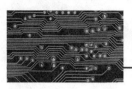

- Headset dual jacks for side-by-side monitoring.

- Supervisor assistance features.

- Easy transfer and conference.

Also, most ACD manufacturers offer a softphone version of their ACD sets, in which telephone set functionality can be accessed through the desktop display.

Real-Time and Historical Reports

Although ACD vendors use a variety of names for ACD reports, they may include:

Strictly real-time reports:

- Number of calls waiting

- Oldest call waiting

- Agent work state

- Number of agents available

Historical reports (based on very recent, rolling data or summary data):

- Average speed of answer

- Number of calls received

- Number of abandoned calls

- Average delay to abandon

- Average time in queue

- Service level

- All trunks busy (number of times and total time all trunks are in use)

- Calls handled

- Time signed in

- Occupancy

- Agent productivity (e.g., workload handled)

As indicated above, some reports that are updated on a real-time basis are actually historical in the sense that the ACD uses recent data to provide rolling reports. (See Interpreting Real-Time Information, Section 3.)

Note: Section 6 was developed with Vanguard Communications Corp., and is drawn from the seminar, *Understanding and Applying Today's Call Center Technologies* and related materials. Contents copyrighted to Vanguard Communications Corp. and/or ICMI, Inc., 2003

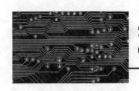

When considering reports from your ACD system (or any technology), be sure you understand the terminology and calculations that are used by the system. For example, ACD vendors have different ways of handling:

- Service level calculations

- Terms for calls offered, service level, after-call work

- How abandoned calls are treated

- How calls are logged that begin in one time interval and end in another

treated

The ACD as "Team Player"

ACD applications have been around since the early 1970s. Since that time, the ACD has been the central nervous system of the call center, making most of the call-routing and call-handling decisions – and having the most information on transactions. Today, the ACD is only one of many technological components that are part of an overall call center solution. As systems are integrated, a variety of databases, Web-based services and other systems are playing a more active role in identifying, routing and handling contacts, and capturing information on these contacts.

Note: Section 6 was developed with Vanguard Communications Corp., and is drawn from the seminar, *Understanding and Applying Today's Call Center Technologies* and related materials. Contents copyrighted to Vanguard Communications Corp. and/or ICMI, Inc., 2003

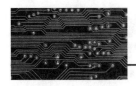

4. Networks

Ready? | 1 | 2 | 3 |

Key Points

- The network is the "pipe" between callers and the call center.

- Network services offer sophisticated call-routing and reporting capabilities for both single and multisite call centers.

- Today, users can directly control network programming.

Explanation

Network carrier Telephone company

In the call center world, the term network is typically used to describe the interexchange (IXC) services that route calls into a center or among several centers. The network is the "pipe" between the caller and the call center, or between call centers. Important criteria when selecting an IXC provider include:

- The features provided

- The total cost of service   *Choosing a Provider*

- Redundancy of the network

- How financially sound the provider is

Typical Capabilities

Network services include features and information, such as:

- **Network routing**: Although ACDs are typically the primary routing mechanism, networks also feature routing capabilities. Routing can be based on factors such as the time of day, day of week, percentage of calls to be handled at each site, area code of the calling party, DNIS, ANI or information gathered from databases via CTI. Additionally, calls can be held (queued) in the network until agents are available and then routed to the most appropriate site. (See ACD Systems, this section.)

- **Network reports**: Provide historical or real-time information on network call activity. For example, network reports can indicate how many network busies were delivered, trunk utilization, call volumes, total traffic (volume multiplied by holding times), calling numbers, etc., for each trunk group or DNIS number.

Note: Section 6 was developed with Vanguard Communications Corp., and is drawn from the seminar, *Understanding and Applying Today's Call Center Technologies* and related materials. Contents copyrighted to Vanguard Communications Corp. and/or ICMI, Inc., 2003

Section 6

- **User control:** Control of network features traditionally has been in the hands of network providers, but in recent years, network technologies have been putting much more control in the hands of users. Today, many call centers have terminals in their facilities that directly control network features.

Multisite Alternatives

Networks also enable multiple sites to be networked, and provide control on how calls are routed. Common types of routing include:

- **Percent allocation:** Calls are allocated across multiple sites based on user-defined percentages.

- **Call-by-call routing:** Calls are routed to the optimum destination according to real-time conditions.

- **Network interflow:** Integrates ACD and network circuits and allows for calls to be queued simultaneously for agents groups in different sites.

An important consideration in managing a multisite network is to ensure that network routing is in sync with schedules in individual sites. In other words, schedules shouldn't be changed without alerting the networks routing manager, and network routing shouldn't substantially be altered without coordinating with individual sites.

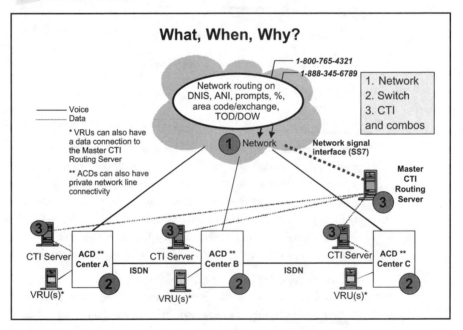

Note: Section 6 was developed with Vanguard Communications Corp., and is drawn from the seminar, *Understanding and Applying Today's Call Center Technologies* and related materials. Contents copyrighted to Vanguard Communications Corp. and/or ICMI, Inc., 2003

As the diagram illustrates, network features can be integrated with other technologies (e.g., CTI, IVR) to provide sophisticated call routing and handling solutions across single or multiple sites. There are three key methods for routing calls to multiple sites: network, switch, and CTI. Network is the simplest method and typically is used when the environment is not very dynamic. Switch is most often the choice when all locations have the same switch type. CTI is used when there is a diverse switch environment, the routing is highly dynamic or the routing is tied to information in databases.

Related Terms

- **ISDN (integrated services digital network)**: A set of international standards for networks, which provides end-to-end digital network services.

- **DNIS (dialed number identification service)**: A string of digits that the network passes to the ACD, IVR or other device to indicate which number the caller dialed.

- **ANI (automatic number identification)**: The network passes the caller's billing number to the ACD, IVR or other device.

- **Number portability**: A shared database among network providers that enables call centers to keep the same numbers even if they change carriers.

(See Technology Infrastructure Components, this section.)

Note: Section 6 was developed with Vanguard Communications Corp., and is drawn from the seminar, *Understanding and Applying Today's Call Center Technologies* and related materials. Contents copyrighted to Vanguard Communications Corp. and/or ICMI, Inc., 2003

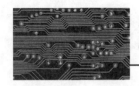

5. IVR/Voice-Processing Capabilities

Ready? | 1 | 2 | 3 |

Key Points

- There are three terms related to "voice-processing systems" that are common today:
  - Auto attendant
  - Voice response unit (VRU)
  - Interactive voice response (IVR)

- Traditionally, these systems turned DTMF (dual-tone multifrequency, otherwise known as touchtone) input into signals recognized by other systems, e.g., the ACD for routing calls, or identifiers such as account numbers for database access. Today, speech recognition is fast becoming an easy and desirable alternative for interacting with these systems.

- IVR systems should be programmed so that they are easy to use and give callers a way to "opt out" to reach an agent.

Explanation

Interactive voice response (IVR) systems are in use in a large number of call centers. The term "voice-processing system" is generically used to describe any system that requests any type of caller input; however, there are actually three general terms – each with slightly different meanings – in use today:

- **Auto attendant**: An auto-attendant system is typically an inexpensive add-on to an ACD and only provides routing capabilities. It does not interact with a database. An auto-attendant is typically used in applications where a caller is asked to "press one for this, two for that."

- **Voice response unit (VRU)**: Often used interchangeably with IVR, the VRU more typically refers to the equipment running the system, rather than the system itself or the capability.

- **Interactive voice response (IVR)**: Systems that enable callers to use a telephone keypad (or spoken commands if speech recognition is used) to access a company's computer system for the purpose of retrieving or updating information, conducting a business transaction or routing their call.

Note: Section 6 was developed with Vanguard Communications Corp., and is drawn from the seminar, *Understanding and Applying Today's Call Center Technologies* and related materials. Contents copyrighted to Vanguard Communications Corp. and/or ICMI, Inc., 2003

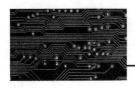

This sample menu emphasizes some of the best practices for a set of menus, such as limited choices and zero to reach an agent.

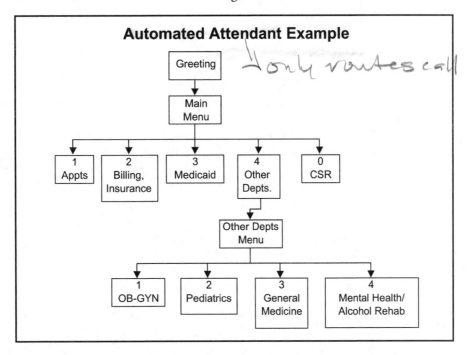

In the past, all these systems worked by turning the distinct DTMF (dual-tone multifrequency, otherwise known as touchtone) codes created by user input on the phone keypad to data bytes that are understood by the system. This is still the most common methodology in use today. However, speech recognition is fast becoming an easy and desirable way of interacting with these systems.

IVR systems can be placed in front of an ACD via direct trunking or they can be connected behind the switch. Either way, the IVR typically interacts with the caller at the beginning of the call. IVR systems can also be used to conduct caller surveys at the completion of calls. IVR architecture enables integration with other systems, including the ACD, databases, network and other applications.

IVR Benefits

The majority of organizations that use IVR systems do so to reduce operating costs and/or extend coverage hours. Examples of the benefits that can be derived from an IVR system include:

Note: Section 6 was developed with Vanguard Communications Corp., and is drawn from the seminar, *Understanding and Applying Today's Call Center Technologies* and related materials. Contents copyrighted to Vanguard Communications Corp. and/or ICMI, Inc., 2003

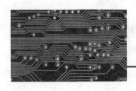

- Capability to handle more call volume

- Reduce staff requirements

- Lower cost per call

- Broaden hours of coverage

- Provide ease of access from anywhere there is a touchtone telephone

- Provide customers with choice and control through self-service

The success of an IVR system is typically measured by an IVR completion rate. This is expressed as the percentage of callers who are fully handled within the system and do not transfer out (voluntarily or involuntarily) to an agent. Completion rates vary widely from one industry to the next. Where calls are more complex (e.g., technical support), the organization may be satisfied with a 10 percent completion rate. In other industries, completion rates of 70 or even 80 percent are common (e.g., bank applications for checking balances or transferring funds).

IVR Architecture

Most IVR systems reside on PCs, using Unix or NT operating systems. Two key elements are the interface to the switch or network and the voice subsystem, which includes applications and processing of audio inputs and outputs. Generally, there is also an interface to external databases or applications. Optional elements, such as speech recognition, text to speech, or fax, are often part of an IVR platform as well.

(continued, next page)

Note: Section 6 was developed with Vanguard Communications Corp., and is drawn from the seminar, *Understanding and Applying Today's Call Center Technologies* and related materials. Contents copyrighted to Vanguard Communications Corp. and/or ICMI, Inc., 2003

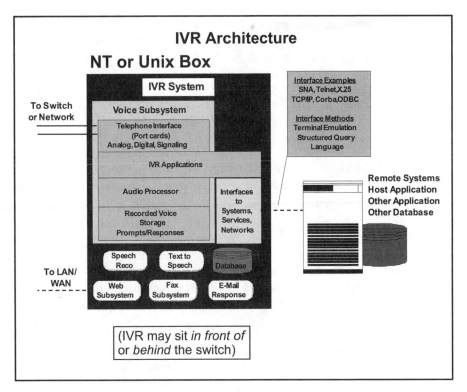

IVR Management

IVR systems are often criticized by users for being too long and/or too complex. There are many best practices in place that keep satisfaction and completion rates as high as possible for a given industry and application. For example:

- **Provide customer education**: Through literature, information posted on the Web and IVR announcements, let customers know how to navigate your menus quickly and easily.

- **Sell the services of the IVR**: Your agents and other personnel should encourage callers to use these services.

- **Keep it simple**: Prompts should get to the point, and menu layers and choices should be kept as few as possible.

- **Allow callers a simple way to opt out**: This ensures that the callers feel in control of the system.

- **Keep messaging short and to the point**: Frequently asked questions and services should be listed first on your menus.

Note: Section 6 was developed with Vanguard Communications Corp., and is drawn from the seminar, *Understanding and Applying Today's Call Center Technologies* and related materials. Contents copyrighted to Vanguard Communications Corp. and/or ICMI, Inc., 2003

Section 6

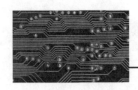

- **Listen to your IVR** (silent monitor via trunk side or station side): Experience what the customer experiences, and use the reporting capabilities to troubleshoot and improve your application.

Overall, easy access to information and the ability to reach agents on demand play the most significant role in customer satisfaction with IVRs.

Advanced Features

IVR systems continue to advance, and are increasingly able to handle transactions simply and effectively. Some of the more advanced offerings found today include:

- **Fax on demand:** The IVR system interacts with the fax server to send forms and other information to a caller without any agent intervention.

- **Post-call surveying:** Callers are notified up front that a survey is available after the call and are sent to the application upon call completion to fill out simple surveys (which generally last two minutes or less).

- **Text-to-speech capability:** The IVR "reads and speaks" information contained in a database back to the caller. An example is reading out a name or address to ensure that a correct match has occurred.

- **Speech recognition:** Rather than relying on DTMF (touchtone) input, the system allows the caller to speak and then turns the spoken words into digital demands that the system can understand.

Speech Recognition

Speech recognition is receiving a tremendous amount of attention today, as it offers the potential to bring IVR systems to new levels of performance. By interacting with databases using spoken language, rather than the telephone keypad, the interface expands and therefore the application opportunities expand. Further, a well-designed speech recognition application will attract customers who would not otherwise successfully complete self-service transactions.

There are two key types of speech recognition used in call centers today:

- **Directed dialogue or structured language:** This type of prompting coaches the caller through the selections. For example, a bank application might say "What would you like to do? You can say 'get balance,' 'transfer funds,' or 'explore specific transactions.'"

Note: Section 6 was developed with Vanguard Communications Corp., and is drawn from the seminar, *Understanding and Applying Today's Call Center Technologies* and related materials. Contents copyrighted to Vanguard Communications Corp. and/or ICMI, Inc., 2003

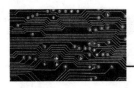

- **Natural language:** This type uses a more open-ended prompt, recognizing what the caller says without as much coaching. The caller can speak naturally, e.g., responding to a prompt about what they would like to do with "Um, I'd like to transfer funds from my checking account to my savings account."

Speech applications are speaker independent, recognizing a variety of accents and colloquialisms. Vocabularies of speech-based systems are in the tens of thousands of words enabling applications that are otherwise too complex for touchtone, such as stock and fund quotes and travel status.

IVR Reports

The IVR, like other call center systems, provides a variety of call center reports, including:

- Port utilization (percent of time ports are in use)
- Calls offered
- Average handling time in IVR system
- Percent completion (percent of callers that successfully self-serve without needing to speak with an agent)
- Number of calls sent to agent groups
- Number of calls that defaulted without using prompts
- Abandonments (callers hang up before finishing IVR routine)
- Exit points (point at which a caller selects to exit and speak to an agent)
- Transfers (to agents from IVR)

A key to using IVR reports effectively is routine analysis tied to a knowledge of the applications. It is critical to track trends – what's working and what isn't – and fine tune applications and scripts to optimize use.

IVR Key Practices

1. **Make the system as easy to use and familiar as possible.**

- Pattern the IVR after familiar methods and procedures. To do this, sit in on agent calls — or even better, put on a headset yourself and field customer calls for a few hours. You'll gain a new understanding of your customer's interactions.

- Keep prompts short and to the point.

(continued, next page)

Note: Section 6 was developed with Vanguard Communications Corp., and is drawn from the seminar, *Understanding and Applying Today's Call Center Technologies* and related materials. Contents copyrighted to Vanguard Communications Corp. and/or ICMI, Inc., 2003

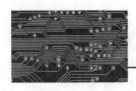

• Permit prompts to be overridden, wherever possible.

• Try to limit the menu to a maximum of five options. Giving callers more than five choices makes it difficult for them to remember all available options and can be frustrating.

• Provide callers with automated feedback and verification of their actions.

• Position the most commonly requested choices first on your menu. In addition, order choices logically, keeping similar things together.

• Use a voice that reflects your corporate image and that is pleasing to callers. Consider using focus groups to evaluate voice talent.

2. Let callers feel in control.

• Don't blame mistakes on your callers. Accusatory error messages will dissuade them from using your application in the future.

• Give callers an easy way to go back to the main menu and all submenus. Provide options that enable callers to repeat information, pause, and move forward and backward throughout the application.

• Automatically repeat each prompt at least once if no action is taken.

• Provide a way for callers to "opt out" to a live agent by pressing 0 during business hours. After hours, silence any options to press 0 so you won't set false expectations. If a caller does press 0 after hours, use a message that tells them the times they can reach an agent. If you'd rather have callers leave messages for a callback, make sure that you have the internal resources to respond.

• Give additional guidance for complex or high-value transactions.

• Don't confuse callers by changing the application frequently. In general, changes to call-flow and logic should not be made more than once every six months. Unless there are compelling reasons, the main menu should almost never be changed.

3. Keep the user interface consistent.

• State the action before the action key.

• Use keys consistently. Don't use whatever keys are leftover at the end of a menu to let callers skip ahead, repeat information or go back to the main menu. Establish specific keys for these actions and enable them throughout the application. We recommend using the IVR "standards" issued in 1990 by the Voice Messaging User Interface Forum. These standards include: 0 to reach an operator; # to skip ahead or terminate an entry; and * to repeat or cancel.

• Handle invalid entries and timeouts the same way throughout the application.

• Make sure that voice quality, including pitch and volume, is consistent throughout the application.

• Use a single voice; multiple voices tend to distract callers from their tasks.

• Don't look at your IVR system in a vacuum. Applications should complement your

Note: Section 6 was developed with Vanguard Communications Corp., and is drawn from the seminar, *Understanding and Applying Today's Call Center Technologies* and related materials. Contents copyrighted to Vanguard Communications Corp. and/or ICMI, Inc., 2003

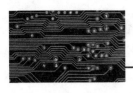

Internet applications, customer materials, screens used by agents, etc., to ensure consistent overall customer contact practices.

4. Talk to callers – don't write to them.

• We speak very differently than we write. Scripts that sound like writing are stilted and frequently discourage callers. Substitute informal words for formal ones, like "stop" for "terminate," or "about" instead of "pertaining to" or "in regards to."

• Always read your script aloud before it is recorded. Test it with a mix of people.

• Use a natural, high quality, intelligible voice.

• Time prompts and options to reflect normal conversation pace.

• Avoid using acronyms or technical jargon that your average caller may not understand.

• Limit concatenation (the linking together of words in a long series) wherever possible by recording concise phrases. Test any concatenated prompts to make sure they sound natural.

5. Don't bore callers with long-winded messages.

• Keep informational messages to one minute or less. Callers tend to lose interest after about 45 seconds.

• Provide disclaimers only if they are required. If possible, refer callers to a handbook or Web site instead of reciting all the legal gobbledygook on the IVR.

6. Leverage technology to personalize the caller's experience.

• Identify callers via account numbers or other methods in order to offer options that are customized to the caller and/or the caller's value to your organization.

• Wherever possible, provide dynamic menus that are tailored to the services available to the caller.

• Don't offer callers options that are not available to them under their specific plan or account. This may drive unnecessary calls into your call center. An exception to this rule is when you want callers to upgrade to a new plan or account level, in which case, offer away.

• If callers opt out of the IVR system, use technology that provides the agent with information about the caller (at minimum an account number on a phone display or "whisper" transfer) and where the caller was in the system when he or she exited.

7. Educate and involve your callers.

• Provide customers with written materials (pamphlets or wallet cards) that instruct them on and encourage use of the IVR system.

• Regularly solicit customer feedback (via phone or mail surveys) regarding the IVR system. Survey them at least once a year.

(continued, next page)

Note: Section 6 was developed with Vanguard Communications Corp., and is drawn from the seminar, *Understanding and Applying Today's Call Center Technologies* and related materials. Contents copyrighted to Vanguard Communications Corp. and/or ICMI, Inc., 2003

• Educate agents on IVR use to help them answer callers' questions about the application. Ask agents to encourage customer use when appropriate.

8. Monitor your IVR system regularly.

• Monitor usage statistics and reports weekly during initial implementation and pilots; monitor on a monthly basis thereafter.

• Specifically, seek reports that provide statistics about:
1. The percentage and number of callers successfully completing transactions in the IVR system. Define success as callers who do not opt out to agents, assuming that these callers received all the information they needed or completed their transaction in the IVR system.
2. The most frequently accessed areas of the application.
3. Areas of the application where callers frequently transfer to agents.
4. Areas of the application where callers are transferred to agents because of caller error.
5. Caller demographics to determine if specific groups in your customer base use the system more than others.

Excerpt from "Key Practices for Optimizing IVR Applications" by Elaine Cascio and Stephen Marshall, *Call Center Management Review*, September 1999.

Note: Section 6 was developed with Vanguard Communications Corp., and is drawn from the seminar, *Understanding and Applying Today's Call Center Technologies* and related materials. Contents copyrighted to Vanguard Communications Corp. and/or ICMI, Inc., 2003

6. Workforce Management Systems

Ready? | 1 | 2 | 3 |

Key Points

- Workforce management systems (WFMS) provide call center managers with a tool to accomplish automated forecasting, staffing projections, scheduling and tracking – key processes within any center.

- The primary value of a WFMS to a call center lies in its ability to maximize the use of available resources and thereby reduce overall staffing requirements and costs.

- Workforce management systems are now able to handle telephone calls, as well as email, text-chat, Web callback and VoIP calls.

Explanation

At a basic level, workforce management systems provide automated support for four key processes in the call center – forecasting, staffing projections, scheduling and tracking.

- **Forecasting:** Forecasting is generally based on time series approaches that assess past patterns and trends and project them into the future. Generally, the user has a variety of options for overriding or changing projections and adding in judgmental criteria. (See discussions on forecasting, Section 5.)

- **Staffing projections:** The "engine" behind staffing projections is generally comprised of a set of Erlang calculations (including Erlang C and Erlang B) or modified Erlang calculations that compute staff and system capacity requirements. Some vendors also provide simulation capability for running complex scenarios. (See Queuing Formulas and Simulation, Section 5.)

- **Scheduling:** Scheduling is generally based on an iterative approach in the software that creates and organizes schedules based on user-defined parameters. (See Scheduling Considerations and Applications, Section 5.)

- **Tracking:** Tracking and reporting provide the capability for users to compare actual results against projections in a real-time mode (tracking) and historically (reporting). Most WFMS not only track and report on volume activity, but also on handling time, adherence to schedule and absenteeism.

[handwritten margin notes:] time series forecasting using historical data to predict — uses Erlang C staffing Erlang B Tracking

Note: Section 6 was developed with Vanguard Communications Corp., and is drawn from the seminar, *Understanding and Applying Today's Call Center Technologies* and related materials. Contents copyrighted to Vanguard Communications Corp. and/or ICMI, Inc., 2003

Section 6

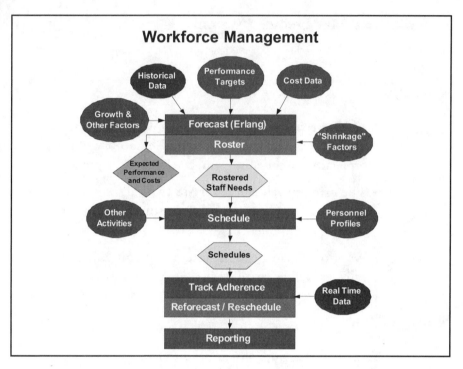

The Business Case

Because of the importance of utilizing staff appropriately, it is typically the call center management team and/or the finance department that drives the decision to purchase a WFMS. The business case for a WFMS usually includes:

- Better, more consistent delivery of service leading to increased revenues and higher levels of customer satisfaction.

- Benefits of more efficient scheduling (e.g., reduction of overtime).

- Reduced telecommunications costs due to reduced queue times.

- Reduction of administrative staff time to manually produce forecasts and schedules. However, this is usually less of a benefit than the above.

The following factors are important considerations when choosing a WFMS:

- Length of time data is retained

- Ability to segment and schedule by skill

- System flexibility in changing schedules

- Ability to provide for flexible hours of operation

Note: Section 6 was developed with Vanguard Communications Corp., and is drawn from the seminar, *Understanding and Applying Today's Call Center Technologies* and related materials. Contents copyrighted to Vanguard Communications Corp. and/or ICMI, Inc., 2003

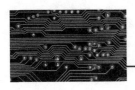

Additional Functionality

While a reduction in payroll expenses is typically the key benefit to a WFMS, most can also automate many other processes in a call center. Typical examples of additional functionality include the following:

- ACD integration
- Vacation approvals and administration
- Shift development
- Real-time adherence
- Meeting/break-time optimization
- Payroll system interfaces
- Networked site capabilities

These features either help to maximize the efficiency of the schedules developed (e.g., meeting/break-time optimization) or automate processes (e.g., vacation administration) that would otherwise be time-consuming. Some vendors have taken these concepts even further with functionality that includes:

- Skills-based scheduling
- Integrated forecasting and scheduling for multiple access channels
- Schedule viewing and shift changes/swapping via the intranet

Implementation Challenges

As with all software, there are integration and implementation challenges. While some systems function as stand-alones, most are at least integrated with the ACD. This integration allows the system to automatically collect data used for forecasting future call loads and for historical reporting. While most of the major WFMS can communicate effectively with most of the major ACDs, occasional problems occur. One example is the difficulty some WFMS have in recognizing different agent states coming from the ACD. The misinterpretation of nonphone time as "logged in and available" time can result in inaccurate adherence calculations.

When implementing these systems, many organizations make the mistake of providing too little support in terms of dedicated staff. Though much of what these systems do is automated, user intervention is required for activities such as "scrubbing" the data. An example is incoming call volume information that is higher than normal due to a one-time event. If this is not adjusted within the WFMS, future forecasts will tend to be inflated.

Note: Section 6 was developed with Vanguard Communications Corp., and is drawn from the seminar, *Understanding and Applying Today's Call Center Technologies* and related materials. Contents copyrighted to Vanguard Communications Corp. and/or ICMI, Inc., 2003

Despite these challenges, most organizations that have installed WFMS have become very dependent on them. When working appropriately, they provide support for critical planning processes that have a direct and significant impact on service level and response time results in a call center.

Note: Section 6 was developed with Vanguard Communications Corp., and is drawn from the seminar, *Understanding and Applying Today's Call Center Technologies* and related materials. Contents copyrighted to Vanguard Communications Corp. and/or ICMI, Inc., 2003

7. Quality Monitoring/Recording Systems

Ready? | 1 | 2 | 3 |

Key Points

- When used properly, quality monitoring/recording systems provide opportunities to substantially improve the call-handling performance of agents as well as improve overall processes and system use.

- Quality monitoring/recording systems can be set up to record all calls, a percentage of calls, a scheduled selection of calls or individual calls on demand.

- Quality monitoring/recording systems can capture screen activity as well as the voice components of a call.

- Quality monitoring/recording systems can also serve as central repositories for all quality-related data.

Explanation

Quality monitoring/recording systems are used to record calls in order to have a permanent record of the complete transaction and to improve the quality of call handling. While all the vendors provide some unique functionality, the ability to record calls is central to these systems. Recording strategies include:

- **Logging**: The taping of every call coming into the organization.

- **Percent**: A certain percent of calls are recorded to enhance the quality review process. The percent of calls can be chosen randomly or from designated types of calls.

- **Scheduled**: Enables the user to schedule calls to be recorded for a certain agent at a certain time.

- **On demand**: Enables the agent or supervisor to activate the recording feature at a moment's notice.

Recording Strategies

The decision on which strategy to use depends on the organization's needs and goals. Logging is appropriate when a single error or dispute can have significant costs or create potential liability, such as in the health care or financial services industries. While logging provides a complete, permanent

Note: Section 6 was developed with Vanguard Communications Corp., and is drawn from the seminar, *Understanding and Applying Today's Call Center Technologies* and related materials. Contents copyrighted to Vanguard Communications Corp. and/or ICMI, Inc., 2003

Section 6

record of what was said, the cost associated with recording and storing all calls can be substantial.

Where only a sampling of calls is required for quality assessment purposes, percent and scheduled recording strategies are typically preferred. These allow for enough calls to be recorded to assess individual performance, without creating the extra expense associated with logging. Organizations that use percent or scheduled recording can augment these strategies with on-demand recording to cover themselves in the event that a critical (e.g., threatening or distress) call is received.

Regardless of the recording strategy, the system must be able to track and search for the call. Where the system is integrated with a CRM or other contact tracking system, a unique identifier can be added to the account of the call to assist in look-up. Without this integration, the system will provide search capabilities by parameters such as agent identification, time of day and date.

The Business Case

Organizations that implement quality monitoring/recording systems do so to improve call handling, make it more consistent and uncover ways to improve processes and systems. Payback is usually defined in terms of reductions in errors, rework and complaints. Some organizations also cite a reduction in call-handling time as a result of being able to identify agents who are struggling with inefficient call-handling methods. Others have been able to reduce handling time by decreasing the amount of documentation required for a call (however, this is possible only with a logging strategy that records every call). Information gathered from quality monitoring/recording systems can also be used to assess the effectiveness of training and make processes more efficient.

Recording systems also reduce some of the inefficiencies associated with silent monitoring. Supervisors and/or quality assurance teams no longer have to deal with issues such as starting a session in the middle of a call, losing a monitored call due to interruption, or waiting for a call to come through during a slow period. Consequently, the call center can monitor more calls with less effort and cost.

Common characteristics of these systems include:

- **Feedback forms:** Most systems allow the user to customize a feedback form to be used by everyone accessing the system.

- **Coordinated data recording:** The system records the screen activity during the call and plays it back to the reviewer, coordinated with the voice part of the call.

Note: Section 6 was developed with Vanguard Communications Corp., and is drawn from the seminar, *Understanding and Applying Today's Call Center Technologies* and related materials. Contents copyrighted to Vanguard Communications Corp. and/or ICMI, Inc., 2003

- **Text-chat/email recording**: Through the data recording capability, the system can also be used for text-chat, email and other nonphone channels.

- **GUI interface for recording/playback**: A user-friendly interface that enables reviewers to set up recording sessions and playback calls.

Successful Implementation

While quality monitoring/recording systems offer a great deal of functionality, they also require a great deal of integration. A robust system must typically integrate with the ACD, workforce management system, CTI system and any desktop tools used by agents (e.g., CRM packages, mainframe applications). As a result, integration difficulties are some of the biggest challenges facing those purchasing a quality monitoring/recording system.

To maximize successful use, call center managers must ensure that the goals of the program are understood and accepted by all members of the staff. Without this understanding, agents may react negatively to the close scrutiny of their work provided by these systems. Communication throughout all phases of the project is a critical success factor that is often overlooked.

New Capabilities

Many of the quality monitoring/recording vendors are working to increase the functionality of their systems. Some of the newer offerings include:

- **Cradle-to-grave customer experience**: Screen shots and voice are captured from the customer's perspective, beginning in the IVR and continuing through any and all systems until the transaction is complete.

- **Integration with e-learning capabilities**: Using data from the performance evaluations contained within the system, the software links with internal or external e-learning systems to identify and provide customized one-on-one training and coaching solutions.

- **Integrated reporting/data mining**: Some systems provide the ability to bring in data from other systems to analyze call patterns in new ways and/or create comprehensive quality reporting.

Despite the integration challenges, many organizations are turning to quality monitoring/recording systems as an effective way to ensure consistent service in an increasingly complex environment.

(For more information on quality monitoring, see ICMI's *Call Center People Management Handbook and Study Guide*.)

Note: Section 6 was developed with Vanguard Communications Corp., and is drawn from the seminar, *Understanding and Applying Today's Call Center Technologies* and related materials. Contents copyrighted to Vanguard Communications Corp. and/or ICMI, Inc., 2003

8. Desktop/Agent System Interface

Ready? | 1 | 2 | 3

Key Points

- Desktop technology options include "dumb" terminals, PCs with terminal emulation, thick clients and thin clients.

- As companies integrate Web-based capabilities into their call centers, many are moving to a thin-client environment with browser-based applications.

- A client-server environment allows for quicker implementation of new applications than traditional mainframe-based environments.

- Companies that still depend on some mainframe applications, but need additional functionality, can utilize PC-based terminal emulation, middleware, a CRM package, browser-based solutions or other options.

Explanation

Agent desktop technologies come in many shapes and sizes, each with their own dependencies and advantages. Primary alternatives include:

- **Fixed-function "dumb" terminal:** The user device (terminal) in a computing environment in which all of the processing occurs on a central computer or mainframe.

- **PC-running terminal emulation:** This duplicates the functionality of the "dumb" terminal in environments that require PCs for some applications, but in which access to a mainframe is still necessary.

- **Client/server architecture:** A networking scheme in which a client application requests information from a server application.
  - *Client*: A computer or computer application that has access to services (data, software) over a network from a server application.

  - *Server*: A computer that shares its resources with other computers on a network. For example, file servers share disk storage with other computers. Database servers respond to requests from other computers on the network (clients).

Note: Section 6 was developed with Vanguard Communications Corp., and is drawn from the seminar, *Understanding and Applying Today's Call Center Technologies* and related materials. Contents copyrighted to Vanguard Communications Corp. and/or ICMI, Inc., 2003

Irish

- **Thick client:** A workstation in a client-server environment that performs much or most of the application processing. It requires programs and data to be installed on it and a significant part of the application processing takes place on the workstation. The client is "thick" in that much of the overall application is running on it.

Low maintain possible with # of servers

- **Thin client:** A workstation in a client-server environment that performs little or no application processing. Often used to describe browser-based desktops. The client is "thin" in that the applications reside on and are run within the server rather than the client.

The following table highlights some of the differences and impacts of these options.

*client impact
/handl 1
will incuase
SL will deans
indiuct
ad home mgst
go down*

Comparing Desktops

Desktop	Architecture	Applications Processing	Desktop Interface	Hardware/Software Requirements & Costs		Software Distribution and Management	Comments
				Desktop	Mainframe or Server		
Dumb Terminal	Mainframe	Mainframe	Character driven, function keys	Low	High	Centralized; Easy	Fast performance; Old approach
PC with Terminal Emulation	Mainframe Access (may be in C/S environment)	Mainframe	GUI	Medium	High	Decentralized; More time required	Done in MF environs where PC needed for other tasks
Thick Client	Client/Server	Mix – PC, Server Mainframe	GUI, may have Browser	High	Medium	Decentralized; Software distribution and updating required	Highest cost desktop but proven approach
Thin Client	Client/Server (Internet/ Intranet-based)	Server (may have some on mainframe)	GUI, Browser	Low	High	Centralized; Software updating required	Requires high bandwidth LAN/WAN; Leading edge

Client-Server Benefits

The use of PCs and PC servers over the past few years has allowed businesses to be more flexible in deploying applications. Systems based on these architectures have the following characteristics:

- Comparatively rapid implementation of or changes to new applications (compared to earlier mainframe-based applications).

- Packaged desktop applications can be leveraged, accessing databases and each other through standard interfaces, protocols and exchange tools.

- Legacy applications on mainframes are impacted less (if at all), coding on

Note: Section 6 was developed with Vanguard Communications Corp., and is drawn from the seminar, *Understanding and Applying Today's Call Center Technologies* and related materials. Contents copyrighted to Vanguard Communications Corp. and/or ICMI, Inc., 2003

Section 6

the mainframes is avoided, and the mainframe-resident data and applications are offloaded for better response times.

• Applications can be integrated more easily and effectively through standard interfaces.

• Access to multiple data sources and applications on multiple computers through the use of middleware.

• Enhanced interfaces and tools at the desktop, e.g., graphical user interfaces (GUIs) and multimedia capabilities.

One of the debates today surrounds the topic of thin vs. thick clients. Thin-client architectures offer lower cost, ease of management and centralized applications. But they require greater bandwidth on the LAN or WAN, and servers need to be more powerful to provide adequate response times loading and unloading applications. The client-server architecture is a two edged sword. If one is to embrace the new Internet-based technologies (e.g., browser, IP network), the work of processing must be moved off the clients.

Performance Issues

The functionality and speed of the desktop have a significant impact on performance statistics. It is critical that the IT team understands the time-sensitive nature of call centers when configuring applications.

Note: Section 6 was developed with Vanguard Communications Corp., and is drawn from the seminar, *Understanding and Applying Today's Call Center Technologies* and related materials. Contents copyrighted to Vanguard Communications Corp. and/or ICMI, Inc., 2003

9. Dialers

Ready? | 1 | 2 | 3 |

Key Points

- Dialers are technologies (hardware/software) for automating the process of making outbound calls to lists of people.

- In addition to placing outbound calls, dialers may provide campaign management and scripting functionality, track the disposition of calls and provide detailed real-time and historical reporting.

- Dialers can operate in several modes, including preview dialing, progressive dialing, predictive dialing and call blending.

- Dialers are evolving from stand-alone systems to become part of integrated call center systems, especially as part of CTI applications.

Explanation

One way to understand the advantages of using a dialer is to consider it as an ACD for outbound calls. Dialers launch calls and deliver them to agents, just as an ACD does. Dialers also provide tracking, real-time monitoring and reporting capabilities for outbound calls similar to those that ACDs provide for incoming calls.

While some experts claim that predictive dialing can double the total talk time per hour of agents, they offer a trade-off. The more aggressive they are programmed to place calls (and increase "productivity"), the more likely that people will hear silence when they answer the phone, causing more people to hang up. Programming should be done with the objective of increasing completed calls. Before purchasing a dialer, conduct manual campaigns to determine your needs. (See Objectives for Outbound, Section 4.)

(continued, next page)

Note: Section 6 was developed with Vanguard Communications Corp., and is drawn from the seminar, *Understanding and Applying Today's Call Center Technologies* and related materials. Contents copyrighted to Vanguard Communications Corp. and/or ICMI, Inc., 2003

Section 6

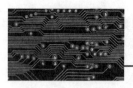

Dialing Modes

Dialing modes include:

- **Preview dialing**: An application that instructs the switch to dial a specific phone number under control of an agent. The agent previews a screen containing information about the person to be called, monitors the call for connection (or other classification), and updates the database accordingly. This is used for callbacks or other contacts in which the agent needs to review information before placing the call.

- **Predictive dialing**: An application that instructs the switch to dial multiple simultaneous calls based upon a preloaded list of phone numbers. A mathematical algorithm is used to predict the correct number of calls to launch and when agents will become available. Then it seeks to match the number of live connected calls with the number of available agents. The system determines when a called party has answered and transfers only live calls (and answering machines, if desired) to agents. Agents also receive a data screen about the call. The system classifies all calls launched (e.g., connect, busy, no answer, answering machine, network tones) and updates the database accordingly.

- **Progressive dialing**: The term is either used as a variation on preview dialing or predictive dialing. Some use progressive dialing to describe preview dialing where the preview is timed before automatically launching. Some use progressive dialing to describe a form of controlled predictive dialing where multiple calls are launched only when an agent becomes available. It is still predictive in that it is predicting how many calls will connect. However, it reduces the chance of a live answer by a customer when no agent is available.

- **Call blending**: The ability to dynamically allocate call center agents to both inbound and outbound calling, based on conditions in the call center and programmed parameters. This enables a single agent to handle both inbound and outbound calls, from the same position, without manually monitoring call activity and reassigning the position. The outbound dialing application monitors inbound calling activity and assigns outbound agents to outbound calling when the inbound volume drops off.

[handwritten margin note: modified Preview Timed / modified Predictive]

Note: Section 6 was developed with Vanguard Communications Corp., and is drawn from the seminar, *Understanding and Applying Today's Call Center Technologies* and related materials. Contents copyrighted to Vanguard Communications Corp. and/or ICMI, Inc., 2003

Call-Blending Considerations

In many cases, call blending is more promise than a reality. The concept seems simple enough to grasp – utilize the idle time between inbound calls to make outbound calls. But when agents are on an outbound call, they are no longer available for the next randomly arriving inbound call. The mathematical laws of probability hold that more agents will therefore need to be scheduled to handle the same workload of incoming calls, if the same agents will be making outbound calls. But the problem presented for the call center manager is "How many more?" Scheduling agents becomes significantly more complex in a call-blending environment. Workforce management systems are only just beginning to address this problem. However, there are cases where call blending works well – most notably in collection departments where customers are being called and returning calls. In this setting, a blended environment is often successful. (See Occupancy and Productive/Nonproductive, Section 4.)

Note: In addition to the traditional definition of blending inbound and outbound calls, call blending can also refer to blending calls with nonphone work, or handling contacts from different channels (e.g., email and phone).

Note: Section 6 was developed with Vanguard Communications Corp., and is drawn from the seminar, *Understanding and Applying Today's Call Center Technologies* and related materials. Contents copyrighted to Vanguard Communications Corp. and/or ICMI, Inc., 2003

10. Fax Servers

Ready? 1 2 3

Key Points

- Despite the proliferation of Web and IVR capabilities, fax is still common in call centers and many customers still use fax as a preferred method of communication for some types of transactions.

- Many companies are expanding their fax-on-demand capabilities to encourage more customer self-service transactions.

- Fax traffic should be planned for and managed along with other types of contacts.

Explanation

Fax-processing systems have the ability to capture, store, manipulate and recreate analog signals, and can be combined on a single platform, but typically are offered by different suppliers to meet a diversity of business applications.

Call centers are rapidly moving from fax machines to fax servers and software solutions running on standard hardware platforms. These LAN-based systems provide inbound and outbound capabilities. Some systems automatically distribute incoming faxes or transfer them to an image processing system for retrieval by an agent.

New Capabilities

New transmission strategies, often using the Internet or Internet protocols (IP) over private networks, dramatically cut transmission costs by converting fax signals into "packetized" data. A new standard is emerging for IP fax that is more effective than existing standards, and will also support current equipment through gateways. Further, new gateways are emerging that enable many advanced features – even for users with ordinary fax machines. Such features include:

- Capture and deliver email messages to fax machines.

- Route fax traffic on and off the Internet.

- Provide advanced reporting, security, guaranteed delivery and receipt.

- Provide broadcast functions.

Note: Section 6 was developed with Vanguard Communications Corp., and is drawn from the seminar, *Understanding and Applying Today's Call Center Technologies* and related materials. Contents copyrighted to Vanguard Communications Corp. and/or ICMI, Inc., 2003

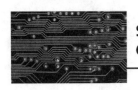

Broadcast fax, from a CPE server or from a service bureau, is used for many outbound customer contact applications. Fax-on-demand systems are an important component for many call centers' self-service strategies. Some products integrate with a Web site, converting an HTML Web page to a fax transmission. Fax servers are used in call centers to send order confirmations or in other fulfillment applications.

Managing Fax Traffic

Managing fax traffic is an important issue in call centers and should not be ignored. (See Definitions and Use of Service Level, Response Time and Quality, Section 3.) Suppliers are developing multimedia queuing techniques, which merge voice calls, incoming fax and email traffic to an agent's workstation for efficient handling. (See Multimedia Routing and Queuing, this section.)

Section 6

Note: Section 6 was developed with Vanguard Communications Corp., and is drawn from the seminar, *Understanding and Applying Today's Call Center Technologies* and related materials. Contents copyrighted to Vanguard Communications Corp. and/or ICMI, Inc., 2003

11. Telecommuting Technologies

Ready? | 1 | 2 | 3 |

Key Points

- While there are relatively few call center telecommuting programs today, interest is growing.

- There are a number of technologies for both voice and data services that make telecommuting feasible.

Explanation

Telecommuting has had an interesting history in call centers. A handful of organizations have had telecommuting programs in their call centers for years, but in the early 1990s, the subject began to become a "hot topic" in call center circles. The potential benefits were compelling: tap into a larger workforce (such as with agents who have physical disabilities), attract and retain employees who need flexible hours, handle peak periods efficiently, have backup for crises such as incapacitating weather, save money and space, and comply with governmental restrictions on commuting.

Dozens, perhaps hundreds, of organizations initiated telecommuting programs in their call centers, many diving in head first. Some were successful and are going strong. Others ran into high costs, inadequate technologies and challenging new management issues. Consequently, even some of the high-profile telecommuting programs were either scaled back or tabled.

There are still few call center telecommuting programs, but interest is steadily growing, and the success stories are mounting. The higher success rate in recent years can be attributed to a number of factors:

- Better planning before launch

- Disciplined pilot studies

- Lower costs (e.g., for network services)

- Improved technologies (e.g., DSL services)

- Well-thought-out HR management plans

Note: Section 6 was developed with Vanguard Communications Corp., and is drawn from the seminar, *Understanding and Applying Today's Call Center Technologies* and related materials. Contents copyrighted to Vanguard Communications Corp. and/or ICMI, Inc., 2003

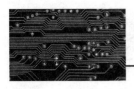

Technology Alternatives for ACDs

There are a variety of technical alternatives available that enable remote agents to be integrated with the call center:

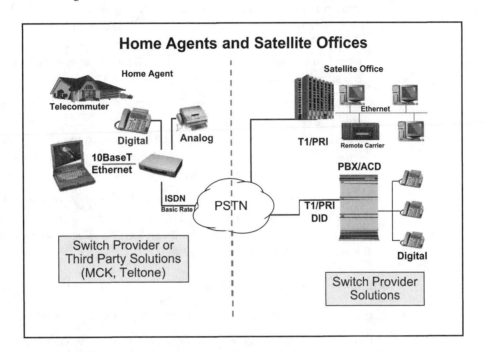

- **IVR-based alternatives:** With this alternative, the remote agent dials into the IVR which designates a port on the ACD. Agents use plain 2500 sets, or virtually any telephone with programmable speed-dial buttons. Not available with all IVR systems.

- **Single-user telecommuter modules:** These products are small book-sized units that have two ports, one that plugs into an ACD line card and the other that connects to a regular switched access telephone line. They enable a remote agent to dial-up and log into the ACD. Agents use 2500-compatible telephones and control status through dial-access codes.

- **ACD extenders:** These extenders enable remote agents to dial-up and log into the ACD over standard analog lines, using regular propriety ACD sets. The host unit (the ACD end) has two ports, one to the ACD and one to the switched line; at the remote unit (the agent end), one port is for the switched line, the other for the digital telephone. Versions are available for regular dial-up lines and for ISDN basic rate interface (BRI) lines.

- **PC-based applications:** These applications deliver all of the capabilities of the ACD to the remote site. Connections to the call center are via a PC

Note: Section 6 was developed with Vanguard Communications Corp., and is drawn from the seminar, *Understanding and Applying Today's Call Center Technologies* and related materials. Contents copyrighted to Vanguard Communications Corp. and/or ICMI, Inc., 2003

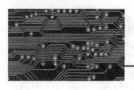

linked to two standard phone lines, an ISDN line or a wide area network.

- **Distributed call center**: Distributed call center software runs on a controller PC and enables users to "build" distributed call-routing systems based on public ISDN services. The switching is done at an ISDN central office, obviating the need for premises-based switching equipment. A virtual packet circuit between each agent's terminal and the controller is established for call control and reports. The agent telephone is a plain 2500 set connected to a PC with a special ISDN card.

- **Central office ACD**: With central office (CO) based ACD, it is inherently feasible to have telecommuters, if they reside in the CO serving area. However, this is rarely the case; as a result, a continuing effort is to link separate COs (signaling system 7, a CO networking technology) to provide virtual ACD service over a large area.

- **Satellite office**: Several ACD vendors enable you to set up a satellite office with full ACD functionality via a T-span connection to the primary ACD and the appropriate proprietary hardware. Call-control management and alarms are handled by the primary ACD.

Technology Alternatives for Data

There are a number of alternatives for providing data to telecommuters:

- **Dial-up line with modem**: Advances in modems have boosted speeds to 56 kbps and higher. Security is addressed by a required log-on sequence. Additional measures can include computer callback to a preauthorized number, encryption and closed user groups. Modems may not be fast enough for some graphical-oriented applications.

- **Leased line**: Dedicated leased lines make sense for satellite offices, but are usually impractical for single users because of the high monthly costs.

- **ISDN BRI lines**: One BRI line can provide both voice and high-speed data. ISDN has been costly and unavailable in some areas, but this is changing. The growth of online services and the Internet has become a key driving force in ISDN proliferation.

- **DSL technologies**: Both competitive local exchange carriers (CLECs) and the regional Bell operating companies (RBOCs) are offering high-speed data network services over standard telephone lines, based on digital subscriber line (DSL) technology. DSL, while not universal, is becoming widely available and can support high-speed applications.

Note: Section 6 was developed with Vanguard Communications Corp., and is drawn from the seminar, *Understanding and Applying Today's Call Center Technologies* and related materials. Contents copyrighted to Vanguard Communications Corp. and/or ICMI, Inc., 2003

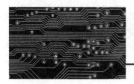

- **Cable modems:** Though rare in call center telecommuting applications, cable modems can conceivably offer the speed and availability many need. Given the shared architecture of cable, security should be assessed carefully.

(Telecommuting is also discussed in ICMI's *Call Center People Management Handbook and Study Guide.*)

Note: Section 6 was developed with Vanguard Communications Corp., and is drawn from the seminar, *Understanding and Applying Today's Call Center Technologies* and related materials. Contents copyrighted to Vanguard Communications Corp. and/or ICMI, Inc., 2003

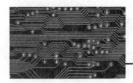

12. CTI Capabilities

Ready? | 1 | 2 | 3 |

Key Points

- Computer telephony integration (CTI) enables the voice and data worlds to share information in a way that allows for enhanced caller treatment.

- Common CTI capabilities include:
  - Coordinating voice and data
  - Intelligent routing
  - Integrated reporting
  - Desktop softphone
  - Outbound dialing

- Business benefits of CTI can include lower operating costs, improved profitability, improved customer service and higher agent satisfaction.

Explanation

Computer telephony integration (CTI) enables integration of previously disparate systems to enhance the customer experience and improve operational efficiencies. CTI integrates the functions of telephone networks, voice switching, data switching, computer applications, databases, voice processing and alternative media. Through this integration, CTI enables the ability to exchange commands and messages between systems. This results in the ability to monitor and control calls, events, applications, information and endpoints.

CTI Functionality

CTI can add or enhance functionality in a number of areas:

- **Coordinating Voice and Data**

  - Screen pops, in which information about the caller, associated database files and the call itself are simultaneously delivered to the agent's desktop.

Note: Section 6 was developed with Vanguard Communications Corp., and is drawn from the seminar, *Understanding and Applying Today's Call Center Technologies* and related materials. Contents copyrighted to Vanguard Communications Corp. and/or ICMI, Inc., 2003

- Intelligent transfers that enable the caller to be transferred along with associated data to another agent or queue group.

- IVR coordination that allows for the customer's voice response transactions and inquiries to be transferred to the agent along with the caller.

- **Intelligent Routing**

  - Conditional routing, which routes calls based on specific criteria such as customer preferences or profiles.

  - Skills-based routing, which routes calls to agents based on information beyond just the ACD (e.g., caller profiles in database systems).

  - Multisite routing, which routes calls between multiple call centers based on predefined criteria available from a variety of systems.

  - Data-directed routing, which routes calls based on information in databases external to the routing system. It is used for applications such as customer segmentation and prioritization.

- **Integrated Reporting**

  - Cradle-to-grave, which captures the entire caller experience from their initial call to the IVR until they end the call with the last agent.

  - Call and transaction data, which capture and report customer information along with the computer transactions processed during the interaction.

- **Desktop Softphone**

  - Telephony features, such as login/logout, workstate changes, hold, transfer, conference and others that can be accessed from a window on the agent's screen.

  - Statistics on agent, queue and group performance that can be made available in a window on the agent's monitor.

- **Outbound Dialing**

  - Preview dialing, in which information about the person being called is presented to the agent prior to dialing.

  - Predictive dialing, in which calls made by the system are routed to agents along with customer information.

  - Progressive dialing, in which calls are dialed when an agent is available.

  - Call blending, which is the capability to allocate resources between the inbound and outbound modes.

Note: Section 6 was developed with Vanguard Communications Corp., and is drawn from the seminar, *Understanding and Applying Today's Call Center Technologies* and related materials. Contents copyrighted to Vanguard Communications Corp. and/or ICMI, Inc., 2003

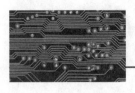

CTI has such far-reaching potential that it's important to note the above are simply examples. The functionality of other systems can be enhanced by CTI implementation. (See discussions on ACDs, networks, IVRs, dialers, desktops and technology infrastructure, this section.)

Business Benefits

There are many business benefits that come with implementing CTI, such as:

- **Reducing costs or keeping costs under control**: Reducing inefficiencies that cost the organization both network and agent time and often affect headcount and overhead.

- **Improving service**: Less time on hold and in queue, faster call handling, fewer transfers, getting to the right person with the right information, not repeating information already provided, and handling multiple transactions on a single call.

- **Increasing revenue**: Provides agents with more time to receive or make revenue-producing calls.

- **New services**: Enables specialized or customized services to meet particular customer needs.

- **Increasing customer retention**: Allows for more personalized and proactive services often leading to increased retention.

- **New customers**: Provides new or additional proactive contacts that can help find new customers.

Customers generally enjoy enhanced service when CTI is implemented. They will not have to repeat information as often, and will be more likely to get to the right person on the first attempt. Through enhanced call-routing options, customers should begin to experience shorter hold times and more personalized service.

Cross-Functional Team

Because CTI "touches" so many parts of an organization, a cross-functional project plan and team play critical roles in a successful implementation. (See Managing New Technology Implementations, this section.) The team needs to have a clear understanding of the company's willingness to adopt the new work processes that CTI allows. There must also be a clear understanding of the current systems' capabilities and what upgrades will be required to implement CTI. And there are key trade-offs in flexibility, reliability, manageability and capability of switch-based vs. computer-based applications.

Note: Section 6 was developed with Vanguard Communications Corp., and is drawn from the seminar, *Understanding and Applying Today's Call Center Technologies* and related materials. Contents copyrighted to Vanguard Communications Corp. and/or ICMI, Inc., 2003

CTI Architecture

CTI architecture can take many forms and is typically dependent on the existing applications used in the center. Two of the most common are client-server (with switch to CTI server connectivity) and a stand-alone communications server.

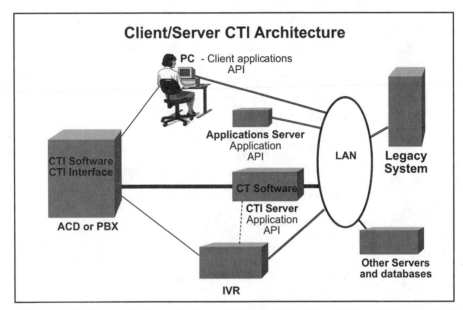

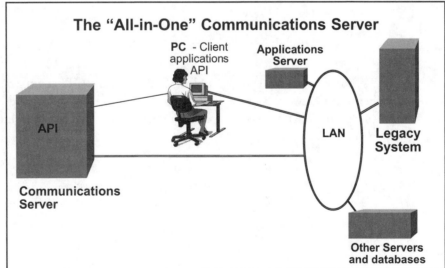

The flow of information in a CTI system involves many sources, which typically communicate as follows:

Note: Section 6 was developed with Vanguard Communications Corp., and is drawn from the seminar, *Understanding and Applying Today's Call Center Technologies* and related materials. Contents copyrighted to Vanguard Communications Corp. and/or ICMI, Inc., 2003

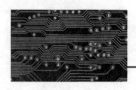

- Entities are designated (dynamically or statically) for monitoring and control.

- The computer and telephone systems send messages back and forth to inform, request action and control calls.

- The CTI server translates messages and converts protocols and interfaces between dissimilar systems.

- The client and server elements of an API (applications programming interface) share information.

- At the desktop, the CTI client and API interact with other desktop applications via standard interfaces.

- The application(s) do the "hard" work:

  - Monitoring

  - Coordinating and accessing information

  - Performing logic or other transactions

  - Initiating actions

  - Delivering information

- Applications may reside on:

  - The desktop

  - The CTI server

  - The applications server

As shown in the following graphic, information in a CTI environment flows between the switch and the CTI server, among the CTI server and other servers (including IVR), between the client and the server, and at the desktop through client-to-client exchanges.

Note: Section 6 was developed with Vanguard Communications Corp., and is drawn from the seminar, *Understanding and Applying Today's Call Center Technologies* and related materials. Contents copyrighted to Vanguard Communications Corp. and/or ICMI, Inc., 2003

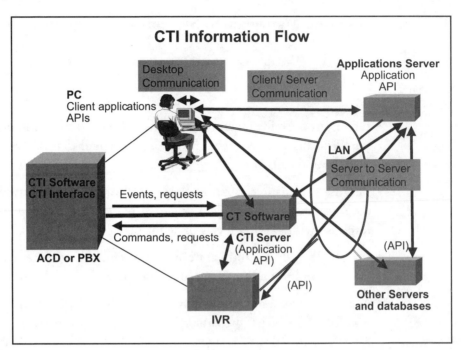

CTI Information Flow

CTI Proliferation

Although fewer than one out of five call centers are currently CTI-enabled, new applications are being developed to tie in other technologies, such as multimedia and CRM. These new applications include additional integration features that allow agents to view and share the customer's Web experience. In fact, Web-enabled call centers are driving much of today's CTI development. CTI is also playing a major role in the current CRM explosion and vendors are enhancing their data warehousing, mining and reporting capabilities. (See CRM Capabilities, this section.)

Section 6

Note: Section 6 was developed with Vanguard Communications Corp., and is drawn from the seminar, *Understanding and Applying Today's Call Center Technologies* and related materials. Contents copyrighted to Vanguard Communications Corp. and/or ICMI, Inc., 2003

13. Email Response Management Systems

Ready? | 1 | 2 | 3 |

Key Points

- Email response management systems (ERMS) perform many of the same routing and reporting functions for email that ACDs perform for inbound calls.

- Because the entire context of the communication is included in the message, an ERMS can help process the message and craft the response with varying levels of agent input.

- An ERMS adds a significant amount of control over the management of email and the resources used to handle it.

- As email increases in popularity as a communication channel, the benefits of an ERMS become more and more compelling

Explanation

Email response management systems (ERMS) control the flow and tracking of email into an organization in much the same way that an ACD controls the flow and tracking of inbound calls. An ERMS can perform the following routing and reporting functions:

- Conditional routing based on skills, customer priority, etc.

- Priority queuing

- Response time tracking

- Management reporting

However, an ERMS can go much further than an ACD in that it can "read" the subject and/or text of the message and then perform further steps based on business rules. The types of functionality provided by this artificial intelligence include:

- **Advanced auto acknowledgment:** An automatic response is sent to the sender indicating that the email has been received, along with the timeframe in which to expect a response.

Note: Section 6 was developed with Vanguard Communications Corp., and is drawn from the seminar, *Understanding and Applying Today's Call Center Technologies* and related materials. Contents copyrighted to Vanguard Communications Corp. and/or ICMI, Inc., 2003

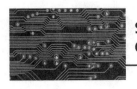

- **Recommended response:** Incoming email messages are interpreted by the system to determine content and an agent is provided with a recommended response.

- **Automated response:** Inbound email messages are interpreted by the system to determine content and an automatic response is sent to the customer. (Note: Accuracy rates are often well below 50 percent.)

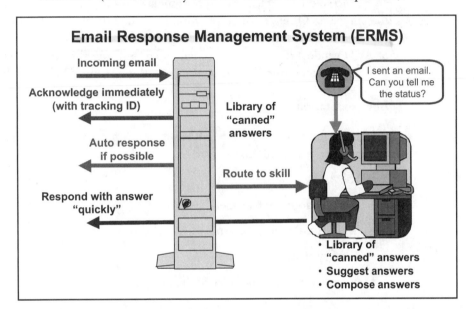

Further, ERMS vendors are continually upgrading their products. Some of the more advanced features include:

- Multiple language support

- Text-chat capabilities (using the same knowledge base for responses)

- ERMS capabilities delivered via an application service provider (ASP)

Primary Benefits

The ERMS offers a call center three main benefits:

- Control over email (routing and content)

- Reduction in the staff required to handle it

- Tracking of response times

The relative value of these benefits is typically dependent on the volume of email received in the center and the emphasis placed on quality and service to the customer.

Note: Section 6 was developed with Vanguard Communications Corp., and is drawn from the seminar, *Understanding and Applying Today's Call Center Technologies* and related materials. Contents copyrighted to Vanguard Communications Corp. and/or ICMI, Inc., 2003

Section 6

For example, where email volume is large, the potential reduction in staff size is often the driver of the ROI calculation and the main benefit of the system. Where quality is of primary importance and errors can cause significant expenses, the ability of an ERMS to encourage/provide consistent and accurate responses is often cited as the key benefit. In organizations in which quick response is crucial and the potential value of each contact is high, the ability of an ERMS to queue, track and report on email is the compelling force behind the purchase. Often, in these environments, the call center will look to integrate the ERMS with a multimedia queue capability (supplied by an ERMS or ACD vendor) to exercise management control over the broad spectrum of communication channels. (See Multimedia Routing and Queuing, this section.)

Implementation

To achieve full functionality, an ERMS must integrate with a number of different systems, including:

- The ACD
- The workforce management system
- SMTP/POP3 email servers
- CRM systems
- Systems with customer contact history

The risk associated with the integration and implementation of these systems is often dependent on how aggressively some of the features are used. For instance, companies that pursue high percentages of end-to-end automation on free-form text email messages (rather than Web form-generated emails) run the risk of inaccurate and incomplete responses if the system is not programmed correctly.

ERMS have proven to be very effective when combined with Web forms. Using this combination, a company can ensure that a form is filled out correctly via the Web with all of the information required by the ERMS or any back-end fulfillment system. The message is then routed to the ERMS, where a standard response is sent out. If applicable, the message will then also be delivered to any other system for completion of the transaction without agent intervention.

The continued acceptance of email as a preferred form of communication makes an ERMS a valuable tool in a call center. As the percentage of contacts by email increases, the use of these systems is expected to rise.

Note: Section 6 was developed with Vanguard Communications Corp., and is drawn from the seminar, *Understanding and Applying Today's Call Center Technologies* and related materials. Contents copyrighted to Vanguard Communications Corp. and/or ICMI, Inc., 2003

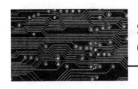

14. Web Communication Channels

Ready? | 1 | 2 | 3 |

Key Points

- The Web offers enormous self-service opportunities, but they rarely succeed without the availability of assisted services.

- There is a large number of channel options associated with the Web, including:
  - Email
  - Text-chat
  - Web callback
  - Web call through
  - Web collaboration
  - Call center initiated assistance

- All channels have at least one drawback, and it is important to understand the drawbacks when choosing and deploying channels.

- Technologies that help manage the complexity created by the proliferation of channels are becoming available.

Explanation

The presence of the Web has opened new ways for organizations to communicate with customers, suppliers, vendors and other stakeholders. Many organizations have recognized that if Web content is accurate, stored appropriately and simple to access, customers can use the Web as a self-service tool. To capitalize on this, many Web sites now offer an enhanced FAQ section that is powered by a natural language input tool. However, while these systems have some success with simple requests, they do not eliminate the need for assisted service – and in many ways, they can increase demand for agent support.

Contact Alternatives

In order to respond to the need for personalized assistance through the Web, new tools have emerged to make the connection easier and more convenient. The various communication channels and possibilities associated with the Web include:

Note: Section 6 was developed with Vanguard Communications Corp., and is drawn from the seminar, *Understanding and Applying Today's Call Center Technologies* and related materials. Contents copyrighted to Vanguard Communications Corp. and/or ICMI, Inc., 2003

Section 6

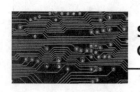

- **Email:** Most Web sites post an email address or they provide Web forms that are mapped directly to the organization's email address.

- **Text-chat:** This allows customers to have a private, real-time, text-based dialogue with a company representative over their Internet connection, without the need for a separate phone line.

- **Web callback:** By clicking on a button, the customer lets the company know that he/she wants to be called back either immediately or at a designated time.

- **Web call through:** Using voice over Internet (VoIP) technology, the customer clicks on a button that establishes a voice line directly to the call center.

- **Web collaboration:** Used in conjunction with any of the above channels (or with a traditional voice call), Web collaboration is a broad term referring to the ability for an agent and customer to share content by pushing/pulling Web pages, and/or whiteboarding and page markup.

- **Call center initiated assistance:** This is a text-chat session initiated by the agent, rather than the customer.

New Challenges

Considering the many choices, it can be difficult for an organization to determine exactly what to provide, and from which vendor to get it. Many Web integration failures are caused by the lack of a clear customer access strategy. (See Establishing a Customer Access Strategy, Section 3.) Others are caused by a lack of understanding of the challenges, which are outlined as follows:

- **Email:** The challenges of handling email are typically problems with routing or content management. Many call centers begin to handle email before obtaining an email response management system. If email volumes grow quickly, the call center may not have the tools to meet customer response expectations. Another routing challenge is how to handle emails with multiple questions that require responses by different people. Content challenges include frequent misunderstandings between customer and agent and legal or regulatory concerns about the permanence of email records. In some cases, email responses that are not "cut and paste" must be reviewed by a supervisor or possibly the legal department. (See Email Response Management Systems, this section.)

Note: Section 6 was developed with Vanguard Communications Corp., and is drawn from the seminar, *Understanding and Applying Today's Call Center Technologies* and related materials. Contents copyrighted to Vanguard Communications Corp. and/or ICMI, Inc., 2003

- **Text-chat:** This channel requires staffing to meet service level objectives. (See Calculating Base Staff for Service Level Contacts, Section 5.) However, agents can sometimes handle more than one chat session simultaneously, so staffing must consider simultaneous sessions as well as average handling time. Text-chat sessions may be slow which can frustrate both the agent and the customer. Also, text-chat sessions tend to drive up workload. Further, as with email, some companies are concerned about the permanence of text-chat sessions.

- **Web callback:** Most customers are looking for an immediate callback, which requires proper service level staffing. Those who don't want or receive immediate service may be hard to reach. Also, this requires a separate phone line on the customer's side apart from the phone line used for the Internet connection. (See Calculating Base Staff for Service Level Contacts, Section 5.)

- **Web call through:** The quality of VoIP calls in many cases does not yet meet customer expectations. Also, the customer must have a microphone and sound card in his/her PC, yet many do not. Another consideration is the time it takes to download the VoIP application. Delays can cause customers to abandon their attempt to reach the center. (See Voice over IP, this section.)

- **Web collaboration:** The complexity of required technology for this channel may be a roadblock to some customers. Also, transaction handling times are typically high, which can create staffing problems for the call center.

- **Call center initiated assistance:** One of the strengths of the Web is the perception of freedom it allows. Any attempts to "reach out" to users without their permission may well create ill will among customers and create privacy concerns.

Despite these drawbacks, these channels continue to increase in popularity. Their presence provides customers with options, those options increase interaction, and the increased interaction often improves customer satisfaction and revenue. The growth of Web-oriented channels, however, is inconsistent. Some channels, such as email, are proving to be much more popular than others, such as call center initiated assistance.

Related Technologies

In order to optimize the operation of the call center with multiple channels, related technologies are emerging:

- **Multimedia queue:** All channels are fed into the same queue and are subject to processing based on business rules. This allows "one view" of

Note: Section 6 was developed with Vanguard Communications Corp., and is drawn from the seminar, *Understanding and Applying Today's Call Center Technologies* and related materials. Contents copyrighted to Vanguard Communications Corp. and/or ICMI, Inc., 2003

Section 6

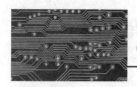

incoming transactions, and provides automation to make moment-to-moment decisions on prioritization. (See Multimedia Routing and Queuing, this section.)

- **Unified reporting:** Data from different channels and systems are included on one reporting tool. This supports better analysis and decision-making in the organization. (See CTI Capabilities, this section.)

- **Customer contact history databases:** Records of all transactions available across the organization. (See CRM Capabilities, this section.)

Note: Section 6 was developed with Vanguard Communications Corp., and is drawn from the seminar, *Understanding and Applying Today's Call Center Technologies* and related materials. Contents copyrighted to Vanguard Communications Corp. and/or ICMI, Inc., 2003

15. Voice over IP

Key Points

- Internet Protocol (IP) is emerging as a technology for voice communications, altering switching architectures and voice transport.

- The use of IP for voice communications and data communications – "convergence" – will deliver economic and other benefits for call centers in the long run.

- The most significant application of IP in the call center will be its role in bringing the Web into the call center most fully for total collaborative voice and data communications.

Explanation

Call center technology architectures are in transition, driven by the convergence of voice and data. The Internet Protocol (IP) is historically viewed as a data protocol, which defines how data systems and networks can communicate openly. Now, that protocol is being used for voice communications as well. And while IP voice communications is just now emerging in the call center environment, it is something to which anyone working with call center technologies must be attuned.

The spectrum below shows the evolution of application and network infrastructure into this converged world. The transition of voice switching from circuit to packet switched, and the transition of voice applications from switch-resident to server-resident are both occurring.

Call centers will not generally be early adopters of the Voice over IP (VoIP) technology, as the risks are too high. (See Creating an Enabling Technology Strategy, this section.) But once the technology is proven, there will be compelling reasons to adopt IP into the call center infrastructure:

- **Freedom from proprietary architectures:** Shift to open architectures will enable vendor competition and allow the call center to purchase various elements from the vendor of choice, driving down costs and spurring technology innovation.

- **Reduced IT/telecom costs:** A common network infrastructure for the wide area or local area network will be easier to manage and maintain.

Note: Section 6 was developed with Vanguard Communications Corp., and is drawn from the seminar, *Understanding and Applying Today's Call Center Technologies* and related materials. Contents copyrighted to Vanguard Communications Corp. and/or ICMI, Inc., 2003

Section 6

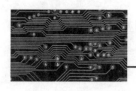

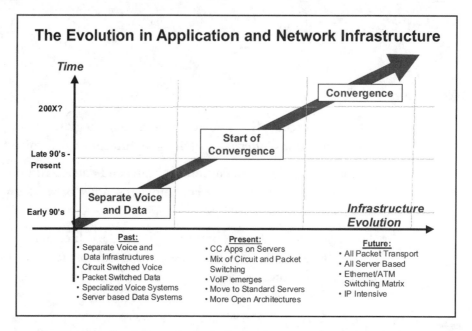

- **Application flexibility**: A platform that leverages the Web and ubiquitous IP infrastructure for communication of information independent of location, enabling customers and agents to connect from any location.

The following two figures show the transition from today's separate voice and data worlds to a fully converged IP infrastructure. Most companies will go through phases to reach a converged environment. First, they will converge the wide area network for IP transport of voice and data, and then transition the on-premise infrastructure to switch voice over IP and move the voice applications to a server attached to an IP switch.

As call centers begin to Web-enable contacts and implement multimedia routing and queuing, the influence of IP becomes greater. The ability for an agent to collaborate with a customer on the organization's Web site is essential to long-term success in merging the various channels of customer contact. Agents communicating via VoIP, co-browsing, and pushing and pulling Web pages is the vision of the future. This vision will become reality when the current quality of service issues for VoIP are thoroughly addressed, and VoIP communication becomes prevalent and accepted as a standard means of communication. (See Web Communication Channels and Multimedia Routing and Queuing, this section.)

Note: Section 6 was developed with Vanguard Communications Corp., and is drawn from the seminar, *Understanding and Applying Today's Call Center Technologies* and related materials. Contents copyrighted to Vanguard Communications Corp. and/or ICMI, Inc., 2003

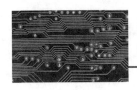

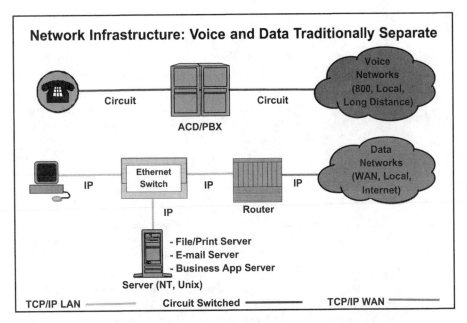

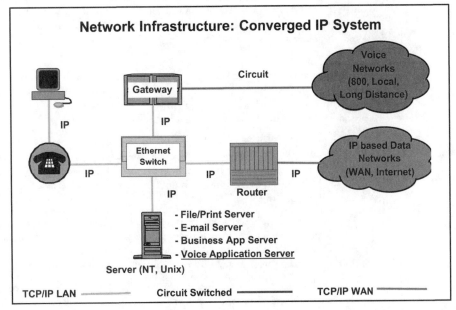

Note: Section 6 was developed with Vanguard Communications Corp., and is drawn from the seminar, *Understanding and Applying Today's Call Center Technologies* and related materials. Contents copyrighted to Vanguard Communications Corp. and/or ICMI, Inc., 2003

The Implementation Options

So how should companies go about implementing VoIP in their call centers? That depends on what stage of development their call centers are currently in.

For example, organizations that are planning their first call center may want to seriously consider creating a full-fledged IP-based environment. Because these companies have yet to invest in any traditional ACD/PBX systems, they are prime candidates for going all VoIP, all the time.

"Clearly [those] establishing a new contact center with no installed legacy system will find it easiest to justify direct implementation of an IP-enabled, unified multichannel contact center," writes the Robert Frances Group (RFG) in a recent white paper titled, "The IP Contact Center."

But most companies aren't new to the call center scene, and thus don't have the luxury of moving directly to an all-IP-based environment. Fortunately for them, tapping the power of VoIP technology needn't be an all-or-nothing proposition. Several options exist for call centers that need to – or want to – wade into IP waters:

• **An Internet telephony gateway.** Call centers with traditional ACDs, IVRs or other call center applications already installed can add an Internet telephony gateway as a front end to the call center switch, explains RFG. "This gateway can then act as a bridge between the PSTN and the Internet. This option will add IP functionality and allow the protection of capital investments in legacy equipment." RFG adds that this is not the ideal solution, but can serve as an interim step to ease the transition to a unified IP-based environment.

• **The "overlay" approach.** In this innovative approach – intended for companies that have a multisite call center environment in place – an IP-based solution is co-located with one of the existing switches and acts as an independent contact center platform while providing overflow support for all other call centers in the network.

According to RFG, "This is a feasible approach for corporations looking to gracefully transition to an IPCC. …System growth can be systematically 'capped' on the legacy switch and transitioned to the new-generation platform(s). Eventually, older switches are retired and [IP-based] products are added until the entire network is based on IP-enabled contact center platforms."

• **The NSP option.** Companies that aren't ready to make any major investments in VoIP may want to consider contracting a network service provider (NSP). NSPs are eager to please call centers and already have the necessary equipment and infrastructure to help them realize the advantages that an IP-based call center solution can offer.

"The rapid expansion of the call center marketplace has attracted the interest of many NSPs including competitive local exchange carriers (CLECS), cable companies, Internet service providers (ISPs) and even some wireless network providers," RFG explains. "All are looking for ways to better leverage their networks and offer enhanced services to the call center marketplace."

Excerpt from "The Emergence of the IP Contact Center" by Greg Levin, *Call Center Management Review*, March 2002.

Note: Section 6 was developed with Vanguard Communications Corp., and is drawn from the seminar, *Understanding and Applying Today's Call Center Technologies* and related materials. Contents copyrighted to Vanguard Communications Corp. and/or ICMI, Inc., 2003

16. Multimedia Routing and Queuing

Ready? | 1 | 2 | 3 |

Key Points

- Multimedia routing and queuing handles contacts across media, including voice, text-based and Web transactions, based on business rules that define how any transaction, inquiry or problem is processed. The key differentiator is not the media, but the customer and his/her need.

- Business rules should be established in regard to service level and/or response time for each alternative media.

- Although multimedia queuing is not common today, it will become so as the multichannel call center continues to develop.

Explanation

Customers are demanding the ability to contact organizations through the media of their choice, and call centers must have technology and processes to enable all types of contacts to be handled efficiently and effectively. Customers should have the same processes, information, steps, interfaces and "look and feel," regardless of the media they choose.

Different types of contacts require different handling. Some types may imply less urgency than others, e.g., a fax vs. a voice call. While contact priorities should be based upon what is known about the customer, decisions must also take into consideration the media used. Business rules define how any transaction, inquiry or problem is processed.

As an example, fax orders today usually take longer to get into the system and receive a response than phone orders. With multimedia queuing and processing, fax orders will be placed in a mixed-media queue along with phone calls, email, voice messages for callback, text-based chat sessions, Web calls, etc. The fax will be processed based on business rules, not on whether someone has time to physically retrieve the fax and enter an order.

Like ACDs that employ sophisticated call-routing capabilities using "if…then" logic and conditional routing, or data-directed routing for CTI, a multimedia queuing system identifies the customer's identity and purpose, and applies business rules to route the contact to the proper skilled resource with the

Note: Section 6 was developed with Vanguard Communications Corp., and is drawn from the seminar, *Understanding and Applying Today's Call Center Technologies* and related materials. Contents copyrighted to Vanguard Communications Corp. and/or ICMI, Inc., 2003

Section 6

proper treatment and prioritization. These contacts may be inbound or outbound, via the various media, depending on the customer's needs and profile.

A typical multimedia queue leverages a common routing engine, based on business rules, to route media to the proper queue. It also uses a common reporting mechanism to track media of all types.

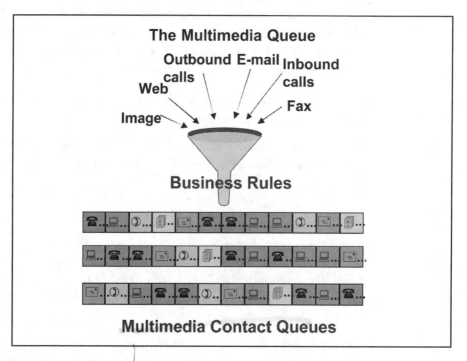

Multimedia queuing is more promise than reality today and it is not necessary to have a multimedia queue to successfully operate in a multichannel environment. However, a multimedia queue is likely to be the most efficient option as agents gain the skills to handle multiple contact types.

also kown as a universal queue

Note: Section 6 was developed with Vanguard Communications Corp., and is drawn from the seminar, *Understanding and Applying Today's Call Center Technologies* and related materials. Contents copyrighted to Vanguard Communications Corp. and/or ICMI, Inc., 2003

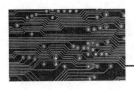

17. CRM Capabilities

Ready? 1 2 3

Key Points

- Customer relationship management (CRM) is a strategy, not a distinct technology. CRM uses advanced technology tools, databases and applications to enable differentiated service to each customer, via a variety of media. CRM uses information about customers to optimize their relationship with the company through personalized sales and service.

- CRM optimizes profitability through revenue growth and customer retention, rather than cost savings.

- Integration is the greatest challenge to an effective CRM solution, and is essential to achieving CRM goals.

- Another key challenge, requiring the collaboration of many people, is building the business rules, workflows, data required and the desktop interface.

- CRM is a central part of the drive today among companies to restructure business processes to tightly integrate service delivery channels and to incorporate new contact methods.

Explanation

Customer relationship management (CRM) has been variously described as everything from "treating different customers differently" to "a strategy for increasing revenue, improving operational efficiencies and winning market share through a better understanding of customers and their behaviors." Thoughtful executives are bound to ask, so what's changed? And at the fundamental level, the answer is, not much. However, today's realities include proliferating channels of contact with customers, distributed organizations, heightened customer expectations and competition that is just a click away. You can't wish excellent customer care into existence; you need the tools, processes, skill sets and organization-wide commitment to make it work.

CRM is a business project, not a technology project, and it requires involvement of people at all levels across the organization. CRM generally grows out of an organization's marketing strategy. Because CRM almost always

Note: Section 6 was developed with Vanguard Communications Corp., and is drawn from the seminar, *Understanding and Applying Today's Call Center Technologies* and related materials. Contents copyrighted to Vanguard Communications Corp. and/or ICMI, Inc., 2003

Section 6

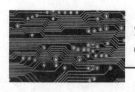

involves the reallocation of budgets, improving crossfunctional processes, restructuring the organization and updating job roles, it requires top-level management commitment. CRM concepts, methods, strategies, technology and customer expectations are changing fast, but the core mission is to build and manage customer relationships to improve customer satisfaction and, in turn, contribute to the organization's success.

The cycle below depicts the key steps in the application of CRM technology to a call center environment.

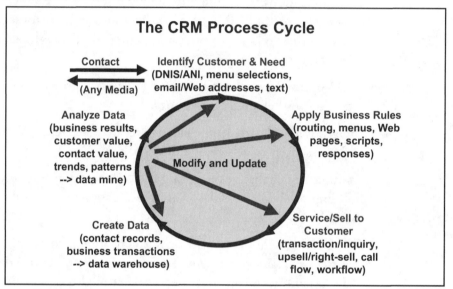

Technology Enablers

Automated sales force and customer service tools make up the backbone of CRM applications. Today, multivendor solutions are typical. Most organizations focus first on the customer-facing, customer-interaction components. Customer information systems, call center technologies, Web-based systems, desktop capabilities and integration tools are examples of the technologies involved. An overall integrated approach is mandatory, including integration with accounting packages and enterprise resource planning (ERP) systems.

Capability and Application Considerations

CRM technology solutions entail numerous capabilities and applications. Some of these elements may be part of a CRM package, others may be applications that you already have in place and want to integrate with the CRM solution, and some may be critical to your business so you'll want to select the best-of-breed components to integrate. Example capabilities and applications include:

Note: Section 6 was developed with Vanguard Communications Corp., and is drawn from the seminar, *Understanding and Applying Today's Call Center Technologies* and related materials. Contents copyrighted to Vanguard Communications Corp. and/or ICMI, Inc., 2003

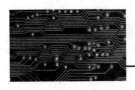

How desirable will it work? will it integrate how long will it take what is the cost

- **Contact management.** This key function is the heart and soul of CRM, allowing you to log contacts, access customer profile data and retrieve contact history. All contacts with a customer (i.e., marketing, sales, service, billing, credit, collections) via any media (phone, Web, email, mail, fax, face-to-face) are logged. This serves two purposes: it creates a single view of the customer and collects data for advanced analysis.

- **Workflow or business rules.** Another fundamental component of CRM is the ability to write business rules or workflows. Where should this contact be routed? What should occur at the desktop based on what we know about the customer? Are there scripts that should trigger? Should other events follow, such as email, calls or mailings? Should the contact be escalated or another group notified after it occurs? This is where CRM draws its power to transform the customer experience and the value derived from customer contacts.

- **Sales Force Automation (SFA).** SFA is one of the key feeder technologies for CRM. It is often thought of as a field sales function, but with contact centers playing a pivotal role in the sales process for many companies, SFA functions have become fundamental. SFA functions track leads or contacts, trigger follow-up contacts, enable win/loss analysis and other evaluations. They can also include scripts and other sales support functions.

- **Service functions.** Help desk tools are another feeder technology for CRM. Help desk functions are a part of service functions. Service functions can include account inquiry and status, billing, shipping and trouble-ticket initiation. These tools can also escalate, track and report on outstanding and closed problems.

- **Knowledge base.** Some CRM systems include an inherent knowledge base with basic functions for online documentation, searches or queries. Others tie into a robust knowledge base or knowledge management system with expert systems intelligence or case-based reasoning. The key elements are the database, search engine and tools for content management. This function is particularly applicable in service environments, but it may also be tied to complex sales environments which need to find the right product to meet the customer needs. A customer interaction can be guided using workflows, scripting and knowledge base interactions.

- **Fulfillment.** Fulfillment can be delivery of a product service, or collateral materials. Materials can be sent via many different channels (mail, email, fax).

- **Scripting.** Scripting is an on-screen agent guide to help manage customer interactions. Scripting can occur on inbound or outbound contacts, and on spoken or written communications. In a CRM environment, scripting is triggered using workflows and intelligently analyzing the customer and business situation. It can be tied to marketing, sales or service steps.

- **Telemarketing.** In a CRM contact center, telemarketing (or "e-marketing" using email) plays a key role. Telemarketing functions within CRM include lead management, campaign management, scripting and reporting.

Beyond these capabilities, when you look at CRM solutions, consider the interfaces and development tools. What will your workflow architects use to develop new business rules? What are your desktop options (i.e., browser, operating system)? What reporting and monitoring tools and capabilities are available? How about optional capabilities, like CTI integration or multimedia (e.g., email, Web integration)?

Excerpt from Call Center Technology Demystified: The No-Nonsense Guide to Bridging Customer Contact Technology, Operations and Strategy *by Lori Bocklund and Dave Bengtson, Call Center Press, 2002.*

Note: Section 6 was developed with Vanguard Communications Corp., and is drawn from the seminar, *Understanding and Applying Today's Call Center Technologies* and related materials. Contents copyrighted to Vanguard Communications Corp. and/or ICMI, Inc., 2003

Elements of CRM

Many elements can fall under the definition of CRM. Some are elements that may already exist and need to be folded in with the new CRM enabling technologies. Others may be new capabilities delivered by the chosen CRM solution.

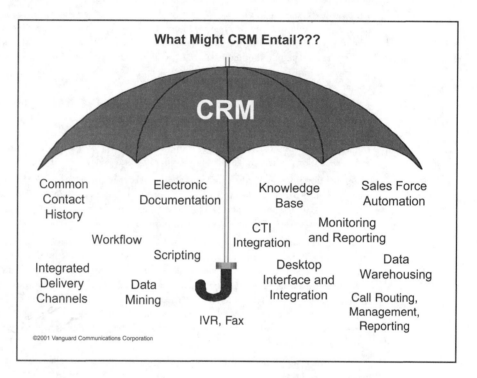

CRM Strategy

There are a number of essential components of a sound CRM strategy, including:

1. Segmenting customers sensibly.

2. Determining the value of different types of customers and how to increase that value.

3. Providing customers with a range of self-service and agent-assisted choices.

4. Integrating all channels of sales and service delivery.

5. Tracking, assessing and, as appropriate, acting on all customer contacts.

6. Providing real-time information directly to sales and service agents.

Note: Section 6 was developed with Vanguard Communications Corp., and is drawn from the seminar, *Understanding and Applying Today's Call Center Technologies* and related materials. Contents copyrighted to Vanguard Communications Corp. and/or ICMI, Inc., 2003

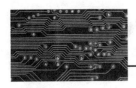

7. Restructuring processes to focus on customer requirements and expectations.

8. Training agents and programming systems to act on information as contacts (events) occur.

9. Establishing and adhering to a sound customer privacy policy.

10. Measuring and continuously improving program effectiveness.

Some of the benefits of a good CRM strategy include:

- Higher customer retention

- Shorter sales cycles

- More overall revenue

- Higher sales per customer

- More targeted marketing, either lowering those costs and/or increasing response rates

- Better retention of sales and customer service agents

- Lower infrastructure costs

- Reduced training times for agents

CRM Is Ongoing

CRM is never final. Workflows, business rules, screen designs, scripts, Web pages, menus and reports all constantly evolve. Data are constantly created and analyzed, leading to more changes. Capabilities and databases may roll out to other parts of the organization. Systems, processes and tools must enable rapid response to changing business needs.

A common misconception of CRM is that it primarily consists of a database or set of technology tools. Technology is an enabler, but CRM includes much more, e.g., processes, organizational structure, information/data and an understanding of what customers you want to serve and how you will address the needs of different types of customers. There's a lot more to it than technology.

Related Acronyms

- eCRM = Electronic customer relationship management

- CIM = Customer interaction management

- EIM = Enterprise interaction management

Note: Section 6 was developed with Vanguard Communications Corp., and is drawn from the seminar, *Understanding and Applying Today's Call Center Technologies* and related materials. Contents copyrighted to Vanguard Communications Corp. and/or ICMI, Inc., 2003

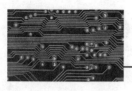

- ERM = Enterprise relationship management

- ERP = Enterprise resource planning

- CIS = Customer information systems

- CTI = Computer telephony integration

The Staffing Impact of CRM

The benefits of any particular customer relationship management (CRM) package are not as important as understanding how it works, why it works and how to make it work better. Service level, staffing and the quality of customer care can and will be affected by the implementation methodology and the degree to which the system is involved at the agent desktop.

Common business practices normally require an analysis of the cost/benefit of the CRM system prior to purchase. This analysis should not be limited to the dollar cost of the software and hardware but should include the impact it may have on the call center.

Labor, technology and toll costs are the three elements that make up the cost of running a call center. Labor is by far the largest expense. In a typical call center, technology, (including CRM) and toll costs make up less than 19 percent of the operating costs. Any changes that impact labor are going to have the most impact on the costs of operating the call center. The addition of a CRM system can and will impact the labor element.

Any CRM suite takes a certain amount of time to find a match, retrieve the desired data and then pass it through the network to the appropriate personnel. This can add time to the current service level. If the current service level for the call center is 80 percent of the calls answered in 30 seconds or less, and a process is introduced that adds X more seconds, the net result is 80 percent in 30 + X seconds. This may represent a significant change in how the call center is managed. To maintain the current service level, it may be necessary to increase staff or restate the service level objective. Given this impact, performance and speed of the system become critically important. In light of these factors, do not shy away from the high cost of any particular CRM package until you understand what it may buy on the labor side of the equation.

Excerpt from "Identify CRM Interfaces to Ensure Smooth Process and Service Level Alignment" by Todd Tanner and Brad Paul, *Call Center Management Review*, 2001.

(For more information on managing customer relationships, see ICMI's *Call Center Customer Relationship Management Handbook and Study Guide*.)

Note: Section 6 was developed with Vanguard Communications Corp., and is drawn from the seminar, *Understanding and Applying Today's Call Center Technologies* and related materials. Contents copyrighted to Vanguard Communications Corp. and/or ICMI, Inc., 2003

Incoming Calls Management Institute
Advancing the Call Center Profession Worldwide

18. Technology Infrastructure Components

Ready? | 1 | 2 | 3 |

Key Points

• In today's technology environment, systems must run on standard platforms with standard operating environments. They must readily integrate with other systems and be extensible and scalable.

• Organizations are increasingly measuring what happened for the lifetime of a contact, regardless of media used or how many contact points were made.

• "Warehousing" and "data mining" enable organizations to uncover correlations between disparate sets of data from the call center environment, and ultimately understand much more about customer trends and desires.

Explanation

The following diagram shows a high-level view of the technology infrastructure components found in today's progressive call center environments.

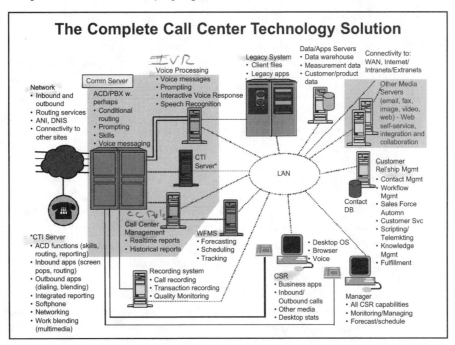

Note: Section 6 was developed with Vanguard Communications Corp., and is drawn from the seminar, *Understanding and Applying Today's Call Center Technologies* and related materials. Contents copyrighted to Vanguard Communications Corp. and/or ICMI, Inc., 2003

In today's technology environment, systems must run on standard platforms with standard operating environments. While it is not always possible to completely replace older, closed legacy systems, functionality can be migrated from these systems to newer client-server systems. The legacy systems become database servers or back-end processors, with desktop computers running front-end applications to access these databases. Data migration and middleware are the two critical components to successfully integrating new technologies with legacy systems.

Some of the characteristics of these newer, open systems are:

- Microsoft Windows on Intel-based computing architectures, usually NT on the server side. (While Windows is becoming the predominant operating system for client-server environments, there are still a substantial number of environments using varieties of UNIX, running on platforms from Sun, Hewlett-Packard or IBM. These platforms and operating systems adhere to standards of protocol and communications compatible with Windows environments, and are therefore mostly compatible in complex, integrated environments.)

- TCP/IP as a network transport protocol.

- Object-oriented and transportable development environments, e.g., C++, Java. (By transportable, we mean that the program code can be recompiled to run on a variety of different platforms.)

- Desktop application-to-application communications protocols (DDE, OLE, ActiveX).

- Open database connectivity (ODBC) databases (Oracle, SQL, Sybase, etc.).

- Standard computer-telephony protocols (TSAPI, TAPI, CT Connect, and S.100).

- Browser-based user interfaces (Netscape Navigator or Microsoft Internet Explorer).

Leveraging Information into Business Success

Companies have begun to rethink the gathering and use of data, and are increasingly measuring what happens for the lifetime of a contact, regardless of media used or how many contact points were made. They are also putting more emphasis on measuring the value vs. the cost of a contact or customer.

Many organizations are turning to increasingly sophisticated tools to gather data into "warehouses" and using these repositories for performing analytical queries and trend analysis. Several types of tools can be used to access and

Note: Section 6 was developed with Vanguard Communications Corp., and is drawn from the seminar, *Understanding and Applying Today's Call Center Technologies* and related materials. Contents copyrighted to Vanguard Communications Corp. and/or ICMI, Inc., 2003

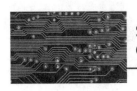

report on the information in the data warehouse, from "shrink-wrapped" reporting packages, to query tools like SQL, to OLAP (online analytical processing) tools for data mining.

Data mining is the growing use of analytical tools to uncover correlation between disparate sets of data. With these tools, an analyst can test hypotheses about data (how many customers who purchased antilock brakes as an option also upgraded their warranty package, for example), and the mining tool can also derive correlation between hypotheses not yet determined. A mining tool may find that, of customers who purchased antilock brakes and an extended warranty, 85 percent were between the ages of 32 and 45 with an average of 2.4 children. This derived information can be fed into scripts, workflows and marketing campaigns to strengthen relationships and enhance customer value. The ultimate objective is to understand and serve customers better.

Section 6

Note: Section 6 was developed with Vanguard Communications Corp., and is drawn from the seminar, *Understanding and Applying Today's Call Center Technologies* and related materials. Contents copyrighted to Vanguard Communications Corp. and/or ICMI, Inc., 2003

19. Creating an Enabling Technology Strategy [Strategic]

Ready? | 1 | 2 | 3 |

Key Points

- The development of an enabling technology strategy begins with a strong, well-informed and educated crossfunctional project team.

- Technology strategies will differ from one organization to the next, but consistent processes should be applied that address a core group of requirements.

- Selling the technology strategy to the rest of the organization requires changing the perspective of the center beyond the traditional viewpoint of a "cost center."

- The impact of a new technology strategy cuts into most, if not all, of the major processes within any call center, so an effective implementation plan must identify and address these impacts.

Explanation

Building an enabling technology strategy – one that supports the overarching customer access strategy – is a cornerstone of a well-run call center. As channels multiply and customer expectations grow, an effective technology strategy becomes more and more vital to an organization. (See Establishing a Customer Access Strategy, Section 3.)

Strategies will differ from one organization to the next, but many processes, steps and critical success factors remain the same. The following table outlines the elements of an effective technology strategy.

Note: Section 6 was developed with Vanguard Communications Corp., and is drawn from the seminar, *Understanding and Applying Today's Call Center Technologies* and related materials. Contents copyrighted to Vanguard Communications Corp. and/or ICMI, Inc., 2003

Steps	Critical Success Factors
Phase 1: Planning the Strategy	
• Form a project team • Develop a project plan • Develop assumptions • Learn	• Representation from key areas including frontline employees • Strong, empowered project manager • "Champion" – credible senior-level manager • Solid support from senior management
Phase 2: Vision and Design for the Strategy	
• Brainstorm • Develop design principles • Create the vision and strategy	• Availability of resources to work with the team and provide information • Open mind to hearing what can be done and thinking differently about the call center • A true commitment to act on the recommendations • Consensus on business direction and participation by all stakeholders
Phase 3: Selling the Strategy	
• Develop the implementation plan • Build the business case • Sell the strategy	• Good workflow analysis of existing operations • Business unit buy-in on the benefits • Good baseline cost figures

Building an effective strategy that exceeds customer expectations while staying within the organization's financial boundaries requires a multidepartmental approach. Successful strategies begin with crossfunctional teams that are large enough to represent all the impacted departments, but are still small enough to make decisions. The group should be educated in the different contact channels that are available and have at least a conceptual knowledge of the technology required.

Building a Technology Strategy

Phase 1: Planning

The first phase in building a call center technology strategy is, in the simplest terms, to get your act together. This is the phase that prepares your team for the real work to follow. It involves the following steps:

• Form the project team. Be sure to include a representative cross-section – vertically and horizontally – of the company and those who influence or are influenced by call center technologies. You'll need a senior-level sponsor or project champion. The team should be

---

(continued, next page)

Note: Section 6 was developed with Vanguard Communications Corp., and is drawn from the seminar, *Understanding and Applying Today's Call Center Technologies* and related materials. Contents copyrighted to Vanguard Communications Corp. and/or ICMI, Inc., 2003

Section 6

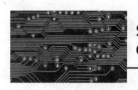

led by an experienced project manager, and should include representatives from the business side (including agents) and technology side (IT and telecom). Also, think about including representatives from marketing, HR or other groups. Consider whether vendor partners or third parties, such as consultants, will strengthen your team.

• Develop a project plan. The project plan should define the business drivers, scope, duration and depth of the planning effort (and its cost, if necessary), as well as key objectives. It should also clearly identify the outcome you are seeking. For example, a target outcome could be: "Approval by senior management of a contact center technology strategy for three years. The strategy will be supported by a solid business case with two-year positive return on investment, and increased customer satisfaction."

• Develop assumptions. It is important to develop assumptions early in the project. This step ensures that everyone is on the same page from the start. Without a commonly understood set of assumptions, you run the risk of each team member working from a different context. Define what is changing and what isn't changing. Will certain technologies be considered to be the building blocks, or is everything fair game? Define the relative weight of design criteria, such as cost vs. increases to customer satisfaction or the ability to grow the customer base. Also, define the elements of the current operation that are considered cherished strengths and, therefore, shouldn't be negatively affected by the strategy.

• Learn. Take time to research technology — there are many ways to do this. Today, online research and articles can provide you with the basic information you need, but you also may need to go on the road. Try to find out what others are doing through benchmarking or site visits. Ideally, talk to customers and, certainly, talk to agents in focus groups. This learning process will provide your team with knowledge of what's needed and what's possible.

Phase 2: Vision and Design

In Phase 2, it's time to apply what you've learned and draw on the brainpower of the team. This part – which is the most fun! – includes the following steps:

• Brainstorm. Get the creative process going with team exercises that will help you to develop a vision for the future – for your customers, agents, managers and supervisors, and the organization. Structure brainstorming sessions so that the group's thinking is not hampered by the past, by projects or processes that have been tried before, or by biases. This is the time to let loose.

• Develop design principles. After conducting brainstorming sessions, analyze the thoughts that have been generated and net out what the team was really thinking. Design principles will emerge. Some examples might be: "We want to give our customers the choice and control they desire, and will do so by offering access via the media of their choice, across extended hours." Or, "We will purchase (not build) applications whenever possible, as it will enable us to be nimble and adapt quickly to our changing business needs." Or, "When necessary and appropriate, we will adapt our processes to the tools rather than adapt tools to our processes. This will allow us to move forward more quickly with new technology capabilities."

• Create the vision and strategy. In this step, the team begins to outline the technology, the organization and the operation. Define the end state and key interim steps. List the key benefits that this environment will create.

Note: Section 6 was developed with Vanguard Communications Corp., and is drawn from the seminar, *Understanding and Applying Today's Call Center Technologies* and related materials. Contents copyrighted to Vanguard Communications Corp. and/or ICMI, Inc., 2003

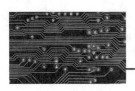

Phase 3: Selling

The third phase is the hardest part. This is where all of the team's ideas need to be incorporated into a solid story that can be communicated effectively to get the senior-level buyin you need to move forward. It involves three key steps:

• Develop the implementation plan. The vision and strategy need to be turned into a plan. This is not intended to be a detailed plan — rather, a plan that will depicts a few (three to five) key phases, and the major events that will occur in those phases. It should include the timeline of what you will do and when, and provide supporting reasons why these steps need to be taken.

• Build the business case. Most companies require a solid business case for deploying an overall technology strategy. Depending on your specific situation, you may need to build a solid budget case for the overall vision, or you may only need to present a laundry list of benefits of Phase 1. In some call centers, entire strategies can be justified on one assumption, such as an increase in customer retention. Others must develop an evolutionary set of benefits over several years, with an ultimate payback in labor cost savings or increases in revenue. Tie the case to the key business drivers, and keep it simple and manageable. It will be compelling in simplicity, not in complexity.

• Selling the strategy. Finally, all of the team's ideas need to be documented, well-laidout and delivered. You will need to create a full, detailed report of your strategy (30 to 50 pages), as well as a brief, two- to three-page version. Keep the story crisp — what, when and why, tied into the defined business goals (or key "pain points"). Remember, you're selling — have your story ready and your closing line planned!

Excerpt from "How to Develop a Customer Contact Technology Strategy" by Lori Bocklund, *Call Center Management Review*, October 2001.

The Technology Adoption Lifecycle

A useful tool in creating the vision and building the design of the strategy is the technology adoption lifecycle, which is generally attributed to Geoffrey Moore, a well-known consultant to the high-tech industry.

The model forms a bell curve with five divisions that describe psychographic buying habits, including:

- **Innovators:** Sometimes referred to as "technology enthusiasts," these folks buy into new technology early and often. They love trying new things, and typically will do what they can to help the supplier bring the product to the marketplace.

(continued, next page)

Note: Section 6 was developed with Vanguard Communications Corp., and is drawn from the seminar, *Understanding and Applying Today's Call Center Technologies* and related materials. Contents copyrighted to Vanguard Communications Corp. and/or ICMI, Inc., 2003

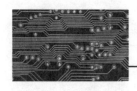

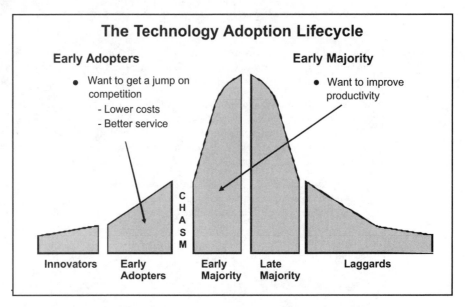

The Technology Adoption Lifecycle

- **Early Adopters:** Also called "visionaries," they are quick to understand and appreciate the benefits of new technologies, and are willing to take some risks to realize potential order-of-magnitude gains that can come from being among the first to embrace new capabilities.

- **Early Majority:** Also referred to as "pragmatists," members of this large group are driven by a strong sense of practicality. They share some of the characteristics of early adopters, but they prefer to wait until the market "shakes out" and the technology is more proven. Moore suggests that once a technology crosses the "chasm" between early adopters and early majority, it will rapidly proliferate, bringing a flood of business to suppliers and competitive pressures to end-users to get on board.

- **Late Majority:** These "conservatives" want solutions that work, with little risk and few implementation hassles. Like the early majority, they have a strong sense of practicality, but would rather wait until turnkey solutions with well-defined ROIs are available.

- **Laggards:** Members of this group resist new technology and distrust conventional competitive and productivity-improvement arguments. These "skeptics" are generally viewed by vendors as not worth the effort.

Using the Technology Adoption Lifecycle

There are a number of uses for the model:

- Viewing your organization, your customers, your competitors and new technologies through the lens of the model will help you identify trade-offs

Note: Section 6 was developed with Vanguard Communications Corp., and is drawn from the seminar, *Understanding and Applying Today's Call Center Technologies* and related materials. Contents copyrighted to Vanguard Communications Corp. and/or ICMI, Inc., 2003

between risks and rewards and establish priorities. For example, early indications are that email management systems and speech recognition capabilities have crossed or are in a position to cross the chasm while Web call-through services and video-equipped call center services may take longer than initially expected to reach the early majority. Assuming that is the case, what are the implications for your call center?

- Any project team is likely to have individuals with differing perspectives. The pragmatists tend to view the visionaries as "dangerous," the visionaries think the pragmatists are too cautious and the conservatives question rationale and the probability of payback. An understanding of these perspectives can help you appreciate differences and produce better decisions.

- The model can help you produce better budgetary proposals. Return on investment is difficult to predict until a technology crosses the chasm and solid case studies emerge. But, by then, the greater opportunities of early adoption will have passed. These are considerations to review with the CFO.

Clearly, the development of a technology strategy requires a significant amount of time, effort and money. Selling the strategy to the executive level requires more than just a simple cost/benefit analysis that is focused on expense reduction. A more effective analysis will include estimates of the impact of the technology strategy on:

- Revenue

- Market share

- Customer retention

- Customer data capture – and the value of the data

- Customer satisfaction

- Employee satisfaction and retention

- Errors and rework

Perhaps most importantly, the analysis will not use today as the basis of comparison, but will instead compare to how tomorrow will look if the access strategy does not change. (See Financial Methodologies, this section.)

Note: Section 6 was developed with Vanguard Communications Corp., and is drawn from the seminar, *Understanding and Applying Today's Call Center Technologies* and related materials. Contents copyrighted to Vanguard Communications Corp. and/or ICMI, Inc., 2003

Section 6

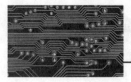

20. Developing the Business Case

Ready? | 1 | 2 | 3 |

Key Points

- A business case is used to provide justification of a technology purchase.

- A key element within the business case will be some version of a cost/benefit analysis. The business case will also typically provide information on benefits that cannot easily be given a dollar value, such as new business opportunities.

- To provide a more complete picture of the recommendation, the business case will also include items such as the project plan, implementation plan and critical success factors.

Explanation

In the course of recommending new technology for a call center, a business case for the purchase must eventually be developed and presented. A business case provides the complete argument behind the recommendation as well as information concerning the implementation plan. Leveraging new business opportunities and/or reducing costs are the two factors that most often drive strategic investments in new technologies.

Central to most business cases regarding technology purchases is a cost/benefit analysis that paints the financial picture of the recommendation. (See Financial Methodologies, this section.) Components of a business case that focus on "hard" dollars include the following:

- Changes in agent staffing and salary expenses

- Changes in support staffing and salary expenses

- Changes in revenue streams

- Changes in telecom costs

- Changes in technology depreciation costs

- Changes in technology maintenance costs

These elements and others are applied to one or more financial calculations used by an organization to determine the financial value of the

Note: Section 6 was developed with Vanguard Communications Corp., and is drawn from the seminar, *Understanding and Applying Today's Call Center Technologies* and related materials. Contents copyrighted to Vanguard Communications Corp. and/or ICMI, Inc., 2003

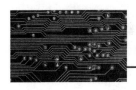

recommendation. Based on the standards and procedures followed, the final result will indicate a dollar value of the investment, a percentage of return on the investment or a period of time in which the investment will be recovered.

A business case is not, however, limited to only financial calculations. Other elements regarding the proposed investment are also taken into consideration, and are typically referred to as the "soft benefits." Examples of these include the following:

- Impact on quality results

- Impact on customer satisfaction results

- Impact on employee satisfaction and turnover

- Value of increased data capture

- Ability to better meet organization's vision/mission

Ideally, some of these soft benefits can be converted to hard dollar estimates, but there are always some benefits that cannot be converted to a dollar value.

A business case for technology may also provide other related information on the project. Examples include:

- A project plan, showing items such as timelines, team members and dependencies

- An implementation plan, providing rollout plans, training schedules and technology support information (See Managing New Technology Implementations, this section.)

- Critical success factors such as integration with current systems, support from executives and an effective communication plan

The goal behind the development of a business case is to communicate and document the complete impact of the technology purchase. Done properly, it provides a starting point for meetings and decision making.

Writing the Business Case

Your business case should include a suite of quantitative benefits and costs. Components to consider include: hardware, software, cabling, facilities, professional services, training (e.g., agent, administration and support staff, supervisors), staffing changes, and ongoing administration and support personnel requirements.

(continued, next page)

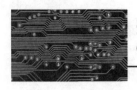

The cost-benefit analysis should contain both financial scenarios of conservative quantitative benefits that have already been signed off on (above-the-line scenarios) and additional potential benefits, including qualitative or more difficult to assess benefits (below-the-line scenarios). The business case can be categorized into:

• **Cost Reduction.** Productivity gains that result in: 1) extractable staff reduction; 2) handling of incremental and, ideally, revenue-generating transactions without requiring additional staff; 3) extractable facility savings; and 4) extractable non-personnel operations expense.

• **Cost Avoidance.** Old or aging equipment and software that require replacement due to manufacturer obsolescence (typically used in below-the-line business case analysis).

• **Revenue Generation.** True incremental revenue realized by new transaction types or measurable additional revenue from existing transactions attributed directly to the introduction of new technology. This would include increased closure rates, upsell and cross-sell opportunities, and customer acquisition.

• **Revenue Leakage.** Legitimate fees that your company can charge an end customer (consumer or business) or cross-charge another department for a service you are providing. The introduction of new technology provides the opportunity to examine your transaction call logging to effectively reclaim revenue that was historically considered lost. For example, if your center takes phone calls for another division in your organization, capturing those transaction types should ensure, at a minimum, cost recovery for the work effort within your operation.

Any impact on service level objectives that may result from the technology initiative should be factored into the business case, as applicable. For example, a new technology may require fewer resources to meet the same service level objective, thereby providing measurable cost reduction. Alternatively, you may wish to enhance your service level, in which case, the introduction of new technology would achieve the higher service level with the same resources compared with the existing technology, which would require additional resources.

The key is to document and examine the applicable business case scenarios for your particular business. Be sure to integrate both one-time and ongoing costs and benefits into a multiyear cost-benefit analysis, which will provide you with such business case metrics as return on investment and internal rate of return for multiple scenarios.

Excerpt from "Developing a Contact Center Technology Project Plan" by Murray Bookman, *Call Center Management Review*, January 2002.

21. Financial Methodologies

Ready? | 1 | 2 | 3 |

Key Points

- A consistent financial methodology needs to be followed to determine the dollar value of investments in technology.

- Organizations use many different types of calculations to come up with a return on investment (ROI).

- Effective ROI calculations take into account the time value of money.

- All ROI calculations depend on a solid set of assumptions and accurate estimates regarding costs and benefits of the technology implementation.

Explanation

Today, there are more technology choices than ever. Vendors are quick to point out the importance of their technologies and the impressive benefits they can bring to any call center. One of the best ways to cut through some of the hype and determine real value is to follow the kinds of analytical processes required for accurate return on investment (ROI) calculations.

Many corporations today have fixed rules in place regarding the kind of ROI calculation used to justify technology purchases, and with good reason. A consistent methodology is important in ensuring that all projects are evaluated fairly and appropriately, and that comparisons can be made between projects that have very different objectives.

ROI Terms

The term return on investment, or ROI, refers not to a specific formula but to a number of different alternatives that are all used to value a technology investment. Examples of commonly used, specific ROI calculations include the following:

- **Net present value (NPV):** The present value of the project's future cash flow less the initial investment in the project.

- **Internal rate of return (IRR):** The discount rate that makes the net present value of a project equal to zero.

Note: Section 6 was developed with Vanguard Communications Corp., and is drawn from the seminar, *Understanding and Applying Today's Call Center Technologies* and related materials. Contents copyrighted to Vanguard Communications Corp. and/or ICMI, Inc., 2003

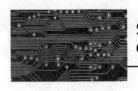

• **Payback period:** The amount of time required to recover the initial investment in a project.

The first two methods, NPV and IRR, both take into account the time value of money. This is a key element of an ROI calculation, and is typically preferred by most organizations. This is especially true because technology investments often take a number of months or years before providing a positive net gain, and technology becomes obsolete quicker now than ever before.

Net Present Value and Internal Rate of Return

The net present value (NPV) methodology delivers a final dollar value of an investment that is either positive or negative. The calculation is as follows:

$$NPV = Present\ Value\ (PV) - Investment\ (I)$$

Determining the present value of monthly or yearly cash flows requires the establishment of a discount rate. This rate is typically set by the financial department and is consistent from one project to the next. Yearly cash flows are reduced by a factor determined by the discount rate, and the final result is then compared to the total initial investment. A positive result means that the project can be recommended. Whether it is actually funded or not depends on the NPV of other projects that are vying for the same pool of money. An example of a NPV calculation is as follows:

Year	Cash Flow	PV @ 10%	PV of Cash Flow
1	$1,000	0.909	$909
2	$4,000	0.826	$3,304
3	$5,000	0.751	$3,755
			Total NPV = $7,968

The project team assumes that the project will return the amounts in the cash-flow column. For this example, the discount rate is assumed to be 10 percent. Multipliers in column three are from NPV calculations available from financial calculators or spreadsheets.

If the initial investment required for this project is $7,500, it would then be approved based on this calculation.

The internal rate of return (IRR) is closely related to the NPV calculation. With the IRR, rather than generating a total estimated gain or loss from the investment, a discount rate associated with the project is calculated. If this rate is higher than the organization's cutoff rate, the project can be accepted. If it is

Note: Section 6 was developed with Vanguard Communications Corp., and is drawn from the seminar, *Understanding and Applying Today's Call Center Technologies* and related materials. Contents copyrighted to Vanguard Communications Corp. and/or ICMI, Inc., 2003

lower, the project is denied.

In order to determine the discount rate of the project, different rates must be used until the present value of cash flow equals the initial investment. An example is included below:

Year	Cash Flow	PV @ 10%	PV of Cash Flow	PV @ 12%	PV of Cash Flow
1	$1,000	0.909	$909	0.893	$893
2	$4,000	0.826	$3,304	0.797	$3,188
3	$5,000	0.751	$3,755	0.712	$3,560
			Total NPV = $7,968		Total NPV = $7,641

If the initial investment of this project is $7,500, then the discount rate would be just short of 12 percent. If the cutoff point for accepting projects is 10 percent, then the investment would be approved.

Payback Period

The payback period differs from the other two calculations in two main ways. First of all, it does not take into account the time value of money, so no discount rates are used. Second, it provides an answer in terms of time – months or years. An example of a payback period calculation is below.

In this example, the initial investment of $115,000 will be paid back after 2.81 years. If the cutoff point for the organization is three years, then the project can be approved.

Initial Investment = $115,000

Year	Cash Flow
1	$40,000
2	$41,000
3	$42,000
4	$43,000
Payback Point	2.81 years

The value of a payback period calculation is in its simplicity and the expression of the result in time – a concept that is easy for almost everyone to understand. The typical payback period calculation expressed above can be improved by discounting the cash flows so that a net present value is supplied.

Note: Section 6 was developed with Vanguard Communications Corp., and is drawn from the seminar, *Understanding and Applying Today's Call Center Technologies* and related materials. Contents copyrighted to Vanguard Communications Corp. and/or ICMI, Inc., 2003

Section 6

Equally as important as the calculation used is the accuracy of assumptions and estimates. Without accurate input, none of the calculations described here will provide worthwhile investment decisions for any organization.

Note: Definitions and some examples are taken from *Finance* by AA Groppelli and Ehsan Nikbakht, Barron's Business Review Series, 1995.

(For more infomation on financial concepts, see ICMI's *Call Center Leadership and Business Management Handbook and Study Guide*.)

Note: Section 6 was developed with Vanguard Communications Corp., and is drawn from the seminar, *Understanding and Applying Today's Call Center Technologies* and related materials. Contents copyrighted to Vanguard Communications Corp. and/or ICMI, Inc., 2003

22. Basic Project Management Principles

Ready? | 1 | 2 | 3 |

Key Points

- Key project management terms include:
    - Scope
    - Project plan
    - Gantt chart
    - Milestone
    - Deliverables
    - Dependency
    - Critical path
    - Owner
    - Sponsor/champion

- Project management software applications can help to organize and track project activity. Such applications range in capability/complexity from basic flowcharting or spreadsheet applications to tools costing hundreds of thousands of dollars.

Explanation

Since call centers are frequently involved in projects, knowledge of project management principles and processes is valuable for call center managers when they participate in, interact with or oversee project teams.

Key project management terms include:

- **Scope:** The boundaries of the project, meaning a statement of what is and is not part of the project. Also, "scope creep" is when a project grows beyond what was originally approved, often because the scope was not clearly defined at the outset.

- **Project plan (also known as work breakdown structure, or WBS):** Listing of all tasks required to complete the project, showing (for each task) start date, completion date, resources required, the person responsible for each task and a task number.

- **Gantt chart:** Visual representation of the project plan, using bars extending

Note: Section 6 was developed with Vanguard Communications Corp., and is drawn from the seminar, *Understanding and Applying Today's Call Center Technologies* and related materials. Contents copyrighted to Vanguard Communications Corp. and/or ICMI, Inc., 2003

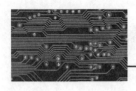

to the right of each task representing the amount of time the task requires. Sophisticated Gantt charts use arrows and symbols to indicate task dependencies, milestones, etc.

- **Milestone**: Measurable point of progress in the project plan. The milestone is listed in the project plan along with the tasks, but is present really as a marker that either has or has not been achieved. For example, "Collect responses to request for proposal."

- **Deliverables**: Completed units of work with tangible results. For example, a report could be a deliverable, as could a software module.

- **Dependency**: Relationship between tasks that makes planning for one task dependent upon planning for the other. For example, "determine number of trunks needed" must be completed before "place order for trunks."

- **Critical path**: The sequence of tasks upon which the project completion date depends. In other words, a change in the duration of any these tasks will change the project's completion date, due to dependencies among the tasks on the critical path. Tasks that are not on the critical path can be delayed without affecting the project end date.

- **Owner**: Person accountable for completion of a task.

- **Sponsor/champion**: Person in the organization with the authority and/or funds to make the project happen, or who advocates for the project to the organization's decision makers.

However, with the requisite knowledge and training, project management software can become a powerful tool for effective project management. Project management software applications are no substitute for understanding project management principles and processes. Indeed, many of the tools are so complex as to require their own training to use them effectively.

(Project management is also discussed in ICMI's *Call Center Leadership and Business Management Handbook and Study Guide*.)

Note: Section 6 was developed with Vanguard Communications Corp., and is drawn from the seminar, *Understanding and Applying Today's Call Center Technologies* and related materials. Contents copyrighted to Vanguard Communications Corp. and/or ICMI, Inc., 2003

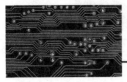

23. Managing New Technology Implementations   Ready? | 1 | 2 | 3 |

Key Points

- When implementing new technologies, a clear strategic vision provides the foundation for success. Stakeholders' ideas and input should be included in the development of a business strategy.

- Vendor responses to a request for information (RFI), request for proposal (RFP) or request for quote (RFQ) should be evaluated against clear, established criteria.

- Oversight of new technology initiatives requires a manager with superior project management skills.

Explanation

All call center technology initiatives should begin with redefinition of the strategic vision of the call center. This vision provides the foundation that will guide the project.

There are many steps to consider when designing and developing a call center technology solution. The path varies depending on extent of changes, whether leveraging existing technology or vendor partners, and the amount of time allocated to the project.

(continued, next page)

when you develop + implement new
technology steps
- divine strategy - why are you doing this?
- divine functional - what you want it to do
  requirements
- select a vendor
- implement

Note: Section 6 was developed with Vanguard Communications Corp., and is drawn from the seminar, *Understanding and Applying Today's Call Center Technologies* and related materials. Contents copyrighted to Vanguard Communications Corp. and/or ICMI, Inc., 2003

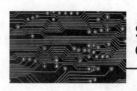

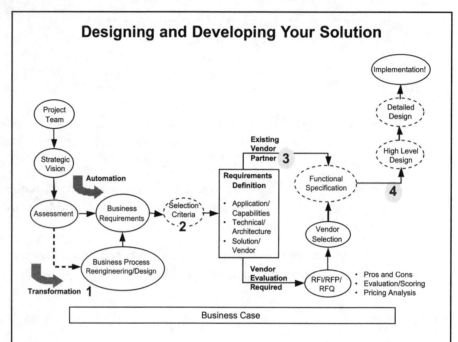

Designing and Developing Your Solution

Notes:
1) For transformation change, process reengineering must be completed prior to defining an automated solution.
2) Selection Criteria is developed when a vendor evaluation is required.
3) The path directly to Functional Specification is more likely when working with an existing vendor partner; to RFI is more likely when a selection process is required.
4) With today's rapid implementations, a functional specification, high-level design, and detailed design, while desirable, are often skipped or shortened, or delivered by the vendor.

As improvement opportunities and their associated technologies are identified, a call center functional requirements plan must be developed. An important aspect of this step is to identify the criteria that will be used in vendor evaluation. Key stakeholders should have a say in criteria and in developing a scoring system.

Once the criteria have been established, a detailed requirements document should be created to outline the capabilities, technical architectures, definitions and expectations. This will usually take the form of a request for information (RFI), request for proposal (RFP), request for quote (RFQ) or some combination. Differences between these approaches include:

- An RFI may be issued to a broad list of companies, and be fairly high level and generic.

- An RFP is generally issued to fewer companies and specifically requests the vendor to propose a solution for the company's environment.

Note: Section 6 was developed with Vanguard Communications Corp., and is drawn from the seminar, *Understanding and Applying Today's Call Center Technologies* and related materials. Contents copyrighted to Vanguard Communications Corp. and/or ICMI, Inc., 2003

- An RFQ can be part of an RFP or RFI, or issued separately, and results in a price for a solution.

These documents should define the following key areas:

- **Selection criteria:** These are the key areas – four to six generally – that are the basis on which a decision will be made. Categories such as functionality, fit with existing environment, vendor experience, and vendor support and relationships are examples of selection criteria categories that could be defined. These categories help focus the questions to the vendors and give the evaluation team clear guidelines for decision making. They also focus vendors on the things that are most important and that will differentiate one vendor from another.

- **Current environment:** The current environment should be described so the vendor knows the environment into which the solution must fit.

- **Requirements:** These should address mandatory features and functions, as well as optional or future plans that may influence a decision. They should also address key system requirements, such as architecture, scalability, and reliability.

- **Professional services:** These should define the role the vendor or their partners are expected to play in the implementation of the system, as well as support and training. With some of the advanced technologies, the professional services costs can exceed the software and hardware costs.

- **Additional vendor information:** Gather vendor qualifications, references, documentation, staffing or other issues that will indicate their fit as a potential supplier or partner.

- **Cost:** Be sure to include purchase price, optional items, implementation costs and maintenance costs. The cost statement should explicitly address what the call center must provide since in many solutions today the vendors provide the software only.

Research is important as you begin to create the requirements document. It is important to gain as much information and insight as possible into how potential products will fit your business requirements. Sources of information on vendors and products include:

- Trade magazines

- Internet sites related to the call center industry

- Industry trade shows

- References

Note: Section 6 was developed with Vanguard Communications Corp., and is drawn from the seminar, *Understanding and Applying Today's Call Center Technologies* and related materials. Contents copyrighted to Vanguard Communications Corp. and/or ICMI, Inc., 2003

Section 6

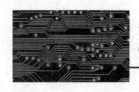

After receiving the vendor responses, each should be evaluated based on the criteria scorecard established by the project team. There may be a need for additional presentations or site visits before one vendor is finally chosen for the project. The project team, along with vendors, then develops functional specifications along with high-level and detailed designs, which provide the "road map" for the technical aspects of the project.

Once all RFP or RFI information has been collected and other research has been completed, methods to evaluate and rank criteria by a weighted scoring system, usually in the form of a matrix, is a generally accepted practice in the call center industry (and for many other technology-related projects).

Example Vendor Evaluation

Scale: 1 = to a very little extent, 2 = to some extent, 3 = to a great extent, 4 = to a very great extent

Criteria	Weight	X	Ratings		=		Score
Product features	10	1	2	③		4	30
Initial costs	5	1	2	③		4	15
Ongoing costs	10	1	2	3	④		40
Usability	10	1	2	③		4	30
Experience with industry	5	1	②	3		4	10
Account team	2	1	2	3	④		8
Support capabilities	10	1	②	3		4	20
Implementation timeframe	8	1	2	3	④		32
Training services	10	1	2	3	④		40
Integration capabilities	10	1	2	3	④		40
Customization capabilities	10	1	2	3	④		40
Financial viability	10	1	2	3	④		40
Totals	100						345

(handwritten note in margin: weighted average)

To determine the score of each vendor, the weighted amount is multiplied by the rating for each item. All of the scores are added together to get each vendor's total evaluation. The vendor with the highest score is typically awarded the project.

Note: Section 6 was developed with Vanguard Communications Corp., and is drawn from the seminar, *Understanding and Applying Today's Call Center Technologies* and related materials. Contents copyrighted to Vanguard Communications Corp. and/or ICMI, Inc., 2003

Using Outside Help

Another important project consideration is whether or not to bring in an outside firm to help implement or provide new technology solutions. Key factors include:

- How complex is the project?

- What other technologies must be integrated?

- How fast can the internal team build the solution? External team?

- Do you have the resources and experience necessary in house?

- Are there better ways to spend your time (what's the "opportunity cost" of dedicating internal resources to the project)?

Whether an outside firm is utilized or not, an implementation plan should be developed based on sound project management principles. (See Basic Project Management Principles, this section.)

Implementation Plan

[handwritten margin note: Application Service Provider ASP – out sourcer for Technology]

Once the plan is in place, the approvals have been received and the project is taking shape, the team also has to develop an implementation plan. This plan should address the details that make the difference between a rough transition and a smooth one. Some examples include:

- Reviewing and revising testing strategies to ensure that selected applicants have the right skills to succeed in the new environment.

- Addressing compensation issues that will arise as assignments change and at least some staff members become proficient in more than one channel.

- Ensuring agents are equipped with the knowledge and training they need to succeed.

- Confirming that new technologies will integrate easily with existing systems.

- Developing forecasting methods that address all the different entry points into the organization.

- Ensuring that technology support processes are in place to address down time and response time issues quickly and effectively for every channel and all supporting hardware/software.

(For more information on vendor selection and contractual arrangements, see ICMI's *Call Center Leadership and Business Management Handbook and Study Guide*.)

Note: Section 6 was developed with Vanguard Communications Corp., and is drawn from the seminar, *Understanding and Applying Today's Call Center Technologies* and related materials. Contents copyrighted to Vanguard Communications Corp. and/or ICMI, Inc., 2003

Section 6

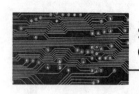

Call Center Technology

Exercises

Key Technology Trends

1. Select from the following words to complete the statements below.

browser-based	media
cost	TCP/IP
implementation	value
integrated	ROI

a. Client-Server Environment
Today, the data communications protocol of choice is ~~TCP/IP~~ , the transport protocol of the Internet.

b. Standards, Open Platforms and Standard Tools
In today's technology environment, systems must run on standard platforms with standard operating environments. They must be "open," that is, readily _integrated_ with other systems and be extensible and scalable.

c. Packaged, Customizable Solutions
The advantages of packaged solutions include lower cost and faster _ROI_ .

d. Adequate and Appropriate Data to Service Customer Needs
Companies need to measure the _value_ vs. the _cost_ of a contact or customer.

e. Improved Desktop Tools
In line with the standard and open approach of platforms, _browser based_ interfaces are becoming the preferred desktop front end.

f. Multimedia Queuing and Transaction Processing
More importantly, response time and action triggered by the transaction need to be similar regardless of _media_ type used by the customer.

Note: Section 6 was developed with Vanguard Communications Corp., and is drawn from the seminar, *Understanding and Applying Today's Call Center Technologies* and related materials. Contents copyrighted to Vanguard Communications Corp. and/or ICMI, Inc., 2003

2. Match the technology with each statement below. You will use some terms more than once.

   a. ACD system
   b. CRM capabilities
   c. CTI capabilities
   d. Desktop/agent system interface
   e. Dialer
   f. Email response management system (ERMS)
   g. Fax server
   h. IVR/voice processing capabilities
   i. Multimedia routing and queuing
   j. Network
   k. Quality monitoring/recording system
   l. Telecommuting technologies
   m. Web communication channels
   n. Workforce management system (WFMS)

G Can automatically distribute or transfer incoming documents to an image processing system for retrieval by an agent.

N The primary value of this technology lies in its ability to maximize the use of available resources and thereby reduce overall staffing requirements and costs.

K Feedback forms, coordinated data recording, text-chat/email recording and GUI interface for recording/playback are common characteristics of this technology.

L The potential benefits of this technology include: tapping into a larger workforce (such as agents who have physical disabilities), attracting and retaining employees who need flexible hours, and handling peak periods efficiently.

H Speech recognition is an advanced capability of this technology.

M Offers enormous self-service opportunities, but rarely succeeds without the availability of assisted services.

C Enables the voice and network worlds to share information in a way that allows for enhanced caller treatment.

B A concept, not a distinct technology, which uses advanced technology tools, databases and applications to enable differentiated service to each customer via a variety of media.

Note: Section 6 was developed with Vanguard Communications Corp., and is drawn from the seminar, *Understanding and Applying Today's Call Center Technologies* and related materials. Contents copyrighted to Vanguard Communications Corp. and/or ICMI, Inc., 2003

Section 6

_A___ The success of this technology is typically measured by self-service completion rates.

_e___ For this outbound technology, a balance must be achieved between increasing agent productivty and minimizing the chance that customers hear silence.

_A___ Routes, sequences and queues calls, and provides real-time and historical reports for planning and management purposes.

_D___ Options for this technology include "dumb" terminals, PCs with terminal emulation, thick clients and thin clients.

_A___ The following reports are generated from this technology: 1) Number of calls today, 2) number of agents in various states, and 3) service level for current period.

_J___ Percent allocation, call-by-call routing and network interflow are multisite alternatives of this technology.

_E___ Hardware/software for automating the process of making outbound calls to lists of people.

_b___ Optimizes profitability through revenue growth and customer retention, rather than cost savings.

_f___ Advanced auto acknowledgment, library of standard responses, intelligent auto response and end-to-end automation are functionalities sometimes provided by this technology.

_H___ There are three common terms related to this technology: auto attendant, voice response unit and interactive voice response.

_j___ DNIS and ANI are features of this technology.

_j___ The "pipe" between callers and the call center.

_F___ Performs many of the same routing functions for email that ACDs perform for inbound calls.

_L___ Central Office ACD, ISDN BRI lines, and DSL Technologies are possible alternatives.

_I___ Identifies the customer's identity and purpose, and applies business rules to route the inbound or outbound contact, regardless of media, to the proper skilled resource with the proper treatment and prioritization.

_N___ Provides call center managers with a tool to accomplish automated forecasting, staffing projections, scheduling and tracking.

Note: Section 6 was developed with Vanguard Communications Corp., and is drawn from the seminar, _Understanding and Applying Today's Call Center Technologies_ and related materials. Contents copyrighted to Vanguard Communications Corp. and/or ICMI, Inc., 2003

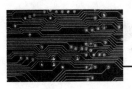

Project Management

3. Match the project management term with the appropriate statement:

a. Critical path
b. Deliverables
c. Dependency
d. Gantt chart
e. Milestone
f. Owner
g. Project plan
h. Scope
i. Sponsor/champion

__H__ The boundaries of the project.

__G__ Listing of all tasks required to complete the project.

__D__ Visual representation of the project plan.

__E__ Measurable point of progress in the project plan.

__B__ Completed units of work with tangible results.

__F__ Person accountable for completion of a task.

__I__ Person in the organization with the authority and/or funds to make the project happen, or who advocates for the project to the organization's decision maker(s).

__C__ Relationship between tasks that makes planning for one task dependent upon planning for the other.

__A__ The sequence of tasks upon which the project completion date depends.

Answers to these exercises are in Section 10.

Note: These exercises are intended to help you retain the material learned. While not the exact questions as on the CIAC Certification assessment, the material in this handbook/study guide fully addresses the content on which you will be assessed. For a formal practice test, please contact the CIAC directly by visiting www.ciac-cert.org.

Note: Section 6 was developed with Vanguard Communications Corp., and is drawn from the seminar, *Understanding and Applying Today's Call Center Technologies* and related materials. Contents copyrighted to Vanguard Communications Corp. and/or ICMI, Inc., 2003

Section 6

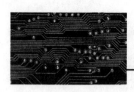

Call Center Technology
Reference Bibliography

Related Articles from *Call Center Management Review* (See Section 9)

Technology vs. Staff Investments: Don't Neglect the People Side of the Equation

Today's ACD: More than Mere Call Routing

Multisite Routing Options: Deciding on the Best Fit for Your Call Center

How to Identify IVR/CTI Performance Problems

Selecting and Implementing Workforce Management Systems

Monitoring Quality in the Multi-Channel Interaction Center

Understanding and Implementing Desktop Productivity Tools

CTI-Enabled Call Centers Enhance Customer Experience

Building the E-Enabled Call Center: It's Time to Get Moving (2 parts)

Web-Chat Emerging as a Leader for Live Online Support Applications

Making Sense of Virtual Customer Care Solutions

Still a Few Barriers to Integrated Multimedia Routing and Queuing

When Is an ASP the Right Solution for Your Center?

A Solid RFP Process Will Ease Vendor Selection and Management

For Further Study

Publications

Bocklund, Lori and Dave Bengtson. *Call Center Technology Demystified: The No-Nonsense Guide to Bridging Customer Contact Technology, Operations and Strategy.* Call Center Press, 2002.

Note: Section 6 was developed with Vanguard Communications Corp., and is drawn from the seminar, *Understanding and Applying Today's Call Center Technologies* and related materials. Contents copyrighted to Vanguard Communications Corp. and/or ICMI, Inc., 2003

Dawson, Keith. *The Call Center Handbook 4 Ed: The Complete Guide to Starting, Running, and Improving Your Customer Contact Center.* CMP Books, 2001.

Dawson, Keith. *Call Center Savvy: How to Position Your Call Center for the Business Challenges of the 21st Century.* CMP Books, 1999.

Special Issue on Technology, *Call Center Management Review*, 2001.

Articles

Bocklund, Lori. "How to Develop a Customer Contact Technology Strategy." *Call Center Management Review*, October 2001.

Bookman, Murray. "Developing a Contact Center Technology Project Plan." *Call Center Management Review*, January 2002.

Levin, Greg. "The Emergence of the IP Contact Center." *Call Center Management Review*, March 2002.

Tanner, Todd and Brad Paul. "Identify CRM Interfaces to Ensure Smooth Process and Service Level Alignment." *Call Center Management Review*, April 2001.

Seminars

Understanding and Applying Today's Call Center Technologies, a public seminar presented by Vanguard Communications Corporation and sponsored by Incoming Calls Management Institute.

Web Sites

A variety of links and white papers is available at www.vanguard.net and at www.incoming.com.

Note: Section 6 was developed with Vanguard Communications Corp., and is drawn from the seminar, *Understanding and Applying Today's Call Center Technologies* and related materials. Contents copyrighted to Vanguard Communications Corp. and/or ICMI, Inc., 2003

Facilities and Disaster Recovery

Operations Management

Section 7: Facilities and Disaster Recovery

Contents

1. Site Selection Considerations [Strategic]

Ready? | 1 | 2 | 3 |

Key Points

- Site selection considerations include:
    - Labor issues
    - Telecommunications considerations
    - Real estate design and cost issues
    - Government incentives, taxation and legislation

- Because labor often constitutes 60 percent or more of call center operating costs, it is the most important site selection consideration. Labor issues include:
    - Size of the labor pool
    - Population inflow or outflow
    - Demographics
    - Skill requirements
    - Quality of life and community

Explanation

There are a number of important factors to consider when selecting a location for your call center. These factors can be grouped into the following general categories:

- Labor issues

- Telecommunications considerations

- Real estate design and cost issues

- Government incentives, taxation and legislation

Labor Issues

Labor issues, including supply, quality and cost, are the most important site selection criteria, partly because of the variance from location to location. Labor often constitutes 60 percent or more of the call center's operating costs. Market size, demographic characteristics (including concentrations of students, second wage earners, military dependents or retirees), wage patterns, turnover rates, skills sets, language capabilities, educational levels and capabilities, training support and the labor relations climate must be addressed.

Section 7

The location's size, demographics, competition and language skills should be considered to ensure that it has a large enough population of people with the required skills to meet customer expectations. Some of the most important labor considerations include:

- **Size of the labor pool:** A guide to understanding if a community can supply enough labor for a new center is to seek areas where the draw of employees is only a small percentage, usually around one percent of the total employed (not population) statistics. Thus, a call center that needs 80 agents would seek a location with at least 80,000 actively employed people.

  Smaller cities and rural communities with populations under 200,000 often have higher than average unemployment rates and offer a loyal workforce. However, smaller communities may not have suitable real estate and the telecom infrastructure to support a large call center. Another consideration is speed-to-market since smaller towns may not have facilities already set up for centers. While downtown areas in larger cities are gaining in popularity as business locations, urban areas should be considered on a location-by-location comparison rather than a generalized evaluation of urban vs. suburban locations. Education and orientation vary widely from city to city.

- **Population inflow or outflow:** Depending on the anticipated turnover rate or plans for future expansion of the facility, consider communities that have more inflowing than outflowing residents. Communities that generally attract new residents have favorable climates and lifestyles, such as Arizona, Colorado or Florida. Also consider cities and towns that are business, commercial, cultural and educational hubs for surrounding areas, such as Sioux Falls, South Dakota, and Boise, Idaho.

- **Demographics:** When considering a community's labor supply, gather unemployment and underemployment statistics for a more accurate picture. Government figures for unemployment come from people who are collecting unemployment insurance, who are actively seeking work or who are working. It doesn't include those who are not in the workforce (i.e., on disability leave, students, stay-at-home spouses, etc.).

  Underemployment, on the other hand, occurs when people take positions for which they are overqualified (e.g., a college-educated person working as a part-time check-out clerk). Finding out whether there is underemployment in an area requires researching the local market, and getting input from local economic development agencies.

In addition to employment statistics, consider the scheduling needs of your call center and the characteristics of your employees. For example, if you will need more staff in the morning hours than late afternoon hours, you may look for a location with a sufficient supply of part-time workers.

When looking at demographics, consider those factors that impact the workforce you need. For example, the unemployment rate for the skilled workers you require is more important than the area's overall unemployment rate. Further, the competitive pay rate for the skilled workers you are seeking is much more important than the community's average household income.

Sources of demographic and labor information are numerous, and include census bureau, chambers of commerce, state and local economic development groups, educational institutions, private sources and government agencies.

- **Skill requirements:** The area under consideration should have a workforce with the skill sets required for the center's customer base. For instance, organizations that serve Spanish-speaking customers will need to have access to agents with those language abilities (e.g., south Texas).

- **Quality of life and community:** Other labor trait considerations involve quality of life and community. Those include:

  - Climate

  - Housing costs

  - Schools

  - Amenities like parks and recreation facilities

  - Traffic and commute times

  - Local business climate

  - Surrounding services including medical

  - Transportation access to buses, airports, etc.

Researching similar employers in each potential location may help you better understand the challenges and advantages of the location. Gauge such factors as recruiting methods, turnover trends, pay and benefit packages, future expansion plans and recent or anticipated location announcements.

Section 7

Payroll Costs

Of course, how much you will need to pay employees in order to attract the skill sets required by your customers is a primary consideration in site selection. A difference of just one or two dollars per hour in labor costs could offset higher facilities costs. Local economic development agencies, local job advertisements, and university and government employment agencies can offer help in determining wage expectations of the labor pool.

Exempt and Nonexempt Labor Considerations

Under the Fair Labor Standards Act (FLSA), federal law requires that employees are to be paid at least minimum wage and overtime for hours worked over 40 hours a week. The law provides for an exemption from both the minimum wage and overtime provisions for employees engaged in an executive, administrative, or professional capacity, certain employees in computer-related positions, or outside salespersons. The FLSA regulations stipulate that the determination of whether an individual is exempt or not is dependent on both job duties and the salary basis tests.

For an employee to be classified as exempt, he/she must meet the Department of Labor's definition of an executive, administrative or professional employee, an outside salesperson or certain highly skilled computer-related employees.

Most commonly known as the white-collar exemption, exempt employees must be paid on a "salaried basis," meaning that the person must be paid the same full salary for any week in which work is performed without regard to the number of hours worked or the quality of the work performed. A salaried employee is not entitled to overtime pay. Nonexempt employees, however, must be paid overtime for any hours they work over a 40-hour work week.

Telecommunications Considerations

Telecommunications often comprises about 20 to 30 percent of a call center's operating costs. Both local and long-distance services must be included in the evaluation. Local phone companies can offer input on current and anticipated needs, such as fiber-optic capability, redundant cable routes, disaster recovery, service delivery times and plans for upgrading switching centers and cabling. If service is being upgraded, the project can be included in these work plans, potentially reducing project costs. Also, consider the location of the long-distance provider's closest switching facilities, or "point of presence." Locating in corporate business parks will likely provide state-of-the-art telecommunications services, as some parks are specifically designed to serve high-tech information-intensive businesses.

Government Incentives, Taxation and Legislation

Government incentives, taxation requirements and legislation can have an impact on operating costs for call centers. These should be considered and compared during the site selection process

- **Incentives:** Many states and communities offer an array of financial and other incentives. By virtue of the company's anticipated employment and investment, your project can begin with a certain level of negotiating leverage. Training is the most sought-after incentive. Some states and communities pay a high percentage of training costs for new employees. Assistance in recruiting and screening of prospective employees for basic qualifications is often available at little or no cost. Other incentives can include tax abatements, loans, grants or facility enhancements.

  Communities that have municipally or regionally owned industrial parks and buildings will package deals that include low-interest loans or outright grants to companies. In some cases, facilities can be used rent-free as interim offices during the planning and construction of the facility.

- **Taxation and legislation:** Make sure you are aware of tax rates and legislation that impacts call centers. Higher taxes can have a direct impact on your organization's costs. Legislation that most directly impacts call centers includes telecommunications legislation, telemarketing laws (if the call center handles outbound contacts) and labor laws. (See Legislation Factors, this section.) (For more information on applicable labor laws, see *ICMI's Call Center People Management Handbook and Study Guide*.)

Facility Design and Cost Issues

The availability of appropriate real estate and the costs associated with it have an obvious impact on site selection. Facilities should be the appropriate size, be aesthetically pleasing, have flexibility for workspace changes, and comply with health and safety regulations. (See discussions of call center design, this section.) You should also consider transportation issues, including expected commuting time and accessibility to public transportation. These issues can be important ones when recruiting staff. The cost of facilities should always be kept in the context of labor costs since labor is such a significant portion of call center operating costs.

Section 7

Economic Development Agencies (EDAs)

Local economic development agencies (EDAs) can provide information about underemployment and offer assistance in setting up the call center. EDAs can put call center management in touch with local resources, such as community colleges and incumbent local exchange carriers (ILECs), and come up with key difficult-to-obtain information, such as number of call centers in the area, the companies that run them and prevailing wages.

Before meeting with EDAs, it's advisable to research the community as much as possible. Keep in mind that the goal of an EDA is to bring new business into the community; therefore, it should never be the sole source of information about a particular community. Take caution in evaluating incentive packages offered by EDAs. Many are private or semiprivate organizations without authority to guarantee planning approval or tax breaks. (Source: *Designing the Best Call Center for Your Business* by Brendan Read, CMP Books, 2000)

The Importance of Labor Cost Considerations

You can find the fanciest, least cost, wow-isn't-it-a-fantastic-deal building, with acres of free parking, Jacuzzi, gym, child care and a 7x24 supermarket in the basement, a three year lease and available now. Yet, if the city or metro area doesn't have the people you need, at your budgeted cost, the property is worthless. You are much better off financially and in your customer service and sales goals if you pay more for real estate to get the labor you want.

Experts say that real estate should represent no more than 10% of your total costs. Susan Arledge illustrated why call centers have to factor labor costs into their real estate planning at the Direct Marketing Association's Telephone Marketing Council conference in June 1999.

In her example, Arledge described a fictitious outsourcer that had a choice between two facilities in two different cities. The outsourcer intended to select one of the facilities only on the basis of real estate costs and labor costs. It planned to provide 150 square feet of space per agent and planned to pay each agent for 2,080 hours of work per year. Each center was to house 300 employees.

Building 1 offered a rental rate of one dollar per sf below the rate for Building 2. Building 2 offered a labor rate of one dollar below that of Building 1. Building 1 therefore cost $150 less in real estate per employee per year, given the difference of one dollar in rental rates between the two buildings and given the 150 sf allotted to each agent.

But if the outsourcer occupied Building 2, it would save $2,239 per employee per year in labor costs. The outsourcer determined its savings from the difference of one dollar in labor rates between the two buildings; from the number of work hours per year for which it would pay each agent; and from the lower employment taxes it would incur as the result of its lesser labor costs.

Section 7

The savings that the occupant of Building 2 experienced from the lower labor costs would be significantly greater than the additional amount of money it spent on real estate. Since each building employed 300 agents, the company that bought space in Building 2 would spend a total of $626,700 less than an occupant of Building 1 over the course of a year.

In the above example, a difference of a dollar per hour in labor savings in Building 2 offsets a difference of $14.93/sf in rent in Building 1. In other words, the rental rates in Building 2 could have been far above those in Building 1, yet, because the occupancy of Building 2 paid lower labor rates, it still would have had lower total operating costs than the company that bought space in Building 1.

Excerpt from *Designing the Best Call Center for Your Business* by Brendan B. Read, CMP Books, 2000.

Section 7

2. Legislation Factors [Strategic]

Ready? | 1 | 2 | 3 |

Key Points

- The federal government and some states require companies to maintain do not call (DNC) lists.

- Given widespread CRM strategies and systems, consumer privacy issues should be a key concern.

- The two main regulations affecting outbound call center operations in the United States are the Telephone Consumer Protection Act (TCPA) and the Telemarketing Sales Rule (TSR).

Explanation

DNC Lists and Privacy Concerns

The federal government and some states require companies to maintain do not call (DNC) lists. The Direct Marketing Association maintains nationwide DNC databases for telephone, email and mail.

Because of the widespread use of customer relationship management (CRM) strategies and systems, consumer privacy issues should be a key concern. Consider posting privacy policies on your organization's Web site and incorporating permission-based marketing strategies (i.e., ask customers for permission to contact them with offers, etc.).

TCPA and TSR

Generally, the two main regulations affecting call center operations in the United States are the Telephone Consumer Protection Act (TCPA), administered by the Federal Communications Commission (FCC), and the Telemarketing Sales Rule (TSR), under jurisdiction of the Federal Trade Commission (FTC).

The TCPA requires call centers making outbound sales calls to place prospects on the DNC list if requested. Companies also must have DNC policies and limit the hours agents can place outbound calls (8 a.m. to 9 p.m.). Companies must also disclose contact information (phone number, mailing address). The law also prohibits unsolicited faxing for sales purposes.

The TSR focuses on outbound consumer fraud. Its provisions include:

1. Telesales agents must inform customers the call is a sales call and identify the company before the sales pitch begins.

2. Telemarketers must be up front about promotion details such as total costs, restrictions, odds of winning, final or nonrefundable offers, etc.

3. Agents cannot charge consumers or withdraw funds from their accounts without their express verifiable authorization.

Other legislation includes the 900 Number Rule, which bans the use of toll-free numbers if they lead to charges to callers.

3. The Phases of Design [Strategic]

Ready? | 1 | 2 | 3 |

Key Points

- Generally, there are 10 key steps or phases involved in designing a call center.

- These steps have not changed significantly in recent years, nor will they in the foreseeable future.

Explanation

Generally, there are 10 phases of design that should be followed in designing and occupying a call center. The size of the call center will influence the amount of time spent on each design phase, but no phase should be eliminated. The phases are:

1. **Objectives:** The single, most important design phase is stating the objectives. Key issues to consider and resolve include physical location, call center's application, geographic cover, new building construction vs. leasing, startup date, relationships between phone area and other departments, expectations of callers and how they are fulfilled, current phone positions and future requirements, and support functions required.

2. **Architect selection:** If the organization has an in-house real estate department, this phase will be much easier. However, depending on the size of the call center and its location, managers may need to find an architect in a different city or be forced to use a preselected architectural firm used by an existing office building. The final selection should be based on references, expertise, services offered and price.

3. **Design development:** The frontline agent must be the core of the design process. Interviews with top management, department heads, clerical staff and the various job classifications in the center should be arranged. The results will offer a better understanding of the call center's structure, office standards, office operations, office environment, flow of work/paper and responsibilities/tasks.

4. **Design selection:** Once all concerns are satisfied with the information gathered during the design development phase, the process of designing the physical space will begin. Generally, several sketches are presented to the company and a choice is made.

5. **Blueprints**: Depending on the size of the call center and whether or not the facility will be newly built or a conversion of existing office space, the number of blueprints can range from one to many dozens. Blueprints are generally divided into the following categories: general requirements, site work, concrete, masonry, metals, woods/plastics, thermal/moisture protection, doors/windows, finishes, specialties, equipment, furnishings, special construction, conveying systems, mechanical and electrical.

6. **Construction bids**: Once the blueprints have been verified, the construction bid phase begins. Generally, contractors receiving bids will be referred by the architect.

7. **Contractor selection**: Selection of the contractor should be based on time required for completion, services offered, references and price.

8. **Construction/renovation**: This phase deals not only with the physical space, but with all furnishings and equipment necessary to make the call center fully operational. This phase requires the most patience. Project meetings must be held to review all necessary modifications to the blueprints due to changes in building codes, call center operations changes, utility needs, telecommunications systems and data installation, or office equipment and furniture installation.

9. **Occupancy**: These plans should include all of the stages of occupancy comfort and functions that the organization would be willing to forgo to meet an occupancy deadline.

10. **Post-occupancy**: The post-occupancy phase begins after the staff is moved in. It can last months or years. This is the time to ensure that all fixes by the contractor will not affect the employees' comfort or be disruptive to the incoming call process. Bills need to be paid and all services contracted for are to be maintained without interruption.

Key Areas of Call Center Design

While there is no definitive answer to the question, "What comprises good call center facility design?" there are several essential design factors that experts say contribute substantially to agent performance and profitability:

1. Overall spatial organization. One of the most effective spacial design strategies in call centers today is the grouping, or "teaming," of workstations into functional clusters of agents who work as a team, according to Rick Burkett, principal of BurkettDesign in Denver, Colo. "We recommend organizing workstations into clusters where each member feels like a part of a cohesive, recognizable team, not just one of 500 worker bees. We also recommend lots of coaching stations [located among clustered workstations] so that spontaneous training can occur in a healthy environment."

(continued, next page)

2. Aesthetics. According to KSBA's Kingsland, "…The money that companies think they are saving by not investing in office aesthetics, they lose twice over in terms of agent turnover." Kingsland and Burkett agree that their are infinite options with regard to enhancing call center aesthetics. They say that little things like hanging colorful art/decorations on the walls and placing plants throughout the center go a long way toward creating positive attitudes among agents and fending off burnout. And painting over drab gray walls with cool bluish green hues has been shown to have a calming effect on agents while enhancing mental alertness.

3. Individual workstation organization/ergonomics. The potential increase in productivity aside, call centers simply cannot afford not to take ergonomics seriously. The Occupational Safety and Health Administration (OSHA) has estimated that employers spend roughly $120 billion annually on direct and indirect costs related to poor ergonomics. The good news is that such exorbitant costs can be avoided by making a relatively small investment of time and money in effective workstation design, including:
• Adjustable chairs
• Workstation height between 710mm and 740mm
• Adjustable keyboards
• Wrist rests
• Foot rests

4. Acoustics. While careful space layout, such as that described previously, will help minimize acoustical interference, other measures are often required. Many well-designed call centers, according to Kingsland, attain "acoustic privacy" by introducing partial height screens, highly absorptive ceilings and walls, and "noise-masking" systems. (Noise-masking is the process by which a sound – such as human speech – is masked by a slightly louder sound.)

5. Lighting. Kingsland explains that call centers require two separate though complementary lighting systems: 1) uniform ambient lighting for VDTs, and 2) task-lighting for hard copy reading and writing. "Computer terminals act as mirrors that reflect ceiling glare, causing eyestrain," says Kinglsand. "Therefore, a uniform light level at the ceiling is important."

He says the best ambient lighting system is "indirect lighting." Such systems are usually mounted between 18 and 24 inches below the ceiling, and shine upward. In addition to reducing glare, indirect lighting creates a calming level of lighting throughout the workspace.

6. Special amenities. Companies serious about enhancing agent performance and retention take call center design beyond good lighting, sound and ergonomics. These centers understand the stress agents face day after day on the phones, and thus provide special amenities to help agents cool down and gear up. Such amenities include "quiet rooms" (equipped with comfortable couches/recliners, books and CD players); fitness rooms/centers, employee cafes, and even outdoor perks like volleyball courts and barbecue pits.

Excerpt from "The Grand 'Design': Four Call Centers Built for Success" by Greg Levin, *Call Center Management Review*, October 2002.

4. Determining Space and Workstation Requirements [Strategic]

Ready? | 1 | 2 | 3 |

Key Points

- The size of a facility is typically determined by using a factor of 100 to 150 square feet per workstation.

- A typical sizing approach for calculating the number of agent workstations is to use 90 to 140 square feet per agent.

- The process for determining how many workstations or seats the call center requires comes from the planning and management process used to meet service level and response time objectives.

Explanation

A typical sizing approach for calculating the number of agent workstations is to use 90 to 140 square feet per agent. (Source: *Designing the Best Call Center for Your Business* by Brendan Read, CMP Books, 2000.)

Besides the main call center operating space, the call center manager should also consider the space required for support functions. The pie chart below shows the percentage of space allocated to the call center and its support functions.

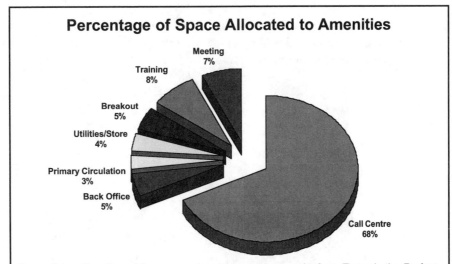

Percentage of Space Allocated to Amenities

Meeting 7%
Training 8%
Breakout 5%
Utilities/Store 4%
Primary Circulation 3%
Back Office 5%
Call Centre 68%

Percentage allocation of floor space based on survey results from Towards the Perfect Call Centre - The Design and Fit Out of the Call Centre Environment, April 2000, ACA Research Pty Ltd, Sydney Australia. Report available at www.callcentres.net.

The process for determining how many workstations or seats the call center requires comes from the planning and management process used to meet service level and response time objectives. (See The Planning and Management Process, Section 3.) Key steps include:

1. **Establish the mission**: Define the call center's role in the organization and the responsibilities it will assume.

2. **Forecast the workload**: Include all channels of contact and look at least three to five years into the future.

3. **Establish service level objectives**: The faster the expected response to the customer, the more resources needed.

4. **Calculate base staff requirements**: Required resources should be determined by using a queuing formula that takes random call arrival into account or through a computer simulation program.

5. **Calculate workstation requirements**: At the busiest point in time, how many agents will need to be at workstations handling the workload? How many additional workstations will be required for supervisors and other support positions?

6. **Repeat the forecast and calculations for alternative scenarios**: Run alternative "what-if" scenarios, and calculate the resources required to handle different possible workloads.

7. **Determine final requirements**: Consider what the consequences will be if the workload is more than expected or less than expected.

It is important to consider the impact of management changes on space requirements. For example, lowering the staff to supervisor ratio will require more supervisor workstations.

5. Floor Plan Design [Strategic]

Ready? | 1 | 2 | 3 |

Key Points

- The average call center worker has half the work space of a typical office worker.

- Workstation designs include delta, single and multiple hexagonal, half-hexagonal, shell and zigzag seating patterns and workgroups.

- The floor design affects the placement of power, voice/data lines and/or heating, ventilation and air conditioning (HVAC), as well as the facility's appearance, costs and ease of change.

Explanation

The support area requirements of the call center will greatly determine traffic patterns and influence interior design. Key support areas include:

- Training room

- Employee facilities

- Administrative support

- Reference library

- Conference room(s)

- Telecommunications/data equipment room

- Reception area

- Facilities for photocopying, mail and file storage

When considering the support area requirements, keep in mind that the quality and placement of employee break rooms can have an effect on overall employee satisfaction. A windowless, cramped break room can often be transformed into a comfortable community room by placing it near the call center entrance (where there are typically windows anyway) and creating a "community center" look and feel.

Workstation Layout and Design

The average call center worker has half the work space of a typical office worker. To keep agents from feeling cooped up and undervalued, managers need to take great care in designing the physical layout of the call center floor.

One of the most effective spatial design strategies in call centers today is the grouping or "teaming" of workstations into functional clusters of agents. Workstations can be organized into clusters where each member feels like a part of a cohesive, recognizable team. Organizing workstations into teams enables agents and supervisors to define their own space and to develop a strong sense of ownership, identity and control. In fact, studies have shown that arranging workstations in groups instead of rows can increase performance.

Workstation designs include delta, single and multiple hexagonal, half-hexagonal, shell and zigzag seating patterns and workgroups. With call centers that need more supervision, rectilinear rows, hub and spoke designs are preferable. Those that require less floor supervision can use the more conventional cube design. However, facility requirements may dictate the use of rows since they take up the least amount of space. Most call centers can operate more efficiently on single floors or floor plates. Besides eliminating the need for supervisors and managers to constantly shuffle between floors, the wiring also can be kept to a single floor.

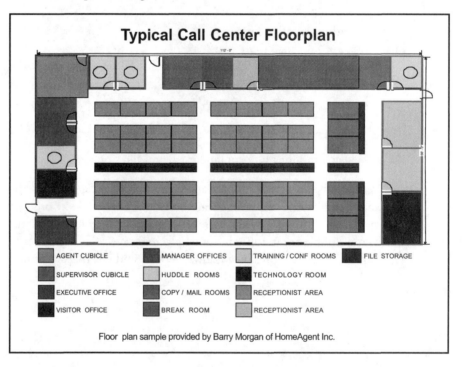

Typical Call Center Floorplan

AGENT CUBICLE	MANAGER OFFICES	TRAINING / CONF ROOMS	FILE STORAGE
SUPERVISOR CUBICLE	HUDDLE ROOMS	TECHNOLOGY ROOM	
EXECUTIVE OFFICE	COPY / MAIL ROOMS	RECEPTIONIST AREA	
VISITOR OFFICE	BREAK ROOM	RECEPTIONIST AREA	

Floor plan sample provided by Barry Morgan of HomeAgent Inc.

Floor Design

The floor design affects the placement of power, voice/data lines and/or HVAC, as well as the facility's appearance, costs and ease of change. The conventional technique is to run HVAC and cabling from ceiling ducts with wires dropping to workstations in poles.

The newer system is raised-access flooring in which a skeletal floor allows cabling and HVAC access to workstations underneath. While raised-access flooring can improve air distribution and offers easy utility access, the facility may also require added ramps to access closets, elevators, stairwells and restrooms (which may require handrails). Raised floors also add 25 percent or more to the leasing price.

Flexibility

Creating as flexible a call center design as possible is important given the dynamic environment in which most centers operate. For example, raised floors, ceiling-mounted indirect lighting, and furniture on wheels contribute to a flexible design. Fixed drywall offices, permanent shelving, and intrusive structural supports (e.g., poles in the middle of a room) limit flexibility.

6. Identifying Health, Safety and Security Issues

Ready? | 1 | 2 | 3 |

Key Points

- Call center leaders have the responsibility to provide a safe and healthy environment for workers.

- The results of a safe and healthy environment include such benefits as:
  - Reduced injuries and occupational illnesses
  - Reduced down time
  - Reduced insurance and workers' compensation costs

- Managers, supervisors and frontline staff must be educated on health, safety and security responsibilities.

Explanation

An organization and its leadership have the responsibility to provide an environment where all workers can operate without injury or occupational illness. This belief must be integrated into the organization and its objectives, at every level. In most organizations, coordination of these issues is important since they are typically handled by more than one manager. When the organization places a high value on the production and comfort of people, the result is a positive culture and staff who tend to reciprocate with high performance.

Other benefits include:

- Reduced injuries and occupational illnesses

- Increased profits

- Reduced down time

- Increased productivity

- Reduced insurance and workers' compensation costs

- Increased employee participation and morale

Managers, supervisors and frontline staff must be provided with the authority and access to relevant information, training and resources they need to carry out health, safety and security responsibilities. Workplace safety and health laws establish regulations that are designed to eliminate personal injuries and illnesses from occurring in the workplace.

7. Lighting and Noise Considerations [Strategic]

Ready? | 1 | 2 | 3 |

Key Points

- Call centers require both uniform ambient lighting for video display terminals (VDTs) and task lighting for hard-copy reading and writing.

- Noise and acoustics are especially important considerations, given the open call center work environment.

- Noise-absorbing workstation partitions, carpeting and ceiling tiles can lower noise levels.

Explanation

Lighting Considerations

Many employee health problems are tied to eye strain caused by lighting that doesn't correspond to the unique requirements of video display terminals (VDTs). Call centers require two separate, though complementary, lighting systems:

1. Uniform ambient lighting for VDTs

2. Task lighting for hard-copy reading and writing

The best ambient lighting system is indirect lighting. Such systems are usually mounted between 18 and 24 inches below the ceiling and shine upward. While natural lighting will help to elevate workers' moods, it also can cause glare and an increased heat load (which can add to cooling costs).

Noise Considerations

Because of the call center's open design, noise and acoustics must be taken into consideration. Given the close proximity of people in call centers, as well as the lower furniture panel heights used, noise problems are compounded. Sound-masking systems reduce noise by emitting a frequency from ceiling speakers that mask the sounds of human voices.

Noise-absorbing workstation partitions, carpeting and ceiling tiles can also lower noise levels. Locating heavy traffic areas away from agent workstations will also

help to keep noise down (doors, time clocks, copiers, fax machines, etc.). Ceilings should be moderately high (10 to 15 feet) to control sound significantly.

Technological advancements in acoustics, plastics and mechanical engineering have enabled manufacturers to make remarkable improvements in the performance and functionality of professional headsets. Good noise-canceling microphones can help immeasurably in blocking out extraneous noise so the customer hears only the agent. An added benefit is the reduction in overall room noise, since agents won't need to speak as loudly to be heard by the customer. (See Individual Comfort and Protection, this section.)

8. Individual Comfort and Protection

Ready? | 1 | 2 | 3 |

Key Points

- Individual workstation design is an important aspect of health and productivity.

- Visual problems stemming from working with monitors can usually be corrected by simply adjusting the settings.

- Headset performance, design and durability are significant contributors to agent health and productivity.

Explanation

Individual Workstation Design

Individual workstation design is just as important as overall spatial organization in the call center. Accommodations should be made for individual workers' comfort, as well. Whenever possible, workers should be able to adjust the temperature of their immediate surroundings – for example, through the use of personal heaters and/or fans.

Other workstation considerations include:

- **Adjustable chairs:** The more adjustable the chair the better. Look for chairs that have seat height adjustments, back adjustments (in both height and tilt) and, preferably, some form of lumbar (lower back) support. The chairs should either have no arms or adjustable arms to ensure that all agents are comfortably seated close to their workstation desk.

- **Workstation height:** The height of the workstation should be around 27 to 29 inches, and the underside of the workstation must be free of any bars or drawers that may obstruct agents' legroom.

- **Adjustable keyboards:** Look for keyboards that tilt and adjust enough for agents to find a comfortable typing position.

- **Wrist rests:** The best wrist rests are those that provide some give, but not too much (such as gel-filled rests). They provide a comfortable feel to wrists in a neutral position without putting undue pressure on the carpal area.

Section 7

Monitors

Visual strain can cause eye strain, headaches, blurred vision, dry or irritated eyes, neck and back aches and other visual disorders. However, visual problems stemming from working with VDTs can usually be corrected by simply adjusting workers' physical work settings. The angle between a computer monitor and the agent's line of vision should be zero degrees – or a maximum angle of 15 degrees below eye level. Agents should not have to look up at all to view the monitor, as this places unnecessary stress on the neck. Monitors with adjustable platforms are ideal. They should be placed 18 to 24 inches from the agent's eyes.

Headsets

Headset performance, design and durability are important contributors to agent productivity. Agents should be able to hear and be heard clearly and feel comfortable in their headsets. Choosing the right headset involves understanding not only how features can benefit the call center, but also how performance factors impact headset investment over time.

Sound quality is one of the most important factors of headset performance. One of the most important measurements of sound quality is "frequency response," or bandwidth capability – the percentage of the telephone voice signal delivered after the sound travels over a local or long distance network. Normally, the network degrades higher frequencies, which gives voice distortion on the receiving end. Therefore, a good headset has a quality microphone that transmits the greatest frequency response, better matching the sound to the original input.

A second factor affecting sound quality is static electricity. As headsets move, they can generate static electricity. Unless the headset has static-resistant components, the static that builds with constant use creates noise on the line. To avoid this, headsets should be designed to resist and eliminate static.

Headset wearers also have a choice of single- or dual-speaker wearing styles:

- **Binaural:** earpiece for both ears

- **Monaural:** earpiece for one ear

In noisy call centers, binaural headsets help the agent to focus on the caller. But not every call center needs binaural; in some call centers, being able to hear surrounding sounds from one ear is important.

9. Primary OSHA Requirements (U.S.)

Ready? | 1 | 2 | 3 |

Key Points

- The main statute protecting the health and safety of workers in the workplace is the Occupational Safety and Health Act (OSHA).

- Under a recent OSHA proposal, about 1.6 million employers would need to implement a basic ergonomics program.

- Section 18 of the Occupational Safety and Health Act of 1970 encourages states to develop and operate their own job safety and health programs. OSHA approves and monitors state plans.

Explanation

Work-related cumulative trauma disorders (CTDs) result when there is a mismatch between the physical capacity of workers and the physical demands of their jobs. Each year 1.8 million workers in the United States report work-related CTDs such as carpal tunnel syndrome, tendinitis and back injuries. The solution to these injuries lies with ergonomics, the science of fitting the job to the worker.

The main statute protecting the health and safety of workers in the workplace is the Occupational Safety and Health Act (OSHA). In November 2000, the Occupational Safety and Health Administration released its Final Ergonomics Program Standard for the workplace. (Whether this program will be enforced is still being debated.) It requires employers to provide employees with basic information about common CTDs and their signs and symptoms.

The proposed OSHA ergonomics program standard relies on a "practical, flexible approach that reflects industry best practices" and focuses on jobs where problems are severe and solutions are well understood. It would require general industry employers to address ergonomics in jobs where employees experience work-related CTDs.

Under the OSHA proposal, about 1.6 million employers would need to implement a basic ergonomics program, including:

- Assigning someone to be responsible for ergonomics.
- Providing information to employees on the risk of injuries, signs and

symptoms to watch for and the importance of reporting problems early.

- Setting up a system for employees to report signs and symptoms and tracking incidents of carpal tunnel syndrome, tendonitis, back injuries, etc.

- Providing training on how to avoid CTDs and individual counseling on ergonomics.

Given the increasing awareness and realities of CTDs and the susceptibility of call center employees to these health risks, it is important for call center managers to stay abreast of legislation, rulings and best practices for protecting employee health. For more information, see www.osha.gov.

Section 7

10. Primary ADA Requirements (U.S.)

Ready? | 1 | 2 | 3 |

Key Points

- The Americans with Disabilities Act (ADA) prohibits discrimination on the basis of disability in employment, state and local government, public accommodations, commercial facilities, transportation and telecommunications.

- To be protected by the ADA, one must have a disability or have a relationship or association with an individual with a disability.

- Under Title I, employers are not required to make existing facilities accessible until a particular applicant or employee with a particular disability needs an accommodation, and then the modifications should meet that individual's work needs.

Explanation

The Americans with Disabilities Act (ADA), administered by the U.S. Department of Justice, prohibits discrimination on the basis of disability in employment, state and local government, public accommodations, commercial facilities, transportation and telecommunications.

To be protected by the ADA, one must have a disability or have a relationship or association with an individual with a disability. An individual with a disability is defined by the ADA as a person who has a physical or mental impairment that substantially limits one or more major life activities, a person who has a history or record of such an impairment, or a person who is perceived by others as having such an impairment. The ADA does not specifically name all of the impairments that are covered.

Title I requires employers with 15 or more employees to provide qualified individuals with disabilities an equal opportunity to benefit from the full range of employment-related opportunities available to others. For example, it prohibits discrimination in recruitment, hiring, promotions, training, pay, social activities and other privileges of employment. It restricts questions that can be asked about an applicant's disability before a job offer is made, and it requires that employers make reasonable accommodation to the known physical or mental limitations of otherwise qualified individuals with disabilities, unless it results in undue hardship.

Section 7

Title I complaints must be filed with the U.S. Equal Employment Opportunity Commission (EEOC) within 180 days of the date of discrimination, or 300 days if the charge is filed with a designated state or local fair employment practice agency. Individuals may file a lawsuit in federal court only after they receive a "right-to-sue" letter from the EEOC.

Architectural Barriers Act (ABA)

The Architectural Barriers Act (ABA) requires that buildings and facilities that are designed, constructed or altered with federal funds, or leased by a federal agency, comply with federal standards for physical accessibility. ABA requirements are limited to architectural standards in new and altered buildings and in newly leased facilities. They do not address the activities conducted in those buildings and facilities.

"Reasonable accommodation" is any modification or adjustment to a job or the work environment that will enable a qualified applicant or employee with a disability to participate in the application process or to perform essential job functions. Reasonable accommodation also includes adjustments to assure that a qualified individual with a disability has rights and privileges in employment equal to those of employees without disabilities.

Examples of reasonable accommodation include making existing facilities used by employees readily accessible to and usable by an individual with a disability; restructuring a job; modifying work schedules; acquiring or modifying equipment; providing qualified readers or interpreters; or appropriately modifying examinations, training or other programs. Reasonable accommodation also may include reassigning a current employee to a vacant position for which the individual is qualified, if the person is unable to do the original job because of a disability even with an accommodation. However, there is no obligation to find a position for an applicant who is not qualified for the position sought. Employers are not required to lower quality or quantity standards as an accommodation, nor are they obligated to provide personal use items such as glasses or hearing aids.

The decision as to the appropriate accommodation must be based on the particular facts of each case. In selecting the particular type of reasonable accommodation to provide, the principle test is that of effectiveness, i.e., whether the accommodation will provide an opportunity for a person with a disability to achieve the same level of performance and to enjoy benefits equal to those of an average, similarly situated person without a disability. However, the accommodation does not have to ensure equal results or provide exactly the same benefits.

An employer is only required to accommodate a "known" disability of a qualified applicant or employee. The requirement generally will be triggered by a request from an individual with a disability, who frequently will be able to suggest appropriate accommodations. The individual with a disability requiring the accommodation must be otherwise qualified, and the disability must be known to the employer. In addition, an employer is not required to make an accommodation if it would impose an "undue hardship" on the operation of the employer's business.

For more information, see www.usdoj.gov/crt/ada/adahom1.htm.

11. Canadian Regulations

Ready? | 1 | 2 | 3 |

Key Points

- Most call centers in Canada fall under the jurisdiction of the provincial labor legislation in their province. Only those call centers in the "federally regulated" sector of the labor force are governed by the federal Labour Program. Federally regulated industries include:
  - Interprovincial and international services such as railways, telephone systems and shipping services
  - Radio and television broadcasting, including cablevision
  - Air transport, aircraft operations, and aerodromes
  - Banks
  - Undertakings for the protection and preservation of fisheries as a natural resource
  - Other undertakings declared by Parliament to be for the general advantage of Canada

- Occupational Health and Safety (OHS) Regulations and the Employment Equity Act cover health, safety, security and disability issues for federally regulated industries. Those industries who are not federally regulated should consult their Provincial Labor Department for similar guidelines.

Explanation

Most call centers in Canada fall under the jurisdiction of the provincial labor legislation in their province. Only those call centers in the "federally regulated" sector of the labor force are governed by the federal Labour Program. This is approximately 10% of the labor force. The rest of the labor force falls under provincial jurisdiction.

The activities that come within federal jurisdiction include:

- Interprovincial and international services such as railways, telephone systems and shipping services

- Radio and television broadcasting, including cablevision

- Air transport, aircraft operations, and aerodromes

- Banks

- Undertakings for the protection and preservation of fisheries as a natural resource

- Other undertakings declared by Parliament to be for the general advantage of Canada

Most federal Crown corporations, such as the Canada Mortgage and Housing Corporation and Canada Post Corporation, are covered by federal legislation. The Government of Canada has stated, however, that the minimum standards of the Code will be met in the public service as a matter of policy.

In most cases, the above guidelines should indicate whether your call center is covered by federal or provincial legislation. However, you may need to contact your Labour Affairs Officer in order to determine if you are covered by federal or provincial legislation.

Canada Labour Code

Most public sector and designated private sector organizations, regardless of geographic location, are governed by a comprehensive set of regulations called the Canada Labour Code. This is approximately only 10 percent of the labor force. The Canada Labour Code details the required guidelines for dealing with the minimum age for employment, hours of work and overtime pay, minimum wages, part-time employees, equal pay, the weekly rest-day, general holidays with pay, annual vacations with pay, parental leave, sexual harassment and individual and group terminations of employment.

In most cases, the above guidelines should indicate whether your call center is covered by federal, territorial or provincial legislation.

Companies not included under the jurisdiction of the Canada Labour Code are not required to comply with the specifics of the code and are governed by territorial and provincial labor regulations based on their geographic location. For more information regarding individual territory and province legislation visit www.hrdc-crhc.gc.ca/.

Occupational Health and Safety (OHS) Regulations

Canada's Occupational Health and Safety (OHS) Regulations are intended to prevent accidents and injury to health in the course of employment. Three fundamental rights of workers underlie the legislation:

Section 7

- The right to know about known or foreseeable hazards in the workplace

- The right to participate in identifying and resolving job-related safety and health problems

- The right to refuse dangerous work if the employee has reasonable cause to believe that a situation constitutes a danger to him/herself or to another employee

The OHS Regulations only apply to federally regulated industries. Most provinces have similar guidelines to govern local employers. Contact your Provincial Labour Department for further information.

The Employment Equity Act

The Employment Equity Act was enacted in 1986. It applies to federally regulated employers with 100 or more employees. The purpose of the legislation is to ensure that employers achieve a workforce that is equitable and representative of four designated groups – women, Aboriginal peoples, members of visible minorities, and persons with disabilities. Employers are required to develop and implement employment equity plans and programs, and to report annually to Human Resources Development Canada on their progress in achieving a representative workforce.

For provincial guidelines concerning equity and disability concerns, contact your Provincial Labour Department.

Note: The information above was compiled from Human Resources Canada, http://employers.gc.ca/. It is provided as an overview of the material and should not be used to create organizational policies. Contact your organization's legal counsel for specific guidance on these issues.

12. Elements of Protection and Recovery

Ready? | 1 | 2 | 3 |

Key Points

- Disaster recovery plans will not work unless people are trained on what to do.

- Duplicate and backup services should be considered, as feasible.

- Protecting service level is a disaster recovery requirement unique to call centers.

Explanation

Call centers should consider the following major areas for protection and recovery plans:

- **Facilities protection:** If possible, secure an alternate disaster site, whether or not the call center is a stand-alone or multisite center. Ensure that potential threats and risks are carefully and realistically identified, such as fire, flood, power losses, etc. Call center staff should be aware of the location of all exits at the facility, and evacuation plans should be visibly posted in each site.

- **Network and systems protection:** Identify how systems will behave if a key component goes down (e.g., what happens to calls when the CTI link fails). Ensure that the facility has adequate backup power and processors (telephony and other mission critical systems). Provide for alternate long distance, local and Internet services and provider coverage.

  Regular record-keeping and backup is critical to prevention. Records should include information such as wiring runs, system and network reconfiguration procedures, lists of alternate systems announcements, and home and mobile contact numbers of key people. Key information and database files should be regularly backed up and stored both onsite and offsite.

- **People protection:** Develop evacuation plans to ensure safe removal of call center staff. Plans must be published and continually tested and updated.

- **Service level protection:** Develop plans to reroute calls within an acceptable timeframe for the business. Identify potential threats and develop the ability to reprogram telephony and IVR systems onsite or from a remote location.

The essentials of protecting service level include:

- Identifying potential threats

- Developing escalation priorities

- Determining economic threat (See Calculating the Cost of Being Out of Business, this section.)

- Identifying preventive measures (See What Disaster Plans Cover, this section.)

13. What Disaster Plans Cover

Ready? | 1 | 2 | 3 |

Key Points

- The purpose of a disaster recovery plan is to avoid or recover quickly from interruptions in call center operations.

- Disaster recovery plans should include:
  - Facilities
  - Networks
  - People
  - Service levels

Explanation

The purpose of a disaster recovery plan is to enable managers to avoid or recover expediently from an interruption in the center's operation. Comprehensive plans should include an approved set of arrangements and procedures for:

- Facilities

- Networks

- People

- Service levels

(See Elements of Protection and Recovery, this section.)

When developing a disaster recovery plan, managers should consider the following questions:

- If the call center is incapacitated, can the business survive?

- Which areas of the operation are mission critical?

- Can staff react quickly and accurately to business interruptions?

- What contingencies are needed to ensure the call center achieves timely resumption of critical business functionality?

Steps to Creating the Plan

There are several fundamental steps to creating an effective disaster recovery plan:

1. Secure the support of senior management for the time, resources and money required to create the plan.

2. Form a disaster recovery team.

3. Identify threats and potential loss of business.

4. Develop and begin documentation for the plan.

5. Test and update the plan often.

6. Provide easy access to the plan on- and off-site and establish criteria for what constitutes a disaster and how to communicate that to staff.

Typical Solutions

Typical disaster recovery solutions include:

- **Remote sites**: Facilities that can provide duplicate services.

- **Service bureaus**: Companies that are prepared to handle the organization's calls in the event of a crisis.

- **Reciprocal agreements**: Arrangements between companies to provide backup services for each other.

- **Multiple data centers**: Centers that provide data redundancy.

- **Redundant network facilities**: Contracting with multiple carriers to provide long distance services. This may also involve established multiple service entry points into the facility and may include alternative channels (e.g., satellite and fiber), sometimes termed dual network routing plan.

- **Multiple pre-recorded announcements**: Having announcements pre-recorded (e.g., "we are currently experiencing technical difficulties") that can be deployed immediately.

When an actual disaster occurs, the most important first step in any plan is to declare an emergency. This requires knowing ahead of time what would constitute an emergency and trigger the subsequent disaster plan. Other steps to take once the disaster occurs include:

- Record an advisory delay announcement (or activate a pre-recorded announcement)

- Ensure back-up routing is functioning properly

- Reforecast the work and required staff

- Identify agents that are available to help

Section 7
Facilities and Disaster Recovery

14. Calculating the Cost of Being Out of Business [Strategic]

Ready? | 1 | 2 | 3 |

Key Points

- Calculating the impact of being out of business provides context and guidance to developing disaster recovery plans.

- In revenue-producing environments, the cost of being out of business is easy to put into economic terms.

- Factors other than revenue that should be considered include:
  - Direct loss of productivity
  - Indirect loss of productivity
  - The impacts on the queue, telecom and handling time

Explanation

Calculating the impact of being out of business for a specific amount of time will provide managers with a benchmark against which to assess the costs of varying levels of redundancy and backup. It will also help them to position the call center within the context of the organization's priorities (e.g., which areas get restored first).

If the call center operates in a sales-oriented industry, a revenue-to-call ratio can be used to calculate the cost of being out of business. For example, a call center that typically receives 100 calls in an hour, and generates, on average, $20 per call, can expect to lose $2,000 in revenue for an hour of down time. (See Average Call Value, Section 4.)

However, revenue-to-call ratios alone won't illustrate the full impact of inaccessibility, especially for those centers in supporting roles (such as help desks, customer service centers, etc.). For a more accurate assessment of outages, the following should be considered:

- **Direct lost productivity**: Without inbound contacts, pure inbound centers will have agents sitting idle. Lost productivity can be directly translated to a dollar amount. If a center is closed for several days, or unable to open, any people costs (benefits, pay, etc.) should be included.

Section 7

- **Indirect lost productivity:** In some cases, agents are moved to non-inbound call center activities during down times. Ultimately, there will be some inefficiencies that will need to be considered, e.g., nonphone work completed by agents not scheduled to perform that type of activity will result in excess capacity.

- **Impact to the queue, telecommunications and handle time:** Customers (internal or external) will normally call back once service has resumed resulting in heavy volumes that require additional staff to maintain service levels.

- **Customer defections and loss of customer confidence:** For most commercial organizations, this is the greatest potential risk, long term. While facilities can be restored and service levels reestablished, winning back customers is potentially much more difficult.

Facilities and Disaster Recovery Exercises

Exercises

Site Selection Considerations [Strategic]

1. Answer the following questions.

    a. What is the most important site selection criteria?

    b. What does the acronym EDA refer to?

    c. What percentage of a call center's operation costs are typically telecommunications expenses?

    d. What percentage are typically labor related?

(continued, next page)

Section 7

Legislation Factors [Strategic]

2. Fill in the blanks to complete each sentence.

   a. The acronym TCPA refers to the _____ _____ _____
      Act.

   b. The TCPA requires call centers making outbound sales calls to place
      prospects on the _____ list if requested. Companies must also
      limit the hours agents can place outbound calls (_____ a.m. to
      _____ p.m.).

   c. The acronym TSR refers to the _____ _____
      Rule.

   d. The TSR provisions include: 1) Telesales agents must inform customers
      the call is a _____ call and identify the company before the sales
      pitch begins. 2) Telemarketers must be up front about promotion details
      such as total costs, restrictions, odds of winning, final or nonrefundable
      offers, etc. 3) Agents cannot charge consumers or withdraw funds from
      their accounts without their express verifiable _____.

Determining Space and Workstation Requirements [Strategic]

3. Select the most appropriate answer to the question:

   A typical sizing approach for calculating space requirements is to use:

   a. 70 to 90 square feet per agent.

   b. 90 to 140 square feet per agent.

   c. 140 to 190 square feet per agent.

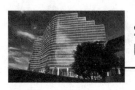

Floor Plan Design [Strategic]

4. Indicate whether the statement typically applies to call centers requiring more supervision (with "more") or less supervision (with "less").

_____ Rectilinear rows, hub and spoke designs are preferable.

_____ Can effectively use conventional cube design.

5. Indicate whether the statement typically applies to the conventional floor design of dropping wires from the ceiling (with "conventional") or raised access flooring (with "raised").

_____ Often improves air distribution.

_____ Offers easy utility access.

_____ Often requires added ramps to access closets, elevators, stairwells and restrooms.

_____ Usually the cheaper alternative initially.

Lighting and Noise Considerations [Strategic]

6. Select the most appropriate answer to the question:

Which type of lighting is best for video display terminals (VDTs)?

   a. Uniform ambient lighting

   b. Task lighting

   c. Natural lighting (although it can drive up cooling costs)

To help reduce noise in the call center, how high should ceilings be?

   a. 8 to 10 feet

   b. 10 to 15 feet

   c. 15 to 25 feet

Section 7

Primary OSHA Requirements and Primary ADA Requirements

7. What do the following acronyms represent?

   a. ABA   Architectural Barriers Act

   b. ADA   American disabilities Act

   c. CTD   Cumalative Trauma Disordes

   d. EEOC   Equal Employment Opportunity Commission

   e. OSHA   Occupational

8. True or false.

   _____T_____ Title I requires employers with 50 or more employees to provide qualified individuals with disabilities an equal opportunity to benefit from the full range of employment-related opportunities available to others.

   _____F_____ Under Title I, employers are required to make existing facilities accessible regardless of cost.

Calculating the Cost of Being Out of Business [Strategic]

9. True or False

   _____ When a call center has been out of business and service is restored, call traffic tends to be higher than normal.

   _____ In sales environments, revenue-to-call ratios illustrate the full impact of inaccessibility.

Answers to these exercises are in Section 10.

Note: These exercises are intended to help you retain the material learned. While not the exact questions as on the CIAC Certification assessment, the material in this handbook/study guide fully addresses the content on which you will be assessed. For a formal practice test, please contact the CIAC directly by visiting www.ciac-cert.org.

Facilities and Disaster Recovery
Reference Bibliography

Related Articles from *Call Center Management Review* (See Section 9)

Success Begins before the Call: Choosing a Call Center Location

Call Center Location: Costs Rule the Site Selection Process

Effective Call Center Design Can Help Drive Agent Performance

Create a Pleasant, Productive Environment that will Boost Agent Retention

Headset Selection: Key Performance Factors to Check Out Before Buying

On Disasters, Plans and Responsibilities

For Further Study

Books

Read, Brendan. *Designing the Best Call Center for Your Business : A Complete Guide for Location, Services, Staffing, and Outsourcing.* CMP Books, 2000.

Articles

Levin, Greg. "The Grand 'Design': Four Call Centers Built for Success." *Call Center Management Review*, October 2002.

Web Sites

The Summit Circuit
http://www.mwprod.com

Site Selection
http://www.siteselection.com

Kingsland Scott Bauer Associates
http://www.ksba.com

Disaster-Resource.com
http://www.disaster-resource.com

Rothstein Associates Inc.
http://www.rothstein.com

Occupational Safety and Health Administration
http://www.osha.gov

Americans with Disabilities Act
http://www.usdoj.gov/crt/ada/adahom1.htm

Human Resources Canada
http://employers.gc.ca

Section 7

Glossary

Acronyms

ACD	Automatic Call Distributor
ACS	Automatic Call Sequencer
ACW	After Call Work
AHT	Average Handling Time
AHT	Average Holding Time on Trunks
ANI	Automatic Number Identification
API	Applications Programming Interface
ARU	Audio Response Unit
ASA	Average Speed of Answer
ASP	Application Service Provider
ASR	Automatic Speech Recognition
ATA	Average Time to Abandonment
ATB	All Trunks Busy
BIC	Best In Class
BRI	Basic Rate Interface
CCR	Customer Controlled Routing
CCS	Centum Call Seconds
CED	Caller Entered Digits
CIS	Customer Information System (also Customer Interaction Software)
CLI	Calling Line Identity
CO	Central Office
CORBA	Common Object Request Broker Architecture
CPE	Customer Premises Equipment
CRM	Customer Relationship Management
CTI	Computer Telephony Integration
DAT	Digital Audio Tape
DDE	Dynamic Data Exchange
DID	Direct Inward Dialing
DN	Dialed Number

DNIS	Dialed Number Identification Service
DTMF	Dual-tone Multifrequency
ERP	Enterprise Resource Planning
EWT	Expected Wait Time
FX	Foreign Exchange Line
GOS	Grade of Service
GUI	Graphical User Interface
HTML	Hyper Text Markup Language
ICR	Intelligent Character Recognition
IP	Internet Protocol
IS	Information Systems
ISDN	Integrated Services Digital Network
ISP	Internet Service Provider
IT	Information Technology
IVR	Interactive Voice Response
IWR	Interactive Web Response
JTAPI	Java Telephony Applications Programming Interface
IXC	Inter Exchange Carrier
LAN	Local Area Network
LEC	Local Exchange Carrier
LED	Light Emitting Diode
MAC	Moves, Adds and Changes
MIS	Management Information System
NCC	Network Control Center
NPA	Numbering Plan Area
OCR	Optical Character Recognition
ODBC	Open Database Connectivity
OLAP	Online Analytical Processing
OLE	Object Linking and Embedding
PABX	Private Automatic Branch Exchange
PBX	Private Branch Exchange
POP3	Post Office Protocol 3
PRI	Primary Rate Interface
PSN	Public Switched Network
PSTN	Public Switched Telephone Network
PUC	Public Utility Commission

RAN	Recorded Announcement Route
RISC	Reduced Instruction Set Computing
RFI	Request for Information
RFP	Request for Proposal
RFQ	Request for Quote
RSF	Rostered Staff Factor
SFA	Salesforce Automation
SMDI	Simplified Message Desk Interface
SMTP	Simple Mail Transfer Protocol
SOHO	Small Office Home Office
SQL	Structured Query Language
SS7	Signaling System 7
TAPI	Telephony Applications Programming Interface
TCP/IP	Transmission Control Protocol/Internet Protocol
TSAPI	Telephony Services Application Programming Interface
TSF	Telephone Service Factor
TSR	Telephone Sales or Service Representative
UCD	Uniform Call Distributor
VOIP/VoIP	Voice Over Internet Protocol
VRU	Voice Response Unit
WAN	Wide Area Network
WATS	Wide Area Telecommunications Service
WFMS	Workforce Management System
WWW	World Wide Web
XML	Extensible Markup Language

Section 8

Glossary

Abandoned Call. Also called a Lost Call. The caller hangs up before reaching an agent.

Active X. A set of technologies developed by Microsoft generally related to Internet capabilities. ActiveX was born out of two technologies, OLE (Object Linking and Embedding – see OLE) and COM (Component Object Model – see COM) which are used for desktop exchange of information between applications.

Active X Controls. A Web-enabled Windows application. Most commonly used over the Web in the form of downloadable applications similar to Java "applets." Active X Controls can be Visual Basic and C++ as well as Scripting languages. Typically used to 'webify' existing client/server applications.

Adherence To Schedule. A general term that refers to how well agents adhere to their schedules. Can include both: a) how much time they were available to take calls during their shifts, including the time spent handling calls and the time spent waiting for calls to arrive (also called Availability); and b) when they were available to take calls (also called Compliance or Adherence). See Real-Time Adherence Software and Occupancy.

After-Call Work (ACW). Also called Wrapup and Post-Call Processing (PCP). Work that is necessitated by and immediately follows an inbound transaction. Often includes entering data, filling out forms and making outbound calls necessary to complete the transaction. The agent is unavailable to receive another inbound call while in this mode.

Agent. The person who handles incoming or outgoing calls. Also referred to as customer service representative (CSR), telephone sales or service representative (TSR), rep, associate, consultant, engineer, operator, technician, account executive, team member, customer service professional, staff member, attendant and specialist.

Agents. See Average Number of Agents.

Agent Features: Features on the switch specific to the needs of a call center agent. Typically include login/logout, changes to work states (available, not available/not ready, after-call work/wrapup), transaction codes, supervisor assistance request, audio trouble indication, call trace indicator (for malicious calls) and queue status.

Agent Group. Also called Split, Gate, Queue or Skills Group. A collection of agents who share a common set of skills, such as being able to handle customer complaints.

Agent Out Call. An outbound call placed by an agent.

Agent Status. The mode an agent is in (Talk Time, After-Call Work, Unavailable, etc.).

All Trunks Busy (ATB). When all trunks are busy in a specified trunk group. Generally, reports indicate how many times all trunks were busy, and how much total time all trunks were busy. What they don't reveal is how many callers got busy signals when all trunks were busy.

Analog. Telephone transmission or switching that is not digital. Signals are analogous to the original signal.

Announcement. A recorded verbal message played to callers.

Answer Supervision. The signal sent by the ACD or other device to the local or long-distance carrier to accept a call. This is when billing for either the caller or the call center will begin, if long-distance charges apply.

Answered Call. When referring to an agent group, a call counted as answered when it reaches an agent.

Application-Based Routing and Reporting. The ACD capability to route and track transactions by type of call or application (e.g., sales, service, etc.) vs. the traditional method of routing and tracking by trunk group and agent group.

Applications Programming Interface (API). A defined set of programming commands that specify a set of actions that can be initiated by a program or application. It allows an application developer access to the capabilities of a specific system without having to understand the details of how it functions. For example, PBX vendors provide APIs so that third party applications can perform additional call-routing functions.

Application Service Provider (ASP). An outsourcing business that hosts software applications at its own facilities. Customers "rent" the applications, usually for a monthly fee. Applications are usually accessed via the Internet.

Architecture. The basic design of a system. Determines how the components work together, system capacity, upgradeability and the ability to integrate with other systems.

Audiotex. A voice-processing capability that enables callers to automatically access pre-recorded announcements. See Voice Processing.

Auto Available. An ACD feature whereby the ACD is programmed to automatically put agents into available state after they finish talking and disconnect calls. If agents need to go into after-call work, they must manually put themselves in this state.

Auto Greeting. Agent's pre-recorded greeting that plays automatically when a call arrives.

Auto Wrapup. An ACD feature whereby the ACD is programmed to automatically put agents into after-call work after they finish talking and disconnect calls. When agents complete any after-call work, they put themselves back into available mode. See Manual Available.

Automated Attendant. A voice-processing capability that automates the operator/receptionist function. Callers are prompted to respond to menu choices by entering digits on their telephone, and their call is routed based upon the selected menu choices. This function can reside in an onsite system (e.g., switch, voicemail or IVR) or in the network.

Automatic Call Distribution/Distributor (ACD). A software application that routes incoming telephone calls. At its most basic, the ACD usually routes calls based on the trunk group of the call or the number the caller dialed (see DNIS) to the longest available agent in a group; it "queues" calls when there is no agent available – usually on a first-in/first-out basis. ACDs can also provide announcements or options to callers while they are in queue, route based on conditional parameters (see Conditional Routing), and route based on agent skills (see Skills-Based Routing). Some provide basic prompting capabilities as well. Most ACDs provide reporting capabilities either as a part of the ACD software or an add-on package. May be a stand-alone system, or ACD capability built into a Central Office, network, LAN or PBX.

Automatic Call Sequencer (ACS). A simple system that is less sophisticated than an ACD, but provides some ACD-like functionality.

Automatic Number Identification (ANI). An enhanced network service offering that provides the calling party's telephone billing number. Often used for caller identification in applications such as IVR, screen pops and intelligent routing.

Auxiliary Work State. An agent work state that is typically not associated with handling telephone calls. When agents are in an auxiliary mode, they will not receive inbound calls.

Automatic Speech Recognition (ASR). A technology that allows people to interface with phone switches, computers, and voice response units using spoken language. Also referred to as Advanced Speech Recognition.

Availability. See Adherence to Schedule.

Available State. Agents who are signed on to the ACD and waiting for calls to arrive.

Available Time. The total time that an agent or agent group waited for calls to arrive, for a given time period.

Average Delay. See Average Speed of Answer.

Average Delay of Delayed Calls. The average delay of calls that are delayed. It is the total Delay for all calls divided by the number of calls that had to wait in queue. See Average Speed of Answer.

Average Handle Time (AHT). The sum of Average Talk Time and Average After-Call Work for a specified time period.

Average Holding Time on Trunks (AHT). The average time inbound transactions occupy the trunks. It is: (Talk Time + Delay Time)/Calls Received. AHT is also an acronym for Average Handling Time, which has a different meaning.

Average Number of Agents. The average number of agents logged into a group for a specified time period.

Average Speed of Answer (ASA). Also called Average Delay. The average delay of all calls. It is total Delay divided by total number of calls. See Average Delay of Delayed Calls.

Average Time to Abandonment. The average time that callers wait in queue before abandoning. The calculation considers only the calls that abandon.

Back-Office Applications. Business applications that encompass functions that are "behind the scenes" to a customer such as finance, accounting, inventory control, purchasing and production. Often associated with enterprise resource planning (ERP) systems.

Base Staff. Also called Seated Agents. The minimum number of agents required to achieve service level and response time objectives for given period of time. Seated agent calculations assume that agents will be "in their seats" for the entire period of time. Therefore, schedules need to add in extra people to accommodate breaks, absenteeism and other factors that will keep agents from the phones. See Rostered Staff Factor.

Basic Rate Interface (BRI). One of the two levels of ISDN service. A BRI line provides two voice-grade channels, known as "bearer" channels, which can be used for voice and/or data (data on BRI bearer channels is limited to speeds of 56 kbps) and one data channel for signaling. This configuration is commonly referred to as 2B+D. See Integrated Services Digital Network.

Beep Tone. An audible notification that a call has arrived (also called Zip Tone). Beep tone can also refer to the audible notification that a call is being monitored.

Benchmark. Historically, a term referred to as a standardized task to test the capabilities of devices against each other. In quality terms, benchmarking is comparing products, services and processes with those of other organizations, to identify new ideas and improvement opportunities.

Best-in-Class. A term to identify organizations that outperform all others in a specified category.

Blockage. Callers blocked from entering a queue. See Blocked Call.

Blocked Call. A call that cannot be connected immediately because: a) No circuit is available at the time the call arrives, or b) the ACD is programmed to block calls from entering the queue when the queue backs up beyond a defined threshold.

Business Rules: A phrase used to refer to various software controls that manage contact routing, handling or follow up. Often used interchangeably with workflow.

Busy Hour. A telephone traffic engineering term, referring to the hour of time in which a trunk group carries the most traffic during the day. The average busy hour reflects the average over a period of days, such as two weeks. Busy Hour has little use for incoming call centers, which require more specific resource calculation methodologies.

Call. Also called Transaction and Customer Contact. A term referring to telephone calls, video calls, Web calls and other types of contacts.

Call Blending. Traditionally, the ability to dynamically allocate call center agents to both inbound and outbound calling, based on conditions in the call center and programmed parameters. This enables a single agent to handle both inbound and outbound calls from the same position, without manually monitoring call activity and reassigning the position. The outbound dialing application monitors inbound calling activity and assigns outbound agents to handle inbound calls as inbound volume increases, and assigns inbound agents to outbound calling when the inbound volume drops off. Note: Call blending has evolved to also refer to blending calls with nonphone work, or handling contacts from different channels (e.g., email and phone).

Section 8

Call-By-Call Routing. The process of routing each call to the optimum destination according to real-time conditions. See Percent Allocation and Network Inter-flow.

Call Center. An umbrella term that generally refers to groups of agents handling reservations, help desks, catalog order functions, information lines or customer service, regardless of how they are organized or what types of transactions they handle. Characteristics of a call center generally include:

- Calls go to a group of people, not a specific person. In other words, agents are cross-trained to handle a variety of transactions.

- An ACD system is used to distribute calls among agents, put calls in queue when all agents are occupied, and play messages while callers are in queue.

- Call centers use advanced network services (e.g., 800 and 888 services) and most use voice-processing capabilities.

- Agents have quick access to current information via specialized database programs (status of customer accounts, products, services and other information).

- Management challenges include forecasting calls, calculating staffing requirements, organizing sensible schedules, managing the environment in real time and getting the right people in the right places at the right times.

ICMI has defined call center as "A coordinated system of people, processes, technologies, and strategies that provide access to organizational resources through appropriate channels of communication to enable interactions that create value for the customer and organization."

Call Control Variables. The set of criteria the ACD uses to process calls. Examples include routing criteria, overflow parameters, recorded announcements and timing thresholds.

Call Detail Recording. Data on each call, captured and stored by the ACD. Can include trunk used, time in queue, call duration, agent who handled the call, number dialed (for outgoing) and other information.

Call Forcing. An ACD feature that automatically delivers calls to agents who are available and ready to take calls. Agents hear a notification that the call has arrived (e.g., a beep tone), but do not have to press a button to answer the call. Also known as "pushing" calls.

Callback Information Capture. Gathering information about a caller to be used in callbacks. Passive capture is done without the caller's knowledge; for example, capturing ANI from abandoned calls. Active capture requests the caller to enter callback information through a voice response system, switch prompting, interactive Web page or voicemail message. Callbacks are then logged and delivered to agents, either through automatically queuing the callbacks to available agents or by providing the callback messages to agents for them to dial.

Call Load. Also referred to as Workload. Call Load is the product of (Average Talk Time + Average After-Call Work) x call volume, for a given period.

Caller ID. See Automatic Number Identification.

Caller Entered Digits (CED). The digits that a caller enters on their telephone keypad. Primarily used in auto attendant, voice response and CTI applications.

Calling Line Identity (CLI). See Automatic Number Identification.

Calls In Queue. A real-time report that refers to the number of calls received by the ACD system but not yet connected to an agent.

Carrier. A company that provides telecommunications circuits. Carriers include both local telephone companies (or Local Exchange Carriers – LECs) and long-distance providers (or Inter-Exchange Carriers – IXCs).

Case-Based Reasoning. Business application that aids the user in analyzing and resolving problems based on a record of cases that are recorded in the database. New cases are dynamically added to the database as additional problems are resolved or resolved in new ways. Includes functions such as problem analysis, problem resolution and case addition. Typically used in technical support areas to help technicians quickly identify previous or similar instances of a problem and identify the most likely steps for resolution.

Cause-and-Effect Diagram. A tool to assist in root-cause identification, developed by Dr. Kaoru Ishikawa.

Central Office (CO). Can refer to either a telephone company switching center or the type of telephone switch used in a telephone company switching center. The local central office receives calls from within the local area and either routes them locally or passes them to an inter-exchange carrier (IXC). On the receiving end, the local central office receives calls that originated in other areas, from the IXC.

Centrex. A central office telephone switch service that serves a defined geographic area. Similar to a PBX, except that it is owned by the local telephone company and is used by multiple business and/or residential customers.

Centum Call Seconds (CCS). 100 call seconds, a unit of telephone traffic measurement. The first C is the Roman numeral for 100. 1 hour = 1 Erlang = 60 minutes = 36 CCS.

Circuit. A transmission path between two points in a network.

Circuit Switching. A method of transferring information across a network by establishing an available path ("circuit") and using that path for the entire period of connection. Typically used to transmit voice (e.g., over the PSTN).

Client. Usually refers to the client in a client/server environment. The client is a computer or computer application that has access to services (data, software) over a network from a server application. See Thin Client and Thick Client.

Client/Server Architecture. A networking scheme in which a client application requests information from a server application. The server application processes the request and delivers the requested information back to the client application. See Client and Server.

Collateral Duties. Nonphone tasks (e.g., data entry) that are flexible, and can be scheduled for periods when call load is slow.

Common Causes. Causes of variation that are inherent to a process over time. They cause the rhythmic, common variations in the system of causes, and they affect every outcome of the process and everyone working in the process. See Special Causes.

Common Object Request Broker Architecture (CORBA). A programming construct that utilizes object-oriented programming.

Communications Server. An alternative to the PBX that manages and routes voice, fax, Web and video communications within a single server. Typically based on a Windows NT platform. Communications Servers are generally seen in small to medium (five to 75 agents) size contact centers that can benefit from an integrated solution that otherwise would be cost-prohibitive as separate point solutions (e.g., IVR, ACD, CTI).

Compliance. See Adherence to Schedule.

Component Object Model (COM). A Microsoft term describing the base model used for building components in an object-oriented programming language.

Computer Simulation. A computer technique to predict the outcome of various events in the future, given many variables. When there are many variables, simulation is often the only way to reasonably predict the outcome.

Computer Telephony Integration (CTI). The functional integration of various computer and telephone system elements that enables voice and data networks to work together and share information. CTI enables a number of useful call center applications, including screen pops, intelligent routing, cradle-to-grave reporting and voice/data transfer.

Conditional Routing. Intelligently routing calls to the right groups(s), position or treatment (e.g., announcements, music, options) based on current call center conditions, defined time/day parameters, information on the call or caller type, or other parameters. Implemented through routing tables and decision trees.

Contact Management. Business application that creates a record of and tracks each contact made with the customer. Also provides contact history information. Creates a database that enables informed communications with customers, database marketing and proactive communications. Includes functions such as contact history database and triggers for followup contacts.

Continuous Improvement. The ongoing improvement of processes.

Control Chart. A control chart sifts out (identifies) two types of variation in a process, common causes and special causes. See Common Causes and Special Causes.

Controlled Busies. The capability of the ACD to generate busy signals when the queue backs up beyond a programmable threshold.

Coordinated Voice/Data Conference. A CTI application that provides the ability to conference a data screen along with a voice call, enabling both parties on the conference to view information about the caller. The computer application coordinates information regarding the call type, caller and destination of the voice call, and delivers the proper data screen to its destination. The conference can be initiated from the telephone or from a PC.

Coordinated Voice/Data Consultation. A CTI application similar to Coordinated Voice/Data Conference, except that the caller is put on hold while the originally called party consults with a colleague.

Coordinated Voice/Data Delivery (also called Screen Pop). A CTI application that delivers an incoming voice call to an agent at the same time as a data screen about the calling party. The call type or purpose is generally identified through DNIS or a prompt selection. The caller may be identified through information such as ANI or customer-entered digits (account number, social security number, etc.). The computer application coordinates the information received from the switch about the call type, caller and destination of the voice call and delivers the proper data screen to its destination as the voice call arrives.

Coordinated Voice/Data Transfer. A CTI application similar to Coordinated Voice/Data Conference, except that the voice call and the data are transferred to a colleague. Often used when transferring a call from an IVR to an agent position with a screen pop.

Cost Center. An accounting term that refers to a department or function in the organization that does not generate profit. See Profit Center.

Cost of Delay. The money you pay to queue callers, assuming you have toll-free service.

Cost Per Call. Total costs (fixed and variable) divided by total calls for a given period of time.

Customer Contact. See Call.

Customer Information System (CIS). An application and database or series of linked databases that enables users to view and interact with all the available information about a customer's relationship with the company, including their transactions with each department in the enterprise. See Customer Relationship Management.

Customer Interaction Software. Another name for Customer Information System (see above).

Customer Relationship Management (CRM). The process of holistically managing a customer's relationship with a company. It takes into account their history as a customer, the depth and breadth of their business with the company, as well as other factors. CRM generally uses a sophisticated applications and database system that includes elements of Data Mining, Contact Management and Enterprise Resource Planning, allowing agents and analysts to know and anticipate customer behavior better. (There are many terms being used for CRM. It is also referred to as eCRM, eRM, ERM, EIM and BRM, and other combinations, where the small "e" refers to electronic, the large "E" refers to enterprise, the "I" refers to Interaction, and the "B" refers to Business.)

Data-Directed Routing. Call (or other media type) routing which is controlled by information in a database. For example, a caller will be automatically routed to a collections group if his account is past due.

Database Call Handling. A CTI application whereby the ACD works in sync with the database computer to process calls, based on information in the database. For example, a caller inputs digits into a voice-processing system, the database retrieves information on that customer and then issues instructions to the ACD on how to handle the call (e.g., where to route the call, what priority the call should be given in queue, the announcements to play, etc.).

Datamart. A subset of a data warehouse, typically with data that is of interest to a particular department of an organization.

Data Mining. The use of sophisticated analysis tools, such as OLAP, to identify patterns within one or more databases (usually data from a Data Warehouse). For example, data mining can be used to identify that customers who purchase superwidgets, generally live in Minnesota. This may provide a sales opportunity to be "flagged" if a caller from Minnesota contacts the company. Data Mining helps companies learn more about their customers and leverage that information to provide customized service and expand relationships.

Data Warehousing. A large database that stores data generated by an organization's multiple business systems. Data can be extracted using report generators, sophisticated decision support systems or other analytical tools (see Data Mining).

Day-of-Week Routing. A network service that routes calls to alternate locations, based on the day of week. There are also options for day-of-year and time-of-day routing.

Delay Announcements. Recorded announcements that encourage callers to wait for an agent to become available, remind them to have their account number ready, and provide information on access alternatives. In some systems, delay announcements are provided through recorded announcement routes (RANs).

Delay. Also called Queue Time. The time a caller spends in queue waiting for an agent to become available. Average Delay is the same thing as Average Speed of Answer. Also see Average Delay of Delayed Calls.

Delayed Call. A call that cannot be answered immediately and is placed in queue.

Desktop Statistics. Real-time and/or historical call center activity accessed from a desktop data device (PC or workstation). This function enables a supervisor to view call center activity, or agents to view their own activity, from a standard desktop. May also include a comparison of individual activity against established targets (e.g., revenue, average handling time, calls handled).

Desktop Telephony. See Softphone.

Dialed Number (DN). The number that the caller dialed to initiate the call.

Dialed Number Identification Service (DNIS). A string of digits that the telephone network passes to the ACD, VRU or other device, to indicate which number the caller dialed. The ACD can then process and report on that type of call according to user-defined criteria. One trunk group can have many DNIS numbers.

Digital. The use of a binary code – 1s and 0s – to represent information.

Direct Call Processing. See Talk Time.

Direct Inward Dialing (DID). A network service offering – generally associated with local service – where a unique set of identifying digits is passed to the customer premises equipment. By mapping each set of digits to an internal extension, the switch can provide direct dialing to a particular extension. See Dialed Number Identification Services.

Directed Dialog. Technology used in speech recognition that recognizes what is being said based on guided or structured interactions. The caller is given examples of phrases to use. Also referred to as structured language.

Dual-Tone Multifrequency (DTMF). A signaling system, used by the standard telephone, that sends pairs of audio frequencies to represent each digit on a telephone keypad. A related term, Touchtone, is a trademark of AT&T.

Dumb Terminal. A phrase used to describe the user device (terminal) in a computing environment where all of the processing occurs on a central computer or mainframe.

Dynamic Answer. An ACD feature that automatically reconfigures the number of rings before the system answers calls, based on real-time queue information. Since costs don't begin until the ACD answers calls, this feature can save callers or the call center money when long-distance charges apply.

Dynamic Data Exchange (DDE). A Microsoft function allowing information from one application to be transferred to another via the Windows operating system. Also referred to as "copying and pasting" or "cut and paste," it involves the temporary storage of information in the Windows Clipboard.

Electronic Documentation. Documentation for an application, product or process that would normally be in the form of paper documentation, but is converted into digital format for display on a desktop computer.

Electronic Mail (Email). Electronic text mail.

Enterprise Resource Planning (ERP). A large-scale business application or set of applications that encompass some or all aspects of a business, such as finance, production, order processing, fulfillment, billing and HR. These are typically referred to as "back-office" functions. There is an evolution within the ERP industry to either provide add-on modules or integrate with third party applications for "front office" functions such as sales, marketing and service. Applications that combine these "front office" functions are generally referred to as Customer Relationship Management applications (See CRM).

Envelope Strategy. A strategy whereby enough agents are scheduled for the day or week to handle both the inbound call load and other types of work. Priorities are based on the inbound call load. When call load is heavy, all agents handle calls, but when it is light, some agents are reassigned to work that is not as time-sensitive.

Erlang. One hour of telephone traffic in an hour of time. For example, if circuits carry 120 minutes of traffic in an hour, that's two Erlangs.

Erlang, A.K. A Danish engineer who worked for the Copenhagen Telephone Company in the early 1900s and developed Erlang B, Erlang C and other telephone traffic engineering formulas.

Erlang B. A formula developed by A.K. Erlang, widely used to determine the number of trunks required to handle a known calling load during a one-hour period. The formula assumes that if callers get busy signals, they go away forever, never to retry ("lost calls cleared"). Since some callers retry, Erlang B can underestimate trunks required. However, Erlang B is generally accurate in situations with few busy signals.

Erlang C. Mathematical tool used to calculate predicted waiting times (delay) based on three things: the number of servers (agents); the number of people waiting to be served (callers); and the average amount of time it takes to serve each person. It can also predict the resources required to keep waiting times within targeted limits. Erlang C assumes no lost calls or busy signals, so it has a tendency to overestimate staff required.

Error Rate. Either the number of defective transactions or the number of defective steps in a transaction.

Escalation Plan. A plan that specifies actions to be taken when the queue begins to build beyond acceptable levels.

Exchange Line. See Trunk.

Executive Summary. A brief summary of the key points of a more detailed report or study.

Expected Wait Time (EWT). A formula that uses real-time and historical queue data to approximate how long a caller will have to wait for an agent. Depending on the wait time, callers may be offered options of staying on hold, hanging up, leaving a callback request or transferring to an IVR.

Expert System. Business application that aids the user in analyzing and resolving problems based on logic trees and known solutions to identified problems. (Also known as Knowledge Based System.) Includes functions such as problem analysis and problem resolution.

EXtensible Markup Language (XML). A language derived from the Standard Generalized Markup Language (SGML), primarily used to pass information between Web pages, applications or systems. A standard for passing data that provides the definition of the type and format of the data, as well as the data, in information passed between systems and applications. Enables very open interchanges between systems.

Extranet. Networks, typically connected via the Internet, providing for direct and secure business-to-business access between suppliers and vendors or other partners.

Extraprise. Refers to a business entity that includes a company, its business partners and suppliers, and its customers.

Fast Clear Down. A caller who hangs up immediately when they hear a delay announcement.

Fax On Demand. Allows callers to select (generally through a voice response system but can also be through a Web site) and receive a fax document providing information about a particular subject, account details, or other information. Once the document is selected, it is sent to a fax machine of their choice either immediately or within a specified period of time. Fax On Demand can be part of a voice-processing application or stand-alone.

Flow Chart. A step-by-step diagram of a process.

Flushing Out the Queue. Changing system thresholds so that calls waiting for an agent group are redirected to another group with a shorter queue or available agents.

Forecasting. In a call center, the process of predicting call (and other types of contact) volumes and workload in order to staff appropriately to meet desired service level and response time goals.

Front-Office Applications. Business applications that deal with customer interactions, such as customer service, help desk, sales or customer relationship management.

Fulfillment. The process of fulfilling a request for literature or other information (e.g., product information, user guides, billing policies, forms, etc.). This can be a manual or automated process and the information may be sent by the customer's preferred choice of media (e.g., mail, fax or email).

Full-Time Equivalent (FTE). A term used in scheduling and budgeting, whereby the number of scheduled hours is divided by the hours in a full work week. The hours of several part-time agents may add up to one FTE.

Gate. See Agent Group.

Gateway. Software that interprets and translates different protocols from different networks or devices.

Grade of Service. The probability that a call will not be connected to a system because all trunks are busy. Grade of service is often expressed as "p.01" meaning 1 percent of calls will be "blocked." Sometimes grade of service is used interchangeably with service level, but the two terms have different meanings. See Service Level.

Graphical User Interface (GUI). An interface that uses icons, menus and a mouse to manage interaction with the system, instead of complex programming languages.

Handled Calls. The number of calls received and handled by agents or peripheral equipment. Handled calls does not include calls that abandon or receive busy signals.

Handling Time. The time an agent spends in Talk Time and After-Call Work handling a transaction. Handling Time can also refer to the time it takes for a machine to process a transaction.

Help Desk. A term that generally refers to a call center set up to handle queries about product installation, usage or problems. The term is most often used in the context of computer software and hardware support centers.

Help Desk Software. Applications that deal with customer interactions usually of a technical nature (e.g., computer support). The application not only captures and manages contact information but also tracks and manages a problem from initial request to resolution. Often has links to an expert system for the purpose of problem analysis and resolution.

Historical Reports. Reports that track call center and agent performance over a period of time. Historical reports are generated by ACDs, third-party ACD software packages and peripherals such as VRUs and Call Detail Recording Systems. The amount of history that a system can store varies by system.

Holding Time. See Average Holding Time on Trunks.

Home Agent. See Remote Agents.

HyperText Markup Language (HTML). A language derived from the Standard Generalized Markup Language (SGML), primarily used to create Web pages.

Imaging. A process whereby documents are scanned into a system and stored electronically.

Immutable Law. A law of nature that is fundamental and not changeable (e.g., the law of gravity). In an inbound call center, the fact that occupancy goes up when service level goes down is an immutable law.

In-band signaling. Passing information about a contact in the same channel as the channel the information passes in. For example, caller ID into a home uses in-band signaling.

Incoming Call Center Management. The art of having the right number of properly skilled people and supporting resources in place at the right times to handle an accurately forecasted workload, at service level and with quality.

Incremental Revenue (Value) Analysis. A methodology that estimates the value (cost and revenue) of adding or subtracting an agent.

Index Factor. In forecasting, a proportion used as a multiplier to adjust another number.

Integrated Reporting. The ability to track a call from its inception to culmination and tie business information and results together with call data (a.k.a. "cradle to grave" reporting). Each point the call touches (e.g., IVRs, announcements, CSRs), and the business results of those transactions (sales, complaints, contact record) are tracked on a single database record and/or via a common tracking identifier. This enables more accurate tracking of caller treatment and contact results.

Integrated Services Digital Network (ISDN). A set of international standards for telephone transmission. ISDN provides an end-to-end digital network, out-of-band signaling and greater bandwidth than older telephone services. The two standard levels are Basic Rate Interface (BRI) and Primary Rater Interface (PRI). Often used in call centers to deliver signaling information quickly for use of ANI and DNIS, and for faster call setup and tear down.

Intelligent Routing. The use of information about the caller, current conditions or other parameters to route calls to the appropriate group, individual, automated system, etc. DNIS, ANI, customer-entered digits and database information all can be used as routing parameters. Can augment or replace conditional and skills-based routing performed on the switch. Generally enabled via CTI.

Inter Exchange Carrier (IXC). A long-distance telephone company.

Interactive Voice Response (IVR). Systems that enable callers to use their telephone keypad (or spoken commands if speech recognition is used) to access a company's computer system for the purpose of retrieving or updating information, conducting a business transaction or routing their calls.

Interactive Web Response (IWR). Systems that enable customers to use their PC and an Internet connection to access a company's computer system for the purpose of retrieving or updating information or conducting a business transaction.

Interflow. See Overflow.

Internal Help Desk. A group that supports other internal agent groups, e.g., for complex or escalated calls.

Internal Response Time. The time it takes an agent group that supports other internal groups (e.g., for complex or escalated tasks) to respond to transactions that do not have to be handled when they arrive (e.g., correspondence or email). See Response Time and Service Level.

Internet. A worldwide, expanding network of linked computers, founded by the U.S. government and several universities in 1969, originally call Arpanet and based on TCP/IP protocol. Made available for commercial use in 1992.

Internet Protocol (IP). The set of communication standards that control communications activity on the Internet. An IP address is assigned to every computer on the Internet.

Intraflow. See Overflow.

Intranet. A company's private data network that is accessed using browser-based technology and TCP/IP protocol.

IP Telephony. Technology that enables voice telephone calls to be carried over a data network (a private intranet or the public Internet) using the Internet protocol. Voice is transmitted in data packets. Generally used today to obtain lower costs for long-distance (often international) calls. Quality of service (latency, delays, lost packets) is the greatest challenge to widespread use for call centers (does not match circuit-switched voice over the public network today), and is being addressed. Also referred to as Internet Telephony.

Internet Service Provider (ISP). A company that provides Internet access to customers, either through a modem or direct connection.

Invisible Queue. When callers do not know how long the queue is or how fast it is moving. See Visible Queue.

Java. An object-oriented programming language developed by Sun Microsystems. It is designed for creating and executing operating system independent applications. Java "applets" – small applications – can be down loaded and run within browsers on virtually any operating system without modification, making them ideal for use over the Internet.

Java Telephony Application Programming Interface (JTAPI). An object-oriented application programming interface for Java-based computer telephony applications. Allows Java applications to initiate, control and disconnect telephone calls.

Judgmental Forecasting. Goes beyond purely statistical techniques and encompasses what people believe is going to happen. It is in the realm of intuition, interdepartmental committees, market research and executive opinion.

Knowledge-Based System. See Expert System.

Knowledge Management. A method of organizing a company's internal and external processes, product, and service documentation, information about customers, prospects, competitors, partners, etc. It searches through company databases to enable access to collective knowledge.

Law of Diminishing Returns. The declining marginal improvements in service level that can be attributed to each additional agent, as successive agents are added.

Legacy systems. Information systems or databases that house core business information such as customer records. May be based on older technologies (e.g., mainframes, mini-computers) but are still used for day-to-day operations.

Linux. A Unix-like open source operating system.

Load Balancing. Balancing traffic between two or more destinations.

Local Area Network (LAN). The connection of multiple computers (usually within close proximity) to enable sharing information, applications and peripherals.

Local Exchange Carrier (LEC). Telephone companies responsible for providing local connections and services.

Logged On. A state in which agents have signed on to a system (made their presence known), but may or may not be ready to receive calls.

Loggers. Tools that automatically record and archive calls in a call center. Can be used to record every call, record on demand or conduct event-based recording. Used by companies such as insurance, financial services and utilities that must keep detailed records of transactions for verification or legal purposes. Today's systems can record both voice and data.

Logical Agent. An agent defined in ACD software by the login, not their physical position or phone number. Enables an agent to log in at any position and receive call types appropriate to their skills.

Long Call. For staffing calculations and traffic engineering purposes, calls that approach or exceed 30 minutes.

Longest Available Agent. A method of distributing calls to the agent who has been sitting idle the longest. With a queue, Longest Available Agent becomes "Next Available Agent."

Longest Delay (Oldest Call). The longest time a caller has waited in queue, before abandoning or reaching an agent.

Look Ahead Queuing. The ability for a system or network to examine a secondary queue and evaluate the conditions, before overflowing calls from the primary queue.

Look Back Queuing. The ability for a system or network to look back to the primary queue after the call has been overflowed to a secondary queue, and evaluate the conditions. If the congestion clears, the call can be sent back to the initial queue.

Lost Call. See Abandoned Call.

Management Information System (MIS). A system that facilitates the capture and reporting of activity within the telephony and computing infrastructure.

Manual Available. An ACD feature whereby the ACD is programmed to automatically put agents into after-call work after they finish talking and disconnect calls. When agents complete any after-call work, they put themselves back into available mode. See Auto Wrapup.

Middleware. Software that provides the means to access and integrate different types of hardware and software within a network. Typically uses open interfaces and applications programming interfaces (APIs) to access and move information.

Modem. A contraction of the terms Modulator/Demodulator. A Modem converts analog signals to digital and vice versa.

Monitoring. Also called Position Monitoring or Service Observing. The process of listening to agents' telephone calls for the purpose of maintaining quality. Monitoring can be: a) silent, in which agents don't know when they are being monitored, b) side by side, in which the person monitoring sits next to the agent and observes calls, or c) record and review, in which calls are recorded and later played back and assessed.

Multilingual Agents. Agents who are fluent in more than one language.

Multimedia. Combining multiple forms of media in the communication of information. (For instance, a traditional phone call is "monomedia," and a video call is "multimedia.")

Multimedia Queuing. Handling customer contacts through different channels (inbound calls, outbound calls, voice messages, email, Web calls, text-chat, fax, video, etc.) in a common queue. Allows customers to choose the method of contact and ensures all contacts are handled according to business rules in a timely way. Requires advanced technology to integrate media, and route and report on it.

Natural Language. Technology used in speech or text recognition that recognizes what is being said or requested through free-form communication (no structure or required words or phrases).

Network Computer. Sometimes referred to as a "thin" client. A computer, usually a PC, with limited or no disk storage, designed solely for connection to servers within a network. Applications reside on and are run within the server rather than the client. See Thin Client.

Network Control Center. Also called Traffic Control Center. In a networked call center environment, in which people and equipment monitor real-time conditions across sites, change routing thresholds as necessary and coordinate events that will impact base staffing levels.

Network Inter-flow. A technology used in multisite call center environments to create a more efficient distribution of calls between sites. Through integration of sites using network circuits (such as T1 circuits) and ACD software, calls routed to one site may be queued simultaneously for agent groups in remote sites. See Call-by-Call Routing and Percent Allocation.

Network Reports. Reports from the network that provide historical or real-time information on network call activity. For example, network reports can indicate how many network busies were delivered, trunk utilization, call volumes, total traffic (volume x holding times), calling numbers, etc. for each trunk group or DNIS number.

Network Routing. The ability to make routing decisions in the network before selecting a location to route the call. Network routing can be based on factors such as the time of day, day of week, percentage of calls to be handled at each site, area code of the calling party, DNIS or information gathered from databases via CTI.

Next Available Agent. A call distribution method that sends calls to the next agent who becomes available. The method seeks to maintain an equal load across skill groups or services. When there is no queue, Next Available Agent reverts to Longest Available Agent.

Noise Canceling Headset. Headsets equipped with technology that reduces background noise.

Non ACD In Calls. Inbound calls which are directed to an agent's extension, rather than to a general group. These may be personal calls or calls from customers who dial the agents' extension numbers.

Object Linking and Embedding (OLE). The ability of Windows to embed an object in another object, and link the two so that when information is updated in one it is updated in the other. For example, an Excel spreadsheet can be embedded in a Word document, and the embedded document will be updated if the original Excel document is changed. In 1997, Microsoft announced that OLE was part of ActiveX.

Occupancy. Also referred to as agent utilization. The percentage of time agents handle calls vs. wait for calls to arrive. For a half-hour, the calculation is: (call volume x average handling time in seconds) / (number of agents x 1800 seconds). See Adherence to Schedule.

Off The Shelf. Hardware or software programs that are commercially available and ready for use "as is."

Offered Calls. All of the attempts callers make to reach the call center. There are three possibilities for offered calls: 1) They can get busy signals; 2) they can be answered by the system, but hang up before reaching a rep; or 3) they can be answered by a rep. Offered call reports in ACDs usually refer only to the calls that the system receives.

Off-Peak. Periods of time other than the call center's busiest periods. Also a term to describe periods of time when long-distance carriers provide lower rates.

On-Line Analytical Processing (OLAP). A category of software technologies that provide dynamic, multidimensional access to consolidated data for the purpose of extrapolating trends. Commonly used with data warehouses.

Open Database Connectivity (ODBC). A standard method of accessing databases on a variety of platforms. Defined by the SQL (Structured Query Language) Access Group.

Open Ticket. A customer contact (transaction) that has not yet been completed or resolved (closed).

Out-of-band signaling. Passing information about a contact in a separate channel from the channel the information passes in. For example, ISDN uses out-of-band signaling.

Outsourcing. Contracting some or all call center services to an outside company.

Overflow. Calls that flow from one group or site to another. More specifically, Intraflow happens when calls flow between agent groups and Interflow is when calls flow out of the ACD to another site.

Overlay. See Rostered Staff Factor.

Packet Switching. A method of transferring information across a network by passing it in small pieces ("packets") of information. Typically used to transmit data (e.g., over the internet). Now being applied to voice, as well.

Pareto Chart. A bar chart that arranges events in order of frequency. Named after 19th century economist Vilfredo Pareto.

PBX/ACD. A PBX that is equipped with ACD functionality.

Peaked Call Arrival. A surge of traffic beyond random variation. It is a spike within a short period of time.

Percent Allocation. A call-routing strategy sometimes used in multisite call center environments. Calls received in the network are allocated across sites based on user-defined percentages. See Call-by-Call Routing and Network Inter-flow.

Percent Utilization. See Occupancy.

Poisson. A formula sometimes used for calculating trunks. Assumes that if callers get busy signals, they keep trying until they successfully get through. Since some callers won't keep retrying, Poisson can overestimate trunks required. See Erlang B and Retrial Tables.

Pooling Principle. The Pooling Principle states: Any movement in the direction of consolidation of resources will result in improved traffic-carrying efficiency. Conversely, any movement away from consolidation of resources will result in reduced traffic-carrying efficiency.

Position Monitoring. See Monitoring.

Post-Call Processing. See After-Call Work.

Predictive Dialing. An application that instructs the switch to dial multiple simultaneous calls based upon a preloaded list of phone numbers. A mathematical algorithm is used to predict the correct number of calls to launch and when agents will become available. Then it seeks to match the number of live connected calls with the number of available agents. The system determines when a called party has answered and transfers only live calls (and answering machines, if desired) to agents. Agents also receive a data screen about the call. The system classifies all calls launched (e.g., connect, busy, no answer, answering machine, network tones) and updates the database accordingly.

Preview Dialing. An application that instructs the switch to outdial a specific phone number under control of an agent or a timer. The agent previews a screen containing information about the person to be called, monitors the call for connection (or other classification), and updates the database accordingly. Used for callbacks or other contacts where the agent needs to review information before placing the call.

Primary Rate Interface (PRI). One of the two levels of ISDN service. In North America, PRI provides 23 bearer channels for voice and data and one channel for signaling information (commonly expressed as 23B+D). In Europe, PRI provides 30 bearer lines (30B+D). See Integrated Services Digital Network.

Private Automatic Branch Exchange (PABX). See Private Branch Exchange.

Private Branch Exchange (PBX) or Private Automated Branch Exchange (PABX). A telephone system located at a user's premise that handles incoming and outgoing calls and provides many features for call routing and management. By adding ACD software, a PBX can provide ACD functionality, such as queuing calls.

Private Network. A network made up of circuits for the exclusive use of an organization or group of affiliated organizations. Can be regional, national or international in scope and are common in large organizations.

Process. A system of causes.

Profit Center. An accounting term that refers to a department or function in the organization that does not generate profit. See Cost Center.

Progressive Dialing. The term is either used as a variation on preview dialing or predictive dialing. Some use progressive dialing to describe preview dialing where the preview is timed before automatically launching. Some use progressive dialing to describe a form of controlled predictive dialing where multiple calls are launched only when an agent becomes available. It is still predictive in that it is predicting how many calls will connect. However, it reduces the chance of a live answer by a customer when no agent is available.

Public Switched Telephone Network (PSTN). The network that interconnects telephones (the good old telephone network we all use every day!).

Quality Monitoring Tools. Tools used to assess agent contact-handling skills, allowing specific or random selection of positions, trunks, queues, or other entities to monitor. Monitoring can be real-time or recorded and may include data as well as voice. Quality monitoring tools now monitor email and Web contacts as well.

Quantitative Forecasting. Using statistical techniques to forecast future events. The major categories of quantitative forecasting include Time Series and Explanatory approaches. Time Series techniques use past trends to forecast future events. Explanatory techniques attempt to reveal linkages between two or more variables. See Judgmental Forecasting.

Queue. Holds callers until an agent becomes available. Queue can also refer to a line or list of items in a system waiting to be processed (e.g., email messages).

Queue Display. See Readerboard.

Queue Time. See Delay.

Random Call Arrival. The normal random variation in how incoming calls arrive. See Peaked Call Arrival.

Readerboard. Also called Display Board or Wallboard or Electronic Display. A visual display, usually mounted on the wall or ceiling of a call center, which provides real-time and historical information on queue conditions, agent status and call center performance. It can also display user-entered messages.

Real-Time Adherence Software. Software that tracks how closely agents conform to their schedules. See Adherence to Schedule.

Real-Time Data. Information on current conditions. Some "real-time" information is real-time in the strictest sense (e.g., calls in queue and current longest wait). Some real-time reports require some history (e.g., the last x calls or x minutes) in order to make a calculation (e.g. service level and average speed of answer). See Screen Refresh.

Real-Time Management. Making adjustments to staffing and thresholds in the systems and network, in response to current queue conditions.

Received Calls. A call detected and seized by a trunk. Received calls will either abandon or be answered by an agent.

Record and Review Monitoring. See Monitoring.

Recorded Announcement Route (RAN). See Delay Announcement.

Reengineering. A term popularized by management consultant Michael Hammer, which refers to radically redesigning processes to improve efficiency and service.

Remote Agents. Fully integrated call center agents residing at home or other remote location. It is transparent to callers that they are remote. Requires both telephony and data connectivity from a main site to the agent's location, and the same features and functions available to agents on site.

Response Time. The time it takes the call center to respond to transactions that do not have to be handled when they arrive (e.g., correspondence or email). See Service Level.

Retrial Tables. Sometimes used to calculate trunks and other system resources required. They assume that some callers will make additional attempts to reach the call center if they get busy signals. See Erlang B and Poisson.

Retrial. A caller who "retries" when he or she gets a busy signal.

Rostered Staff Factor (RSF). Alternatively called an Overlay, Shrink Factor or Shrinkage. RSF is a numerical factor that leads to the minimum staff needed on schedule over and above base staff required to achieve your service level and response time objectives. It is calculated after base staffing is determined and before schedules are organized, and accounts for things like breaks, absenteeism and ongoing training.

Round-Robin Distribution. A method of distributing calls to agents according to a predetermined list. See Next Available Agent and Longest Waiting Agent.

Sales Force Automation (SFA). A class of business applications designed to automate the marketing and sales process. Historically, they were limited to such areas as "opportunity management" and "interactive selling." Today, the term usually refers to any technology-enabled sales tools and often includes contact and customer relationship management. See Customer Relationship Management.

Satellite Office. A call center location that operates using a cabinet or carrier of a switch from a main location. Used to extend one switch to another site to operate virtually without purchasing a second switch.

Scatter Diagram. A chart that graphically depicts the relationship between two variables.

Schedule Compliance. See Adherence to Schedule.

Scheduling. Allocating call center agents and other resources in a way that will meet service level and other goals for specific days and times. Scheduling is generally based on historical call center activity, agent skills and performance, and knowledge of planned events.

Scheduling Exception. When an agent is involved in an activity outside of the normal, planned schedule.

Screen Monitoring. A system capability that enables a supervisor or manager to remotely monitor the activity on agents' computer terminals.

Screen Pop. A CTI application. See Coordinated Voice/Data Delivery.

Screen Refresh. The rate at which real-time information is updated on a display (e.g., every five to 15 seconds). Note, screen refresh does not correlate with the timeframe used for real-time calculations. See Real-Time Data.

Scripting. Sometimes referred to as "dialog manager." An application that provides scripts to agents to aid in call handling (e.g., product description, promotional offer, wrapup information). Can generally be controlled and modified to accommodate various situations and individuals (e.g., different levels of experience, full scripts vs. reminder lists, generic or customized).

Seated Agents. See Base Staff.

Server. A computer that shares its resources with other computers on a network. For example, file servers share disk storage with other computers. Database servers respond to requests from other computers on the network (clients).

Service Bureau. A company that handles inbound or outbound calls for another organization.

Service Level Agreement. Performance objectives reached by consensus between the user and the provider of a service, or between an outsourcer and an organization. A service level agreement specifies a variety of performance standards that may or may not include "service level." See Service Level.

Service Level. Also called Telephone Service Factor or TSF. The percentage of incoming calls that are answered within a specified threshold: "X percent of calls answered in Y seconds." See Response Time.

Service Observing. See Monitoring.

Shrink Factor. See Rostered Staff Factor.

Signaling System 7 (SS7). A method of signaling within the voice network that uses a separate packet-switched data network ("common channel signaling") to communicate information about calls. In a multisite virtual call center environment, SS7 can be used to pass information in order to decide which site is "best" to route the call.

Silent Monitoring. See Monitoring.

Simplified Message Desk Interface (SMDI). An industry standard method of integrating voicemail systems with digital PBXs. The standard is defined by Bellcore for use with Centrex style technologies, and is a common method of integrating the two systems. It uses a data communication link to permit transfer of information over an RS-232 link to the voice-processing module.

Simulation Tools. Tools used to replicate call activity in order to test applications and resulting impact on call center performance.

Skill Group. See Agent Group.

Skills-Based Routing. A specific form of intelligent routing that matches the skills of each agent with information about the caller to route a call to an appropriate agent. When an agent logs in, the database associates a defined skill set with that position and the application routes call types that match the skills to that position. An agent can have multiple skills, preferred skills and unique combinations of skills.

Smooth Call Arrival. Calls that arrive evenly across a period of time. Virtually non-existent in incoming environments.

Softphone. The ability to access telephony functions, through the desktop computer interface of a PC instead of a telephone. For a call center agent, softphone can include login/logout to both the voice and data systems via a single action on the PC, point-and-click changing of work states (available, unavailable/not ready), visibility into availability and statistics, outbound calling and entry of transaction codes via the PC. Softphone is a CTI-enabled function.

Special Causes. Variation in a process caused by special circumstances. See Common Causes.

Speech Recognition. See Automatic Speech Recognition (ASR).

Split. See Agent Group.

Stand-alone ACD. A switch with software specifically designed to perform ACD routing and other call center functions. Stand-alone ACDs typically exclude many PBX capabilities, such as least-cost routing, camp-on or other functions targeted toward general business use, and may co-reside with a PBX in many office environments.

Structured Query Language (SQL). A language developed by IBM for requesting data from relational databases.

Supervisor Monitor. Computer monitors that enable supervisors to monitor the call-handling statistics of their supervisory groups or teams.

Supervisor. The person who has frontline responsibility for a group of agents. Typical ratios are one supervisor to every 10 to 15 agents. However, help desks can have one supervisor for every five people, and some reservations centers have one supervisor for every 30 or 40 agents. Generally, supervisors are equipped with special telephones and computer terminals that enable them to monitor agent activities.

T1 Circuit. A high-speed digital circuit used for voice, data or video, with a bandwidth of 1.544 megabits per second. T1 circuits offer the equivalent of 24 analog voice trunks.

Talk Time. The time an agent spends with a caller during a transaction. Includes everything from "hello" to "goodbye."

Telecommuting. See Remote Agent.

Telephone Service Factor. See Service Level.

Telephony Application Programming Interface (TAPI). API developed by Microsoft to enable computer telephony functions on Windows-based systems. It is one of the de facto standards by virtue of Microsoft's large installed base.

Telephony Services Application Programming Interface (TSAPI). API developed by Lucent (Avaya) and Novell to enable computer telephony functions. Generally used only by Avaya in today's market.

Text Chat. Allows agents and customers to have a "conversation" over the Internet by typing on their computers. Generally enabled through a "click-to-chat" button on a Web site, and then a separate window opens for chatting (via a Java Applet or Active X control).

Text-to-Speech. Enables a voice-processing system to read the words in a text field aloud using synthesized – not recorded – speech. Sometimes used for large, dynamic database applications in which it is impractical to record all speech phrases. Also used to "read" email or other text-based information over the telephone.

Thick Client. A workstation in a client-server environment that performs much or most of the application processing. It requires programs and data to be installed on it and a significant part of the application processing takes place on the workstation. The client is "thick" in that much of the overall application is running on it.

Thin Client. A workstation in a client-server environment that performs little or no application processing. Often used to describe browser-based desktops. The client is "thin" in that the applications reside on and are run within the server rather than the client.

Threshold. The point at which an action, change or process takes place.

Tie line. A private circuit that connects two ACDs or PBXs across a wide area.

Toll-Free Service. Enables callers to reach a call center out of the local calling area without incurring charges. 800 and 888 service is toll-free. In some countries, there are also other variations of toll-free service. For example, with 0345 or 0645 services in the United Kingdom, callers are charged local rates and the call center pays for the long-distance charges.

Touchtone. A trademark of AT&T. See Dual-Tone Multifrequency.

Traffic Control Center. See Network Control Center

Transaction. See Call.

Transmission Control Protocol/Internet Protocol (TCP/IP). Protocols that support internetworking. TCP/IP specifies how information that travels over the Internet should be divided and reassembled.

True Calls Per Hour. Actual calls an individual or group handled divided by occupancy for that period of time.

Trunk. Also called a Line, Exchange Line or Circuit. A telephone circuit linking two switching systems.

Trunk Group. A collection of trunks associated with a single peripheral and usually used for a common purpose.

Trunk Load. The load that trunks carry. Includes both Delay and Talk Time.

Trunks Idle. The number of trunks in a trunk group that are non-busy.

Trunks in Service. The number of trunks in the trunk group that are functional.

Un-PBX. An term sometimes used for communications server. See Communications Server.

Unavailable Work State. An agent work state used to identify a mode not associated with handling telephone calls.

Uniform Call Distributor (UCD). A simple system that distributes calls to a group of agents and provides some reports. A UCD is not as sophisticated as an ACD.

Universal Agent. Refers to either: a) An agent who can handle all types of incoming calls, or b) an agent who can handle both inbound and outbound calls.

Virtual Call Center. Multiple Networked ACD systems that operate as a single logical system even though they are physically separated and geographically dispersed. A resource at one site can handle a call from any of the other sites. This permits economies of scale in call handling, as well as supporting disaster recovery, call overflow and extended hours coverage. Ability and degree of networking varies with system type, similarity of systems and approach to integration. Can be enabled to varying degrees using network features, switch features or CTI.

Visible Queue. When callers know how long the queue is that they just entered, and how fast it is moving (e.g., they hear a system announcement that relays the expected wait time). See Invisible Queue.

Voice Over Internet Protocol (VoIP). Transmitting voice signals as packets of data from one computer to another over a TCP/IP network. See IP Telephony.

Voice Processing. A blanket term that refers to any combination of voice-processing technologies, including Voicemail, Automated Attendant, Audiotex, Voice Response Unit (VRU) and Faxback.

Voice Response Unit (VRU). See Interactive Voice Response. Note: VRU is sometimes used to refer to the piece of equipment, while IVR is used to refer to the capability.

Web Call. A VoIP transaction that is initiated by a customer from a company's Web site.

Web Callback. Transaction in which the customer clicks a button on a company's Web site, which initiates an automatic callback from an agent.

Web Integration. Incorporating Web contact into the call center by providing access to a live agent over the Internet when needed. Provides the customer with additional support, information and guidance during a self-service transaction. Can be enabled through text chat, Web callback or a Web call. Email is sometimes included offered as part of this integration. Often includes "co-browsing" or "pushing" Web pages to the customer.

Wide Area Network (WAN). A data and/or voice network that covers a large geographic area.

Work Flow Management. Business application that enables work tasks to be created and assigned, both manually and through automation. Because Work Flow Management is driven by business rules, it ensures that transactions are accomplished through proper and consistent steps. The movement of each task can be tracked throughout the duration of the process providing both current status and historical activity. Work Flow Management can be used to track contact handling at specific stages or for the life of a contact.

Workforce Management System (WFMS). Forecasting, scheduling, tracking and adherence monitoring tool used in a call center. Enables the manager to project work volume and corresponding resource needs based on historical information and other parameters (e.g., growth). Workforce management can be performed for a single site or for networked sites. In a multisite environment, forecasting and scheduling may be performed at a central site or in a decentralized fashion at each site. Tracking and adherence monitoring is generally a local function.

Workload. Often used interchangeably with Call Load. Workload can also refer to non-call activities.

World Wide Web (WWW). The capability that enables users to access information on the Internet in a graphical environment.

Wrap-up. See After-Call Work.

Wrap-Up Codes. Codes that agents enter on their phones to identify the types of calls they are handling. Generally entered at the completion of each contact. The ACD can then generate reports on call types, by handling time, time of day, etc.

XML. See EXtensible Markup Language.

Zip Tone. See Beep Tone.

Reference Articles

The following articles are from the pages of *Call Center Management Review* (formerly *Service Level Newsletter*), the journal for ICMI members. They were selected to provide you with further information on some of the key areas of operations management.

A Primer on Developing Effective Call Center Strategy: Part 1

"Making strategy, once an event, is now a continuous process."

– Thomas Petzinger Jr.
The Wall Street Journal

What differentiates truly great organizations – and by extension, truly great call centers – from those that are just "okay"? How can an organization create tangible advantages that make the whole greater than the sum of the parts? How do you adapt and thrive in a fast-evolving networked economy? While there are many possible answers to these questions, an effective strategy clearly plays a key role.

Unfortunately, mention strategy, and many managers justifiably conjure up images of an overused business buzzword, the latest management trends or the last conference session they sat through with too much fluff and not enough substance. All the while, many organizations struggle to create viable, sustainable strategies. Many are currently working on their approach to customer relationship management or on redefining core businesses. Some are focusing on individual components of strategy, such as organization, resources or processes. And others are taking stock of what comes after mergers, industry restructurings or shifting budgets and priorities.

Developing effective strategy is not only possible, it's a pervasive characteristic of organizations that create sustainable customer loyalty and marketplace value. Still, many organizations are grappling with fast-changing markets and technologies, and struggle to leverage the

"pieces and parts" into a sustainable business advantage. Somewhere between strategy and tactics, the vision too often gets lost – or at least diluted – in operational realities. That seems to be especially true in developing cohesive, customer contact solutions.

What's needed is a mechanism for extending corporate strategy into tangible, realistic applications. In the call center realm, strategy is embodied in what is often termed a "customer access strategy," which is *a framework – a set of standards, guidelines and processes – defining the means by which customers are connected with resources capable of delivering the desired information and services.* The customer access strategy is an extension of corporate strategy and often, in turn, also helps to shape corporate strategy. When approached with the right commitment and buy-in, a customer access strategy is a powerful tool for unleashing the potential of the call center.

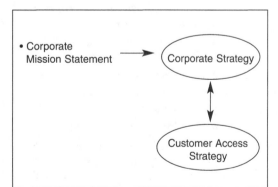

- Corporate Mission Statement → Corporate Strategy ↕ Customer Access Strategy

The need for a cohesive customer access strategy is clear. Multiple access methods are evolving. As services evolve, they become far more complicated from both the customer's and organization's perspectives, and as multiple technolo-

gy "owners" exist, telling customers the same story is an important concern. Caller tolerance is evolving rapidly, and customers are growing increasingly more savvy and well informed. And being "easy to do business with" is of paramount importance.

Developing a customer access strategy has broader implications than may first meet the eye. By nature, it positions the call center as the communications hub of the organization, and customer loyalty as the primary objective. It is an effort that will touch virtually every business unit, so it must be supported by top-level management. In fact, top management must be actively involved, along with any organization accessible to customers, all technology and process owners responsible for customer services and customers (ask them how they want to be served!).

As with corporate strategy, a customer access strategy can take many different forms. And, as with corporate strategy, there is a lot of

Section 9

confusing and conflicting advice on how to best approach the process of developing a customer access strategy and the form it should take. But the most sustainable strategies cover, in one form or another, 12 key business processes:

Developing *customer profiles* is, by necessity, a first step. Who are your customers and prospective customers; what do they want and need; and how can you best service those needs? While a strategy document generally doesn't go into individual detail, it should define specific customer types and their evolving expectations (see the discussion of customer expectations, Service Level Notes, January 2000).

Customer communications broadly describes how the organization plans to communicate with customers and establishes guidelines for developing those messages and ensuring that the organization is in sync (e.g., that the call center is properly informed of marketing campaigns).

Defining *contact types* anticipates the types of interactions with customers. General categories include such things as placing orders, changing orders, checking account status, problem resolution, etc., but most organizations wisely break these categories into more detail.

Identifying *access channels* is where strategy really begins to hit home for call centers. All channels of contact should be itemized: telephone, Web, fax, e-mail, IVR, kiosk, handhelds, face-to-face service, postal mail and anything else that comes along, plus corresponding telephone numbers, Web URLs, e-mail addresses, fax numbers, postal addresses, etc.

Routing and distribution plans naturally follow. How – by customer, type of contact and access channel – is each contact going to be routed and distributed? (While these terms have inbound connotations this also applies to outbound; e.g., when the organization originates the contacts, through which agent group or system will the contact be made?). Next, *service level objectives*, which in application includes both service level and response time objectives, are agreed to and specified.

Defining *required resources* takes strategy from the realm of "getting the customer's contact to the right place at the right time" into the realm of "doing the right thing." What resources, including people, technologies and databases, are required to provide callers with the information and assistance they need? This aspect of strategy will help guide hiring, training, technology deployment, database development and many other operational considerations.

Outlining the *organization and processes* necessary to support customer access requirements runs the gamut, from specifying how many call centers you will have to defining agent groups, responsibilities and planning requirements.

Capturing customer data identifies the methods used for capturing information on each customer interaction, and defining how that data will, in turn, be used to strengthen customer profiles, identify trends and improve products and services.

Finally, the strategy document should establish an agreed-upon *technology architecture*, (corporate standards and technology migration plans), *investment guidelines* (priorities and plans for operational and capital expenditures) and a *framework for deploying new services* (timeframes and approaches for expanding customer contact services).

Clearly, developing a sound customer access strategy is not something you throw together during a weekend retreat. It takes leadership, persistence, participation from across the organization, and a lot of collaboration and cooperation.

Each of the 12 processes addressed by the customer access strategy are interrelated, and when you focus on one, you will inherently be impacting and shaping others. And it's not something that happens in a vacuum; call center strategy cannot develop independent of broader corporate strategy.

But the payoffs of developing a cohesive strategy are compelling. From a customer's perspective, a good strategy will result in simplified access, consistent services, ease of use and a high degree of convenience and satisfaction. From the organization's perspective, the benefits translate into lower overall costs, increased capacity, higher customer retention and a workable framework that guides ongoing developments.

Next month, I'll focus on the process of putting these pieces together into a cohesive whole. In the meantime, I would encourage you to take stock of where your customer access strategy (whatever you may call it) stands.

CCMReview

A Primer on Developing Effective Call Center Strategy: Part 2

As discussed in Part 1 of this two-part series, a thoughtful customer access strategy is an essential aspect of developing a cohesive, effective customer contact environment. Broadly defined as "the standards, guidelines and processes defining the means by which customers are connected with resources capable of delivering the desired information and services," a customer access strategy generally considers these business processes:

- Customer profiles
- Customer communications
- Contact types
- Access channels
- Routing and distribution
- Service level objectives
- Required resources
- Organization and processes
- Capturing customer data
- Technology architecture
- Investment guidelines
- Framework for deploying new services

Thoughtfully addressing these issues, as discussed in Part 1, is essential to making the link between corporate strategy and the call center's ongoing activities and direction.

But developing an effective customer access strategy is no easy task. Because it touches virtually every traditional business unit, it requires an immense amount of collaboration, cooperation and leadership. And, as each of the processes are interrelated, changes to one will impact all others. In short, developing strategy is not a once-and-done event; it's an ongoing process. Without a system or approach for ongoing development, strategy quickly becomes out of date and ineffectual.

Figure 1, on the facing page, illustrates "The Strategic Develop-

ment Process" as taught by Incoming Calls Management Institute. Despite its somewhat lofty (stuffy?) title, it is an approach that is simple, effective and enduring. (If you are familiar with this process, you'll notice that although we have retooled some of the labels, the steps in the process remain the same). It will provide focus to your efforts to keep strategy current, along with an approach for tying the pieces together. Here's how it works:

1. Create a Connected Vision

Vision comes first. Vision is the creative ability to see past current circumstances to "what could be." As much as the concept of vision has been overused by some in business circles and consequently pooh-poohed by others,

> *Developing strategy is not a once-and-done event... Without a system or approach for ongoing development, strategy quickly becomes out of date and ineffectual.*

vision remains the undisputed motivation behind any human change or action.

We refer to a "connected" vision because it must be appropriate for today's fast-changing, networked economy. Key questions often serve as a useful catalyst in this effort. For instance, how do your customers define great service? What sort of organizational structure best supports the integration of e-commerce and traditional

telephony services? How else can the call center help the organization understand customers better? How can the call center's vision and purpose be better communicated? What is a call center?

2. Shape the Supporting Strategy

It is within this context that the customer access strategy is created and/or refined. The customer access strategy is a mechanism for turning vision into operational reality, and will serve as a framework for developing the steps that follow. (For a more complete discussion, please see Part 1 of this series, *CCMReview*, Feb. 2000.)

3. Build Skills, Knowledge and Leaders

This first involves developing a "map" of resident vs. required competencies for every key requirement (position) in the call center and identifying areas where you may be vulnerable (i.e., areas in which only a few key people possess important management or technical know-how). Other important aspects of this step involve developing appropriate hiring and training plans; implementing a systematic process for recognizing and cultivating management and leader-

Section 9

ship competencies; instilling an understanding of queuing dynamics and unique call center planning and management implications into the culture; establishing appropriate performance standards; and defining and developing attractive career- and skill-path alternatives.

4. Implement Connected Plans and Processes

This refers specifically to putting the planning and management processes in place which are necessary to support the customer access strategy. In today's environment, this usually involves forecasting, scheduling and real-time management across all channels of contact; simulating "what-if" scenarios given increasingly complex routing and distribution requirements; redefining agent group structure to move toward a true multimedia queuing environment; and improving collaboration and planning across the organization.

5. Apply Enabling Technologies

The obvious focus of this step is to specify the technology infrastructure required to turn vision into reality. However, a less-stated but equally important aspect of this process is to address the "technology conundrum," consisting of three important questions:

• *Should we buy now or buy later?* If we buy now, we begin conquering the learning curve now and will enjoy the benefits sooner. However, if we buy later, the technology will be cheaper, faster and better, and more organizations will have worked out the kinks.

• *Is the capability a sea change or diversion?* For instance, widespread video capabilities in call centers have, thus far, proved to be illusive while e-commerce services are quickly and fundamentally changing the customer service environment.

Figure 1
The Strategic Development Process

- Create a Connected Vision
- Shape the Supporting Strategy
- Build Skills, Knowledge and Leaders
- Implement Connected Plans and Processes
- Apply Enabling Technologies
- Make the Required Investments
- Unleash Innovative Quality

• *Who's in charge of specification and implementation decisions, the technology people or the marketing people?* (Note: There are questions within these generalized categories as well – e.g., should the data people or telecom people generally dictate direction?)

The point here is not to answer these questions, but to ensure they are addressed as a part of the process.

6. Make the Required Investments

Money, money, money. Here's where vision, strategy and all of our lofty ambitions and plans can run into cold reality. For that reason, some say, this step should occur much sooner in the process. But I respectfully disagree. Why have a call center – or, for that matter, why have an organization, if budgetary allocations predetermine possibilities? No one in his or her right mind would choose to spend money in any of these areas unless there is a reasonable return for both customers and the organization. Therein is the point: We don't even know what the possibilities are without going through the previous steps.

Yes, return on investment (ROI) analysis, FTE staff budgeting and capital planning play an important role in good management. And in

the end, it's all semantics anyway because no step, including budgeting, is inseparable from any other. But as a matter of principle, the budget should not short-circuit vision and strategy before new possibilities get a chance to make their case.

7. Unleash Innovative Quality

When it comes to quality, three prevailing questions continue to surface:

• What are customer expectations?

• Are we meeting them?

• Are we using the fewest possible resources to do so?

Quality has never consisted only of the attributes of a product or service; it must always be defined within the context of the customers' needs, wants and expectations. The invention and application of toll-free services, ACD capabilities, Internet-based services, speech recognition – the list can go on and on – all have raised expectations to new levels (see "Customer Expectations in 2000," *CCMReview*, Jan. 2000). And that takes us back to the beginning: What's our vision?

A Continuum

Business analyst and former *Wall Street Journal* Editor Thomas Petzinger Jr. was right when he proclaimed that: "Making strategy, once an event, is now a continuous process." Webster's New World Dictionary defines *continuum* as: "A continuous whole, quantity, or series; thing whose parts cannot be separated or separately discerned."

The key to effective strategy development is to see each step as part of a continuum. Developing good strategy is hard work. But, given the fundamental changes taking place in how organizations serve their customers, it has never been more important.

CCMReview

Section 9

Service Level Notes with Brad Cleveland

How Incoming Call Centers Behave: Back to the Basics, Part 1 of 3

SLN is dedicated to periodically reviewing the "basics," the core knowledge call center managers must have in order to manage effectively. This three-part series will review the fundamental, underlying principles that shape incoming call center behavior. It will address such questions as: How are service level and occupancy inter-related? How does agent group size affect productivity? How does staffing affect network costs? These principles will be discussed in the context of recent industry developments.

Just as the laws of physics define the parameters for air travel, there are fundamental, underlying principles that apply to the call center environment. Inappropriate group configuration, inefficient network designs and inherently-unfair standards for telephone agents are signals that one or more of these principles has been either misunderstood or ignored. This article reviews random call arrival and caller tolerance — key driving forces in incoming call centers — and it identifies important immutable "laws" that shape what occurs within a call center and how they impact staffing and service levels.

Random Call Arrival

Theorem One of incoming call center management is that "Calls Bunch Up." For virtually any call center, calls arrive in predictable repeating patterns, by time of day, day of week and season of year. With appropriate interdepartmental coordination and judgment — i.e., what's the marketing department doing? how is the call mix changing? — forecasts for the aggregate workload can be quite accurate, down to specific half-hour increments.

But even with near-perfect fore-casts, the actual moment-to-moment arrival of calls within the half hour is a random phenomenon — the luck of the draw. It is ultimately the result of countless individual decisions made by callers, based on a myriad of individual habits and motivations.

Because of random call arrival, staffing must be calculated using either a queuing formula that takes random arrival into account, typically Erlang C, or computer simulation. The widely-used Erlang C formula, developed in 1917 by A.K. Erlang, a Danish telephone company engineer, assumes random call arrival and that calls will go into queue if a server (agent) is not immediately available.

More specifically, Erlang C assumes "infinite sources of traffic"

> *Simulation is the call center equivalent of a flight simulator – you can learn how to program an intelligent ACD without suffering the consequences of bad design.*

(infinite trunking capacity — i.e., no busies) and that "lost calls are delayed" (infinite caller patience — i.e., no abandoned calls). The formula has been criticized for its tendency to lead to overstaffing because, Erlang's findings notwithstanding, busies and lost calls are a reality in many call centers. Fortunately this has become less of a problem with definitions of

"acceptable" service levels, which minimize abandonments and busies.

Erlang C is currently the basis for staffing calculations in virtually all of the workforce management software packages on the market. However, computer simulation has the potential to provide greater flexibility, and to account for issues such as busies, abandonments, skill based routing, overflow, etc. Simulation is the call center equivalent of a flight simulator — you can learn how to program an intelligent ACD without suffering the consequences of bad design.

Currently, a small but growing percentage of call centers is utilizing simulation. While general-purpose simulator software has been available in a variety of formats for years, a handful of vendors provide packages designed specifically for call center modeling, and more are under development.

Either Erlang C or simulation is a stark contrast to a common "wrong" approach to calculating staff — taking the average calls reps can now handle in a half hour or hour and dividing that into projected future traffic volumes. This approach ignores both random call arrival and service level. Poor staffing results in either idle reps or a long queue for callers, with the associated repercussions. Further, because staffing impacts the load

Section 9

the network and system must carry, miscalculated staff can also mean miscalculated system and network resources. In short, calculating staff correctly is essential.

Even with good forecasts and solid staffing calculations, random call arrival means that call center systems operate in a "demand-chasing" mode — there are either more calls to be answered than resources available, or more resources than calls. Because supply and demand are rarely equal, demand must be "chased" with the supply of answering capabilities. Systems and networks can help by making useful historical and real-time data available on trends and queue dynamics; providing flexibility to respond to changing traffic loads; and enhancing call answering capabilities. Likewise, flexibility in staffing — getting the right people in the right place at the right times — is imperative.

> ## Because supply and demand are rarely equal, demand must be "chased" with the supply of answering capabilities.

Seven Factors of
Caller Tolerance

Random call arrival, the fact that calls "bunch up," makes answering every call immediately highly impractical for most call centers. Accordingly, caller tolerance is another important driving force in incoming call centers. How long are callers willing to wait in queue? How many will abandon? Further, caller tolerance affects such things as how callers will react to automation, such as a voice response unit (VRU), and how favorably they perceive the service they get. Caller tolerance is influenced by seven major factors that are not static.

They include:

1. Degree of motivation: Callers to airlines wait longer during special price promotions than at other times. Callers with power-outages will wait longer to reach their utility than those with billing questions.

2. Availability of substitutes: The World Wide Web, fax, mail, other numbers and other selections in the VRU are examples of potential substitutes that callers try to reach the primary group. If a primary queue backs up, callers may dial other numbers available, choose incorrect routing selections in an automated attendant (press one for this, two for that...) or even call the company's main number (switchboard). If callers are highly motivated and have no workable substitutes, they will retry many times if they get busies, and will generally wait a long time in queue.

3. Competition's service level: This factor applies when callers have the alternative of using a competitor's services.

4. Level of expectations: The reputation that an organization or industry has for service (or the level of service being promoted) has a direct bearing on tolerance. For example, callers to catalog companies generally expect comparatively high levels of service, and are much less tolerant of queues than, say, callers to utilities or software support centers.

5. Time available: Doctors who call insurance providers are infamous for being intolerant of even modest waits. Retirees calling the same companies may have time to chat.

6. Who's paying for the call: In general, callers are more tolerant of a queue when the call is free to them.

7. Human behavior: The weather, the caller's mood and the day's news all have some bearing on caller tolerance.

Some call centers have discovered that telling callers how long the queue is can lower abandonment, generally if the queue is no more than two or three minutes. When the wait is unknown, a caller may wait 90 seconds in queue and hang up in frustration, when he or she would have been

cut through to an agent in 95 seconds. In the mid-80s, Word Perfect pioneered the use of "queue jockeys" to announce queue times to incoming callers, play music, deliver informational announcements, and generally entertain callers on hold. A handful of others companies have followed Word Perfect's example.

Although this approach is impractical for most, a small but growing number of call centers are using an

> ## We'll probably look back on these pioneering '70's, '80's and '90's and smile at how little we knew as callers.

automated approach, whereby the ACD looks at real time data, calculates the expected wait and relays that information to callers via intelligent system announcements. You need an ACD that has this capability. You also need a reasonably straightforward environment; if you're using some form of complex contingency-based routing (such as skills-based routing), the ACD generally cannot predict wait times accurately.

In the future, visible queues will be common. In fact, we'll probably look back on these pioneering '70's, '80's and '90's and smile at how little we knew as callers. With multimedia technologies, the queue will most likely be represented graphically on the caller's computer or video screen.

These driving forces behind us, the next articles in this series will cover such issues as staffing, service level, occupancy, group size, system configuration and the fundamentals of getting the right people and supporting resources in the right places at the right times.

SLN

Section 9

How Incoming Call Centers Behave: Back to the Basics, Part 2 of 3

In any inbound call center, there are predictable, fundamental laws at work. And just as you would need to understand such principles as gravity, lift and velocity in order to design or operate an aircraft, it's imperative to understand the laws that shape how call centers behave in order to manage effectively. Part 1 of this series reviewed random call arrival and caller tolerance, important "driving forces" in incoming call centers. This article will introduce key "laws of call center nature" and discuss their importance in planning and management decisions.

> *When adherence to schedule improves (goes up), service level will get better and occupancy will drop.*

Occupancy, Service Level and Group Size

Service level is expressed as "X percent of all calls answered in Y seconds." Occupancy is the percent of time during a half-hour that agents who are on the phones are either in talk time or after-call work (wrap-up). The inverse of occupancy is the time agents spend waiting for calls, plugged in and available.

Tables 1 and 2, which are based on Erlang C calculations, illustrate the relationship between service level and occupancy: for a given call load, occupancy goes up when service level goes down. In Table 1, for service level of 80/20, occupancy is 78 per-

cent; if service level drops to 14/20, occupancy goes up to 97 percent. What's the reason for this inverse relationship? If occupancy is high, it's because the agents on the phones are taking call after call after call, with little or no wait between calls. In other words, calls are backed up in queue and service level is low. In the worst scenario, occupancy is 100 percent for a long stretch of time because service level is so low that all callers spend at least some time in queue.

The size of the agent group also affects occupancy. At comparable levels of service, a large airline reservation center will have higher occupancy than a small call center serving a regional insurance company. Table 1 shows that 15 agents are required to handle 100 calls at a service level of 80/20; agent occupancy is at 78 percent. In Table 2, 40 agents are required to handle a call load three times as large and at the same service level, with occupancy at 88 percent.

Occupancy cannot be directly controlled. That can be a tough case to make in the budgeting process. The reality, though, is that the time agents spend waiting for calls — nine seconds here, 18 seconds there, two seconds there – is a necessary part of a good service level and is driven by how calls are arriving. Sure, even with very good forecasts and schedules, there will be times when you either have too many or too few agents; it only makes sense for them to do other activities when there is time to do so. But don't expect them to get other work done and still meet your service level objective if, according to Erlang C or computer simulation, you have no more than the minimum staff required to handle the call load.

At the individual level, standards

on number of calls handled are usually inherently unworkable or unfair. Agents can't control occupancy, and those assigned to larger groups, busier shifts or shifts that have lower service levels, will naturally have the opportunity to handle more calls. On the

> *At some point, the cost of adding additional staff outweighs the small improvements in service that they would bring.*

other hand, agents should be responsible for their, "adherence factor," or how well they adhere to their schedules. The terms occupancy and adherence factor are often incorrectly used interchangeably. But they have very different meanings and actually have an inverse relationship — when adherence to schedule improves (goes up), service level will get better and occupancy will drop.

As anyone who's handled calls knows, extended periods of high occupancy are stressful. Studies gen-

Section 9

Table 1

	Talk Time: 180 sec; Work Time: 30 sec; Calls: 100			
	SL %			Trunk
Agents	In 20 Sec.	ASA	Occ.	Load
12	14%	561	97%	41.2
13	46%	97	90%	15.4
14	67%	37	83%	12.1
15	80%	17	78%	10.9
16	89%	8	73%	10.5
17	94%	4	69%	10.2
18	97%	2	65%	10.1
19	98%	1	61%	10.1
20	99%	0	58%	10.0

erally conclude that agents begin to burn out when occupancy is higher than around 90 to 92 percent. Unfortunately, occupancy tends to feed on itself. When it's high to begin with, agents need and will often increasingly take breaks from the action. They may sign-off or, more subtly, stretch out talk time and/or after-call work time, which will cause service level to drop and occupancy to go higher still. (If you are running into this problem, see the suggestions in the third column on this page.)

The Law of Diminishing Returns

The law of diminishing returns says, "When successive individual telephone agents are assigned to a given call load, marginal improvements in service level that can be attributed to each additional agent will eventually decline." For example, Table 2 shows that 36 agents will provide a service level of 26 percent answer in 20 seconds with an ASA (average speed of answer) of 171 seconds. With just one more agent, service level jumps to 46/20 and ASA drops to

68 seconds — a quantum improvement. Adding one more person yields another big improvement. But keep adding staff, and the returns begin to diminish. At some point, the cost of adding additional staff outweighs the small improvements in service that they would bring.

Call centers that struggle with a low service level ought to like this law — it often doesn't take a lot of resources to improve things dramatically. On the other hand, those who want to be the "best of the best" in terms of service level find it takes a real commitment in staffing. That is why many call centers have target service levels such as 80/20 or 90/20 versus 100/20 or 100/0.

If you find yourself short-staffed, you'll notice that delay grows exponentially and occupancy quickly becomes high. Here are three proven strategies for avoiding these problems:

• Ensure that your staffing calculations are as accurate as possible. If service level is volatile throughout the day and week, or frequently below your objective, the fix may go to the fundamentals of managing a call center — a good forecast and schedules that better match staff to the workload.

• Make every agent aware of how much they contribute, even if they are tempted to feel like just "one of many." Explain service level and show them the call load patterns so they know how important schedule adherence is.

• Provide real-time queue information to supervisors and agents so they can adjust their activities according to real-time conditions.

In Part 3 of this series, we'll pick up with these and other immutable laws and further discuss their implications on planning and management.

Table 2

	Talk Time: 180 sec; Work Time: 30 sec; Calls: 300			
	SL %			Trunk
Agents	In 20 Sec.	ASA	Occ.	Load
36	26%	171	97%	58.4
37	46%	68	95%	41.4
38	61%	36	92%	36.0
39	72%	21	90%	33.6
40	81%	13	88%	32.2
41	86%	8	85%	31.4
42	91%	5	83%	30.9
43	94%	4	81%	30.6
44	96%	2	80%	30.4
45	97%	1	78%	30.2
46	98%	1	76%	30.2

SLN

Service Level Notes with Brad Cleveland

How Incoming Call Centers Behave: Back to the Basics, Part 3 of 3

There are predictable, fundamental laws at work in an incoming center. In order to manage effectively, it's imperative to understand how these laws shape how call centers behave. Part 1 of this series reviewed random call arrival and caller tolerance, important "driving forces" in incoming call centers. Part 2 discussed the relationship between service level and agent occupancy, and the impact of staffing levels on service level and agent occupancy. In Part 3, the last in this series, we'll look at how staffing levels impact the load on the trunks (and therefore, network costs), and discuss the management decisions surrounding the "powerful pooling principle."

Agents Impact Trunk Load

When more telephone agents are assigned to handle a given call load, the load that the trunks (telephone lines) must handle goes down. The converse is also true: when fewer agents are available to handle a given call load, trunk load goes up because delay increases (see Figure 1). Consider checking in for a flight — fewer agents at the counter means longer lines. In a call center, each person waiting in queue requires a trunk. You can see this relationship in the last column of Table 1, which gives the load to be carried by the trunks, expressed in erlangs (hours) — (talk time + average speed of answer) X number of calls in an hour (calculations are based on Erlang C). To determine ACD system capacity required, the following inputs are necessary:

• Calling load, which includes the number of calls the ACD will be required to handle at peak capacity, average talk time, and average after call wrap-up. Note, since wrap-up does not show up on trunking reports, trunk reports alone are insufficient to predict ACD capacity requirements.

• Service level objective, or "X percent of calls to be answered in Y seconds."

• Agent scheduling factors that accommodate absenteeism, lunch, breaks, training and other realities that will keep agents from the phones. Call center managers should know these numbers — often factors of 1.2 to 1.5

(for example, if Monday's 9:00 am factor is 1.3 and 20 agents need to be "plugged in," 26 agents will need to be scheduled, or 20 X 1.3). For more information, see *Service Level Notes*, November 1995.

Once the above inputs are used to calculate staff, trunks can be configured to carry the load (plus any VRU load not reflected in delay, etc.). Since delay is a function of staffing, staffing must be calculated before trunking. Further, the costs on the network are directly related to staffing levels (for information on calculating these costs, see *Service Level Notes*, February 1996). The major message from this immutable law is that staffing, system, and network resources must be planned and calculated in sync because they are inextricably associated. (For more information on calculating trunks, see *SLN's Q&A* column, December 1992).

The Powerful Pooling Principle

The pooling principle is a mathematical fact, based on the laws of probability. It states: any movement in the direction of consolidation of resources will result in improved traffic-carrying efficiency. Conversely, any movement away from consolidation of resources will result in reduced traffic-carrying efficiency. Note the efficiencies illustrated in Table 2; for

Figure 1

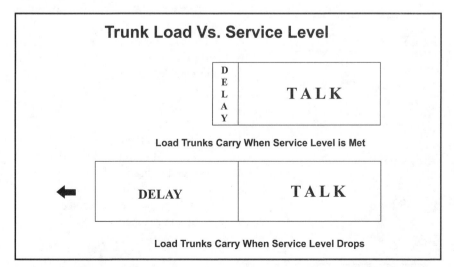

Trunk Load Vs. Service Level

DELAY | TALK

Load Trunks Carry When Service Level is Met

DELAY | TALK

Load Trunks Carry When Service Level Drops

Section 9

example, one combined group of 15 agents can handle the same call load at the same service level as two groups of nine agents.

To the degree you can combine smaller groups of agents into larger groups without increasing average handling time, you can A) handle more calls, at the same service level, with the same number of agents, B) handle same number of calls, at the same service level, with fewer agents, or C) handle the same number of calls, at a better service level, with the same number of agents.

The pooling principle is a consideration at the highest levels of strategic planning (i.e., call center consolidation or networking multiple sites) down to more specific decisions about how far to proceed with cross-training. In one sense, pooling resources is at the heart of what ACDs do. In fact, when ACDs first came into the market in the early 1970s, the big challenge was to get users to abandon the "clientele" approach, or the need to reach specific individuals. Further, geography no longer matters. In some cases, agents can work out of their homes if the proper telecommuting environment is established. And, networked-ACDs are virtually a "must-do" for organizations with multiple call centers.

Intelligent call processing capabilities in modern ACDs provide the means to bring diverse resources and skills together at just the right time. For example, skill-based routing enables the skills of each agent (i.e., knowledge of products or services or languages spoken) to be defined and identified to the ACD. Then, specific types of incoming calls can be matched with specific skills — assuming a good planning and management process is in place so the right agents are in fact available at the right times.

But it's important to remember that the most efficient environment would be one where any call could be handled by any agent. Further, if capabilities such as skill-based routing are implemented poorly, the number of contingencies can multiply beyond the call center's ability to manage them, reducing efficiencies and causing poor service. One thing is certain — as real and pervasive as the pooling principle is, it is not an all-or-nothing proposition. There is a continuum between pooling and specialization. Call centers should specialize when it clearly is necessary – i.e., for different languages or significantly different product lines — but should also look for cross-training opportunities wherever practical.

In a Nutshell

This series reviewed random call arrival and caller tolerance, important "driving forces" in incoming call centers. It then summarized important immutable laws:

• When service level goes up, occupancy goes down (at a given call load).

• With more staff, delay goes down and therefore trunk load goes down (at a given call load).

• The law of "diminishing returns."

• The "powerful pooling principle."

• Larger groups have higher occupancy (at a given service level).

These immutable laws shape the way call centers behave, and understanding them is a prerequisite to understanding the call center environment and managing it effectively.

Table 1

Talk Time: 180 sec; Work Time: 30 sec; Calls: 300				
Agents	SL % In 20 Sec.	ASA	Occ.	Trunk Load
36	26%	171	97%	58.4
37	46%	68	95%	41.4
38	61%	36	92%	36.0
39	72%	21	90%	33.6
40	81%	13	88%	32.2
41	86%	8	85%	31.4
42	91%	5	83%	30.9
43	94%	4	81%	30.6
44	96%	2	80%	30.4
45	97%	1	78%	30.2
46	98%	1	76%	30.2

Table 2

Calls	SL	Agents Req.	Occ.
25	80% in 20 sec.	5	58%
50	80% in 20 sec.	9	65%
100	80% in 20 sec.	15	78%
500	80% in 20 sec.	65	90%

*Assumption: Calls last 3.5 minutes.

Section 9

Service Level Notes with Brad Cleveland

Real-Time Management... without the Hangover

Real-time management is a fact of life in call centers. Take steps to avoid perpetuating resource management problems.

Real-time management must augment even the most accurate call center planning. That means monitoring events as they happen and making adjustments to plans and resource allocations as necessary.

Real-time management, though essential, has a serious downside. Real-time tactics that enhance supply or curb demand can also undermine the organization's ability to create accurate resource plans. These tactics — adjusting call handling processes, overflowing calls to secondary groups, postponing breaks and training, or reassigning agents to unplanned work — can create skewed activity reports. They can defer essential work or training. And they can complicate future workload and schedule predictions. In short, real-time management can create a hangover — perpetuating the imbalances that created the need for reactionary measures.

That doesn't mean that real-time tactics shouldn't be used. But you should employ them judiciously, and be alert to their implications on planning and management.

Preventative Steps

Many variables in the internal and external environments influence the numbers and types of inbound contacts. Call centers responsible for handling inbound calls operate in a "demand-chasing" environment. Each minute, the workload arrives randomly, subject to the whims of callers. At any moment, there are more calls to be answered than resources available; or there are more resources than calls. Call centers continually straddle the line between waiting agents and waiting customers.

Because supply and demand are rarely equal, and because situations in which demand outpaces supply create problems for both callers (long queues) and the call center (elevated network traffic and high agent occupancy), the supply of contact handling capabilities — properly skilled agents, IVR ports, database information, etc. — must "chase" demand to ensure supply remains adequate.

Effective resource planning can help meet this challenge. Sound workforce management principles enable you to predict resource requirements in advance. And they let you match resources to evolving workloads with what should be a high degree of accuracy.

The key to minimizing real-time measures is to establish a good foundation before contacts come crashing in. Translation: Ensure that you aren't, for lack of planning, creating crises you are reacting to.

One important foundational issue is to ensure that everybody understands the relationship between service level and quality. Although these performance measures may seem to be at odds in the short term, poor quality will negatively impact service level over time by contributing to repeat calls, waste and rework.

Supervisors and agents may feel the pressure of the moment forces them to trade between seemingly competing objectives. ("Hey, you train us to do a quality job, but then you emphasize service level. What do you really want?")

The answer: Look at the calls in queue; make certain you are as available as feasible; and do what's possible to arrange non-phone activities around the call load as it arrives. Above all, handle calls right the first time. If agents handle contacts cleanly and correctly, contacts don't repeat through other channels.

A related issue is to ensure that everybody maintains a consistent approach to handling calls, regardless of queue conditions. Each agent impacts the components of call load (including average talk time, after-call work, and volume) and, therefore, the data used for forecasting and planning call loads. When the queue is building, one is tempted to postpone after-call work (wrap-up). This skews reports, causes planning problems and may lead to increased errors. The solution is to define what work should follow calls and which tasks can wait.

It is also important for everybody to be aware of how much impact each person has on the queue. As the figure on the facing page demonstrates, each additional agent impacts the queue. With 41 agents, service level is low — agents answer about 5 percent of calls in 20 seconds (note, because Erlang C assumes no busy signals or abandoned calls, the problem could be somewhat overstated). But each additional person contributes to service level. The message is clear: When a queue begins to build (or when it's well-developed) each person makes a measurable difference — up to a point. As the chart indicates, the percentage service level gain with each additional agent diminishes. At 52 agents, service level effectively plateaus.

Agents must understand this relationship between agents and service level so they know what to look for, how to react and keep queues from spinning out of control. To handle calls and contacts properly, agents must have real-time information, typically via wall-mounted displays, displays on telephones or in a window on the desktop.

Monitoring Trends

Service level — a high-level measure of the queue callers encounter — is a primary focus in call center planning. Ser-

The Relationship of Agents and Service Level

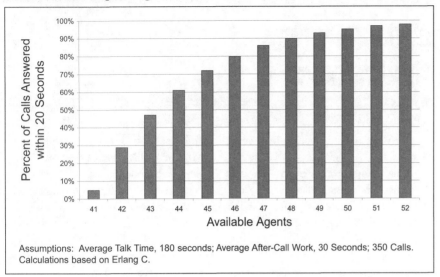

Assumptions: Average Talk Time, 180 seconds; Average After-Call Work, 30 Seconds; 350 Calls. Calculations based on Erlang C.

vice level represents historical data (e.g., calls during half hours, hours, or days) provided by the ACD. Service level is also historical when reporting "real time": The ACD must look back some number of calls (e.g., 20), or some amount of time (e.g., 10 minutes) to make the service level calculation. (Note: Determine where these thresholds are set in your system.) Ditto for average speed of answer and average time to abandonment.

However, the number of calls in queue is a real-time report, as is longest current wait and current agent status. Understanding the distinction between reports that are real time and those that must incorporate recent history explains apparent contradictions.

For example, service level may read 45 percent in 20 seconds even though there are no calls in queue. Keep watching the monitor, though, and service level will begin to climb. Or service level may look high at the moment even though an enormous amount of calls are stuck in queue. Give it a few minutes and, unless circumstances change, it will have dropped significantly. In short, service level as reported "real time" does not immediately reflect new developments.

One should pay closest attention to the number of calls in queue and the longest current wait because these variables foretell where service level will go (unless conditions change). As circumstances dictate, assess the mode agents are

in — signed off, auxiliary, handling calls, etc. — and make appropriate adjustments. If you focus only on service level, it may be too late to prevent a sizable traffic jam.

Escalation Plans

Because preventative steps alone won't always cure problems, effective real-time management also requires a workable escalation plan that outlines other steps. The best plans typically define a three-tiered approach. The first level of response involves steps immediately and easily available. For example, agents who are unavailable or involved in flexible activities are reassigned to the queue.

The second level of response includes such tactics as adjusting breaks, lunch, meeting, and training schedules; reassigning agents from one group to another; or having supervisors and managers help handle the call load. These tactics go beyond the readily available responses defined by level one, but are still within easy reach.

The highest-level response engenders tactics that are increasingly severe in cost, deviation from plans or impact on customer perceptions. Examples include significant adjustments to overflow or call routing thresholds; calling in reinforcements from other departments (sometimes called a "swat team"); making announcements to callers of "unusually heavy call volumes"; or taking messages

for callbacks or generating busy signals (extreme tactics that are generally not recommended).

The key is to identify all tactics that are feasible within the context of the environment and to categorize them appropriately. You thereby follow a logical progression when the dust starts flying. Minor resource imbalances merit level one response; more serious resource problems call for escalation to more involved tactics.

Revising Reports and Plans

An important but sometimes neglected aspect of real-time management is to analyze what happened once the crisis has passed, and to revise workforce management plans as necessary. How well did the escalation plan work? Were the right tactics deployed? Do schedules need to change?

Essential to this process is adjusting the data used for forecasting resource requirements. For example, calls overflowed from one agent group to another will impact the volume and average handling times of both the primary and secondary groups. Generally, schedule forecasts should reflect what is most likely to happen, not what occurred due to real-time tactics. In short, those involved in forecasting and scheduling will need to revisit historical data used in projections. Using the reports as they are may perpetuate the circumstances that created the problems.

Real-time management is a fact of life in call centers. But taking steps to prevent real-time reactions, and developing sensible escalation plans, will ensure that your approach to real-time management isn't creating the very problems it is supposed to solve!

CCMReview

Brad Cleveland

Brad Cleveland is president of Incoming Calls Management Institute (ICMI) and publisher of Call Center Management Review. *He can be reached at 410-267-0700 (ext. 958), or bradc@incoming.com.*

Measuring Individual Agent Performance

Editor's Note: Due to the numerous requests from readers for information about how to fairly and effectively measure individual agent performance, we're running this popular article that was originally published in April 1996.

Want to start a lively discussion among call center managers? Float the issue of performance measurements for agents by them. Since performance measurements are usually tied to expectations and standards, that will raise issues about fairness, what agents can and can't control, why people have different capabilities and drives, and the processes that they are working within. Few subjects elicit such strong and varied opinion.

Consequently, there are about as many different sets of performance measurements and standards as there are call centers. Here, we will look at three types of performance measurements — calls per hour, adherence and qualitative measurements — commonly used in assessing individual performance. We'll also discuss why calls per hour is fading, while the other two types of measurements continue to gain acceptance.

Calls Per Hour

Traditionally, calls per hour has been an almost universal produc-

tivity measurement. In fact, many call center managers have viewed calls per hour as virtually synonymous with "productivity." Sure, there have always been concerns about sacrificing quality for quantity. But in practice, calls per hour has been the preferred benchmark for establishing productivity standards, comparing performance among agents and groups, and assessing the impact of changes and improvements to the call center.

However, as a measure of performance, calls per hour is, and

> As a measure of performance, calls per hour is, and always has been, problematic.

always has been, problematic. Many of the variables that impact calls per hour are out of agents' control: call arrival rate, type of calls, knowledge of callers, communication ability of callers, accuracy of the forecast and schedule, adherence to schedule (of others in the group), and absenteeism.

There are also mathematical realities at work that are not within the control of an individual agent. For example, smaller groups are less efficient (have lower occupancy) than larger groups, at a given service level (see Table 1). Since the number of calls changes throughout the day, so does average calls per hour for a group or an individual in the group.

And, as is often pointed out, if calls per hour is over-emphasized, quality can suffer. Agents may even "trick" the system to increase their call count and achieve a set standard. (Many call center managers get a sheepish smile when this point comes up in discussion. One could surmise that more than a few, once upon a time, have "accidentally" clicked off or erroneously transferred a call or two.)

Some call center managers convert raw calls per hour into an adjusted measurement that is more fair and meaningful. For example, occupancy, which is not within the control of an individual, can be "neutralized" by dividing calls handled by percent occupancy. Using the numbers in Table 1, 5.6 average calls per agent divided by 65 percent is 8.6 "normalized" calls, as is 6.7 calls divided by 78 percent,

Section 9

Table 1

Calls In 1/2 Hour	Level:	Reps Required:	Occupancy:	Avg. Calls Per Rep:
50	80/20	9	65%	5.6
100	80/20	15	78%	6.7
500	80/20	65	90%	7.7
1000	80/20	124	94%	8.1

Assumptoions: Calls last 3.5 minutes. Calculations based on Erlang C for 1/2 hour's calls.

7.7 calls divided by 90 percent and 8.1 calls divided by 94 percent. Others go a step further and develop statistical control charts to determine whether the process is in control, what it's producing, and which agents, if any, are outside of "statistical control."

But even with further analysis, calls per hour begins to lose meaning as technologies such as CTI, skills-based routing and Web integration, which enable increasingly sophisticated and varied call- handling routines, proliferate. For many who have depended on calls per hour, this has left a vacuum: How can we measure productivity in an increasingly varied and com-

> ## Calls per hour begins to lose meaning as technologies such as CTI, skills-based routing and Web integration, which enable increasingly sophisticated and varied call-handling routines, proliferate.

plex environment? Enter adherence and qualitative measurements, which are gaining increasing acceptance.

Adherence Measurements

Adherence factor, or signed-on time, is a measurement of how much time an individual is available to handle calls versus the time he or she was scheduled to handle calls. If adherence factor is 85 percent, an agent would be expected to be in adherence .85 x 60 minutes, or 51 minutes on average per hour. Adherence consists of all plugged-in time including talk time, after-call work (wrap-up) time, time spent waiting for the next call and making necessary outgoing calls. Lunch, breaks, training, etc., are not counted as time assigned to handle calls. Adherence factor should be established at a level that is reasonable and that reflects the many things that legitimately keep agents from the phones. It should also be flexible (adjustable downward) when call volumes are low.

Some have developed adherence factor into a more refined measurement that also incorporates timing — when was a person available to take calls, in addition to how much time they were available. The idea here is to ensure that people are plugged in mid-morning when calls are barreling in, and are saving special projects for Thursday and Friday afternoon when calls slow down. ACD and forecasting/scheduling software has improved adherence reporting significantly in recent years.

The advantage of adherence factor is that it is reasonably objective. Agents cannot control variables such as the number of staff scheduled to answer calls, the number of calls coming in, the distribution of long and short calls or the distribution of easy and difficult calls. But they can generally control how available they are to take calls.

Qualitative Measurements

In most call centers, qualitative criteria, which focus on knowledge of products and services, customer service and call-handling skills, and the policies of the organization, continue to become more refined and specific. Most use some form of monitoring (i.e., remote, side-by-side, or record and review) to evaluate individual performance and identify training and coaching needs.

An important and developing aspect of quality is that agents take the necessary time to do the job right — no more, no less. This means not rushing calls, but also not spending excess time on calls over and above what is necessary to satisfy callers and handle them completely and correctly. If qualitative measurements are refined enough to ensure that agents are spending the appropriate amount of time handling calls, then adherence and qualitative measurements make a powerful pair. In fact, measuring calls per hour becomes unnecessary.

This is easier said than done in environments where qualitative measurements are vague and indeterminate. And many managers still believe that tracking production

> ## Well-defined qualitative measurements are beginning to erode reliance on measurements that are after-the-fact outputs.

outputs, such as calls per hour or average handling time, is necessary. But the trend is clear: well-defined qualitative measurements are beginning to erode reliance on measurements that are after-the-fact outputs.

Cultivating Success

Calls per hour, which used to be an almost ubiquitous productivity measurement, is fading. It is increasingly being replaced by focused and specific qualitative and adherence measurements. Agents can concentrate on being available and on handling each transaction according to its individual needs. If implemented well, qualitative and adherence measurements can cultivate a better working environment, better quality — and higher productivity.

CCMReview

Service Level Notes with Brad Cleveland ▬▬▬▬

How Key Performance Indicators (KPIs) are Evolving

It takes a significant amount of information to effectively manage a call center. That has always been the case, even in the relatively straightforward telephone-centric centers of yesteryear. But throw in proliferating channels of communication, an ever-increasing range of responsibilities and the competitive necessity to track customer interactions at deeper levels, and the task of collecting and interpreting call center reports becomes even more daunting.

Enter KPIs – key performance measurements. The purpose of KPIs is to enable you to climb above the detail and assess overall performance – a compelling concept to call center managers buried in data. Unfortunately, the high-level nature of KPIs is also their biggest weakness – as measures that summarize a lot of detail, they don't pinpoint specific problems. However, if chosen and interpreted wisely, they can indicate general trends that will often point the way to more detailed reports which, in turn, will enable you to isolate and address specific problems and improvement opportunities.

Following are summaries of 12 KPIs recommended by Incoming Calls Management Institute and brief descriptions of how they are evolving to address the demands of today's changing customer interaction environment.

> *Like the key flight instruments on an aircraft instrument panel, KPIs must be interpreted together – the best-managed call centers are continually looking for connections and relationships between the variables.*

Customer Satisfaction/Loyalty

Customer satisfaction has long been a priority of well-run call centers. However, there is a trend today to go beyond satisfaction, to measure and improve customer loyalty. A prerequisite to accurately assessing satisfaction/loyalty is to collect data on a representative sample of customer experiences and perceptions across the full range of contact channels and issues. Accordingly, many firms continue to conduct ongoing customer satisfaction surveys via outbound calls, mail and fax, even as they add e-mail, Web and automated VRU-based samples. (To read about the most recent research on customer satisfaction with electronic contacts, see "Companies Not Managing E-Contact Satisfaction" on page 1.)

Assessing loyalty – a burgeoning art and science which, by nature, involves predictions of consumer behavior – is more difficult than gauging customer satisfaction. However, a growing bevy of organizations are providing resources related to defining and measuring loyalty, including e-Satisfy.com (formerly TARP at tarp.com), SOCAP (socap.com), ICSA (icsa.com), CustomerSat.com, and many others. *CCMReview* will also continue to focus on the this evolving discipline.

Agent Satisfaction

It has been proven time and again, in a wide range of organizations, that customer satisfaction tends to move in the same direction as agent satisfaction. "The Customer Comes Second!" declared Hal Rosenbluth over a decade ago (*The Customer Comes Second*, Quill, reissue edition, 1994). Certainly makes sense. (See "Evaluating Pride of Workmanship," *CCMReview*, August 1998.)

Turnover

Turnover should be differentiated by internal turnover (going to other positions within the organization) and external turnover or "negative attrition" (going to other organizations).

Service Level/Response Time

Service level and response time are time-tested measures that, between them, gauge the organization's accessibility via any channel of contact. While they can be measured down to specific increments of time for operational purposes, they are most usable as KPIs when summarized by individual contact channel, according to how many half-hour results were at, above or below target objectives. (See "Service Level and Response Time in a New Era," Parts 1 and 2, *CCMReview*, July and August, 1997.)

Percent Abandoned

Abandonment has long been a concern in call centers. And with the growth of new channels of contact, additional classifications of abandoned contacts are emerging, ranging from callers who bail out of VRU menus to e-shoppers who abandon shopping carts before checking out. However, a fundamental truth remains: Abandonment is a customer behavior that is difficult to forecast. You can't directly fix abandonment. But you can fix the things that contribute to abandonment, e.g., long queues or

Cost Per Contact

The basic formula to calculate cost per contact is to divide total costs associated with each contact channel, by total contacts received over a given period of time (e.g., a month). You will need to agree on assumptions related to assigning costs (e.g., how to allocate equipment and facilities).

Further, the KPI should differentiate by each channel or combination of channels of contact (i.e., inbound call, VRU only, VRU to rep, Web only, Web to rep, etc.) and by general services provided (i.e., placing orders, changing orders, checking account status, problem resolution, etc.).

Once you get an approach in place you can live with, there is great value in tracking cost per contact vis-à-vis the factors driving it upward or downward, and in assessing the impact of changes in the contact mix. There is also a trend toward tracking the cost per incident or issue, or the total costs across media to make a sale, resolve a customer service issue or provide a service. These costs can then be compared to a variety of customer demographics to create more focused products and services.

Errors and Rework/
Handled on First Contact

Errors and rework and a related measure called "handled on first con-

Key Performance Indicators

- Customer Satisfaction/Loyalty
- Agent Satisfaction
- Turnover
- Service Level/Response Time
- Percent Abandoned
- Cost Per Contact
- Errors and Re-work/
  Handled on First Contact
- Actual to Forecasted Call Load
- Actual to Scheduled Staff
- Adherence to Schedule
- Average Handling Time
- Average Value of Contact

tact" are a lasting outgrowth of the quality movement. Errors and rework or repeat transactions are particularly troublesome in call centers. They consume valuable staff time, which can lead to insufficient staffing to handle the workload; insufficient staffing tends to lead to high occupancy, unhappy callers and increased stress on the staff – which contribute to additional errors and rework. This cycle is further compounded in a multi-channel environment, e.g., insufficient service via e-mail often turns into telephone calls.

There are a variety of alternatives for producing this KPI. For example, the database may allow you to track repeat calls, unresolved issues and errors in data entry. Monitoring or side-by-side coaching should detect and track specific problems that are occurring during call handling. Call coding in the ACD (where reps use codes to track specific types of calls and issues) can trace problems. And transferred calls, escalated calls, customer complaints and correspondence (both to and from customers) can provide additional sources of information.

Actual to Forecasted Call-load

Forecasting the workload is a high-leverage activity that is fundamental to managing a call center effectively. Common practice is to blend quantitative "time series" forecasting (projecting out existing patterns for each contact channel) with judgmental forecasting (e.g., what is the expected impact of a new marketing campaign? New terms and procedures? Process changes? The weather?). If your forecasts are routinely off by more than 3 percent or 5 percent, you will need to identify the variables causing the inaccuracies, and work on better anticipating or resolving them.

Actual to Scheduled Staff

This measure is independent of whether you actually have the staff necessary to achieve a targeted service level. How well do the staff you do have adhere to schedule, overall?

If this is a problem, why?

Adherence To Schedule

Adherence factor is a measure of the time an individual is handling or available to handle customer contacts. It generally consists of all plugged-in time, including the time waiting for transactions to arrive.

Today, with multiple channels of contact and growing responsibilities, it is more important than ever for agents to be "in the right places at the right times, doing the right things." Not all systems provide seamless reports across all channels of contact, so some piecing together of data may be necessary.

Average Handling Time

Average handling time (AHT) traditionally brings together two components, including talk time (everything from hello to goodbye) and after-call work (work that must immediately follow the contact).

Average handling time, and the ratio of talk time to after-call work (if applicable) varies significantly from one call center to another and usually varies from one channel of contact to another. Tracking AHT is essential to forecasting, process improvement and other aspects of planning and management.

Average Value of Contact

This measure, which applies specifically to sales and reservations environments, is generally calculated by dividing total revenue generated by number of contacts.

Conclusion

Any individual KPI, by itself, can be misleading. Like the key flight instruments on an aircraft instrument panel, KPIs must be interpreted together – the best managed call centers are continually looking for connections and relationships between the variables. But together, they paint a fairly complete, high-level picture of your call center's performance.

Technology Focus with Jay Minnucci
Forecasting and Scheduling: Beyond the Basics

Even if the forecasting and scheduling in your call center is fairly accurate, you may be ready to take it to the next level.

So just how good are your forecasts? Typically within 7 percent? Usually under 3 percent? Hitting a target of 5 percent?

Those are nice-sounding numbers, but I'm less interested in the number than the timeframe. So my followup question is: "Over what timeframe is that accuracy measured?"

This is where things tend to get a little shaky. Good call center managers are used to reviewing individual agent results over a week or month, since that provides the most accurate picture of performance. So the assumption is made that longer timeframes are always better for any kind of analysis. As a result, forecast accuracy is usually measured by the week, month or even quarter. But where forecast accuracy measurements are concerned, longer timeframes serve only to dilute the results. Even daily accuracy measurements don't tell the true story.

Table 1, below, provides an example to illustrate the point. This scenario shows performance results over three different half-hour intervals. During each interval, the average handling time (AHT) projection is perfect and adher-

ence is 100 percent. The only difference in this exercise is the projection accuracy for each interval. While the projection for the first interval is perfect, actual volume in Interval 2 is 10 percent under projection, and it is 10 percent over for Interval 3. The column on the far right shows the service level result for each interval.

The problem comes into play when you focus on the last row – overall results. Here's a case where the overall projection for the three intervals is right in line with actual results, the AHT projection is perfect and adherence is 100 percent (this is the call center manager's version of the stars being in perfect alignment!). Yet with what seems like a scenario that is too good to be true, service level is only 63 percent – well below the goal of 80 percent. What happened?

The answer is that the summary results are simply hiding the problems that exist throughout the day. Over-projecting during one interval masks the under-projecting that occurred during another interval, so the summary appears fine. Unfortunately, service level isn't able to follow the same pattern. When volume is 10 percent under projections, you will likely see service level results that are a bit above your goal (in this case, 17 percentage points above the goal). But when volume is 10 percent over projections, the penalty can be severe. In this case, service level is 59 percentage points under the goal during this interval.

There Are Better Ways

to Measure How Good You Are

The previous exercise demonstrates how important it is to measure accuracy correctly. And the only correct way to do it is to focus on the interval level. Of course, most people don't want to see a report that shows accuracy by every interval throughout the day for every distinct call group in your center (too much paper!). So how do you provide the key contacts in your center with a simple report that accurately displays your forecasting results?

Table 2 shows a way to clearly and accurately display your forecast performance over time. By grouping results into categories, you can provide a very

Table 2. Performance Over Time

Accuracy Rate	% of Intervals
98.0% to 100%	12.5%
95.0% to 97.9%	25.0%
90.0% to 94.9%	34.4%
85.0% to 89.9%	21.9%
Under 85.0%	6.2%

accurate representation of your forecasting efforts. And you should not focus on volume alone. Handle time (both talk and after-call work) has just as much impact on staffing as volume, so a similar chart can be used to track AHT accuracy, as well.

Volume and handle time are the key inputs (along with your service level objective) to staffing requirements, so the measurements in Table 2 will provide you with the information you need to start improving these inputs. And those of you who are responsible for forecasts will understand the impact of the results. But that may not be true of everyone who is dependent on your forecasts.

To help display the importance of forecast accuracy, it is important to put it into terms that everyone in the call

Table 1. Performance Results for Three Half-Hour Intervals

Interval	Projected Volume	Actual Volume	Projected/ Actual AHT	Scheduled Actual Staff	Actual Service Level
1	305	305	300	57	80%
2	305	274	300	57	97%
3	305	336	300	57	21%
Total	915	915	300	57	63%

Section 9

center understands. To do this, we recommend some "after the fact" calculations to compare scheduled staff to what was actually needed during the interval. An Erlang chart (or your own workforce management system) can be used to generate this information. Simply use actual volume and handle time results to determine what the staffing requirement should have been, and compare it to the scheduled staffing requirement. Table 3, below, shows this comparison along with the percentage of error between scheduled staff and required staff.

Where Do You Go From Here?

Most call center managers are familiar with the adage "what gets measured, improves." The methodology previously discussed will paint an accurate picture of forecast and scheduling accuracy, and will help drive the organization to find news ways to improve the planning process. That's reason enough to measure accuracy in this manner, since a solid planning process can go a long way to achieving service level goals. Even if there were no more value to be derived from this exercise, these improvements would be well worth the time and effort.

But there is so much more that we can do with this data. Accuracy measurements can be used to pave a path to further workforce management improvements. By generating valid data on accuracy, we are, in effect, handing ourselves one more piece of information that can be used to generate better schedules. To understand that, we have to first accept one of the shortcomings of our current forecasting methods – ignoring our own inaccuracy.

Getting the Most Out of Your Accuracy Results

Think about it – an awful lot of data goes into our volume and handle-time projections – historical trends, planned events, growth rates, etc. We take all of those ingredients, run them through all our fancy calculations and software, and come back with a number – one single number – which becomes the staffing projection for that interval. Do we really believe that we can accurately take into account all of those different factors that affect volume and all of those different factors that shape caller behavior and, time after time, deliver a staffing requirement that is absolutely perfect?

Unless you've been taking lessons from Nostradamus, the answer should be "no." So rather than ignore the degree of error that we know exists in our projections, instead, let's start using that data to generate even better schedule requirements.

One simple way to do this is to look at the average percentage of error (by interval) in our forecasts. The far right column in Table 3 shows how to arrive at this calculation. Notice that we are ignoring whether the error is positive or negative. In this example, the weighted average of our error rate for this time period is 4.5 percent.

Once we know that, we can put the number to work. Rather than sending out a schedule that says we need 110 people from 10:00 to 10:30, we can send out a schedule indicating that we need

at least 105 (110 - 4.5 percent), and maybe as many as 115 (110 + 4.5 percent), agents on the phone. And while, on the surface, this may sound a little indecisive, any concerns surrounding that will disappear once everyone understands how this information can drive performance improvements.

Consider the possibilities. Rather than putting 110 agents on the phone, hoping that's right and scrambling if it isn't, the call center can take a completely different approach. It can schedule 105 agents for the phone and let them know there is little or no chance that they can get off the phone for other activities during that time period (it may not be what they want to hear, but at least it gives them clear information about how they'll be spending the half-hour). The call center manager can take another five agents and tell them that they will probably be needed on the phone, but there's a chance they'll be able to sign off and do some other work at their desk. So now they can be prepared and have the work available if they are not needed. And the manager can inform a second group of five people that they probably won't be needed, but they should stay near the phone and sign on if there are X number of callers in queue. We call this approach "tiered scheduling" – using it, the call center can substantially reduce the chaos that surrounds real-time management. Tiered scheduling replaces this chaos with a more disciplined methodology that not only responds more quick-

Table 3. Comparison of Actual Volume and Handle Time Results with Percentage of Error

Interval	Projected Volume	Actual Volume	Projected AHT (secs)	Actual AHT (secs)	Scheduled Staff-Based on Projections	Required Staff-Based on Actuals	Percent Scheduling Error
10:00	592	590	310	299	110	106	3.8%
10:30	617	631	312	317	115	120	4.2%
11:00	638	683	315	316	120	129	7.0%
11:30	622	614	322	317	120	117	2.6%

Section 9

ly to the peaks and valleys within an interval of traffic, but also gives agents more advance notice about their scheduled activities.

Finally, if you're the type who wants to get even more value out of the data, you may be wondering if there is a better approach than using averages. You'll be glad to know that there is. Measuring this kind of variance is an excellent application for standard deviation, which is the measure of how tightly a set of values is clustered around the average. By using standard deviation, you can produce schedule ranges that have a certain level of confidence associated with them, which further reduces reliance on real-time schedule adjustments. Standard deviation can be very powerful when working with projections – but it is also a bit too detailed to discuss in this article.

Accurate Schedules Make for a Well-Run Call Center

Good forecasts lead to good schedules, and an accurate schedule is the backbone of a well-run call center.

The first step to improving forecasts and schedules is to start measuring accuracy in the appropriate manner. Once you've done that, a world of possibilities opens up to take your planning processes to the next level and beyond. CCMReview

Jay Minnucci

Jay Minnucci is the Director of Consulting for Incoming Calls Management Institute. In this role, he provides strategic and tactical consulting for call centers in all different industries. Jay can be reached at (610) 966-4700, or at jaym@incoming.com

Section 9

The Pain and Gain of Skills-Based Routing in Call Centers

by Greg Levin

Skills-based routing – the strategic routing of customer calls to the most qualified agents available to handle those calls – is one of the hottest trends in call centers today. It is also one of the most misunderstood.

Skills-based routing (SBR) is a potentially powerful call center tool that breaks through the boundaries of traditional call distribution. In doing so, it can present daunting challenges for call centers. Most managers struggle enough trying to simply match the right number of staff to the incoming call load for each ACD group. Throw in the added objective of routing calls based on individual agents' specific knowledge and skill levels, and the call center can become a breeding ground for chaos.

While some call centers have faltered in their SBR ventures, others have hurdled most of the challenges on the way to bolstering performance and customer satisfaction. Their success was the result of carefully examining the intricacies of SBR and deciding how best to implement it in their specific environment. But even those with proven SBR applications say that the challenges never really stop.

Too many companies implement SBR without fully understanding the impact it has on virtually every major aspect of call center management – forecasting and scheduling, training and motivating agents, etc. Instead, managers get sold on vendors' well-versed descriptions of the benefits SBR will bring to the call center – quicker, more personalized service, higher first-call resolution percentage, and more agent career-path opportunities.

These potential benefits may be real, but can be realized only after the call center undergoes a rigorous planning process, which includes:

- Identifying callers' needs (call types)

- Defining and prioritizing agents' skill sets to meet those needs

- Learning to consistently and efficiently match callers' needs to agents' skills on a daily basis (i.e., forecasting/scheduling and programming appropriate call-routing plans).

Before even beginning the planning process, managers must determine if SBR is appropriate for their call center environment.

"Don't implement skills-based routing just because it's fashionable," warns Marty Prunty, director of consulting and implementation services for ALLTEL Call Center Solutions in Little Rock, Ark. "Implement it because your center handles a variety of call types and because you need to improve the efficiency of your existing staff. But count on having more administrative tasks to contend with if you decide to implement it."

Filling the Gap between Universal Agents and ACD Groups

SBR is not a "perfect world" scenario for call centers handling diverse call types. A more ideal solution would involve universal agents, where every agent knows everything about every product/service and can speak every language the call center handles, says Prunty. While this would result in the highest efficiency, a true universal agent environment is next to impossible to achieve, considering the amount of agent turnover in most centers and the amount of training time required to cover the diversity of skill sets.

The least efficient call center environment – and perhaps the most common – involves ACD groups, where separate groups of agents each handle a specific call type or product

type. According to Prunty, the more ACD groups a call center has, the less efficient it is.

SBR, when well-implemented, can help fill the gap between the elusive universal agent concept and the inefficient ACD group concept, Prunty explains.

"For example, let's say you have a call center that handles customer service, sales, and product support calls for two products in English and Span-

> *SBR, when well-implemented, can help fill the gap between the elusive universal agent concept and the inefficient ACD group concept*

ish. Without SBR (or universal agents), you would need several different agent groups to have each call handled by the most qualified agents. And wait times can get long if one group gets slammed. With SBR, you may have an agent qualified to handle customer service and sales calls for both products in English, another qualified to handle customer service and product support calls for product 2 in English and Spanish, another who can handle all three call types for product 1 in English, and so on. By tapping the potential of your agents' diverse skills and staffing/routing appropriately, your center can dramatically improve service levels with no additional staff."

But doing so is no simple task. Take the straightforward call center example above: the number of possible combinations of requirements that callers might present to the center is shown in the box below.

In an SBR environment, ensuring that you have the right mix of staff trained to handle all call types efficiently can be difficult. Complicating matters is the fact that traditional staffing calculations go out the window once you add SBR to the mix. Traditional workforce management tools rely on Erlang tables, which assume that calls entering the queue are random and unknown. But SBR identifies the caller and/or the caller's needs, thus countering Erlang's assumptions. "The real 'fun' in SBR is matching up the resources necessary to handle that forecast when you have agents with a wide variety of skill sets," says Prunty.

How do call centers do it effectively? "Many of them who have been dealing with SBR for a while take their Erlang C calculations and tweak the heck out of them based on what they know about their calling patterns," says Prunty. "They learn by trial and error." He adds that call-by-call simulation technology can help lessen the call management complexity brought on by SBR. Simulators enable call center managers to run hypothetical call scenarios on a PC to see how the center will perform under various conditions.

SBR Survivors Speak

Most call center managers with successful SBR applications in place refer to themselves as survivors. "We had to endure significant growing pains to get it to work the way it does today," says Rick Welch, vice president of reservations, sales and services for Certified Vacations' call center in Ft. Lauderdale, Fla. "[SBR] can't be taken lightly, especially when you first implement it."

Deborah Charlton, director of subscriber relations for Media General Cable's call center in Fairfax County, Va., offers a similar sentiment. "We've lived through the numerous

challenges involved in [SBR]. We had to adapt to a whole new call center environment."

Despite the struggles with SBR, both managers say they now would

"If you don't take the time to do it right, you can create a disaster. You really have to study this process and make a commitment to the training before you roll out a full application."

Rick Welch

not operate their centers any other way.

Certified Vacations, a wholesale tour operator that handles vacation tours for several airlines as well as American Express and AAA, implemented SBR in late 1995. The 300-agent call center has six "destination desks," such as Florida/USA, the Caribbean, Hawaii and Europe. Within each destination desk there are various products and call types. Using Lucent's Expert Agent Skills product,

Certified is able to maximize the capabilities of its agents and shorten callers' wait times. "It gives us the ability to efficiently route calls based on the training and skill sets we have developed for agents in our center," Welch says. "Because we have agents with numerous 'back-up' skills, I can cut back on my headcount when staffing for each destination and/or call type." To help determine how best to route each call, the center uses dialed number identification service (DNIS). "For example," Welch explains, "if we run a promotion for travel to Disney World in the newspaper, we'll include a special 800 number. Whenever a caller dials that number, the call is quickly routed to an agent specially trained to handle that call type." In addition to DNIS, the center uses IVR prompts to pinpoint what each caller wants and to which agent to route the call.

Media General also uses DNIS and IVR prompts in its SBR application, which features Siemens' ResumeRouting product. The Siemens product is programmed to route each call to an agent who specializes in handling that particular call type. If no "specialized" agents are available, the call is routed to an agent who has been trained to handle the call type. Each agent in the call center is specialized in one or two call tracks – i.e., customer service or service repair – and spends most of their time handling those call types (within each

Possible Combinations in a Simple SBR Scenario

1. English-speaking callers requiring customer service for product 1
2. English-speaking callers requiring sales assistance for product 1
3. English-speaking callers requiring product support for product 1
4. English-speaking callers requiring customer service for product 2
5. English-speaking callers requiring sales assistance for product 2
6. English-speaking callers requiring product support for product 2
7. Spanish-speaking callers requiring customer service for product 1
8. Spanish-speaking callers requiring sales assistance for product 1
9. Spanish-speaking callers requiring product support for product 1
10. Spanish-speaking callers requiring customer service for product 2
11. Spanish-speaking callers requiring sales assistance for product 2
12. Spanish-speaking callers requiring product support for product 2

track there are several skills/call types). But agents are also trained to handle calls in as many as three or four other call tracks to provide back-up whenever agents who specialize in those call tracks are unavailable. The center also has a few agents who handle Spanish and Korean calls. "You have to carefully program 'resumes' for each agent within the Resume Routing product so that calls are routed quickly and effectively," explains Media General's Charlton.

Prior to implementing SBR in February 1996, the 145-agent call center consisted of several different groups that each handled specific call types. "We wanted an efficient way to combine some of these groups because we had times when agents in one group were sitting idle while others were jamming," Charlton recalls. "[SBR] has enabled us to enhance service and reduce staffing."

Training and Scheduling Sometimes Scary

Both Certified Vacations and Media General train new hires to handle the most common call types, then later encourage them to learn additional skills as they gain experience. Because of the importance of having numerous multi-skilled agents in place, the call centers provide incentives to motivate agents to acquire new skills. "We have different pay levels and bonuses for different skills, so there is a definite and defined career path for agents," Welch explains. "The challenge isn't in motivating agents to obtain new skills, but in finding time to train agents for those new skills. We work hard to meet agents' training needs."

Media General takes the training load off managers and supervisors by employing a dedicated trainer who often works one-on-one with agents

seeking new skills. To ensure that agents don't overload on skills too quickly, Media General requires each agent to spend several months between new training sessions.

The biggest challenge regarding SBR, according to the managers of both call centers, is scheduling the right number of agents with the right skills to best handle the forecasted call load. "When we first implemented [SBR], we had to have people in our 'ACD Office' pick-off calls and route them by hand until we got the scheduling and routing down pat," says Welch. While the call center has since gotten a better handle on these tasks, challenges still exist. The call center has to constantly monitor the queues to ensure that one or two call types aren't waiting excessively while all other calls are answered promptly, according to Welch.

Charlton agrees. "There are some delicate balances involved in making sure that certain people are getting calls before or after certain other people."

Charlton also acknowledges that occasionally customers have to wait in queue for a while because qualified agents are unavailable. In such instances, however, the assistance is often provided by four supervisors who work in the center's "command center" – an area equipped with monitors that show real-time information. "Those four folks keep an eye on all the call activity," explains Charlton. "If they see a call waiting for a long time, using Resume Routing they can take it out of queue and handle it themselves."

Avoiding Disaster when Taking the Plunge

As survivors, Welch and Charlton offer advice to other call center managers who are considering taking the

SBR plunge.

"If you don't take the time to do it right, you can create a disaster," says Welch. "You really have to study this process and make a commitment to the training before you roll out a full application."

Charlton reminds managers of the importance of clearly communicating to agents why the center is changing to an SBR environment and how the change will affect their jobs. "We thought that we had done a good job of walking our agents through our plan for implementing [SBR]," she says. "We learned later that we should have done a lot more preparation with them to see how they felt about the change and to see what they did and didn't understand. We had been immersed in this project for so long and were so excited to get it off the ground, we forgot to focus more on the agents."

ALLTEL's Prunty says that managers considering SBR must ponder the unique paradox involved. "The more skills in your call center, the more complicated SBR gets. But the more skills, the more benefit there is to be gained by SBR. You have to evaluate the pain vs. the gain. The gain is that you're going to improve efficiency and customer satisfaction if you do it right; the pain is that it is going to require a lot more administrative work."

CCMReview

Service Level Notes with Brad Cleveland

Calculating Staff Required to Meet E-Contact Response Time Objectives

Editor's note: Over the past few months, we've received numerous inquiries for information on how to staff for the growing e-contact volume (i.e., e-mail, Web forms, "Click for Callback," etc.). Judging by the extremely poor response times generally reported across industries (see page 3), we felt it might be helpful and timely to run this column again.

Effectively managing customer inquiries via the Web takes commitment, planning, skilled agents, the right processes and enabling systems. Getting the "right number of skilled people and supporting resources in place at the right times" is at the heart of effective incoming call center management. This article provides a primer on how to accurately calculate the staff required for response time transactions.

Three Types of 'Response'

There are three categories of response to a customer inquiry or contact that comes into the call center via the Web:

1. Automated reply — this is a system-generated response that automatically sends a reply to customers acknowledging that the e-mail or message they sent was received and informing them of when to expect a response. This establishes appropriate expectations and minimizes telephone calls or other additional contacts inquiring about the status of the original message.

2. Response — this refers to the response the customer receives when the transaction is actually handled by the call center. The time that elapses between the customer's original message and the call center's response is measured as "response time."

3. Resolution — this is a measure of when the problem or issue is actually resolved. It is used in environments where the call center's initial response may not fully resolve the issue. For example, in a help desk environment, additional research may be necessary; the problem is "resolved" when the matter is handled to completion and the "trouble ticket" is closed.

This discussion focuses on the staff required to meet response time objectives. If additional research or contacts are required for complete resolution, this activity should be reflected in the workload forecast of this group, or another if handled by other agents.

Two Types of Response Time

There are two types of response

Calculating staff requirements for a workload that does not have to be handled at the time it arrives is generally based on the centuries-old "units of output" approach.

time: "rolling" and "scheduled" (see Figure 1). *Rolling* response time is hinged on the specific times when each message arrives. For example, if you establish a four-hour response time, a customer who sends a message at 9:03 a.m. should get a response by 1:03 p.m., and one who sends a message at 9:12 a.m. should receive a response by 1:12 p.m.

Scheduled response time, like a dry-cleaning service, is geared around blocks of time. For example, you may commit to handle all messages received up to noon by 5 p.m., and to respond to messages received between noon and 5 p.m. by 10 a.m. the next morning.

Today, many call centers are establishing straightforward 24-hour scheduled response time objectives, but some in more competitive envi-

FIGURE 1

The Two Types of Response Time

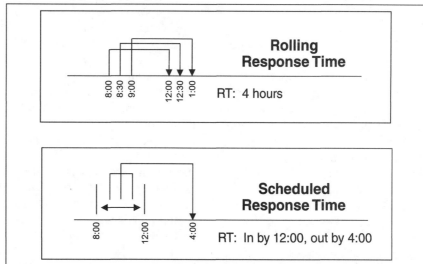

Rolling Response Time — 8:00, 8:30, 9:00 ... 12:00, 12:30, 1:00 — RT: 4 hours

Scheduled Response Time — 8:00, 12:00, 4:00 — RT: In by 12:00, out by 4:00

Section 9

ronments are targeting rolling response times of four and even two hours. In fact, a small but growing number of call centers are handling e-mail messages as they arrive or soon thereafter. If your call center is new to handling customer e-mail, we recommend beginning with a manageable, obtainable objective, such as 24 hours. You can then move toward more aggressive objectives once you are familiar with this aspect of planning and management, and as customer expectations and your business mission dictate.

Base Staff Requirements

Calculating staff requirements for a workload that does not have to be handled at the time it arrives is generally based on the centuries-old "units of output" approach. Here's the logic: If you get 60 messages that have an average handling time of four minutes, that's four hours of workload. One agent working non-stop could handle the load in four hours. If you need to complete the transactions within two hours, you will need a minimum of two agents working over a period of two hours. So, as with service level and inbound telephone calls, the e-mail workload and response time objective dictate staff requirements. Accordingly, the basic formula for calculating the minimum staff required is:

$$\frac{Volume}{(RT \div AHT)} = Agents$$

Volume is the quantity of transactions you must handle, AHT is the average amount of time it takes agents to handle the transactions (the equivalent of average talk time and average after-call work for inbound telephone calls) and response time is the time you have to respond to customers after receiving their messages. Using the formula, you could handle the 60 messages above in two hours with $60(120/4) = 2$ agents.

As with any basic formula, there are potential "upgrades" that may

better reflect the real-world environment. For example:

$$\frac{\left(\dfrac{Volume}{(RT - F) \div AHT}\right)}{Efficiency} = Agents$$

In this variation, F represents the forecast increment, the units of time down to which you forecast the workload (e.g., 30 minutes).

If you include the forecast increment in the calculations as shown, the formula will determine the staff you need from the end of the forecast period to the initial promised response time for those messages. In other words, if you receive the messages between 7:00 and 7:30 and have a four-hour response time objective, the formula will calculate the staff you need from 7:30 to 11:00 (four hours after the messages began arriving). This option adds a conservative component to rolling response time calculations; it ensures that, regardless of when the messages arrive in the course of the half-hour, you will have the staff necessary to handle them within the next 3.5 hours.

Efficiency is a factor that acknowledges that agents cannot handle one transaction after another without any breathing time in-between. We recommend using an efficiency factor of .9 (90 percent) which means agents will have a 10 percent allowance between messages to collect their thoughts and prepare for the next transaction. (You can achieve a similar result by building extra time into AHT before using the basic formula, and leaving efficiency out.)

Figure 2 provides an example of the complete formula. The calculations you make for each forecast increment must be added in layers to arrive at the base staff you need throughout the day. Also, the base staff requirements for any other type of work that your agents handle should be added to these figures.

There are several additional notes to keep in mind:

FIGURE 2

Base Staff Formula

Input:
95 messages, 8:00-8:30
Rolling RT, 120 min.
Forecast Incr., 30 min.
Efficiency factor, .9

$$\frac{\left(\dfrac{95}{(120-30)\div 6}\right)}{.9} = 7$$

Therefore, 7 agents required, 8:30 to 10:00

■ The approach outlined here is just one alternative; there are many ways you can slice and dice base staff schedules to achieve your objectives. In fact, for the case illustrated in Figure 2, you could have 95 agents rush in and handle all 95 transactions just before the promised response time and still meet your objective. What you are really doing is looking for an efficient way to pour 570 minutes of workload (95 messages x 6 minutes AHT) into your schedules within the promised response time.

■ When response time objectives are less than an hour, traffic engineers generally recommend using Erlang C or computer simulation to calculate base staff. This would be a queuing and service level scenario, like inbound telephone calls.

■ Breaks, absenteeism and other activities that keep agents from the work need to be added to base staff calculations.

The key point is to get a handle on the e-mail workload and ensure that you are producing sensible staffing and scheduling alternatives. And, as with service level contacts, be sure to periodically glance in the rearview mirror — when all the dust settles, are you accomplishing your objectives as planned?

Section 9

Service Level Notes with Brad Cleveland

Getting People in the Right Place at the Right Times (Part 1): Rostered Staff Factor

Have you ever looked at a supervisor monitor or counted your reps on the floor and wondered, "Where in the world is everybody?" If so, you're not alone. I don't know of a call center manager who hasn't asked that question at one time or another.

Where are they? On break? In the restroom? Maybe they ran out of something they need or are in training. Maybe they are doing non-phone work, getting help from someone or helping somebody else. Or maybe they went home sick. The list could go on and on. The reality is, you can do a good forecast of exactly how many people you need on the phones, and still miss your service level objective by a long shot because you don't have the staff you expected on the phones.

In some respects, this issue is becoming even more challenging (or at least more critical) than ever before. For example, a growing number of organizations are serving customers through online services. This traffic is growing by leaps and bounds and, in most cases, is being handled by a small but proliferating number of call center staff. And although this activity is less time-sensitive than randomly arriving incoming calls, it is a type of non-phone work that must be planned for. Further, the trend toward skills-based routing and other forms of custom call-handling which require specific skills means that service level will deteriorate more quickly if reps aren't plugged in when expected.

An important part of the solution is to accurately calculate rostered staff factor (RSF). RSF, alternatively called "shrink factor" or an "overlay," is a numerical factor that leads to the minimum staff needed on schedule over and above the staff required on the

phones to achieve a targeted level of service. It is calculated after base staffing requirements are determined and before schedules are organized (see Figure 1).

Figure 2 (next page) illustrates the simple mechanics necessary to calculate rostered staff factor. Staff required on the phones from previous planning steps are entered into the first column. The next three columns reflect absen-

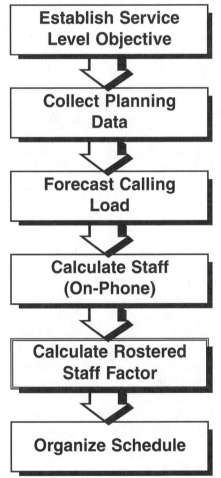

Figure 1: Basic Planning Process For Staffing and Scheduling

teeism, breaks and training as they now occur. (Note: You may want to break these columns down further. For

example, absenteeism can be divided into planned absenteeism, such as vacations, and unplanned absenteeism, such as sick leave). The "On Schedule" column is the sum of all previous columns. Finally, the "Rostered Staff Factor" column is the result of dividing staff required on schedule by staff required on the phones.

The result is a set of RSFs that you then multiply against the number of people you will need on the phones when assembling future schedules. For example, if you are putting together a schedule that begins several weeks from now, and you need 32 people on the phones between 8 a.m. and 8:30 a.m., you will need to schedule 40 reps (32 x 1.25) for that half-hour, plus any staff required to be in special training or to do non-phone work or anything else not included in the RSF calculation.

Why bother with RSF if you know how many reps you will need by adding the columns together? Because, you are coming up with a table of factors that will prevent you from having to add these columns together in the future, as base staffing requirements change. RSF not only improves accuracy, it is a big time saver.

RSF should be calculated for each half-hour (or for added accuracy, each 15-minute increment), for each day of

Rostered Staff Factor Calculations

	Agents on Phone From Erlang C	Absent	Break	Training	On Schedule	Rostered Staff Factor
08:00-08:30	28	3	0	4	35	1.25
08:30-09:00	30	3	0	4	37	1.23
09:00-09:30	37	3	4	4	48	1.30
...						
...						

$$\text{Rostered Staff Factor} = \frac{\text{On Schedule}}{\text{On Phone}}$$

Figure 2: Rostered Staff Factor Calculations

the week. However, some call center managers use an ongoing, fixed percentage for RSF (such as 15 percent or 20 percent). That will not be acceptably accurate because the things that keep staff off the phones fluctuate throughout the day and week. For example, absenteeism is usually higher on Mondays and Fridays. And the number of staff on breaks will vary throughout the day.

> ## RSF...is a numerical factor that leads to the minimum staff needed on schedule over and above the staff required on the phones to achieve a targeted level of service.

The major assumption behind rostered staff factor is that the proportion of staff off the phones for reasons accounted for by RSF will stay constant in the future, relative to onphone staff requirements. In other words, if one person is on break in a group of 10, 10 people will be on break in a group of 100.

While breaks and absenteeism should almost always be included in RSF calculations, other activities often require a measure of good judgment. For example, Figure 2 shows training included in RSF. Should it be? Clearly, if training schedules frequently change and/or require differing proportions of staff, keep it out of RSF and instead factor it into schedules on a case-by-case basis. But if it happens in predictable proportion to the staff required on the phones, include it.

The same holds true for any type of non-phone work. If it happens in proportion to the base staff required (i.e., correspondence or outbound calls that are associated with, but do not have to immediately follow, inbound calls), it can feasibly be included in RSF. If not, it should be scheduled independently of RSF (in either case, remember that after-call wrap-up is already accounted for in base staffing requirements). Assess it against the core assumption, which is that it will happen in proportion to the on-phone staff requirements.

In many incoming call centers, RSF ranges between 1.1 and 1.4 throughout the day, meaning that a minimum of 10 percent to 40 percent additional staff are required on schedule over those required on the phones. If non-phone activity is included in RSF, and there is a lot of it, RSF can be as high as 2.0 (common in small, specialized help desks with extensive off-line research). Like any planning, go back and check how accurate the RSF cal-

> ## RSF not only improves accuracy, it is a big time-saver.

culations were compared to actual results and adjust accordingly. Further, you will have to adjust RSF over time for things like vacation season and major changes in training schedules.

An added advantage of calculating RSF is that it will force you to assess these activities. Should they be happening when and to the degree that they are? Some changes may provide better coverage or make scheduling easier or more acceptable.

SLN

From The Field with George Nichols

Call Center Scheduling: Practical Tips for Today's Environment

The nature of inbound contacts has changed — accurate scheduling is more important than ever.

There's no doubt that scheduling is more of a challenge in today's environment than it was in call centers of yesteryear.

Modern call centers support a broader range of products and services than they did in the past. Technology has enabled many simple transactions to be automated, leaving agents to handle more varied and demanding calls that often require additional off-line research and followup. Add to that ongoing training and a variety of customer access channels including telephone, email, fax, Web and even video.

There are many areas that need to be addressed prior to, during and after a new scheduling process has been created.

The Planning and Management Process

Scheduling is one component of an overall planning process. It can only be effective if it's placed in the proper sequence relative to other activities in the process. Those activities include:

1. Choosing a service level objective
2. Collecting data
3. Forecasting call load
4. Calculating base staff
5. Calculating trunks (and related system resources)
6. Calculating rostered staff factor (shrinkage)
7. Organizing schedules
8. Calculating costs
9. Repeating for higher and/or lower levels of service

Creating and Implementing a New Scheduling Process

Let's look at an 11-step process that will help you to develop a more effective scheduling process:

1. Educate all staff on the need for a

Scheduling Facts

- 65 percent to 75 percent of a call center's budget is allocated to supporting employees.
- Inefficient scheduling (e.g., breaks, lunches, etc.) can waste up to 15 percent of the center's budget.

new scheduling process. Changes in the scheduling process, naturally, affect your agents. Education and communication from the start will help you create and maintain effective schedules and agent motivation.

2. Form a taskforce or scheduling process committee. Include representation from those who affect — and are affected most by — the scheduling process.

3. Analyze the existing methods of forecasting, scheduling, reporting and operations. Then document the flow and processes supporting them.

4. Gather employee feedback using a simple analysis model. Ask agents: "What's working; what's not working; and what's missing?"

5. Develop solutions to identified problems by trouble-shooting the existing scheduling process.

6. Build the framework for a scheduling team that will have ownership of the scheduling process.

7. Determine your scheduling strategy.

8. Define the scheduling rules and communicate them to everyone involved.

9. Investigate the need for supporting tools, such as workforce management technology. If required, do your homework by seeking input not only from the top vendors, but also from colleagues, industry publications and electronic news sources. During the research and purchase stages, determine which system is best for your center based on business and employee needs.

Benefits of Accurate Scheduling

- Reduced payroll related expenses generated by either doing the same amount of work with less people or doing more work at the same service level with the same number of agents. Big payback when you consider the cost per agent and the cost per transaction!
- Decreased telecommunication costs — generated by taking more calls with the same number of resources by "having the right people, in the right place, at the right time."
- Increased revenues from previously lost sales.
- Increased employee morale.
- Decreased rate of employee turnover.
- Increased customer satisfaction by reducing the time in queue and providing a faster response.
- Simplified processes for adjusting schedules on the fly.
- Administrative timesaving — generated by comparing manual or semi-automated methods to automate data collection, processing, management and information distribution.
- Increased productivity in support of meeting and/or exceeding service level and response time objectives.
- Improved customer and employee satisfaction.

10. Create "test" schedules and review for accuracy.

11. Ensure ongoing education and awareness of the new scheduling process. Changes need to be shared with the entire center. When change is communicated and embraced at a peer level, buyin comes much more easily.

Investigate Supporting Tools

Once the planning process is complete, you'll need a supporting workforce management tool. (If you already have a WFM system in place, you'll need to ensure that you maximize its capabilities). For smaller call centers, there is effective spreadsheet-based software available, which is reasonably priced (such as, ICMI's Easy Start Call Center Scheduler, www.incoming.com).

No matter which type of tool you're considering, make sure you fully understand its capabilities. Following is a list of common workforce management features and a brief explanation of each.

■ **Real-time adherence.** A feature that monitors agents to ensure they are adhering to the prepared schedule. If deviations occur, many workforce management products include alarms or alerts that notify supervisors.

■ **Forecasting.** A mathematical equation — combined with historical data, service level goals and operating parameters — that determines staffing and scheduling requirements.

■ **Web-enabled schedule viewer.** Enables agents to view and modify

---

Scheduling to Handle Multimedia Work

In a multimedia call center, there are three different group design options that need to be considered: 1) separate groups, 2) blended groups, and 3) multimedia queuing.

- In separate groups, determine staff and schedule by the two separate access channels: email plus telephone.
- In blended groups, determine separate base staff and then schedule as one group.
- In a multimedia queue, use one scheduling model (because you are in a single queue environment).

---

schedules over a corporate network using a Web browser. Some WFM products allow agents to request schedule changes by sending an email message directly to a supervisor.

■ **Open database connectivity (ODBC).** Provides the ability to pull information from various databases to create comprehensive schedules and reports.

■ **Multisite management.** Software that accommodates a single point of control over the entire network or allows for decision making at individual sites. Site information can be consolidated or viewed on a site-by-site basis, and maximizes staffing and scheduling capacity throughout the enterprise.

■ **Intra-day management.** Tracks the call center's performance throughout the day so that adjustments to staffing and schedules can be made to maintain efficiency.

■ **Scheduling.** Generates employee schedules in a graphic format by predetermined time segments. Breaks, lunches, absences and offline work are included.

■ **Vacation planner.** Enables agents to enter vacation and holiday requests in advance of schedules and await approval from a supervisor.

■ **Skills-based routing.** Offers the ability to segment customers and match them with the appropriate agents. Accurate staffing and scheduling is extremely important when using skills-based routing since the impact of random call arrival and variable workload is more volatile.

The Future of Scheduling

An effective scheduling process is more important than ever. In the future, there'll be more types of transactions for agents to handle, and those transactions will be more complex. CCMReview

---

George Nichols

George Nichols is the founder of Career II Marketing Inc., a call center consulting firm based in Kingston, Ontario, Canada, and a Certified Associate of Incoming Calls Management Institute. He can be reached at 613-389-4283 or careercc@sympatico.ca.

Technology Vs. Staff Investments: Don't Neglect the People Side of the Equation

Balance call center technology spending with staff investments. Focus on the tools that help agents do their jobs better.

Over the past decade, technology has been the dominant thrust in the call center world. CTI, IVR, CRM, call routing/queuing and a host of other systems have entered the picture, each designed to improve efficiency, heighten sales and reduce waste.

According to Datamonitor, the global call center software market will reach $8.5 billion by 2003, up from $2.9 billion in 1999.

Unfortunately, many technology investments do not always pay off. For instance, even with all of the interest generated by customer relationship management applications, studies show that more than half of those projects fail, according to Gerhard Waterkamp, executive consultant for IBM's Siebel Practice. Instead, he says, "it is essential to focus on applications that make it easier for staff to do their jobs."

Invest Wisely: Look at Staff-Enabling Tools

Call routing/queuing technology is probably the best example of a staff-enabling tool. By routing calls to centers where agents are available and queuing them correctly, call wait time is minimized and organizational results improved.

Take the case of Continental Airlines. Its previous percent-allocation service, provided by an 800-network carrier, lacked the ability to align agent skills and availability with inbound calls. Inhouse staff had to monitor service levels at each site and manually change routing patterns. It was a constant struggle for management – with 200,000 calls coming in every day to five contact centers staffed by more than 5,000 agents.

"The previous approach kept us in reactive mode," says Jane Beeby, Continental's senior director of reservations operations. "We would make a change based on one set of conditions and, by the time that change took effect, a different problem surfaced. There were days when we changed the percent allocation more than 100 times."

To solve the issue, Continental implemented contact management software (Cisco Systems' Intelligent Contact Management). Their new system routes calls based on the number dialed and voice prompts activated, directing callers to agents grouped by specific skills who are located in call centers around the country.

The result? "We can now route real-time based on skills and on formulas, such as next available agent and minimum expected delay," says Beeby. "Callers are less likely to be put in a queue and more likely to be connected immediately to an agent who can meet their needs."

Focus on Ease of Use

Comprehensive, large-scale solutions – like the one Continental Airlines implemented – are not cheap. The cost can run hundreds of dollars (sometimes thousands) per seat. Considering the number of impressive-sounding applications currently on the market and the high ante fee, how do companies decide which technologies to purchase?

Two top considerations are ease of use and return on investment. Some applications fall into the "bells-and-whistles" category rather than the "must-have" classification for call centers.

For example, Web-based call center products have stimulated much interest, but not everybody needs them. However, in organizations where a growing number of sales are conducted on the Web site, online customer support functions should be phased in.

Consider the case of Coldwater Creek, a multichannel retailer of women's apparel, footwear, jewelry, gift items and soft home accessories. The growth of its Internet-based ecommerce business prompted the organization to implement a Web-based application to allow agents to interact in real time with site visitors.

"Even though the Internet channel is an efficient and powerful sales tool, we had no ability to interact with the customer," recalls Dave Gunter, the company's director of communications.

Coldwater Creek turned to Avaya Inc., a provider of enterprise communications systems and software. They implemented Avaya's Interaction Center, a integrated multimedia contact center solution that routes, manages, records and reports on customer interactions across a variety of communication channels. It supports up to 6,000 agents and has a per-seat price that ranges from $500 to $3,500, depending on the configuration.

In Coldwater Creek's case, the investment has paid off. Forty full-time agents are now dedicated to answering customers' questions via live chat, taking part in about 600 chats per day. Agents were able to begin using the new system with minimal additional training. What type of results has the center achieved? Online abandonment is significantly lower and cross-selling revenue has soared. Overall, Web sales have leapt to 15 percent of the Coldwater Creek total, and 1 percent to 1.5 percent more customers migrate from the traditional channels to online options each month.

So what's the bottom line on technology purchases? "Companies need to ensure they are investing their dollars wisely," says Rod Johnson, service director for the customer management strategies practice of Boston-based AMR Research. "To avoid overbuying and mismatched vendor selection, determine your organization's best fit by focusing on usability over functionality."

Technology Alone Isn't the Answer

Using technology alone to solve call

Section 9

center problems is an incomplete solution at best. In many cases, call centers find this technology reliance leads to additional expenses and, for some, budgets spiraling out of control. Clive Burrows, an analyst at London-based consulting firm Ovum Ltd., offers this analogy: "It's like a vendor assuring you that they are selling you everything you need to play tennis, you purchasing a racquet and then being told that you'll have to build your own court if you want to play on grass."

Technology expenditures are often wasted by neglecting the people side of the equation. With turnover rates exceeding 30 percent in many call centers, consider the thousands of dollars squandered on training agents on the technology tools only to have them walk out the door before they adequately learn the job. (It costs between $5,000 and $18,000 to recruit and train a call center agent, according to figures released by Purdue University's Center for Call Center Excellence. Add to that the average annual agent compensation of $32,000 per year, and the total is staggering.)

Effective Scheduling Can Impact Budgets

Another aspect of the people side that can reap rich rewards for call centers is agent scheduling. Instead of rigid shifts, schedule fluidity can improve agent performance and increase retention.

For instance, one call center that found a balance between business and employee needs improved job satisfaction ratings 36 percent to 82 percent while also reducing turnover and absenteeism.

"The traditional eight-hour schedule, five days a week, no longer works," says Larry Swain, principal consultant, at Coleman Consulting in San Francisco. "Agents these days are often attending school or have young children. It is important to offer them a variety of shift lengths, start times and off days that fit their lives."

Once a good schedule is worked out that both management and agents can live with, he recommends investing in workforce management software.

Here again, it's important to avoid technology that is difficult to implement. "Some call centers only utilize 20 percent

Salaries Are the Biggest Call Center Expense

Streamlining agent recruiting, hiring and training processes can have a greater impact on the call center budget than technology initiatives. At Inteleservices Inc., a Tampa, Fla.-based call center, attrition rates were cut in half when the company brought in Clearwater, Fla.-based Belleair Custom Resources to improve personnel screening, hiring and training. New screening procedures were so thorough that out of 1,000 job applicants, only 50 made it to interview and 35 were finally employed.

Ron Benson, president of Inteleservices says that, normally, he would have hired a lot more of the applicants, wasted time and money training and paying people who were destined to leave, and taken far longer to end up with productive staff. According to his figures 90 percent of these new-hires immediately joined the ranks of the top 10 percent of performers. "The proprietary screening procedure of Belleair Custom Resources involved tailored questionnaires based on the strongest attributes of our top performers," says Benson. "They hired individuals who matched these characteristics then trained them on self-paced courses."

Benson's recruits underwent a training program that addresses study techniques and communication skills developed by humanitarian L. Ron Hubbard. "Although new recruits spend more time than before on training, it's costing us a lot less due to high retention and performance," says Benson. "These study methods really speed time to competence."

Such results stand in stark contrast to typical call center training programs. Why? According to a Deloitte and Touche study, call center training is primarily instructor-led. Eighty-four percent cite standup instruction as their main method of delivery. On average, there is one trainer to 121 employees.

That's just not good enough, says Belleair Custom Resources President Matthew Feshbach. "The retention rate from instructor-led training is only 15 percent (i.e., agents understand 15 percent of the job)," he said.

Feshbach points out that wages are by far the biggest call center expense. No company today can afford to waste 30 percent of its annual compensation budget paying people who produce little or nothing. By being more selective and investing wisely in effective training methods, recruits become effective in weeks rather than months.

Such accelerated productivity directly assisted the agents at Inteleservices who are paid a bonus for every call correctly handled. Instead of spending months getting to know the job before they earned a decent wage, they hit the floor running and rapidly became high earners. "The people we hired could see we were being very choosy," says Benson. "Those selected felt they had really achieved something. They valued the job much more than typical hires and wanted to perform well from the start."

to 25 percent of the features of their scheduling software because you need a Ph.D. to understand it," says Swain.

Finding the Middle Ground

Clearly, there is a middle ground between technology spending and personnel investment. Technology must be chosen with a view to ease of use rather than width of functionality. It must actively assist personnel in performing their jobs better without bogging them down with unwieldy tools that take months to master.

Similarly, if you are recruiting people, choose wisely. But once hired, invest heavily in proven training methods that will develop talented agents into real assets.

"Don't over-invest in technology that is more complex than the agents are trained for," says Feshbach. "And if existing technology is complex, it must be matched by the thoroughness of the training." *CCMReview*

Drew Robb

Drew Robb is a Los Angeles-based freelance writer specializing in technology and business. Originally from Scotland, he graduated from Strathcycle University in Glasgow.

Section 9

Today's ACD: More than Mere Call Routing

by Dave Morris

The first thing you'll discover when looking for an ACD today is that most vendors have absorbed their ACD products into an integrated call center "solution." On the Web site of one of the most renowned ACD companies — www.aspect.com — the word "ACD" does not even appear. Neither does the word "product." Be careful, though: while one-stop-shopping solutions are everywhere, they are not necessarily the right choice for everyone.

The second thing you'll find is that vendors are giving more attention to smaller call centers. Rockwell, for example, has just released its Spectrum 100 for call centers of 50 to 100 agents. All the nifty graphical workflow tools/reporting packages available to larger call centers are included.

Here's a survey of such nifty tools and capabilities that can enable call centers of any size to significantly enhance productivity and customer service.

Intelligent Routing

Back in the days when all customer interaction was done face-to-face down at the corner hardware store, if a customer needed some special piece of equipment, he asked one of the clerks, who then called the appropriate person up front for help. We in the call center business often forget how effective that arrangement was. It is nowadays quite simple to route a call based on Automatic Number Identification (ANI) or Dialed-Number Identification service (DNIS) using "splits." But that is no longer good enough for many call centers, who are implementing more complex routing schemes using data obtained from a CTI link.

Consider this example: A customer purchases something over the telephone and then calls back in five minutes. Isn't it likely that the second phone call is going to be a question or change related to the order

just placed? Should that call be routed to the original agent who took the order if the agent is available? Or at the very least, might we display that order to an agent immediately? Let's assume the customer calls on

> *The incredible power and speed of current computing platforms, combined with sophisticated new software, is enabling a revolution in telephony and ACD applications.*

the day after the order's delivery due date. Wouldn't we naturally assume he either didn't get the product, or that the product is defective?

This type of routing depends on

having a CTI link between the ACD and a server that can access the necessary databases to look up the information about the customer and his transaction history. Through the CTI link, the application program can tell the ACD to redirect the call to a specific queue, or even to a specific agent, and to pop a specific screen. This feature enhances the customer's experience with the call center and reduces talk time, and thus cost-per-call.

ACD Workflow Programming

New workflow tools enable administrators to define how the ACD system routes calls using simple graphical toolkits. With these tools, steps such as playing an announcement or selecting an agent are represented as icons in a palette. Work flows are constructed by dragging the icons onto the workspace and linking them, to graphically depict how calls will be routed. The attributes of each step are then defined using pop-up property sheets. Gone are complex procedural programming languages; no code must be written. There are standard

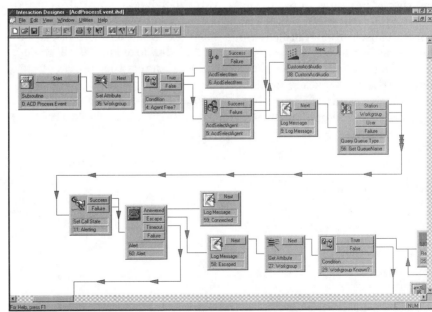

Products like Interactive Intelligence's *Interactive Designer* enable call centers to define ACD workflow using simple graphical toolkits.

Section 9

controls such as scroll bars, zoom tools, and other icons that will be familiar to anyone who has worked with Windows. Often, the new workflow can be tested immediately and then implemented when the time is right.

Examples of products offering such functions are Aspect's Architect, and Interactive Intelligence's Interaction Designer (see diagram on previous page). The benefits of these tools are lower cost of workflow modification, quicker deployment, easier debugging, and more sophisticated workflow options that result in improved customer satisfaction.

Automatic E-mail Distribution

E-mail is one of the most popular uses for the Internet, and customers will use it more and more to complain, ask questions, make suggestions, and order products (see article on page 6 for a more in-depth look at e-mail management). A study by Forrester Research claims that in 1996, only 15 percent of the U.S. population communicated by e-mail, but that this figure will increase to a whopping 50 percent by the year 2001.

Companies that attempt to handle non-telephony customer transactions without a compatible ACD will find thorny problems to overcome. For example, how does an agent remove himself from availability on the phone system in order to reply to an e-mail without distorting ACD reports that show worker productivity via average handle time, after-call work time, and other metrics?

Call center vendors are scrambling to offer unified message-handling capabilities in ACDs, CTI solutions, customer interaction software, etc. In addition to simple e-mail routing software, a few companies are beginning to experiment with automated e-mail response, using either simple keyword matching and rules-based canned responses or sophisticated natural language comprehension systems that will answer e-mail automatically, without human intervention. There are still monumental linguistic problems to overcome in this area before it will be possible to produce 100-percent accurate answers to every e-mail. But the results of such automation will be higher customer satisfaction and improved access to customers.

Some examples of these capabilities are found in Mustang Software's Internet Message Center AutoAgent, and IsoQuest's NetOwl Extractor.

Telecommuting Capabilities

One way to maintain a flexible staffing strategy is to incorporate off-premise and work-at-home agents into the call center's routing and staffing systems. These agents may be allocated to the call volume on an as-needed basis, or they may simply be telecommuters with ordinary work schedules. Many call centers have disaster plans that allow for a select group of off-site agents. These workers are linked to the call center through routers that provide both voice and data connections through a single ISDN or analog phone line. Many systems can disconnect the

phone line when the agent is not using it. The results are improved call center staffing flexibility and disaster survival.

Some sample products include Lucent's DEFINITY Extender and Nortel's Meridian HomeOffice.

Tapping Technology for Competitive Advantage

The incredible power and speed of current computing platforms, combined with sophisticated new software, is enabling a revolution in telephony and ACD applications. As companies discover the importance of excellent customer service and relationship-building, they are using these new technologies to make the ACD part of a total call center solution, giving them a strong competitive advantage.

CCMReview

Dave Morris is chief technologist for The Brady Group, Inc., a Dallas-based consulting firm specializing exclusively in call centers. He has 23 years' experience in telecommunications and computer technology. He can be reached at 972-404-0800 x 213 or at davem@thebradygroup.com.

Technology Focus with Lori Bocklund and Dave Bengtson
Multisite Routing Options:
Deciding on the Best Fit for Your Call Center

Editor's note: The following article is excerpted from Call Center Technology Demystified: The No-Nonsense Guide to Bridging Customer Contact Technology, Operations and Strategy *by Lori Bocklund and Dave Bengtson, published by Call Center Press.*

As with single-site routing options, multisite routing involves various levels of sophistication and a range of complexity, value and costs. It ranges from simple percentage-based network allocations to customer-specific, real-time, event-based routing decisions using CTI.

There are three basic multisite routing technology options: 1) Carriers provide pre-arrival routing, which routes a call before it goes to a site; 2) PBX/ACDs provide post-arrival routing, which routes a call after it arrives at a site; and 3) CTI-based applications, which provide both. These three technologies can also be combined into other options.

Carrier-Based Multisite Routing

Carrier-based routing is available from interexchange carriers (IXCs), such as AT&T, MCI Worldcom and Sprint. Provisioning services from these carriers is essentially outsourcing your multisite technology – you rely on the hardware and software capabilities of their network and the carrier manages and maintains the infrastructure. The provider typically charges flat monthly and per-usage fees for these advanced features.

Carrier-based capabilities include:

■ **Allocation.** Calls route to various centers with predefined rules, usually on a percentage or threshold basis (e.g., in a three-site call center environment, 20 percent of calls route to one location, 50 percent to a second site and 30 percent to the third center).

■ **Area of call origination.** Calls route between centers based on location. For example, East Coast calls go to Charlotte, Midwest calls to Omaha, Mountain states calls to Denver, and West Coast calls to Seattle. Calls can be routed based on the caller's phone number, which can be differentiated down to the area code and exchange.

■ **Caller identification.** Calls are routed by identifying the caller using prompted digits (e.g., account number) or ANI matching. This is typically used in a customer segmentation routing strategy (e.g., send VIP customers to one site and all other customers to another site).

■ **Time-of-day and day-of-week.** Calls route to sites based on the time and the day. This is often combined with one of the other routing capabilities. For example, from 6 a.m. to 10 a.m. (EST), all calls route to a site in New Hampshire. Starting at 10 a.m., calls are split 50/50 between that site and one in Oregon. Starting at 7 p.m., all calls route to Oregon until 10 p.m. After hours (nights and weekends), all calls route to an outsourcer who provides extended coverage.

■ **Network transfer.** This option provides the capability to transfer the call to another center after it is received by the initial center. It can be invoked automatically (prior to agent answer – conditional routing logic in the switch or IVR signals the network to take control of the call and transfer it to another center) or manually (the agent enters a feature access code signaling the network to transfer).

■ **Combinations.** Network features are often combined for routing. Typical combinations are time-of-day/day-of-week routing with various allocation schemes.

■ **Real-time management.** The network carrier provides a dedicated terminal, dial-in access or Web browser access to the network-based routing logic. Your organization designs and changes the routing routines; changes and updates typically take effect in less than 15 minutes. So, for example, when a center needs to hold an all-hands meeting or is hit by a snowstorm or the flu, calls to that site can be quickly reallocated to other locations.

Switch-Based Multisite Routing

Switch-based multisite routing technology makes extensive use of the conditional routing statements, skills management, scripting tools and logic available in the vendor's single-site routing software. It also leverages intelligent signaling between sites, typically using ISDN and/or TCP/IP.

PBX/ACD-based multisite routing uses signaling messages to poll the alternate switches in the organization. The messages can inquire about existing conditions (for example, number of calls in queue, anticipated wait times, agents available, agents staffed), or about ability to take the call.

The decision to reroute the call is controlled by either the sending switch or the receiving switch. When the decision to reroute the call is at the receiving switch, the call is only moved when the "OK to accept" is sent by the receiving switch. It uses conditional routing logic to make its decision. When the sending switch controls the decision, it requests information about the status of queues at other locations. Upon obtaining the status information, the sending switch software determines the best site to take the call. For example, in a three-switch network, if a call is received in Denver and there are already 15 calls in queue, the Denver-based PBX/ACD queries sites in Seattle and St. Louis. If Seattle has 20 calls in queue and St. Louis has 10 calls in queue, the Denver switch sends the call to St. Louis.

The drawback to switch-based multisite routing is that the polling/querying methodology is proprietary – vendors implement this technology in a way that only their products understand. If you have switches from a single manufacturer, consider this option. If you have a mix of switches, you'll have to look at the carrier or CTI-based solutions.

CTI-Based Multisite Routing

Network-based routing primarily

addresses pre-arrival routing while PBX/ACD-based routing applies to only post-arrival routing. CTI-based multisite routing addresses both.

CTI-based routing works with various vendors' PBX/ACDs and a variety of IXCs. Consider this option if your center has (or will have) a mix of switch and long-distance vendors. It can also be used in a homogeneous environment.

In addition to pre- and post-arrival routing, this option delivers advanced reporting, the ability to load-balance traffic among geographically dispersed voice-response units, desktop CTI (softphones, screen pops), and the ability to make data-directed routing decisions across the enterprise. So while CTI is the most complex (and costly) option, it is also the most robust and sophisticated.

CTI-based routing uses the same underlying CTI capabilities as data-directed routing. This multisite routing alternative uses three key technology elements: CTI event monitoring, CTI control and Signaling System 7 (SS7). The first two are used for post-arrival routing and all are used for pre-arrival routing. Following is a brief description of the role of each in pre-arrival routing:

■ **CTI event monitoring.** CTI monitors state changes of call center resources on the voice switch. The switch real-time events may be provided passively or the CTI server may query the switch for the information. The key types of information monitored are: 1) Agent-related events – login and logout, work states; and 2) skill, group or application-related events – number of calls in queue, number of calls being handled.

■ **Signaling System 7.** When a caller dials an 800 number, the call is routed from the local exchange carrier to the IXC. The IXC's signal control point (SCP) queries a network routing database for routing instructions, and the database tells the SCP to get routing instructions from the CTI master router. If the data-directed (customer-specific) routing option is enabled, the SCP also sends ANI and/or network-prompted digits to the master router in the "get route instructions" message.

Multisite Routing Options, Strengths and Issues

Routing	Strengths/Best Fit	Issues/Limitations
Network	• No additional hardware or software to manage and support • Operational costs instead of capital costs • Relatively easy to implement • Good low-cost learning option as a first step • Carrier infrastructure is extremely reliable and robust • Good in combination with other solutions for post-arrival routing	• Very basic multisite routing capabilities; does not provide any automatic adjustment to current call center conditions (staffing level, queue length, etc.) • Service fees may not be economical in large volume environments • Lacks control needed in dynamic environments without routing management capabilities • Additional set of management reports to monitor • No visibility between other IXCs and LECs • Provides primarily pre-arrival routing capabilities; take back and transfer is the only post-route option
Switch	• Good option if all switches from same vendor • Provides dynamic routing based on current call center conditions • Uses administrative and management tools of existing infrastructure, leveraging familiarity with the system for each site • May take advantage of existing reporting tools if networked reporting ability provided by vendor • Can be combined with carrier-based services; for example, use carrier-based percentage allocation at the network level (pre-arrival routing) with switch post-arrival routing capability • Good uptime and reliability	• Must have homogenous switch environment • Increases network complexity due to additional private lines and/or switched access between sites • May require significant upgrades, additions, reengineering to existing infrastructure • Poor design can severely limit scalability due to heavy processor demands • Provides post-arrival routing capabilities only; call must be sent to a site based on network features first (DNIS, prompting, percent allocation, etc.) • Connectivity requirements become complex for more than three sites
CTI	• Provides most dynamic routing; can base routing decision on current call center status, as well as on information about the customer stored in a database • Can also be used for balancing IVR traffic among multiple sites (pre-arrival routing) • Excellent reporting; can follow call from site to site, can combine call information with IVR information and business data, also provides common reporting across a diverse switch environment • Good fit for heterogeneous switch environments (but can also be used in homogeneous environment) • Can be used for heterogeneous network providers (IXCs and LECs) • Provides pre-arrival routing and post-arrival routing capabilities • Very nice fit with other CTI applications (screen pop, soft phones)	• Complex solution; many servers and software modules to manage • Most expensive of the three multisite options; costs include hardware, software, system support and SS7 network charges • Significant new skills, knowledge and system support required • May require significant upgrades/additions/reengineering to existing switch infrastructure • Not as reliable as carrier- or switch-based options

Section 9

The link between the SCP and the master router is a special circuit called Signaling System 7 (SS7). When the SCP queries for the routing instructions, the CTI master router delivers the routing address back to the SCP via the SS7 link (this query and response is performed in 250 to 500 milliseconds). The SCP executes the routing destination and routes the caller to the "best" center or even the "best" agent. If the CTI master router doesn't respond quickly enough, the network will follow a default routing path.

■ **CTI control.** When CTI is in control of routing, the network or switch basically asks: "What do you want me to do with this call?" The CTI application gathers the data, applies routing logic, determines the best place to route and tells the switch what to do. In pre-arrival routing, a master router is in control and talks to the network. The routing application goal is to get the caller to the right center the first time.

So why would you use post-arrival routing capabilities if you are using pre-arrival routing? Post-arrival routing applications fit with pre-arrival routing in situations where:

• Lengthy queues exist at all sites when the pre-arrival routing decision executes. The post-arrival routing is a "second look" to see if any sites are clearing their queues quickly.

• Significant traffic is generated by callers who "zero-out" of the IVR for agent assistance. In this case, the pre-arrival routing decision originally looks for IVR port availability, not agent availability.

• Large numbers of transfers and conferences occur between specific agents and other skill groups. At the time of pre-arrival routing, the decision focused on the availability of the original agent or skill group.

CTI is used just for post-arrival routing in many cases (no pre-arrival routing occurs). There are also environments based on "best-of-breed" approaches that use one CTI solution for pre-arrival routing and another for post-arrival routing. Pre-arrival routing using CTI can be expensive because of the network fees for the signaling interfaces. Therefore, some companies use basic network features, such as percent allocation for pre-arrival routing, and then use the switches or CTI for post-arrival routing. Mix-and-match can sometimes be

the right answer, but be sure to recognize the cost and management tradeoffs. This decision is best supported by carefully analyzing the pros and cons tied to your business needs and analyzing the costs of the options.

Making Your Decision

Multisite routing can take place at many levels, using a combination of the options described here. Be sure to consider scalability, manageability, reliability and support in conjunction with functionality. Cost-analysis and modeling tools can help you to determine the best approach for your virtual call center environment. CCMReview

Lori Bocklund and Dave Bengtson

Lori Bocklund is Vice President for Vanguard Communications Corp., and a certified associate of ICMI. She can be reached at 703-242-3001 or lbocklund@vanguard.net.

Dave Bengtson is a Consultant for Vanguard Communications Corp. He can be reached at 303-618-4647 or dbengtson@vanguard.net.

Section 9

How to Identify IVR/CTI Performance Problems

Expand monitoring processes beyond agent interactions. Voice systems have a great impact on caller satisfaction.

The growing sophistication of today's IVR and CTI applications has created new opportunities to increase efficiency and quality in contact center operations. Unfortunately, it has also created more opportunities for things to go wrong.

In this new, often distributed technological environment, contact center managers are discovering that their agents can't perform efficiently unless the entire system is performing efficiently. For example, a major U.S. bank that processes about 70 percent of its customer calls in its IVR discovered that a single 20-minute slowdown creates about four hours of agent overload. Faced with invalid prompts, delays and dead air, frustrated customers give up on the IVR and "zero out," thereby raising queue times and toll charges while swamping agents with transactions that should be fully automated. The bank in question estimated that this recurring problem was costing them more than $2 million a year — until they started monitoring the per-formance of their voice system and IVR self-service applications.

Caller Satisfaction with IVR Self-Service Remains Low

Across industries, managers are working to achieve greater efficiency and lower operating costs by increasing the number of self-service applications handled by their voice systems.

A recent study by Purdue Research found that IVR self-service applications now account for a majority of a company's contact with its customers. But even with IVR self-service transactions accounting for up to 80 percent of customer contacts in some sectors (such as the travel industry), customer satisfaction with call center transactions remains much lower. Even the highest-ranked sector (financial services) manages only a 57 percent average satisfaction rate for IVR self-service transactions. For the telecommunications industry, the satisfaction rate is a shocking 20 percent. With most consumers required to interact with self-service service applications on a frequent basis, frustration with IVR/CTI technology has become a cliché of modern life: Nearly everyone has a personal horror story of getting stuck in endless IVR loop, having a call dropped for no apparent reason, being asked multiple times for the same information or being forwarded to the wrong agent.

Call Centers Not Monitoring IVR Transactions

So why is it that, despite their high cost, these performance problems so often go unnoticed and unrepaired until angry customers report them? Prompt errors, database slowdowns, incorrect routing and other similar problems are only caught by monitoring voice system performance from the customer's perspective — all the way from the public switched telephone network to the back-end databases and out to the agent. Yet, until recently, the primary focus in call center monitoring has been on agent interactions rather than on the applications and infrastructure that play such a crucial role in improving agent productivity and maintaining the overall quality of experience (QoE) for call center users.

However, the biggest impediments to efficiency and quality in contact center operations are as likely to be found in the automated systems as with human agents. Empirix recently conducted a benchmark study of the credit card industry. The study showed that slow or unavailable databases were a common problem across all companies accounting for 20 percent of failures (see box, left). In addition, more than 37 percent of all transaction failures were due to switch problems — primarily at one company. Poor quality or wrong prompts accounted for roughly 26 percent of failures. The remaining 15 percent of failures were caused by routing errors, in which calls were accepted by the ACD, but were never connected to the voice application.

Finding All the Problems All the Time

Many call centers still rely on manual monitoring (having agents dial in to an application) or on network management tools that monitor individual system com-

Types of Transaction Failures

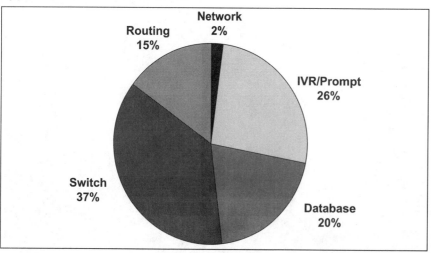

- Network 2%
- Routing 15%
- IVR/Prompt 26%
- Switch 37%
- Database 20%

ponents. Yet manual monitoring is fraught with liabilities — it is subjective, expensive and rarely performed with adequate frequency or intensity. As a result it yields little in the way of detailed, consistent data about system performance. By contrast, network management tools can miss a majority of potential performance problems because they report only on individual components, not on whether these components are interacting seamlessly in order to provide the customer with a high QoE.

For example, the IVRs at a large wireless contact center were flooding agents with self-service calls even though the IVR was still reporting as active and below capacity. The company implemented a performance monitoring solution and quickly found out that when customers called in, they were greeted by a sound clip of an opera singer rather than the expected opening prompt. A quick analysis revealed that the load balancer was configured to think that each IVR only had a single T1 in each

The Rise of Automated Performance Monitoring

The use of manual monitoring or network management tools alone simply cannot identify or correct expensive and aggravating problems in many of today's highly advanced voice systems.

The test and monitoring industry has been responding to this challenge with a new generation of monitoring solutions designed to offer detailed performance assessment at every step in a contact center transaction. These automated solutions measure carrier, host and database response times, verify that the right prompt is playing at a sufficient quality level and that the call has been routed to the appropriate agent. If a problem is detected, it will immediately issue an alert to the appropriate technical resource. The alert identifies both the type of problem and its location, and allows technical personnel to take corrective action before the problem begins to adversely affect the caller's QoE — and before a performance problem in the IVR, CTI or network escalates into an expensive degradation of overall contact center efficiency.

Measuring Up to Customer Service Expectations

In addition to monitoring voice systems performance within one or more linked contact centers, managers can use benchmarking to track performance relative to industrywide performance levels, thereby ensuring that they meet or exceed customer service level expectations. Empirix's Voice Performance Index rates performance by collecting benchmark data of three simple customer QoE metrics that measure the end-to-end performance of voice applications. These metrics and their importance are:

- **Transaction failure rate** measures how often a customer encounters a problem when trying to complete an automated transaction. Failures in the automated system greatly increase the risk that a $.35 automated call will turn into a $5+ agent call. Additionally, frustrated customers may choose to conduct their business elsewhere, resulting in lost business revenue for that particular transaction or loss of the customer entirely.

- **Transaction length** measures how quickly an experienced customer can complete an automated transaction. Speed is an essential element of customer satisfaction and this measurement provides insight into whether a call flow is optimized for a particular transaction. Additionally, variation in call length can reveal underlying performance issues within the voice system infrastructure or application.

- **Customer delays** offer an aggregate measure of how long a customer is kept waiting over the course of a transaction. Long silences or an inability to bypass promotional prompts often frustrates customers and may train them to avoid the IVR. Additionally, long delays add unnecessary toll charges to every call.

Using these three simple metrics, contact center managers can quickly assess the performance of their voice systems. Companies with high failure rates are running the risk that customers may choose to take their business elsewhere.

trunk group when in reality it had 2 T1s per trunk group. The result was that, at only 50 percent capacity, the load balancer would think the IVR was full and route calls directly to agent queues — yet the components all appeared to be acting normally.

The incorrect prompt in this example is a case of a "discrete" failure, which might have been detected with frequent and intensive manual testing. The load-balancing error, on the other hand, is a classic example of a systemic bottleneck that would have remained invisible to manual testing.

Rapid Detection Reduces Downtime and Slowdowns

Finding out about failures is important, but making sure that the time, cause and symptom of the failure are all relayed to the appropriate technical support person or system in real time is critical to increasing service uptime and customer QoE. Immediate, intelligent alerting allows contact centers to quickly detect, diagnose and resolve issues — saving toll charges, agent costs and technical resources.

While immediate access to performance data helps contact center managers

detect and respond to performance issues, the identification and correction of systemic performance bottlenecks requires consistent historical archiving and data analysis.

The Bottom Line

The increasing complexity of contact center voice systems — network, switch, IVR, CTI, middleware and databases — has created a growing potential for performance bottlenecks, outages, failures and errors that can frustrate customers while generating unnecessary toll charges, overinvestment in capital equipment and bandwidth, and inefficient use of agent and technical resources.

In an increasingly competitive business environment, companies should therefore adopt a more stringent monitoring process to find and fix IVR/CTI performance issues in order to reduce costs, improve agent productivity and enhance the caller's quality of experience. CCMReview

Pieter Boelhouwer

Pieter Boelhouwer is Director of Contact Center Services at Empirix, a provider of integrated test and monitoring solutions for Web, voice and network applications. He can be reached at PBoelhouwer@ Empirix.com

Section 9

Selecting and Implementing Workforce Management Systems

by Todd A. Cotharin and Daryl A. Gonos

Workforce management is an operating philosophy, not just software that resides on a server. Simply automating your existing manual or semi-automated workforce management process by installing a workforce management system ignores the power of these systems to help your call center achieve greater results.

The selection and installation of workforce management systems must be coupled with specific goals that reflect the corporate objectives of your business. While acquiring and installing the appropriate tools enables you to start a cultural evolution towards better customer service and optimal efficiency, it's only the beginning. Having the right system in place merely points you in the right direction; it doesn't produce dramatic results in and of itself.

Effectively implementing workforce management software requires a thorough understanding of your call center objectives and culture. Your type of business plus the service your industry demands, and the characteristics of the available workforce, create a unique mix of workforce management challenges.

Implementing a workforce management software system is a step toward gaining control over these factors, but choosing and effectively installing such systems isn't easy. This article is intended to identify the key factors to guide you in your selection and implementation efforts.

Find the Right Fit for Your Call Center

Every business operates differently. So does every workforce management software package. While surveying call center users of the package you are considering will help to shed some light on the quality and reliability of the product, it's more important to consider your own specific call center environment when selecting the right workforce management system.

Here is a list of questions to ask yourself to help determine the ideal product for your organization:

- Does marketing drive your business?

- Is your business cyclical, seasonal, or both?

- How volatile is your call volume?

- How flexible are your agents?

- Are your agents' schedules permanent or do you change them to meet call volume requirements?

- Do you rotate weekends? If so, how?

- Is seniority the only consideration for assigning schedules?

- How are lunches and breaks assigned?

- Do your agents perform other tasks besides answering calls? If so, when and who?

- What is the mechanism for schedule changes such as vacation, meetings, etc.?

- Do you measure agent adherence to schedules? If so, how?

- What information is management expecting from the system?

- What is the implementation strategy for introducing automated scheduling to the existing environment?

Take an Active Role in Project Management

It is essential that your call center team designate an internal project manager for the implementation of your workforce management system. Do not leave the responsibility for the integration solely in the hands of your selected vendor. As strong as your vendor's experience may be, your vendor cannot understand the intricacies of your business. The skills required for a successful implementation include a thorough understanding of your call routing tables, workforce management culture, specific scheduling requirements and IT expertise.

Put together a team of internal experts to ensure a smooth installation. Failure to develop a strong team may result in a poor implementation and ineffective initial use of the software. The project manager should be responsible for keeping the team on schedule and making sure that individual goals are met. If your company does not staff professional project managers, it may be helpful for you to bring in outside expertise for this project.

Your technology department should be given ownership over the application server; they need to understand the configuration and any third-party software components (i.e.,

Features of Today's Workforce Management Systems

- Historical reporting and data manipulation
- Robust forecasting algorithms
- Powerful "what-if" analysis tools
- Budgetary information
- Flexible scheduling mechanisms
- Meeting planners
- Off-phone activity scheduling
- Real-time data feeds featuring:
  -Adherence data
  -Actual vs. forecasted data
  -Scheduled vs. actual
- Imbedded report writers
- Powerful day-of-operation mechanisms
- Timeclock and payroll integration
- Web-enabling capabilities

ORACLE, Carbon Copy, Crystal Reports) to confidently support your environment down the road.

Ensure Effective ACD Integration

Automatic call distributor (ACD) integration is an absolutely essential element for effectively implementing workforce management software in your call center. The product vendor you select probably has a good basic understanding of your ACD, but not of your call flow patterns. Sit down with your ACD administrator and ensure that you have a complete understanding of where calls get counted before you implement a system. The vendor you select will probably be able to correctly count your calls if you are able to explain the data, but you may be facing additional charges for a "non-standard" interface. All too often, it is only after the initial interface is in place that a call center realizes the numbers do not add up correctly, thus requiring a cumbersome interface modification.

Select and Train a Strong System Coordinator

The individual(s) you select to run your workforce management system should possess good analytical skills and a strong grasp of your telephone system's routing and reporting processes. Understanding the relationship between the reported phone system data and how it relates to the workforce management perspective is key. A common mistake is to name an administrative worker as the workforce management coordinator. This position is an analyst-level job, not a data entry position; the administrative worker is likely ill-equipped to handle the heavy analytical responsibilities of the job.

Training the analyst(s) is a standard part of any workforce management implementation. How the training is managed will have a long-lasting impact on the overall project effectiveness. The training sessions need to include more than an overview of how to navigate within the application software. The focus should be on how to apply the sys-

> *Do not leave the responsibility for the integration solely in the hands of your selected vendor.*

tem to meet the needs of your culture.

A consultative approach to your workforce management training class – where "what-if" scheduling scenarios and analysis are strongly encouraged – will result in analysts who are curious and will push the limits of the product's functionality. Remember, you aren't trying to merely automate your current manual workforce management process, rather to push your call center to a more powerful forecasting/scheduling strategy.

Consider inviting senior management to participate in these training sessions to help them better understand how the workforce management system works and the key information it can provide. One of the underlying problems in many call centers is that senior managers who lack a solid grasp of the intricacies of workforce management often override solid decisions made by the call center analyst. By taking time to edu-

cate upper management on forecasting/scheduling processes, such political struggles can be avoided.

Solid Strategy Needed to Maximize Tools

Effectively implementing a workforce management system requires careful analysis and planning across a broad spectrum of the organization. Give serious considerations to corporate goals, call center culture, the needs of your customers and agents, technology and integration, training, personnel, and daily operations. Your workforce management vendor will provide the tools and basic support, but not the strategy and objectives that drive improved call center operations. That part's up to you.

CCMReview

Daryl Gonos (top) and Todd Cotharin are founding partners of The WorkForce Management Group, Inc. - an independent consulting firm specializing in the selection, implementation and optimal use of automated scheduling systems for call centers. Together, they have over 30 years' experience as workforce management professionals. They can be reached at 561-243-0440. Daryl can be reached via e-mail at dgonos@wfmg.com. Todd can be reached at cotharin@wfmg.com.

Section 9

Monitoring Quality in the Multi-Channel Interaction Center

by Matthew Page

The Internet has opened new avenues of communication for customers to communicate with your company. Call centers are evolving to interaction or contact centers, handling multiple types of inquiries through multiple channels. E-mail, Web chat, collaborative browsing, and Web call-back are the new media your call center may have or perhaps are considering implementing.

While these new communication technologies provide a competitive advantage that your customer can benefit from, they present new challenges to your interaction center management team. The issues are:

■ How do we effectively manage and monitor all media types for quality?

■ How do we know that our representatives are consistently delivering the brand promise in written and phone interactions?

In this article, we'll examine the new recording and monitoring tools and technology available to call centers. By effectively deploying these tools, you can look forward to creating a contact center in which interaction quality across all channels of contact meets or exceeds your company's standards, and your reps consistently deliver the brand promise to your customers.

Process and Systems

Deploying a recording solution requires a clear monitoring and quality strategy, combined with the tactical processes to effectively implement and leverage the benefits that the tool offers.

We have found that many companies have installed the latest recording solution only to discover that they are under-utilizing the tool's capabilities, and drowning in recorded interactions that they can't possibly monitor! Supervisors and managers in these interaction centers complain that they do not have the time to listen to the recorded calls. In most cases, the problem arises from a lack of processes or guidelines to effectively sample, analyze, score and,

most importantly, provide feedback to each representative. These companies need to begin by defining their brand and how it's applied during customer interactions for their representatives. Next, they need to ensure that the brand and quality service are provided through implementation of a concise and manageable monitoring and coaching process that leverages the technology tool.

Value of the Interaction

Companies have begun to realize the value of each individual customer/prospect interaction. The interaction center is a goldmine of information – who's buying, future product opportunities, brand definition or dilution (and brand valuation), and how responsive a company is to its customers.

In the past, access to this information has been driven primarily through exhaustive database analysis. But customer data represents only a small piece of the overall picture. Imagine marketing and senior executives learning about their customers through hearing and reading selected customer interactions. Is the company delivering on or diluting its brand promise? Are the millions of dollars spent promoting and advertising the brand being leveraged through phone and online interactions? Does your product or service provide real value to your customers? What improvements can be made to your products and services that will drive additional value to your customers? The best resource for remaining competitive is often the information gathered when a customer engages your interaction center.

Help is On the Way?

There are two ways to monitor the quality of an interaction – real-time (live monitoring) or by reviewing the interaction through voice and data recording. The traditional recording vendors have solutions that simultaneously record the voice and the representatives' use of the customer man-

agement tool. This way, managers get a complete picture of each customer interaction when monitoring representatives, for instance:

■ Does the new customer management system speed up or slow down each customer interaction?

■ Is data verified for accuracy?

■ Does the system usage help the call flow?

■ Was training effective? Can the representative put all the pieces in place for each call?

Beyond the Screen Scrape

Initially, data recording was just a series of captured screen graphics, commonly referred to as "screen scrape." Recently, vendors rolled out solutions that provide a screen scrape, as well as event and application integrated solutions. Imagine interaction center managers and supervisors having access to the voice and data recording of all orders or hot leads. These interactions can be saved in a file (in an AVI file format) for distribution for training purposes or for system improvements.

The New Media

The next step to providing full media coverage is recording online interactions: Web chat, e-mail and collaborative browsing. The quality of these text-based interactions is proving increasingly crucial to most call centers. Customers frequently save the written records from e-mail interactions and Web chat sessions (if transcripts are provided at the completion of chat sessions). The quality, accuracy and tone of these interactions is critical because they are documented and provide irrefutable proof of interaction quality, delivering (or not) of brand promise, and overall service quality.

Companies that have deployed interaction management software, such as Kana, eGain or Servisoft, have embedded tools to review e-mail and text-chat content for accuracy. Each online representatives' interaction

Special Technology Issue 2001 ■ **Reprinted with permission from CCMReview®**

logs can be accessed for content review, coaching and training purposes. Live interactions such as Web chat sessions can be monitored in real-time in addition to after-the-fact access to session archives. Call centers need to carefully evaluate and define the most effective method for monitoring and reviewing e-mail and chat content. Some examples, include:

■ All recording vendors have products that integrate with the leading ACD manufacturers including: Avaya (formally Lucent), Nortel, Aspect, Rockwell and Siemens. Additionally, Comverse, Witness and Nice have taken steps to integrate with the leading CRM and interaction management solutions. Thus, marketing, sales, R&D or product development – as well as the senior executive team – can learn first-hand from their customers. For instance: An interaction center manager wants to analyze the quality of calls for those customers waiting in queue for more than two minutes. Most recording applications will provide the tools (CTI bridge) to listen to recordings based on ACD metrics. In this case, the call center manager can listen to how representatives handle calls with long hold times. These recordings can be used for training new and existing representatives by pulling the best calls for later replay.

■ Companies using Nice's Call System Analysis can go beyond the traditional CTI based recording analy-

Monitoring Systems Vendors

Comverse Info Systems Inc.
516-677-7400
www.cominfosys.com

Dictaphone (recently acquired by Lernout & Hauspie)
800-447-7749
www.lhsl.com

Envision Telephony
(206) 621-9384
www.envisiontelephony.com

Eyretel, Inc.
(800) 895-0803
www.eyretel.com

Nice Systems LTD
888-577-6423
www.nice.com

Witness Systems Inc.
888-3-Witness
www.witness.com

sis. Call-routing data can be used to provide call recordings. For example, a report can be run on all calls that were transferred more than two times. Management can drill down in the report to learn more about the reasons for multiple transfers. Once the reasons are understood, these issues can be addressed and resolved proactively – through training, call flow and/or IVR design, service level agreements or other appropriate measures.

■ CRM integration – Comverse's

recording solution allows companies using Siebel to access the call history data as entered by a representative and listen to the call directly through the Siebel application. Comverse offers an add-on product that can analyze the recording "stress level" (in other words, the tone of the call, the voice quality of the representative) and forward applicable recordings to a manager based on a set of pre-defined business rules.

Interaction Center Performance Evaluation System

Look for tools that can automate your current system. Your monitoring forms should be easily re-created using the recording and monitoring tool, and your scoring system should be readily supported. A fully integrated system will allow forms to be shared with the representatives, with the digitized voice recording allowing reps to listen to their calls and view their scoring and feedback forms concurrently.

Brand Reality

Innovations in the recording industry are driving closer examination of policies and procedures implemented in the interaction center. Interaction recordings can and should be shared with various groups outside of the interaction center, including senior executives. What better way to demonstrate the marked differences between the organization's vision, the brand and the operational realities that drive overall execution? Key customer interactions can provide eye-opening opportunities for your executive team and set the stage for strategic and operational changes that will enable your interaction center to more effectively deliver your brand promise to your customers.

CCMReview

Making the Right Decision: Tips for Vendor Selection

Clearly the functionality and depth of recording solutions has increased significantly in the last year. With the pressure to quickly develop and release product, some vendors have announced functionality that has yet to be fully implemented.

Advanced functionality such as event-driven recording, integration with CRM and Interaction Manager solutions are still in development or, in a few cases, have reached beta-testing stage. Most vendors will begin shipping these advanced solutions in 2001. However, according to Comverse spokesperson Linda Dunlea, the company began installing Siebel integrated solutions at the beginning of 2000.

Making the right selection decision and understanding clearly what functionality is currently available is best achieved through a formal Request For Proposal (RFP) process in which your interaction center's recording and monitoring needs and functionality requirements are clearly defined. A key component to the RFP process is to schedule site visits to centers using the solution you choose. Make sure that the site visits reflect a similar deployment of the tool to how it will be deployed in your contact center. After all, nothing replaces real-world experience when it comes to installing and setting up new technology!

Matthew Page

Matthew Page is a Senior Consultant with Initiatives Three Inc., a leading call center consulting company committed to the significance of delivering your brand at the point of interaction. He can be reached at 207-761-2400; Web site: www.initiatives3.com.

Section 9

Understanding and Implementing Desktop Productivity Tools

by Bruce Calhoon

During the last 10 years, we have witnessed a dramatic increase in the requirement for sophisticated tools and information for call center agents. These tools and information are most often presented on a PC, or desktop.

Interactive voice response (IVR) has reduced the number of repetitive, redundant tasks; and speech recognition and e-commerce will cause further reductions. The requirements are increasing for call center agents to have substantial customer relationship management skills, sales skills, Web transaction skills, writing skills for e-mail/text chat, and presentation skills for video sessions. The call center desktop has evolved from being a data input and information access terminal to a multimedia command center for customer relationship management. (See diagram on next page)

This evolution has been marked by an explosion in the number and type of desktop productivity tools, which can provide the following capabilities:

- Presentation of information based on call flows and business rules

- "Softphone" functions to provide single login and telephony functions on the desktop

- Scripting and FAQ questions/ answers

- Online help and electronic access to documentation

- CTI, e.g., screen pop, conditional routing, etc.

- Automated fulfillment and workflow management for fax server as well as letter/forms generation.

- Easy access (no logon or logoff required) to business applications such as order entry

- E-mail management

- Outbound campaign management and dialing technologies

- Web coordination/call-back

- Access to dispatch and paging

- Measurement of real-time individual and group performance statistics

The call center desktop has evolved from being a data input and information access terminal to a multimedia command center for customer relationship management.

What's Out There

Some products are designed for a specific function, such as e-mail management and routing. Vendors of such products include Mustang Software, Kana Communications and Acuity.

Other products deliver a more comprehensive solution, incorporating numerous capabilities or supplying them via partnerships. A sampling of such "customer information system" (CIS) vendors includes Clarify, IBM, IMA, Pegasystems, Quintus, Sieble, and Vantive (see Lori Bocklund's CIS article on page 10). The back-office automation, or ERP (enterprise resources planning), vendors such as SAP and Baan as well as database vendors such as Oracle are partnering with or acquiring these CIS vendors to provide comprehensive front-office automation.

Call centers that find that the above vendors do not meet their desktop automation needs often build their own systems using tools such as Visual Basic. We are also seeing the emergence of browser technology (e.g., Netscape or Microsoft Internet Explorer) to provide the desktop framework using JAVA to build a common access layer for all of the required applications and tools.

There is a debate going on concerning "fat" versus "thin" clients for agent desktops. In general, these terms refer to where the software that drives the desktop applications resides. In a "fat" client world, much of the software resides on the PC on the agent's desktop. The "fat" client was popular when LANs were not so reliable. The downside to a "fat" client is that software must physically exist on each desktop, which means that it must be *maintained* on each desktop. The other "fat" downside is the constantly increasing processing power and hard disk requirements needed whenever adding/upgrading software.

In the "thin" client world, the software resides on a server that is accessed by the agents' desktop computers equipped with a browser and/or minimal software. These computers do not require exceptional processing power or disk space, and are often referred to as "network" computers. The advantage is that the software is maintained, upgraded and augmented on the server as opposed to multiple (often hundreds) of desktop computers. In addition, the pressure to upgrade to new chips, faster processing speeds, and expanding disk drives is minimized.

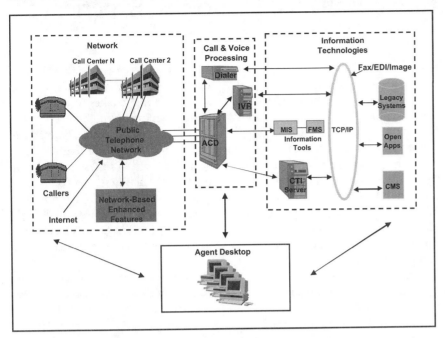

The call center desktop has evolved.

The Golden Rules of Selection/Implementation

If this is not enough to confuse you, attend any of the tradeshows or conferences and check out the vast array of vendors and solutions providers hawking their wares. The confusion is amplified by esoteric discussions about emerging standards: Netscape versus Microsoft, Sun versus Microsoft, the scalability of NT, etc.

However, such technology decisions will be greatly simplified if you follow two "Golden Rules": (1) drive your desktop application with a clear business imperative and (2) design it yourself.

1) *Drive Your Desktop Application with a Clear Business Imperative*

Before you charge out and start buying high-powered PCs for everyone's desktop and Windows NT, make sure the desktop project is part of a total strategy for delivering business results. Ensure that your investment in a desktop productivity tool, or set of tools, is driven by a clear link to improved customer service and productivity. For example, focus on how having an automated fulfillment tool can reduce fulfillment

cycle times, or on the productivity enhancements that come from reducing wrap-up time by having fax-server access from the desktop.

2) *Design It Yourself*

Once the business case for your investment in desktop tools is made, conduct a thorough analysis of your specific user requirements. It is best to do this in a vendor-free environment to ensure that the requirements are based on your needs rather than on a vendor's capabilities.

Take inventory of all the technology you have in place. Check with your corporate information technologies/telecommunications departments and see what they have planned. Make sure they give you a detailed picture of the enterprise technology architecture that will support your customer service system over the next three years.

With the above information in hand, try building a detailed technical specification for your desktop tool(s). Once again, this should be built on your specific performance requirements. If you feel you and your organization do not have the necessary knowledge base to build

a technical specification, try it anyway and then:

- Use a vendor-independent desktop technology expert; or...

- ...Put out a Request for Information, but be prepared for the vendors to descend on you.

While the technology decisions will begin to become clear at this stage, we still encourage you to go through the Request for Proposal (RFP) process for four reasons:

1. To clarify any differences in approach

2. To ensure you have the most current information on alternatives

3. To verify your analyses

4. To foster price competition

You will be amazed by how much vendors will come down in price if you keep them vying against each other throughout selection process. You will also be pleased with how your desktop tool selection fits your business requirements.

CCMReview

Bruce Calhoon is vice president of strategy and technology for Quintus Corporation, which provides consulting and software solutions for call centers. During his 12 years in the call center industry, Bruce has published numerous articles on effective call center management and has delivered talks at a wide range of industry trade shows and seminars. He can be reached at 919-469-0982 or at bruce.calhoon@quintus.com.

Section 9

CTI-Enabled Call Centers Enhance Customer Experience

by Theresa VanLaeken

Computer Telephony Integration (CTI) that oft-maligned stepchild of the public telephone network and organizations' data processing infrastructures, has been huffing and puffing along for more than a dozen years. Some of the initial CTI-enabled technologies are processes that we now take for granted, such as voice mail, network fax and e-mail. As CTI evolved, more cost-saving applications arrived on the desktop. The phone functionality left the proprietary desk set and appeared on the computer screen, driven by mouse clicks.

Interactive voice response systems (IVRs) gathered customer information that enabled data to pass from their handset to your customer database, and to allow that data to automatically appear on the agent's PC. IVRs also increased call center efficiency by up to 30 percent by starting to enable customer self-service. Answers to repetitive requests were automated, never reaching a live agent, driving down call center operating costs while greatly increasing agent productivity.

Automated call distributors (ACDs) emerged that enabled callers to reach the most appropriate resource based on any number of variables including ANI, DNIS, time of day, length in queue, or even special requirements such as language or a given skill set. And much, if not all, of this ACD functionality migrated from the PBX or PBX adjunct to an NT server on the data network.

Unified messaging arrived soon after merging voicemail, fax and e-mail into a single entity, accessible via a single unified interface. Users could access voice, text and data messages initially as e-mail attachments, and later via their cell phones using text-to-speech technology. Unified messaging spawned multimedia contact routing in the call center, where customers could call, fax or e-mail and have the contact treated the same way regardless of the media method employed.

Further CTI development added the Web to the call center where customers could browse, ask questions via e-mail or web chat, request a live agent callback, or launch a Net-Meeting session. Agents had the ability to see what Web pages the customer had been browsing, and could even "push" appropriate pages back to the customer, enabling the customer to initiate further self-service, reduce the time required in handling questions, and potentially increase incremental revenue through cross-selling or upselling.

The latest CTI revolution is IP (Internet Protocol) telephony, where voice signals are distributed over the data network in packets. This can dramatically reduce transmission costs in a distributed enterprise.

Even with all this CTI technology readily available, fewer than one in five call centers is currently CTI-enabled. This is expected to change dramatically fairly soon, however, and predictions from market research groups such as Datamonitor suggest that CTI deployment by 2004 will grow by 100 percent.

CTI Growth Factors

Driving this rapid adoption of CTI-enabled technology are several factors. The first and perhaps foremost factor is competitive pressure resulting from the global commoditization of goods and services. As it becomes increasingly difficult to differentiate one's offerings, and as discount pricing strategies "bottom out," marketers have turned their attention to what may be the last bastion of differentiation, the customer experience.

Organizations wishing to survive must employ technologies focused on enhancing the customer experience and providing an environment that empowers the customer. If the customer feels in control of the relationship, the relationship will thrive and grow. The customer must be able to determine the method of contact and how long it takes to acquire the required information, service or product. The customer must be made to feel comfortable with the transaction, as it is far too easy these days to simply take the business to a competitor. With "shopping cart" abandonment rates of nearly two-thirds of all Web-based sales interactions, creating the ultimate customer experience is critical.

The pace of CTI deployment could not be possible without another important factor – the emergence of "standardized" CT middleware. This middleware is the glue that provides for the interchange of information between hardware and software in a heterogeneous, or multi-vendor environment. Organizations like the Enterprise Computer Telephony Forum (ECTF), comprised of the leading hardware and software vendors in the CT sphere, are creating brand-independent, interoperability specifications that can be used to build applications where disparate hardware and software solutions can communicate to provide a complete customer solution. Intel's acquisition of Dialogic last year is also paving the way for a "standardized" CT platform which could at long last start the CTI market on the road to true plug-and-play compatibility.

Another major factor is simply economics. A CTI-enabled call center gains efficiency in a number of ways. Web sites, IVRs and automated e-mail response systems promote customer self-service and can dramatically decrease costs by reducing the number of agents required to interface with the customer. Customer data can appear on the agent desktop with the call, eliminating the need to manually enter information each time the customer calls.

Customer data combined with data-mining can build targeted predictive dial lists that create up-sell and

Special Technology Issue 2001 ■ **Reprinted with permission from CCMReview®**

cross-sell opportunities, which can make each call less costly while potentially incrementing revenue.

The changing nature of the call center is also contributing to the growth in CTI-enabled applications. They are becoming more distributed – even globally. While large single-site call centers continue to thrive, the largest growth is in small to mid-size call centers, in the 30- to 100-agent segment, according to Datamonitor. And many of these call centers will be distributed around the globe, but will be networked together for maximum blended efficiency, as well as for centralized management. Informal call centers, smaller groups of agents that currently do not employ CTI-enabling technology, are also on the rise. These smaller centers will become increasingly networked and will require the same technologies used to manage larger distributed formal centers.

The Five Fastest-Growing CTI-Enabled Technologies

There are five "hot" CTI-enabled technologies that are critical to the success of forward-looking call centers. Effective deployment of one or more of these applications can turn a call center from a cost center into a profit center.

■ **Screen Pop.** The most common technology is the screen pop. Based on information inherent in the call, i.e., the number called from (ANI), or acquired via touch pad or even voice input, customer records in legacy databases can be matched and sent to the agent desktop as the call is presented to the agent. This increases productivity by saving the time required for an agent to enter this information. Customer history is available to the agent, who can automatically assume some familiarity with the customer, enhancing the customer experience.

■ **Warm Transfers.** A complementary technology to the screen pop, a warm transfer enables data to be transferred along with the call to another agent, department or site, eliminating the need to ask the caller to repeat information.

■ **Intelligent Call Routing.** Intelligent call routing is the ability to send the call to the most appropriate resource and can reduce costs dramatically by optimizing time per call. This can enhance the customer experience by matching them with an agent best suited to serve their needs.

Manage E-Mail/Web Site Volume With Automated Response Technology

Customers today are very demanding. They want enterprises to respond to their non-voice contacts with the same sense of urgency as their voice contacts. They don't want to wait in queue to get answers to mundane questions (e.g., Where do I send my payment?). And when they visit a Web site, they expect to be able to access a live agent immediately, at any time of the day, if they have a question.

As a result, the volume of e-mails and Web inquiries organizations receive is skyrocketing. Most organizations are not equipped to adequately handle any level of e-mail, much less the number they're experiencing.

One immediate solution to this problem is to implement an automated response system, which will ensure that e-mail or web contacts are being received by a centralized system, acknowledged immediately, potentially answered automatically, and routed to the most appropriate person if live intervention is required.

Designed to automate responses to fairly predictable and repetitive e-mail and Web inquiries from customers and prospects, the systems often utilize advanced artificial intelligence and linguistic techniques to examine the inquiries, look for matches in a database of frequently asked questions, and automatically respond if an appropriate match is found (see graphic, below). They also enable customers to service themselves a majority of the time. This significantly reduces the amount of e-mails and Web inquiries now requiring a live response, allowing employees to focus on the more complex issues that require personalized responses.

Automated response technology allows organizations to address this situation much more efficiently while greatly improving the quality of their online customer service.

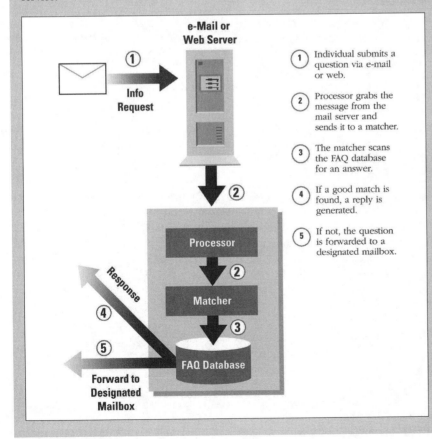

e-Mail or Web Server

Info Request

① Individual submits a question via e-mail or web.

② Processor grabs the message from the mail server and sends it to a matcher.

③ The matcher scans the FAQ database for an answer.

④ If a good match is found, a reply is generated.

⑤ If not, the question is forwarded to a designated mailbox.

Processor

Matcher

FAQ Database

Response

Forward to Designated Mailbox

■ **Call Blending.** Call blending can radically reduce costs and increase productivity, especially in telesales applications. Marketing campaigns traditionally cause peaks and valleys in any call center. There will always be some periods when agents will be idle and not taking calls. Blending outbound campaigns with inbound calls can fill in these valleys. Agents will take more calls per hour, the cost per call will decrease and revenue per agent will increase. Outbound agents can also be automatically moved to inbound applications during peak call-in times, lowering call waiting times and raising service levels.

■ **Web-Enabled Call Centers.** Web enabling your call center is a recent phenomenon that is starting to create rapid growth in many markets. It also can be a way to significantly decrease call center costs by empowering the customer to initiate self-service over the web. If your call center is tightly integrated with your web site, the customer experience can be rewarding. This puts the customer in charge of the relationship. The customer can determine how much time he or she takes to acquire needed information. If the customer has a question, he or she may choose to e-mail it right from the Web site.

If the request is urgent, a Web chat could be initiated or a callback can be scheduled with a live agent. Unfortunately this is an area where many new organizations are failing and losing potential customers. In order to provide premium service, more than a pretty Web site is required. There must be a way to contact live agents or customer service representatives, and the choice of media and urgency must be able to be made by the customer.

What Does CTI Mean to You and Your Customer?

What does CTI mean to you? It is a technology strategy that enables you to more effectively and efficiently acquire and retain customers. It can significantly decrease your call center costs by reducing the number of required agents by automating answers to repetitive requests. It can dramatically increase agent productivity by driving the call length down, thus increasing the calls taken per agent. It can enable customers to help themselves, further reducing costs. It can empower agents with access to data and tools necessary to more effectively up-sell and cross-sell. It can help enhance the total customer experience, thus reducing customer abandonment and attrition. It facilitates the optimization of your technology and human resources. It

means a leveling of the competitive landscape and wider access to your market.

What does CTI mean to your customers? It means they will no longer have to repeat account information multiple times per contact. It means they won't have to explain their contact history each time a new agent gets the call. It means that customers have more choices on how to do business with you. It is a technology-based way to effectively empower the customer to have more control over the relationship, and this perception will lead to increased customer loyalty, repeat business and incremental sales. *CCMReview*

Theresa VanLaeken

Theresa VanLaeken is senior product manager at Cincom Systems Inc. She is responsible for Cincom Encompass, a multi-channel customer interaction application suite that enables companies to achieve their customer relationship management goals through their call centers. For more information on Cincom Encompass, call 800-2CIN-COM, visit their Web site at www.cincom.com/encompass or send an e-mail to: info@cincom.com.

Service Level Notes with Brad Cleveland

Building the E-Enabled Call Center: It's Time to Get Moving (Part I)

Editor's Note: This article was co-authored by Jay Minnucci, a Senior Consultant with Incoming Calls Management Institute.

In August 1996, our firm partnered with Angus Telemanagement Group to launch "Call Centers on the Internet" (CCOTI), the first major conference focusing on the impact of the Internet on customer services and the prospect of integrating call center and Internet-based services (CCOTI has since been acquired by Advanstar).

Planning for the event had been in the works since 1995, but forecasting attendance was difficult. Those were the days when Internet security and reliability concerns abounded and some pundits were predicting that the Internet would collapse under its own weight. The word on the street was that nobody, save the purveyors of "adult material" and some financial services firms had or would make money on the Internet. Further, some influential technology firms, e.g., Microsoft, had been slow to embrace the Internet.

All considered, we expected around 200 to 300 attendees. As it turned out, more than 700 executives crammed into the conference facility. There was an overwhelming belief among attendees that we were discussing a development destined to forever change the delivery of customer services.

Vision Vs. Reality

What's happened in the four years since – a long, long time given the pace of development? If *bona fide* cases of integrated call center/ Internet applications are the measure of progress, then the answer is, *not much*. There are cases, but they are

few and far between. Meanwhile, there has been literally thousands of articles published on call center/ Internet integration, dozens of conferences every month dedicated to the subject and billions of dollars poured into the development of products and services.

CASE STUDIES OF INTEGRATED CALL CENTER/INTERNET SERVICES

Nobody in their right mind would argue with the proposition that the Internet has pervaded our lives, and changed our economy and organizations to an extent few predicted in the mid 1990s. But Internet-enabled call center applications have largely been stuck at the starting gate.

Few doubt the eventual proliferation of fully connected call centers, which, ironically, stands in stark contrast to many significant call center developments of days gone by. For example, quite a few customer-service directors initially questioned the value of ACDs, VRUs, desktop productivity tools and other call center capabilities as they were introduced to the market. But acceptance of the *vision* of call center/Internet integration has been rapid and widespread.

So, if the collective spirit is willing – end users, suppliers, consultants and customers all want to see these channels come together – what's the holdup? And where are things... *really*?

Slow Goes It... So Far

We have used the technology adoption lifecycle as a lens through which to assess the progress of developments (for more on the technology adoption lifecycle, see Service Level Notes, *CCMReview*, Sept. 1999). There are few statistically valid studies estimating the current penetration of these capabilities, which leaves the true state of progress to debate. But judging by the information that is available, we would describe and place general capabilities as follows (see figure 1):

Information-only and basic transaction-capable **Web sites** not integrated with the call center are referenced here to provide context. Information-only Web sites, often described as online, glossy brochures with only static information, represent the first level of Web development.

Basic transaction-capable Web sites represent a legitimate service-delivery channel, and enable customers to place orders, retrieve some user-specific information (e.g., account status, shipping progress and purchase history) and review basic FAQs. While more advanced applications such as Amazon.com's "One Click" ordering capability or Dell's Ask Dudley technical assistance feature (an enhanced FAQ powered by Ask Jeeves technology that allows natural language input to search for answers) are clearly in the early phases of development and adoption, basic capabilities are in the late majority category.

Section 9

While the majority of call centers handle customer e-mail, far fewer have implemented **e-mail response management systems**, that provide "ACD-like" capabilities: identifying, routing, queuing, tracking and reporting. However, these systems are rapidly penetrating the market and soon will cross into the early majority category.

Text-chat enables customers to exchange real-time text messages with agents while visiting an organization's Web site. While few applications exist, the enabling technology is feasible and available. Given the enormous popularity of instant messaging and chat groups, this channel will likely grow rapidly as customers come to expect and demand it.

Although many organizations enable customers to request a follow-up contact, **Web call-me** capability connotes integration with call center systems; the agent and customer can both converse and share a view of the Web site – services still at the innovator-stage of adoption. Generally, the customer must have an Internet connection and a separate telephone line available.

Web call-through enables a customer to click a button while viewing a Web site and establish a voice connection. The caller and agent can then converse and share Web pages. But bandwidth remains a barrier: Voice-over-IP quality remains erratic, and not all customers are equipped with the necessary hardware to make this feasible.

Web collaboration broadly refers to capabilities that enable the agent and caller to share web content by pushing pages back and forth, and/or doing some whiteboarding and page markup. It's used in conjunction with other communication channels – text-chat, Web call-me and Web call-through – and enhances the interaction by adding a shared visual element.

Given the development of the multichannel call center, the **multimedia queue** – all transactions being routed and handled based on business rules, regardless of channel – is compelling. Service level and response time can be managed from a single source, and a truly integrated view of the organization's workload can be achieved. This may be held up more by organizational and agent capability issues than technology.

Unified reporting, unfortunately, remains an innovator-only application. Few deny the importance of good data, but reporting all too often falls victim to the "let's-just-get-the-thing-up-and-running-and-we'll-worry-about-reporting-later" line of thinking that has become commonplace in the ever-changing call-center environment. Clearly, this is one of the reasons to choose an "all-in-one" solution from a single vendor, since that reduces the likelihood of integration problems on the reporting end.

There also are a variety of future capabilities envisioned. **Video over the Internet** would bring full multimedia capabilities to these transactions. Video is constrained by bandwidth issues and the need for the proper equipment at the customer's end. If and when these issues can be resolved, this represents an ultimate means of customer service interaction – and introduces the element of visual imagery into the agent selection process.

And as cultural acceptance grows, **call center-initiated assistance** could become more common. But the cultural hurdle may prove to be too formidable – especially since the unrequested appearance of a cyber-salesperson works against the vision of the anonymous surfing that helps differentiate web shopping from phone-based and bricks-and-mortar retailing.

Conclusion

Given the current state of flux, many organizations seem resigned to just let things happen as they will. As one call-center director told us, "We've got plenty to do in the meantime."

However, considering the widespread state of customer dissatisfaction with their e-contact experiences, and the impending changes in the competitive environment that e-enabled services will bring, waiting too long can be dangerous. In Part 2, we will identify common barriers to developing e-enabled call center services, and how they can – and must – be surmounted. There's been enough hype and talk. It's time to get things moving. *CCMReview*

Figure 1

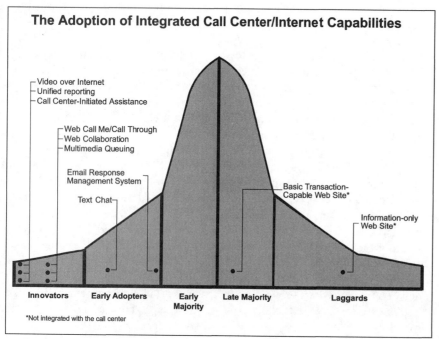

The Adoption of Integrated Call Center/Internet Capabilities

- Video over Internet
- Unified reporting
- Call Center-Initiated Assistance

- Web Call Me/Call Through
- Web Collaboration
- Multimedia Queuing

Email Response Management System

Text Chat

Basic Transaction-Capable Web Site*

Information-only Web Site*

Innovators   Early Adopters   Early Majority   Late Majority   Laggards

*Not integrated with the call center

Service Level Notes with Brad Cleveland

Building the E-Enabled Call Center: It's Time to Get Moving (Part 2)

Editor's Note: This article, along with Part 1, was co-authored by Jay Minnucci, a Senior Consultant with Incoming Calls Management Institute.

The e-enabled call center will become a widespread reality. That is without question. But, as discussed in Part 1, even though acceptance of the vision of call center/Internet integration has been rapid and widespread, few bona fide cases of integrated call center/Internet applications exist.

Given the current state of flux, many organizations seem resigned to let things happen as they will. But waiting too long can be dangerous, for a number of reasons:

■ As survey after survey bears out, overall customer satisfaction is at its lowest state in years – ironic, given the widespread emphasis on Customer Relationship Management (CRM) and customer lifetime value.

■ Developments will not happen in linear fashion. Despite the slow start, new Web/call center integration possibilities will present themselves at breakneck pace. Forward-thinking companies will identify and embrace those that offer promise but organizations that don't do the necessary planning and positioning in advance will fall behind.

■ A "one-channel-at-a-time" approach to the new environment is likely to produce lackluster results and a tangle of systems that have little chance of presenting a clear, integrated vision to your customers or your employees.

■ Datamonitor has estimated that businesses lost $1.9 billion last year due to the failure to Web-enable their customer service operations. Whatev-er the actual number, these lost opportunities are becoming a bit too much to stomach, particularly for organizations that have seen their stock valuation punished by investors.

In our studies of the market and our work with organizations planning and implementing Web-enabled solutions, we have found that a number of common barriers exist. Identifying and addressing these issues is key to getting things moving:

Lack of Organization-wide Strategy. Developing a solid customer access strategy is essential to effectively building an e-enabled call center (for background on strategy, see "Service Level Notes," *CCMReview*, February, March and May 2000). Creating strategy is not a simple process. Integrated delivery channels cause ownership boundaries to overlap, which can bring progress to a grinding halt. Those that have adequately addressed this and related issues have done so with a strong message and active involvement from the leadership ranks to bring potential factions together.

Budgetary Priorities. The door to the CFO's office is lined with VPs and directors vying for the big piece of the budget pie. And as you already know, or will soon find out when you start researching the technology, call center/Web integration won't happen without one of those big pieces.

But there is little value in competing with other parts of the organization that are also trying to address evolving customer service challenges. For example, initiatives such as CRM or supply change management offer a similar promise to help the organization meet customer expectations, now and in the future. Progressive organizations are working hard to avoid the trap of viewing and valuing these initiatives individually.

Current Workload. Technologists are stretched to the breaking point trying to maintain today's platform while at the same time designing and developing tomorrow's ideal environment. Call center managers are struggling just to maintain their support of existing channels – a recent ICMI study of 579 call center managers found that only 23 percent of the respondents regularly meet their inbound telephone service level goal.

The resources available are often barely able to meet existing challenges – heaping further responsibility on call center managers is not the answer. The development of the connected call center requires competent associates from the technical and managerial disciplines fully dedicated to the integration project to get it done right.

Technology in a State of Flux. Given the many alternatives, sorting through the maze of technology alternatives can be confusing. Further, call center technology is in a state of development unprecedented in the history of the industry (see box, page 17). But many suppliers offer impressive functionality that all too often comes with fine print, e.g., features that won't be available until the next release ("…it's due for general availability 'real soon'"). Further, consultants and other experts can't seem to come to any agreement – one that we spoke with described a well-known vendor's offerings as "tightly integrated," while another described the exact same solution as "bolted together." Concerns about risk

Section 9

abound, and with good reason.

A big part of the solution is to turn Moore's Law on its head. Yes, tomorrow's version will be faster and cheaper, but progressive organizations recognize that the risk associated with moving forward may be far less than the risk of sitting on the sideline waiting until everything shakes out – by that time, you may already be left behind. Getting into the arena gets you moving on the learning curve. The lesson may be costly, but far less so than ignorance.

Agent Skill Sets. This is causing great concerns in call center management circles, and for good reason. Finding trained, effective staff just to handle the inbound telephone channel has become a major challenge. Many managers are sweating over the prospect of having to fill hundreds or thousands of positions that require not just oral communication skills, but written ones, as well. Ongoing technology – and, especially, process improvements – may diminish the skill requirements somewhat. But that's of little comfort in today's tight job market.

Here again, it's time for organizations to face the inevitable. Revamping recruiting, hiring, training and career path initiatives to encourage the creation of a more Web-enabled workforce is the only sure way forward.

No competitive mandate – yet. The slow adoption rate of Web-enabled call center applications has, to some extent, become a self-fulfilling prophecy. "The competition's not doing it yet, so why should we?"

Further, though customers are clamoring for better service, they have not clearly dictated en masse the integrated mix of channels that suits them best. Of course, that evokes a chicken-and-egg question: How can they "embrace" anything before it becomes more commonplace? Industry leaders will recognize and leverage this opportunity to help shape expectations by offering customers as

The Many Technology Choices

While suppliers are migrating to a similar vision of the e-enabled, multichannel call center, they are getting there from different perspectives.

- **Traditional ACD/PBX Systems,** e.g., the Lucent (Avaya) Definity, Nortel Meridian or stand-alone ACD systems from Aspect and Rockwell still dominate the call center market. These vendors are building on their presence. Web channels are being "pushed" into the inbound call-queuing system to provide the users with a unified look at the incoming workload. But critics wonder about how tightly integrated these solutions really are.

- **Communication Server Vendors** such as Interactive Intelligence and Apropos are offering server-based solutions that provide tight integration of channels and a unified view of contacts. But critics often cite the high level of reliability of traditional ACD/PBX systems, and cast doubt on the reliability of server based systems in mission-critical environments.

- **IP-Based ACDs,** e.g., those from Cisco and Cosmocom, approach the multichannel ACD environment from the IP perspective. They enjoy a high level of recognition from high-tech organizations, dot-coms and other Web-centric companies, and afford tight integration between channels. But these solutions are subjected to the same reliability questions from those favoring more traditional ACD systems.

- **CTI Vendors** such as Genesys (now part of Alcatel) and Davox are building on their experience with integration solutions to make the e-enabled call center a reality. They have a strong presence in many large call centers, but many view them as niche players, a perception they are trying to change.

- **Alternative Channel Vendors** include companies that got their start by focusing on a "non-phone" channel. E.g., E-gain and Kana entered the market by offering E-mail Response Management Systems (ERMS). Through acquisitions and/or product developments, this category of suppliers is evolving to offer complete communication solutions. As with CTI vendors, they are trying to move beyond the perception that they are niche players.

- **CRM Vendors,** often through mergers, acquisitions, and partnerships, are offering multichannel/CRM integrated solutions. Examples include Lucent/Siebel, Nortel/Clarify, Cisco/Oracle, Quintus/Nabnasset, Cosmocom/Onyx, Kana/Silknet and others. These providers offer a broad range of capabilities but face the challenge of ensuring end users that they can focus solutions and support on specific call center requirements.

much as possible – and relentlessly surveying them to determine what is working.

Conclusion

Last year's holiday shopping season (1999) proved to be a publicity disaster for dot-com companies. Orders shipped late or never arrived, glaring incompatibilities between retail outlets and Web sites became obvious, and customers were trapped in poorly designed tangles of services when trying to reach organizations to resolve problems. A couple of

months later, investors begin to punish "E-tail" stock prices.

These experiences created a positive point of demarcation for call centers: Before last Christmas, the call center's value in the networked economy was questioned; after last Christmas, the need for a prominent role for "call centers" was firmly established. Now is the time to build on that promise.

Section 9

Web-Chat Emerging as a Leader for Live Online Support Applications

by Greg Levin

While call center managers were busy breaking their backs to tame the e-mail monster, the issue of live-agent assistance via the Web cruelly crept up. Today e-business is booming, and many customers are calling for more than three-day-old e-mail responses or sterile self-help applications. They are on your Web site ready to spend real money, and they want real-time interaction with real reps.

In a recent study conducted by Jupiter Communications, more than 40 percent of online shoppers stated that having a live-agent support option via the Web would significantly impact their purchase decisions. And Forrester Research has found that nearly 70 percent of customers who fill their online shopping baskets never complete the sale due to a lack of real-time support on the Web site.

The demand for live-agent support online isn't likely to subside. According to International Data Corp (IDC), there will be 500 million people online by 2003, and the value of e-commerce is expected to rise to $1.3 trillion.

Companies that don't cater to these customers' online needs won't be taking part in the e-commerce explosion. As Gartner Group explains, "Internet-based customer service is imperative for any enterprise that wants to compete effectively in the new millennium."

Features and Functions of Effective Chat Applications

Most Web-chat applications work in the following way: A customer clicks on a "chat" icon that's been strategically placed on a Web site. A dialogue box pops up on his screen in which he writes his initial inquiry and submits it. Back in the call center, a dialogue box containing what the customer has written opens on an available agent's desktop.

(Depending on the application, other relevant customer data that's been captured can be displayed on the agent's desktop as well, helping him or her to provide more personalized service). The agent responds with an "I'll be happy to help you with that" message, and the real-time (or near real-time) text-based transaction is under way. (Note: Call centers that don't have "chat agents" on staff 24 hours a day should highlight the hours that chat is available. Another option is to program the chat icon to appear on the Web site only at the times when such transactions can be handled.)

Some chat applications feature a "visitor monitoring" capability, which enables agents to see when customer begins browsing the Web site. The agent can then proactively engage the visitor in a live chat by typing "need any help?", which appears in a dialogue box on the page the visitor is viewing. This can be a good way to let new customers know of the live-support option and facilitate the sales/service process, but some customers may find it to be overly aggressive.

The most effective Web-chat applications contain powerful knowledge bases filled with frequently used

---

Leading Web-Based Support Applications

While call center professionals are well aware of customers' desire for real-time online assistance, most have sat back and waited to see which of the "big 3" Web-based support applications will lead the way:

- Voice over Internet protocol (VoIP) – enables online customers to speak with a live agent via their PCs.
- Web "call-back" – lets online customers choose when they would like an agent to call them.
- Web chat – allows for real-time, interactive text conversations between an online customer and an agent.

VoIP is an attractive solution at first glance, but the technology is still in its infancy. The handful of call centers that have implemented it report that the quality of the voice connection ranges from awful to mediocre. In addition to the technical limitations, VoIP applications require customers to first download the software they need before connecting with your call center. And many customers don't have the required hardware (i.e., soundcard, speakers, microphone) in their PC to make the application work.

Web call-back applications enable online customers and agents to conduct natural voice conversations, but the technology requires customers to have a second phone line. This is a big drawback when you consider the fact that only about 40 percent of American homes – and even fewer in most other countries – are equipped with a second line.

This brings us to live Web chat. It's not as "sexy" as VoIP and it doesn't provide the natural voice advantage of web call-backs, but guess what – it works. It works today, and it doesn't require your customers to search for any software nor install any hardware or any extra phone lines.

Though live Web chat brings with it some challenges – particularly with regard to hiring and training suitable agents – it appears to be the early leader in the online customer support game.

Nearly 10 percent of Web-enabled call centers already handle Web-chat transactions, and International Data Corp (IDC), expects the technology to reach near-saturation – exploding to 90 percent – in less than five years.

phrases to help agents save time during routine chat conversations. These systems can analyze the content of each customer inquiry/statement and suggest appropriate text templates to be incorporated into the agent's response. Call centers can also fill knowledge bases with entire pages and files that can be "pushed" to the customer's desktop during the chat session to provide him with detailed information on relevant products and services. The most vigorous Web chat applications are coupled with "shared browsing" and "form sharing" capabilities, which enable agents and customers to see the same screens simultaneously and to fill out order forms together.

"The ability to application-share while chatting is one big innovation," says Neal Goldman, director of Internet Computing Strategies for research firm The Yankee Group. "[It's a huge benefit when] the customer support person can see directly what's happening on the user's machine in real time."

Because of the speed that such features can add to the Web-chat process, agents in some call centers handle multiple chat sessions simultaneously. "[In same way that] many PC users juggle checking their e-mail, sports scores and stock reports at one time on their screen, Web-enabled CSRs can handle up to four customers at once in a real-time setting," says Chris Stanvick of Kowal Associates, Inc., a Boston-based telemanagement consultancy.

This is the real advantage of chat, says John Hunter, senior vice president of customer services for e-retailer iQVC (www.iqvc.com), whose Web agents have been handling chat transactions since November 1999. "Being able to do several transactions at one time is where you get productivity gains."

Another advantage of Web chat is that, like e-mail, all interactions with customers can be easily archived by the call center, enhancing the company's CRM efforts. Having past chat sessions handy in written form also facilitates the quality assurance

process. Call center supervisors can quickly go over chat transcripts with agents, pointing out strengths and weaknesses of the agents' responses.

The Need for a New Breed of Agent

None of the advantages of Web chat mean a thing without agents who can effectively handle the real-time text transactions. Herein lies the biggest challenge for call center professionals interested in adding chat to the service mix.

"Your chat application is only as good as your agents' writing and analysis skills," according to Valentina Guergova, customer service manager for Art.com. "Recruiting agents with these skills and bringing your existing agents up to speed on how to quickly and effectively handle text-chat transactions isn't easy."

Call centers serious about customer service on the Web are revamping their hiring programs to attract a new breed of agent. The recruiting process has become a quest for career-minded customer support and sales professionals with strong writing skills and Internet savvy. Some centers have even started screening applicants online via e-mail and Web chat to weed out weak candidates.

Such changes to traditional hiring methods are essential for call centers that want to succeed in e-business, says Wanda Sitzer, executive vice president of Initiatives Three Inc., a consulting firm specializing in phone and Web initiatives to improve customer support.

If you're launching an Internet venture and think that you can simply promote or transfer your best phone agents – think again! Even if some of your current employees have the potential to "morph" into Net Reps, they will need to meet productivity and service standards that are far higher than anything they have experienced before.

In addition to screening and interviewing potential Net Reps, Sitzer recommends that call centers conduct customer/agent role plays via Web chat to test candidate's real-time writ-

Chat Technology Note

Chat can come in many forms. Chat technology can consist of an HTML form, a Java applet, a browser plug-in, or a stand-alone application. Standards such as H.323 also support chat, enabling interoperability between H.323 compliant applications. If chat is to be supported within a customer service environment, it is most prudent to support a range of approaches, enabling customers with less sophisticated chat capabilities installed on their computers.

— *Genesys Telecommunications*

ten communication skills in a customer service situation. "Look for ease of chat session use and familiarity with "netiquette," good typing skills, the ability to interpret questions while online, appropriate paraphrasing or questioning, and a simple, concise writing style."

While the search for agents who can thrive in a chat environment is no simple task, it may get easier in the near future as chat becomes a common form of communication in general society. According to a recent white paper by Genesys Telecommunications, "A whole new generation of chat users has entered the workforce over the last few years, and many more are in high school and college today."

Getting Net Reps Web-Ready

It's unlikely that this new generation of chat users will come readily equipped with online customer support and sales skills. That's why Web-enabled call centers need to begin modifying their existing training programs now. Having a staff of Web whiz kids who can write dialogue as smoothly as they speak is great, *if* they can "connect" with your valuable customers. To ensure that they do, Sitzer recommends the following modules be incorporated into the Net Rep training program:

■ Your company's Internet strategy – today and tomorrow.

Section 9

- Introduction to e-commerce: what it is, how it affects your business, the Net Rep's role.

- "Netiquette."

- Adapting traditional sales and service skills to the needs of online customers.

- The basics of Web technology.

- Knowledge of your Web site and your online competition's sites.

Training programs for agents who will be handling chat transactions should include sufficient practice using text templates and page-push tools. Effective use of such features can enhance the quality of online customer service that's delivered while reducing handling time – and agent burnout – significantly, says Goldman of The Yankee Group. "Enabling agents to quickly paste FAQs into their chat responses and/or push appropriate pages to customers is a big time-saver. It's the equivalent of phone agents not having to repeat the same information over and over to callers."

Further Challenges in Forecasting, Staffing

Once you have a team of agents who are qualified to tackle chat transactions, you still must manage some important forecasting and staffing issues. Predicting initial chat volume is tricky business; there is usually little or no historical data on which to base calculations. Call centers that already handle customer e-mail transactions may decide to use the same agents for chat sessions, though additional staff may be needed to meet the real-time demands of chat.

Most managers embarking on live Web support ventures rely on a combination of common sense and guesswork when forecasting and scheduling. "At first, you have to make educated guesses based on past Web site traffic and customer e-mails," Bruce Seago, vice president of E*Trade Canada's call center in Toronto. "Pretty soon, patterns start to develop, just like with regular phone calls, and you'll get a good idea of how many agents you need to have in place."

Even with forecasting figured out, managers must make an important staffing decision: a) to use a separate team of dedicated Net Reps to handle only Web-based transactions (chat and e-mail); or b) to use a broader team of "super agents" who can handle all Web *and* phone transactions. While the super-agent approach appeals to most call center professionals in theory, many feel that it is difficult to implement from a hiring and training standpoint. Others, like The Yankee Group's Goldman, still feel that the super-agent approach is the only way to go.

"I haven't found using separate [Web and phone] groups to be an effective strategy because handling chat and e-mail only, like handling phone calls only, can get very rote quickly, and this affects employee turnover." He adds that, as much as chat and e-mail are growing, "they will never supplant phone calls," thus it doesn't make good business sense to have a large team of agents who can handle only Web transactions.

Chat's Currently Where It's At

While the best way to staff for Web chat is still a subject of debate, few deny that chat makes sense for call centers looking to offer reliable live support online *today*. This is not to say that VoIP and Web call-backs aren't viable applications with a future, but they currently don't provide the same quality and/or coverage as chat, which anybody with a Web browser can easily use.

True, getting the right agents in place to handle chat isn't easy, but there's a long-term payback after the pain, says Art.com's Guergova.

"Offering live support on the Web via chat has greatly enhanced sales and service for us. Customers like being able to contact an agent immediately while online, and we are able to show them things that we cannot show them over the phone." CCMReview

Greg Levin

Greg Levin is the former editor of Call Center Management Review. *Greg is a regular contributor to the publication, and also writes the "In Your Ear" call center humor column. He is currently a freelance writer based in Spain.*

Making Sense of Virtual Customer Care Solutions

by Sydney Burton

Lately, it seems that the one constant in the call center industry is change. Key questions surfacing for call center managers include: "How can we handle more inquiries?" and "How do I maintain quality control over remote locations?"

Probably the most heralded change taking place industrywide is the need to handle multiple media types. However, there is another key development that is also causing significant transitions in call centers – the move to a virtual call center environment. Existing call center architecture is now being impacted by an impressive array of available alternatives to link agents into physical and logical groups, regardless of their location.

Call Distribution Solutions Are Varied and Diverse

The benefits of geographically distributing a call center are well-known. Virtual environments allow companies to: 1) locate call centers where the workforce exists; 2) extend service hours across time zones; 3) tap into a larger staff to cover peak demands; and 4) provide coverage for

call centers during major (or minor) disasters, such as hurricanes or snow days.

Today call centers are no longer limited to a handful of individual architectures. The virtual call center may blend together multiple distribution alternatives into unique designs: Entire agent groups in one location, single agent groups spread across multiple corporate locations, and individual agents working from remote locations.

Conventionally distributed call centers use ACD (Automatic Call Distribution) systems that are interconnected with overflow and interflow to move calls between groups of agents. Although this is a significant advancement toward expanding a call center across multiple locations, it occasionally may result in sending calls from one overloaded queue into another overloaded queue.

Some ACD systems have solved the initial interflow problems by employing a "look ahead" routing method that uses statistical routing to check for even call distribution. These methods evaluate such things

as the queue depth, longest waiting call and number of available agents at each location, and measures the queue-time disparity across those locations. However, this design is still somewhat limited since it routes calls based on queue information rather than agent information.

Another recent development in ACD technology allows agents to be identified across a network of associated PBX systems with call routing controlled by a single ACD system in that network. This technology gives call centers the advantage of being able to route calls directly to the most appropriate agent.

As an alternative to the conventional distribution and interconnection of call centers, network-level resources may be used for call routing and distribution. One variation relies on network-level applications to route calls to agents at multiple call centers served by multiple (vendor-independent) ACD systems. The application communicates with each individual location to monitor the real-time state of each call center, which then provides the basis for the application to route each call to the most appropriate agent, regardless of location. A

Elements of a Virtual Call Center

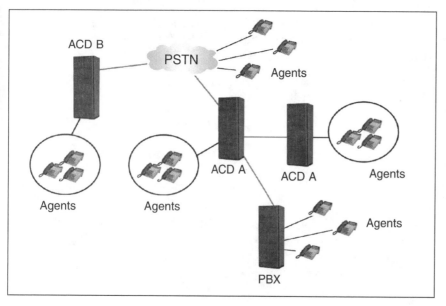

second variation uses ISDN (Integrated Services Digital Network) services to define the entire ACD at the network-level. In this arrangement, calls are routed directly to agents without requiring premises-based customer switching equipment.

Revisiting the Remote Agent

Another viable alternative for call center distribution is to use remote agents. This is most usually associated with telecommuting, but could be used to meet other requirements.

Telecommuting was the "killer app" of the early 1990s, but declined in popularity as companies discovered that administration of agent-at-home programs often resulted in management nightmares. Many of the early programs suffered from the use of immature technologies, inadequate planning and unexpected costs. Recently, however, there has been a quiet resurgence in telecommuting and agent-at-home programs. The technology has matured, costs have come down and management teams have taken lessons from early pilot programs and are now better prepared to face the administration issues.

Technology can enable communications to the remote agent in two forms – each using either existing phone lines or ISDN services for connectivity. One variation uses a PC-based application to provide a softphone with agent features. The other uses extender modules (analog, digital or ISDN) to place a digital agent telephone at the remote location.

The key to success with either solution is to have the agent logged directly in to the ACD system from the remote location. This means that the agent appears to the ACD system just like any other agent – thus, calls are routed to the remote agent no differently than to any other agent; data is gathered on the remote agent no differently than any other agent; and all other call center features such as emergency recording, quality monitoring, etc., are available to the remote agent no differently than to any other agent. This provides seam-

---

Challenges to Creating a Virtual Call Center

Virtual call centers face other management challenges in addition to technology. Some issues for consideration include:

- Creation of a unified culture in the organization.
- Communication of cohesive goals and objectives for the entire organization.
- Development of confidence and commitment within the organization.
- Definition of reporting arrangements and agent group structures.
- Definition of compensation and benefits across geographical boundaries.
- Communication of news and information simultaneously to all members.

---

less functionality to both the agent and the call center manager, as well as call-handling that is transparent to the customer.

Organizational Requirements Dictate Architecture Selection

When designing a call center, there is no single right or wrong architecture. Decisions must be based on the requirements and objectives of the call center organization, and its preferences with respect to owning equipment or purchasing services. Also, various architectures lend themselves to the use of centralized or decentralized supporting technologies (such as interactive voice response, workforce management, quality monitoring and recording, etc.). The organization's requirements for redundancy and disaster recovery options, or perhaps the desire to reduce or eliminate duplication of resources will establish values for the various alternatives.

The use of multiple contact types – voicemail, fax, e-mail, Web callback, Web chat and/or Web calls – also adds both opportunity and complexity to the virtual call center. While

the design nature of an center handling customer contacts from a variety of locations may more easily adapt to handling multiple contact types, conversely, the range of media types may require additional technology and new integration to enable agents in diverse locations to effectively manage customer contacts. One straightforward solution is to employ a single communication platform that can process all customer contacts with multimedia queuing. This solution allows one set of queues to contain all types of contacts, each with the appropriate routing criteria, prioritization and data gathering.

Let the Data Be Your Guide

The integration required to deploy a virtual call center often results in an assortment of systems connected at various levels to generate the desired handling of customer contacts. Unfortunately, data collection and reporting may not be as tightly integrated as call routing.

The ability to adjust to real-time demands depends entirely on information. A virtual call center must depend extensively on system data to understand organizational performance – for instance, how long calls wait in queue at each location; what the average handle time is and how it is affected by agent location; and whether or not agent activities can be tracked for transaction validation or performance evaluation. Systems that can provide centralized data gathering, reporting, administration and control, regardless of the call center's architecture, are the ones that can best enable managers to respond to changing conditions and to plan for future demand.

The addition of multiple contact types makes the collection of data even more crucial in making decisions on how to handle the various customer contacts. Some considerations include:

- How long do contacts of different types (such as e-mail or Web-chat) wait in queue?
- What is the average handle time

for each contact type?

- Can the activities of an agent who handles multiple contact types be tracked for transaction validation or performance evaluation?

While it's possible to set service level goals in the absence of such data, it's not possible to determine how well those goals are being met. Single systems performing multimedia queuing have the advantage of being able to continuously track contacts within a single framework. Integrated systems have a greater challenge to track contacts as they are handed off from one system to another.

The Goal: Provide A Seamless Customer Experience

Consistency is the key to developing a virtual call center. Maintaining consistent functionality for both customers and agents across diverse mediums is imperative. Customers can and should expect personalized, high-quality service regardless of the technology involved.

Call centers have an obligation to closely examine their approaches to customer service through each contact medium and to make intelligent decisions to ensure the handling of each contact type is consistent. For instance, customers who phone a call center typically receive a message to indicate their call is in queue and may receive information on how long they can expect to wait before talking with an agent. Similarly, customers requesting service via e-mail should receive an acknowledgement that their request has been received.

Managing business information is another significant challenge in operating a virtual call center. In order to provide consistent service to customers across diversely located agents and across multiple contact types, all agents handling contacts must have access to the same information with the same frequency of updates, the same level of detail and the same access tools.

In addition, documentation on customer status and transactions must be current and available to the next agent in contact with a customer, regardless of the location of the agent. Likewise, the same information should also be available to the agent regardless of what contact type the customer selects. For example, a customer should be able to place a voice call to an agent to complete a transaction that began with a Web contact – without placing any additional requirements on either the customer or the agent.

Regardless of architecture, the virtual call center is dependent on unique and still-emerging technology, processes and management practices to operate effectively, which introduces integration and coordination challenges for call center organizations. However, meeting these challenges is worth the investment in time and resources when it results in improved efficiency and enhanced service. CCMReview

Sydney Burton

Sydney Burton is responsible for marketing NEC America Inc.'s call center and customer contact center product portfolio. She has extensive knowledge in PBX products and applications, multimedia products, public networks and data communications. Sydney holds Bachelors' Degrees in both Chemistry and Computer Science from the University of Texas, and an MBA from the University of Dallas.

Still a Few Barriers to Integrated Multimedia Routing and Queuing

by Susan Hash

Over the next few years, most call centers will need to adopt a multimedia routing and management approach to handle the growing volume and complexity of inbound contacts. The debate between vendors and industry analysts is how soon the technology and business processes will reach a level of maturity to make multimedia queuing and routing systems a viable call center investment.

Vendors stand ready to take on that challenge now with numerous e-service enabled call center packages; consultants and analysts caution that the business processes and technologies still have some kinks to work out.

The GartnerGroup characterized 1999 as a banner year for the release of call center products by leading vendors. And it seems likely that 2000 may even surpass 1999 for e-service product releases.

Industry experts agree that developing a comprehensive approach to managing all inbound customer contacts, regardless of the type of media used, is key to business survival. But figuring out exactly how to do that can be a bewildering process for managers.

"I think it's probably one of the most confusing parts of the market right now because there are so many different ways to approach it," says Lori Bocklund, call center practice manager for Vanguard Communications, based in Morris Plains, N.J. "The concept is to create a common routing and reporting tool for managing all media and delivering it to a collection of agents. Although that's the same concept call centers have been dealing with for 10 years, we've added a new dimension with the other media. Now you've got to figure out who's contacting you, why and how, and then segment agent skills for call type and function, customer type and medium type."

Analysts Skeptical

of Current Market Offerings

Probably the key obstacle associated with integrating multiple channels is that the alignment of business strategies and technology is still largely in the early adoption stage – even by the more pioneering organizations. Vendors are currently rolling out multimedia routing and management applications to technologically aggressive organizations, most of which are, or expect to be, competing heavily in the e-business arena (i.e., dot-coms, high-tech organizations, financial services, catalog retailers).

But do the current market offerings meet the needs of more mainstream call centers dealing with a high volume of voice calls?

"I don't think anyone [vendors] is there yet. They're all taking different paths to move to the same space – multimedia routing capabilities tied to CRM [Customer Relationship Management]," says Bocklund. Ultimately, though, key differences will begin to emerge depending on the vendor's core competency, for instance, coming from a CTI or switch perspective vs. e-mail routing and management.

"The effects of work balancing the different live contact channels, as well as integrating real-time live contacts with time-delayed asynchronous channels, such as e-mail, are not yet well understood by platform vendors," according to Bernard Elliot, an industry analyst with GartnerGroup. "Few vendors have modeling and simulation applications to assist in the complex programming of contact routes and queues." However, he adds, "enterprises should expect rapid evolution of modeling, simulation and other tools that support work balancing."

The GartnerGroup estimates that the adoption rate for electronic channels by mainstream call centers will pick up speed in two to five years. The research firm predicts that:

- By 2002, only 20 percent of call centers will have integrated, live Web contacts or e-mail response management systems with their

Baby Steps: Ease into Multimedia Integration

In many cases, managers are taking a piecemeal approach in an effort to keep pace with the technology while bringing the people and process components up to speed, says Yung Chen, product manager, Enterprise Routing Solution, Enterprise Applications Business Unit, Genesys. "We've seen a definite trend in which call center managers are starting out by keeping the various media separated," she says. "Then, as they improve the operation and agent productivity, they can move to a universal queuing engine for an environment that supports the various media in a neutral fashion – with each contact moving through a common queue."

She also suggests rolling out multimedia applications to a small group of agents initially, and then pulling in more agents as the processes fall into place.

Also, consider how the new media will impact your staff. "Be careful not to overload your agents when scheduling integrated media," says Jody Wacker of Apropos Technology. "Try to balance your various service levels with agent skills – you don't want to force customers back to the phone when you wanted them to use e-mail."

Cisco Systems' Firdauf Bhathena recommends managers pick solutions that solve a specific problem they're dealing with today, such as e-mail or Web contacts, while keeping in mind that, eventually, they will need to migrate to a solution that integrates multiple points of contact.

Inevitably, agrees Lawrence Byrd of Quintus Corp., "no single channel approach is going to work. The customer expects multiple channels; you've got to make them work."

telephone-based agents.

- By 2005, 70 percent of call centers in geographic areas with high Internet adoption rates, such as North America and parts of Europe, will support integrated, live Web contacts and/or e-mail response management systems for their telephone-based agents.

Estimated Timeline for Multimedia Adoption

The combination of technology maturity and the level of adoption of media types in call centers will be key in differentiating among multimedia products and functions.

David Peterson, president of PowerHouse Consulting, an independent call center consulting firm based in Bedford, N.H., sees multimedia routing and queuing capability evolving in three stages. He pegs traditional e-mail as the No. 1 multimedia queuing application currently being implemented in call centers.

"E-mail queuing and distribution is probably the hottest item in this whole multimedia business today," says Peterson. "The main reason for that is everybody has the capability to send an e-mail – it doesn't require any special software or hardware on your computer. As a result, we're seeing a lot of call centers getting inundated with e-mail."

The second stage for call centers is likely to be interactive chat sessions over the Web, which is similar to e-mail in that customers who have an Internet connection generally have the capability for text-chat.

While not many Web sites are currently offering Web chat, "it's not because they can't – it's simply because they haven't," Peterson says. "The demand on call centers will be to distribute chat sessions to agents in a live fashion, as you would a phone call."

Peterson estimates that Web chat will start to take off over the next year, and soon will be almost as prevalent as e-mail.

In fact, Web chat is already "the second most requested multimedia feature that we're seeing," says Todd Tanner, senior consultant for The Tanner

Group Inc., an independent telecommunications consulting and call center modeling firm in Salt Lake City. "The best programs allow agents to chat with up to three individuals simultaneously. However," he says, "there aren't any systems currently out there that I'm aware of – specifically, from the four largest ACD seat manufacturers – which do a good job of holding multiple chats on the mainstream telecom."

The third level of multimedia applications for call centers, which is getting a lot of attention today, is Voice over Internet Protocol (VoIP) – transmitting voice as packets over an IP network. Peterson estimates VoIP will begin to surface in call centers in about two years after several technological issues have been resolved.

The VoIP Development Debate

Vendors are already gearing up for VoIP, many of whom say it's a viable solution in use today.

Cisco Systems' Internet Communications Software Group is currently conducting field trials with IP PBXs and ACDs, says Firdauf Bhathena, director of engineering.

"Our Web strategy is to help migrate companies' internal voice communication from a PSN (Public Switched Network) to a VoIP network, because that will allow call centers to leverage that same IP ACD to handle multiple points of contact down the road."

Aspect Communications also has beta customers using VoIP technology in its Aspect Portal Multimedia solution, says David Puglia, vice president of product marketing. He expects VoIP capability to take off when it evolves from a point-to-point solution to many-to-many.

"Today, the VoIP works as a point-to-point," he explains. "If I go to a URL with a specific data connection, the agent can't transfer me like you would in a call center." This year, Aspect expects to introduce VoIP technology that's integrated with the Portal to allow agents to transfer callers to Web chat, as well as over the center's PSN network.

Peterson, however, remains highly skeptical about current VoIP capabilities and quality.

"It's going to be a horror show," he says. "There's no control over latency and delay. Granted, if you're using the Internet to call your relatives overseas, you might put up with a little delay and choppiness, but if you're running an enterprise business, you're not going to have that kind of tolerance. Call centers can't afford to have retransmits, errors and latency in the communication path."

Tanner agrees with that assessment, stressing that VoIP is "nowhere near ready for prime time."

On the consumer side, another potential obstacle is that VoIP would require callers to have the appropriate software to talk to call centers. And although Microsoft is bundling a real-time collaboration and conferencing product, called NetMeeting, with its Windows 2000 operating system software, "it's a cumbersome application to use," Peterson says.

Call Centers Still Working Through Organizational Barriers

Vendors generally acknowledge that call centers need to focus attention on their business processes before turning to technology as a solution.

"The biggest issue is not the technology necessarily, because that's coming along quite quickly," says Jonathon Farmer with Nortel Networks' Clarify eBusiness Applications unit. "However, all of this technology is outpacing call center managers' abilities to segment the skill sets within their centers, as well as to find the types of agents who can handle multiple types of media."

That's because, historically, the hiring practices in most call centers have been focused on voice and people skills, says David Fuller, director of marketing, Call Center Applications, Interactive Intelligence. He believes call centers initially need to look at ways to pull staff with Internet skills into the center to handle the e-mail volume, at least in the short term. Once they're part of the center, they can begin to transfer those skills to other agents.

Often, the organizational structure and communication among senior-level management is the biggest hurdle, says Lawrence Byrd, vice president of strategy, Quintus Corp.

"The first challenge for organizations is to create a relationship between the call center manager, customer service director and the czar of e-commerce," he says. "Typically, they're different people in different locations with different reporting structures who haven't gotten around to talking to each other yet. The fact that we've arrived is the first time they're in a room together. It shouldn't be technology that causes that to happen."

Generally, call center managers know that, eventually, they'll have to plan for and implement multimedia routing, queuing and reporting systems. But, says Bocklund, "they're probably not ready yet. There are huge organizational and operational implications for call centers – they might have to rewrite job descriptions and change compensation plans – those will be prerequisites for doing a lot of this."

Technology Will Evolve Quickly

While most experts agree that the call center industry is just seeing the beginning stages of integrated multimedia applications, the pace of development is expected to far outstrip previous technology.

"With CTI, the vendors pushed the technology before the application," says Peterson. "But, with e-mail and Web chat integration, the customer is pushing the application, so it's going to develop much faster. It's the freight train that's rumbling down on you." CCMReview

Section 9

When Is an ASP the Right Solution for Your Center?

by Steve McCullough

Remember when the biggest decision you had to make with regard to software applications was whether to buy or build? Indeed, this was never an easy decision to make, but now it's being further complicated by another question – should you buy or rent?

The Application Service Provider (ASP) alternative has become very appealing to many call center operations, but navigating the complex issues involved in answering that question is quite another matter.

One of the key reasons businesses consider using an ASP solution is the potential savings in the upfront costs involved in purchasing, implementing and integrating new systems. While these savings can range from thousands of dollars to hundreds of thousands, what most companies eventually discover is that the real value proposition lies in the fact that application outsourcing eliminates a lot of procurement and implementation hassles.

Instead of spending time managing a technology headache, management can focus their efforts on the call center's core competencies and tactical execution – which are the areas that frequently create more sustainable improvements than new software applications. And it's these intangible benefits that provide the most attractive reasons to consider an ASP solution.

Technology Advancements Spurring the Growth of ASPs

The ASP phenomenon is upon us now because only recently has technology reached the point of feasibility for true application outsourcing. Some of the contributing factors are:

■ **Acceptance of outsourcing.** Outsourcing as a strategic model for procuring services has demonstrated its worth in the new economy. The need to be fast and flexible has forced businesses to focus on core competencies while outsourcing non-core services to service providers and business partners. Information technology has been one of the most logical and widely adopted choices for outsourcing.

■ **Ubiquitous access.** The Internet is almost universally accessible, while connection charges continue their rather steep downward trend. Bandwidth also continues to increase at a considerable pace.

■ **Browser accepted GUI (Graphical User Interface).** Well over 90 percent of Internet users have Microsoft's Internet Explorer or Netscape's Navigator. These products are virtually ubiquitous and their users demonstrate high levels of comfort and familiarity.

■ **Internet is more secure and reliable.** Today's Internet is much more powerful, reliable and secure than it has ever been. The infrastructure gains in the last few years alone have evolved the Internet from little more than an information resource (Web sites, portals, etc.) to a powerful commerce engine (business-to-consumer and business-to-business e-commerce sites) and now finally to a true enterprise-ready, data infrastructure tool (intranets and ASPs).

The Buy vs. Rent Proposition

When deciding whether or not to use an ASP, the first step is to determine which applications you can and/or might outsource. Typically, it's a good idea to look at applications that require a high level of availability or technical expertise that your company doesn't have or doesn't wish to maintain inhouse as a core competency.

While this is certainly a good place to start, it's not the only consideration. When examining the buy-or-

What Is an ASP?

The ASP (Application Service Provider) Industry Consortium defines an ASP as an organization that "manages and delivers application capabilities to multiple entities from a data center across a wide area network (WAN)." In plain English, an ASP owns the software license and leases access to the application to its customers for a monthly or annual fee. Of course, the most common method an ASP application is delivered today is via the Internet with a browser as the frontend "client."

While the concept of running an application on a central server is certainly not new (ever hear of a mainframe?), the idea of using the Internet as a hosting and distributing mechanism is fairly recent. And it's quickly becoming extremely popular. According to International Data Corp., I/T industry analysts, more than $296 million was spent on ASP services in 1999. That is expected to reach $633 million this year and will rise to $7.8 billion by 2004.

rent issue, there are several thoughts to keep in mind.

For instance, some of the more attractive benefits of using an ASP include:

■ **Reduced total cost of ownership.** Because of the economies of scale the service provider can leverage, it is typically less expensive to go with an ASP than purchasing and installing the software yourself. Your first step should be to list all of the costs associated with licensing the software – licenses, upgrades, implementation, hardware costs, internal and external support, network connectivity, etc. – and weigh those against the costs of using an ASP.

But to understand the complete costs of the rent-an-application model, you also have to know the total price of outsourcing the software over a specific time period. An ASP's contract may require a minimum number of users to sign up for the service and may force clients to commit to a specific length of time in the contract. If an ASP's monthly rental fee for an Enterprise Resource Planning (ERP) suite is $100 per user, and the outsourcing service provider specifies that customers must have at least 100 users over a three-year period, the cost of outsourcing the application starts at $360,000. Be sure to read all of the fine print.

■ **Ability to focus on strategic business initiatives.** Perhaps the greatest advantage of the ASP model is that you will be able to focus more time on the elements that really drive success in your call center (i.e., cor-

porate strategy alignment, workforce management, measurement, customer feedback and agent training). Technology, while increasingly important, is only one element in the overall mix that contributes to the creation of a world-class call center.

■ **Freeing of I/T resources.** Perhaps the costliest and most challenging aspect of leveraging technology in a call center today is the availability and management of technical personnel. Organizations typically fight over a limited pool of trained technical resources, within and without the organization. Using an ASP puts the burden on the service organization to attract, maintain and manage those personnel.

■ **Remote availability.** The ubiquitous availability of the Internet combined with the use of a browser as a thin client creates a simple and cost-effective model for connecting resources distributed across a wide geographic area. Adding an additional call center requires little more than purchasing desktops and Internet access.

■ **Faster implementation.** An ASP application can usually be deployed within 30 to 60 days – a fraction of the time it takes to design, customize and implement a system purchased in the traditional way. This increased speed gives organizations a tremendous competitive advantage, allowing them to realize the benefits of new applications sooner.

■ **Even cost allocation.** Since most ASP contracts are written with a monthly or annual fee, costs are computed and charged on a regular, timed basis. This allows for more accurate budgeting and frequently corresponds directly to the number of individuals accessing the system. In contrast, traditional software licensing requires a significant investment in infrastructure and implementation costs at the early stages, which can be a significant cash drain for many small to medium-sized organizations.

■ **Scalability.** Typically, ASP licenses are computed on a per-user basis. This

means that, as your call center grows, you simply purchase additional licenses. There is no additional software to load, no hardware to install and no changes to be made in server configuration. This simplifies the scalability issue for fast-growing organizations. It also means smaller companies with a rather limited user count can better afford the software because there is no need to invest heavily in upfront infrastructure costs.

■ **Trouble-free revision management.** Staying current with software license revisions is a tedious and troublesome task. By managing all the software at the server level, the ASP dramatically simplifies upward portability. Training issues still need to be addressed for enhancements and programmatic changes, but the traditional I/T burden of rolling out new software to multiple desktop clients is eliminated.

Selecting a Service Provider

If you've decided that using an ASP can benefit your call center, there are a few areas to research when selecting a particular provider.

Your first concern should be security. If you're going to trust someone to handle critical aspects of your customer management applications, you should pay particular attention to making sure your data is in good hands. Look for an ASP with a dedicated security officer, a written set of policies and regular security audits. And make sure that all audit results will be available for your inspection.

Along with physical security and employing technology such as Virtual Private Networks (VPN), firewalls and intrusion-detection software, ASPs must also provide safeguards to ensure that each client sees only its own data. At present, virtually all ASPs do this by setting up each client with its own set of hardware, which is most often housed in the collocation facilities of a top-rung hosting facility. You'll know if you're dealing with one of the better ones if they insist on taking you on a tour of their facilities. If they do, take them up on it

Don't Overlook Potential Drawbacks

In addition to the numerous benefits associated with Application Service Providers (ASP), there are a few concerns, as well. For instance, one of the major drawbacks of using an ASP is the relatively limited opportunity to customize the application to your specific needs. Success in applications, such as CRM (Customer Relationship Management), requires extensive customization capability for large enterprises. The ASP approach doesn't allow much room for customization, particularly in dealing with small customers.

Another potential obstacle is integration with other systems. Many times, you'll want the application you're implementing to integrate with one or more related systems. For instance, you may want a knowledge management system to interface with a customer support application. ASPs have had difficulty in being flexible enough to integrate to other platforms within an organization's enterprise infrastructure. This is gradually changing, but can be a severe limitation in many cases.

and don't be afraid to be a little nosy!

Most ASPs contract with outside data centers to actually host the applications that you'll be accessing from within your company. So your due diligence has to go beyond just the ASP you're thinking about using.

Also consider where the data center is located. Who's actually hosting the equipment? Is there redundancy built into the system?

How will you know if an ASP is reliable and service-oriented? Be sure to request a list of customers who are purchasing a similar level of service and the Service Level Agreement (SLA) that goes along with that spending level. Talk to those customers and see if they are satisfied with the level of service they are receiving. Be sure to ask how proactive the ASP was in reporting service failures.

In fact, it's a good idea to pay particular attention to the SLA. Keep in mind that you are purchasing a service, not a product, in the truest sense. The service levels you negotiate will be critical to the success of your relationship. These contracts should clearly define the specific quality and performance levels you will expect from the service provider. It may include everything from expected response times for software applications to minimum bandwidth provided over a dedicated line. It should completely detail the nuts-and-bolts of day-to-day service.

The SLA may also include financial penalties that serve as incentives for ASPs to meet or exceed those minimum requirements. In some cases, ASPs may be allowed to offset those penalties against performance bonuses when they exceed the contract's terms. Keep in mind that the more critical the application is to your delivery of customer service, the more likely you'll be interested in higher service levels as opposed to cheaper monthly fees.

The last two points to consider will be the toughest to evaluate in your process of due diligence: 1) your ASP's integration capabilities, and 2) after-sale service. These are absolutely critical to its long-term success with you. Again, look to other customers for testimonies of how well they've done in these areas. Hint: Research some of the older press releases on their Web site and call customers not included on their reference list. This will give you a truer picture of their integration capabilities and commitment to service.

A Viable Option, If Approached Correctly

Using an ASP is a very attractive option for many call centers. It can be inexpensive, quick and relatively painless, if approached correctly. It can also be a nightmare. Approach it no differently than you would approach any other mission critical software purchase.

If you apply the pointers mentioned here along with a sizeable measure of common sense, you may just find yourself joining the growing list of evangelists for this exciting movement in application software distribution. **CCMReview**

Steve McCullough

Steve McCullough is a principal partner in Atlanta-based Xperio Inc., a consulting services firm specializing in the full lifecycle of customer care management. Previously, Steve was the founder and president of Close the Distance Inc., a marketing and sales consulting firm focused on the high-tech market. Also, in his previous work at Support Technologies Inc., a provider of technical support outsourcing, consulting and educational services, he was instrumental in launching Help Desk 2000, an education and certificate division that trains service and support professionals internationally. Steve can be reached at 877-973-7461 or steve@xperio.com.

A Solid RFP Process Will Ease Vendor Selection and Management

by Greg Levin

You can select technology products for your call center without going through a strategic request for proposal (RFP) process. You can also go on a lion safari wearing clothes made out of meat. In both cases, you are asking for trouble.

The call center supplier market is a wild domain with new products leaping out almost daily. But, keep in mind, choosing the right vendor and product for your call center takes time. Rushing through technology acquisitions could lead to damaging service glitches and vendor support problems in the long run.

Developing and implementing an effective RFP process enables you to pinpoint your specific technology requirements, evaluate and compare vendor candidates up close, and decide which supplier/products will best support your center's needs.

"Having an RFP levels the playing field," says David Peterson, president of PowerHouse Consulting in Bedford, N.H., and a specialist in call center technology acquisition. "All vendors must respond to the exact same set of specifications, which goes a long way toward getting an 'apples to apples' comparison."

The Initial Steps

The more you know about what you want prior to contacting vendor candidates, the better off you'll be throughout the RFP process. Take the time to document what you need the technology to achieve for your call center. For example, if it's an automated monitoring system you're after, determine which specific features and functions the product must have: i.e., selective recording; voice and screen monitoring; integration with CTI; voice compression (to maximize disk space for recordings); customized agent performance reports; etc.

Arming yourself with clear objectives will allow you to be proactive when dealing with vendors. As one ex-vendor executive advises, "Without a formal specification, vendors are left to their own devices to decide what is important, typically emphasizing the things that they do well and de-emphasizing those functions which are more difficult or impossible for them to provide."

In addition to determining what you need the technology to do, make a list of criteria that the vendor must meet to qualify as a candidate for your business. For instance, you may require the vendor to have a certain number of clients already using the product in question, or that the vendor has an office within reasonable driving distance of your call center.

Once you have an initial list of your "must have" criteria documented, send them as part of a "pre-RFP" (just a page or two) to a variety of vendors that offer the product. Ask each to tick the criteria that they or their product meet and to return their responses as soon as possible. This will enable you to eliminate some vendors early on. Those who meet all the initial criteria are the vendors to focus on during the formal RFP process.

"Keep the field down to five or six vendors maximum," says Peterson. "That gives you plenty of diversity, but keeps you from having to review an endless stream of RFP responses."

Writing Rock-Solid RFPs

The RFP document itself is the most crucial piece of the vendor selection puzzle. If poorly written or incomplete, you will not receive all the information you need, which leads to less than optimal selection.

While the exact content of the RFP depends on the type of product/service the call center seeks, the most effective RFP documents share several key characteristics:

1. A concise description of the call center's RFP objectives. Briefly describe the specific type of technology/service you're seeking, and explain that you are inviting the vendor to submit a proposal regarding its specific offering. While you may have already done this in your pre-RFP document, be sure to include it in the formal RFP document, as well.

2. Vendor "instructions." Clearly explain your project timeline to vendors, including:

- When written responses are due.

- When vendor presentations/interviews will be held.

- When you will select a vendor.

- When you want the technology to be implemented.

When choosing an RFP due date, be sure that it gives vendors enough time to produce comprehensive responses, Peterson advises. "A one-week turnaround on RFP responses will usually mean that the good vendors will 'no-bid' and the rest will do a lousy job. Any complex bid should have three to four weeks allotted for the RFP response."

Your instructions should include key contact information (name, address, phone, fax and e-mail), as well as how many copies of the responses you require from each vendor.

The instructions should also include a standard "right to reject" disclaimer, which basically tells vendors that, even if they meet all the requirements, the call center reserves the right to reject their response. In addition, the instruction section should include the essential "legalese" that protects you against potential product/vendor problems which may occur later on, including insurance requirements, reasons why you won't pay, indemnification, etc.

3. Key background information on the call center. Include all infor-

Plan to Manage Vendor Relationships Long-Term

It's important to keep communication open and take a proactive role in the partnership with the selected vendor – particularly in the beginning – to ensure that the installation and cutover go smoothly. "Organize regularly scheduled project status meetings with detailed action steps published after each meeting," advises David Peterson of Powerhouse Consulting. "Be clear on your expectations, have a lucid plan laid out with well-established milestones and deliverables, and manage it closely."

And don't lose contact with your vendor after the technology's in place and running smoothly. Stay in the loop with regard to product and vendor news. Most vendors will contact you about system upgrades and new add-ons, but that isn't enough to maintain a solid relationship with your vendor over the long term. It's a good idea to schedule regular meetings (i.e., quarterly) with your vendor to discuss/check the status of your system/software and to ask any questions you have about the product. You may also want to attend user meetings to network with other call center professionals who have the same or similar product in place. This is a good way to compare notes on your product's functionality and the vendor's service consistency.

Managing the vendor relationship is not a difficult task when you treat your vendor like a partner, says Peterson. "It's all about respect. I like to believe that we have selected a professional group, and I always treat them that way."

mation that will help vendors better understand your call center environment, such as:

■ Number of call centers

■ Call volume data

■ Number of agents/trunks

■ Hours of operation

■ Existing technology

4. A comprehensive list of questions about the product. Here's where you drill the vendor on the ins-and-outs of their offerings and the various features. While you may already have determined that the product meets your basic requirements, you still need to ask detailed questions to find out if the technology truly is a match for your center. In well-written RFPs, these questions are separated into specific categories, which helps the vendor to organize their responses – and you to evaluate those responses – in a logical manner. The box on the right provides one example of the categories under which questions might be organized in an RFP for a workforce management (WFM) system.

5. Questions about product installation and maintenance. Find out exactly what the vendor's policies are in terms of product delivery and testing, as well as customer/system support. Ask vendors what tasks they perform during the installation and

what tasks your call center needs to perform. How long does a typical installation take? Also, ask what's included in the vendor's support and maintenance program. Is online support available? In addition, ask about warranty information, product upgrades, training on use/maintenance of the system, and user meetings.

6. Pricing forms (or "bid sheets"). The most thorough RFPs ask vendors to fill out a detailed pricing form, which should include the base purchase price of the product, as well as listing each feature, the price of that feature and whether or not the feature is optional or mandatory.

Peterson highly recommends using an itemized approach to gathering pricing information, as it enables call centers to pick and choose the pieces they need. "I insist on itemized pricing for my clients so we can configure the product the way they want it," he says.

In addition, ask vendors to list any one-time or annual costs associated with the product, such as installation, maintenance and training fees.

7. A request for client references. Ask vendors for the contact information of at least three customers using the product you are considering. You will need this information to check references in the later stages of the RFP process.

Evaluating Vendor Responses

To ease the strain of evaluation, Peterson recommends creating a vendor evaluation matrix before the RFP responses come back. The matrix is a spreadsheet that includes every question asked in the RFP, the name of each vendor, and a column in which to rate their responses. (The rating can be a simple "pass/ fail" or "yes/no" score, or a more detailed rating based on a 1-10 scale. In addition, some call centers "weight" each question in terms of its importance.)

"I organize the matrix around major groupings like system features, vendor capabilities (installation/support, references, etc.) and pricing," says Peterson. "And I typically break down pricing into three components: purchase price, maintenance price for 10 years and costs for the most frequently added parts after cutover."

Even with a helpful matrix, analyzing responses takes time and effort. Peterson advises that the entire call center management team participate in the evaluation process. This helps to promote open discussions and to lessen the impact of individual biases among managers.

When evaluating RFPs, check whether or not vendors meet your requirements, but also if they provide comprehensive and clear responses to your questions. "The response is a good indicator of a vendor's commitment to working with you," explains Peterson. "If they take the time to carefully assemble a cogent, cohesive response, they will most likely apply the same approach when implementing and supporting the solution."

After narrowing the vendor candidates to three or four, call some of their clients listed in the RFP to find out their level of satisfaction with the product. Keep in mind that vendors usually only list their most satisfied and loyal customers as references, so have some good, tough questions prepared to reduce the amount of "scripted" praise you hear. Also, ask if you can visit their center to see the system in action.

Focusing on the Finalists

Once you've completed the RFP

analysis and site visits, invite the vendor finalists to your call center to give a presentation and to answer any additional questions you have. Most call center professionals feel that it's best to hold these "bidder conferences" with each vendor individually to help you to carefully focus on each candidate's offering and reduce the vendor's fear of revealing key information to competitors.

Use these meetings to clear up any questions you have about the vendor, the product's features and the price. Take note of the level of comfort and trust you have with the vendor. "The one-on-one interviews with vendors is the way to determine if there is 'chemistry,'" says Peterson. "The final choice of a vendor is not just about the system, but about the relationship."

Sealing the Deal

After you make that all-important final choice, it's time to seal the deal. The contract signing shouldn't be too stressful an event if you've taken the time to go through all the key stages of the RFP process. The completed RFP document itself already contains the reasons why you are choosing the vendor – as well as "delivery" dates and legal jargon – thus Peterson strongly recommends that this document be included as part of the final contract.

He adds that call centers should not waste time haggling over the price of the product this late in the game. "I try not to do too much price negotiation at the end of the process. I asked to receive the best pricing up front in the RFP response; if I didn't get it, the vendor wouldn't

have made it to the final round."

Peterson also doesn't believe in the use of "performance bonds" – special legal documents that hold vendors accountable (and prescribe specific penalties) for problems or poor performance, i.e., delayed installation, a faulty product or lack of client support.

"In this business, [performance bonds] are just an added expense that create mistrust," he says. A detailed contract – one that contains the standard legalese listed in the RFP, is all the protection a call center needs against non-performance, he adds.

The products you put in place today will have a lasting impact on customer service, loyalty and revenue for years to come. Rushing through technology acquisition without a for-

mal RFP process is a dangerous practice. Keep in mind, when it comes to technology, nothing positive happens overnight. `CCMReview`

Possible RFP Question Categories for a WFM System

SOFTWARE CAPABILITIES

Sample question: Describe the basic and optional components of the system, generally describing the role of each component and its interaction with the others.

SYSTEM REQUIREMENTS

Sample question: Is your system compatible with all ACDs? Do you have co-market and/or technical agreements in place with major ACD producers? If so, list some.

FORECASTING CALL VOLUME

Sample question: How is current data weighted when averaged with historical trends? Can the weighting be user-defined? What assumptions are made in cases where limited or no historical data are available?

SCHEDULING

Sample question: Can the system re-optimize schedules after the known exceptions are taken into consideration?

Source: Taken from a sample RFP provided by TCS Management. For the complete RFP, visit www.CRMXchange.com and click on "white papers."

Greg Levin

Greg Levin is the former editor of Call Center Management Review. *Greg is a regular contributor to the publication, and also writes the "In Your Ear" call center humor column. He is currently a freelance writer based in Spain.*

Section 9

In the Center

with Andrew Brown

Success Begins before the Call: Choosing a Call Center Location

Andrew Brown is the director of community economic development for GTE Telephone Operations, based in Irving, Texas. His responsibilities include helping communities attract call centers to create new jobs. Andrew also assists GTE's site selection for national call and customer service centers. GTE provides local telecommunications services in 28 states.

Selecting the best site for a call center is a very sophisticated matchmaking exercise that can determine success or failure even before the doors open. In today's competitive environment, companies know that site selection is an increasingly strategic factor in making the bottom line.

If management asked you today to lead or assist in selecting a location for a new call center, where would you begin? Existing facility? Another community? Another state? Another country? What location screening factors would you use? You will quickly realize this is not an easy process or decision.

Step into the role of site selector, but consider these three basic principles before you begin the selection process:

Site Selection Issues:
Labor supply
Labor quality
Labor cost
Telecommunications requirements
Facilities
Regulations
Utility costs
Taxes
Transportation
Employee incentives
Economic Incentives

• The location decision process should be designed to uncover your company's unique business objectives and operating requirements. The name of the game is knowing as much about your company's proposed operation as possible.

• Take an objective approach. While your existing locations and company experiences are good indicators, look beyond them to maximize your options. Sites that worked yesterday may not meet today's financial and competitive requirements.

• Evaluate criteria in a planned fashion. Prioritize screening factors. Establish a project timeline that allows ample time for the screening and decision-making process and is consistent with management's implementation schedule. Competitive factors can often lead to a very compressed timeframe. This could compromise your decision.

Seeking a Site Step by Step

Once you've considered these principles, you are ready to begin the formal selection process. Here are the key steps to follow:

1. Determine how to manage the selection process. Establish an internal site selection team comprised of representatives from finance, human resources, internal telecommunications and real estate. Taking a collaborative approach fosters greater objectivity and reduces internal biases. Reach a general agreement on the site selection methodology. If this is a new experience, you may want to consider retaining outside expertise. There are national site selection consultants who offer objective, confidential and comprehensive site selection services for proposed call centers.

2. Define the mission of the call

Andrew Brown

center. Do this in 25 words or less. For example: "This center will primarily process inbound calls for orders and secondly, process customer service calls through to satisfactory completion." Keeping the mission clear will help you narrow your site choices.

3. Define the project scope and screening criteria. Identify your geographic parameters. For example, will this be a national search or do you have time-zone preferences? List all labor factors. Include telecommunications network requirements, building and space requirements, transportation, taxes, regulations and other business costs. Rank your location criteria from most important to least important.

4. Don't wait to act. Proper research and analysis take time. Begin your search by reviewing articles about similar companies that have moved or expanded. Daily newspapers and business journals are full of announcements on call center location decisions. Subscribe to site and real estate periodicals. Solicit information from communities and counties that you read or hear about.

5. Collect data: Obtain and focus on critical information at the outset. Sources of demographic and labor information are numerous. Cover all the bases: U.S. Census Bureau, other government agencies, chambers of commerce, state and local economic development groups, education institutions, and private sources.

Here is a list of the specific factors you should research:

Labor, labor, labor. Almost all companies rank labor issues, including supply, quality and cost, as the most important site selection criteria, partly because of the variance from location to location. Labor constitutes 60 percent of the center's operating costs and likely will drive the final decision. Market size, demographic characteris-

---

> *The name of the game is knowing as much about your company's proposed operation as possible.*

---

tics (including concentrations of students, second wage earners, military dependents or retirees), wage patterns, turnover rates, skill sets, language capabilities, training support and labor relations climate must be addressed. Match these against the staffing profile you have defined for your proposed call center.

In considering market size, don't overlook smaller areas. Successful centers are operating in non-urban areas with populations of 20,000 to 75,000. These areas can be attractive because the competition for labor is minimized and communities are recruiting call centers as a diversification strategy.

An area's labor supply outlook and competitive demand are also essential screening factors. Companies that project future as well as current supply will be able to recognize and evaluate the potential for meeting future

requirements before a decision is made.

Training Resources: Examine college and vocational programs. Are programs relevant to your company's needs? If not, can they be customized? Community colleges are invaluable. Many communities also have a number of business colleges, trade schools and training institutes.

Collaborations between business and education to train and staff call centers are on the rise. Earlier this year, for example, 30 employers in Tampa Bay, Fla., including GTE, launched a Customer Service Academy with Hillsborough County Public Schools to design curriculum and training to help students learn key communications skills, including data entry, diction and conflict resolution.

Telecommunications: Telecommunications comprises about 20-30 percent of a call center's operating costs. Both local and long distance services must be included in your evaluation. The local telephone company can consult with you on current and anticipated needs, such as fiber optic capability, redundant cable routes, disaster recovery, service delivery times, and plans for upgrading switching centers and cabling. If service is being upgraded, your project can be included in these work plans, potentially reducing your project costs.

Check on the location of the long distance provider's "point of presence." Consider locating in corporate business parks that provide state-of-the-art telecommunication services. Some of these parks are specifically designed to serve high-tech information-intensive industries, such as call centers.

The Facility: The size of the facility is generally determined by using the factor of 100 to 150 square feet per work station, i.e., 200 work stations = 20,000 to 30,000 square feet. Allow 10 parking slots for every 1,000 square feet of space. How important is access to highway or air transportation? Is proximity to daycare and public transportation important to employees?

Economic development organiza-

tions and commercial real estate agents maintain current information on building availability and costs. A call to these organizations will usually result in a flood of materials. Note: former retail centers like K-Mart and Wal-Mart are frequently used for call center activity.

Incentives: Many states and communities offer an impressive array of financial and other incentives. By virtue of your company's anticipated employment and investment, your project can begin with a certain level of negotiating leverage. For call centers, training is the most sought-after incentive. Some states and communities pay 100 percent of the training costs for new employees. Assistance in recruiting and screening of prospective employees for basic qualifications is often available at little or no cost.

> *In today's competitive environment, companies know that site selection is an increasingly strategic factor in making the bottom line.*

The more quality jobs your call center provides, the better the incentive package. Incentives are often tied to starting wages and benefits. Many states require that new jobs be permanent and that the company offer employees basic health insurance benefits to qualify.

Other incentives can include tax abatements, loans, grants or facility enhancements. Communities that have municipally-or regionally-owned industrial parks and buildings will package deals that include low-interest loans or outright grants to companies. In some cases, facilities can be used rent-free as interim offices during the planning and construction of your facility.

Your Competition: Research similar employers in each location you are considering. Gauge recruiting methods, turnover trends, benefit packages, future expansion plans, recent or anticipated location announcements. Recheck this information before making the final location decision.

The Envelope, Please

Now the fun begins. What do you do with all this data and information?

1. Analyze the Data. This process will vary depending on the site selection methodology you agreed upon and whether you have consulting support. As a general rule, your data needs to be compiled and compared across all locations based on the criteria you've identified. Assign weighting values to help narrow the candidate list. Ideally, you should end up with a "short" list of two to four locations.

2. Make Site Visit(s). Your initial screening phases may have already taken you to some of the candidate locations. Even so, you'll need to make a final visit to all finalist sites to confirm or revise your initial information and impressions, including any new competitive information. Coordinate with local economic development officials to facilitate meetings, help negotiate incentive packages and most importantly to maintain and ensure the confidentiality of your project.

3. Make the Decision. Tabulate the scores. Shorten the list. Complete the final site visits. And the winner is..........

If you develop a plan and methodology and follow the basic steps outlined here, you just may be selected to manage the new center. Congratulations!

As part of its economic development program, GTE is publishing a manual to help communities assess their opportunities to attract call centers and other back-office operations. You can obtain a copy of the manual in June by writing to: Community Economic Development Manager, GTE Telephone Operations, P.O. Box 152092 - HQE04M24, Irving, TX 75015-2092.

SLN

Section 9

Call Center Location: Costs Rule the Site Selection Process

by John H. Boyd

The call center industry is the fastest growing industry in the U.S. today in terms of new job creation and white-collar corporate investment in new facilities and equipment. Indeed, call centers and related telecommunications-intensive operations have dominated my firm's corporate site selection workload over the past several years.

Today, there are some 70,000 call centers in the U.S. and Canada employing over 2.5 million people. We at Boyd forecast that by the year 2003 there will be some 105,000 North American call centers with over 4.0 million employees.

The phenomenal growth of the call center industry is being driven by a number of "engines," including:

■ **Customer service strategy.** Many of our clients are targeting customer service as a means to distinguish their products in a competitive marketplace. Call centers and help desks provide an effective way to achieve this goal. This trend crosses many industry lines.

■ **E-commerce.** Direct consumer sales via the Internet and traditional off-line direct channels are fueling a great need for call centers and fulfillment operations by our clients. Direct sales to the home exceeded $190 billion in 1998 and could account for over 20 percent of all retail sales by 2010.

■ **PC explosion.** Throughout the 90s, help desks providing computer software, hardware and related tech support have been a major engine of growth for our booming call center site-selection workload.

■ **Financial services.** Banking by phone and trading online have made many of our banking, brokerage and insurance clients major players in the call center industry.

With call centers booming, companies are seeking optimum locations for their new operations. This article will provide you with the key trends and practices you need to understand and embrace to maximize your call center site selection process.

> *While the fundamentals in call center site-selection continue to hold true, comparative operating costs tend to dominate today's site selection equation.*

Bottom Lines Dominate Location Equation

While the fundamentals in call center site selection continue to hold true (see Call Center Site Selection Checklist on page 9), comparative operating costs tend to dominate today's site selection equation. Even with the current attention focused on all-time low unemployment rates and tightening labor markets, comparative economics rule the site selection process for the vast majority of our clients. These companies are reacting to a number of bellwether industry and market trends by making bottom-line economics the pivotal determinant in the search for new call center sites. Our clients' preoccupation with bottom line economics can be linked to:

■ **Corporate reengineering.** There is currently a huge corporate reexamination of sales, marketing and customer service in light of the changing business landscape brought on by the Internet. Cost/benefit analyses are being run on many call center functions that are deeply rooted in traditional sales and direct marketing techniques. In addition, many of Boyd's Fortune 500 clients have already reengineered their manufacturing units through downsizing and offshore migration. These same corporations have also completed major white-collar reorganizations through layoffs and attrition at the corporate headquarters. Now these corporations are focusing their reengineering and cost audits to their sales and customer service functions, including call centers.

■ **New players/ease of entry.** The booming call center field and the affects of deregulation in the telecommunications industry are causing an influx of new companies entering the teleservices industry. Low interest rates, the affordability of packaged start-up tele-communications equipment (including a booming secondary market for used telephony equipment), and the ready availability of call center software and management expertise are contributing factors to the ease of entry into the call center field.

The upshot of all these new inbound and outbound teleservices agencies entering the market is tight operating margins and white hot, dog-eat-dog price competition. As a result, companies' site selection efforts place a premium on finding a location that offers a very low operating cost-profile.

■ **Free trade.** With free trade, companies are taking a world-view of their competition and concluding that they must be as cost-efficient and lean as possible in order to survive and flourish in the new world

November 1999 ■ Reprinted with permission from CCMReview®

Section 9

Table 1
Cost Rankings for Call Center Sites

Location	Total Annual Operating Costs
San Francisco, Ca.	$12,807,978
New York, N.Y.	12,741,386
Washington, D.C.	12,698,809
Los Angeles/Long Beach, Ca.	12,436,139
Stamford, Conn.	12,203,906
Jersey City, N.J.	12,154,500
Boston, Mass.	12,041,083
Chicago, Ill.	11,878,886
Middlesex/Somerset/Hunterdon, N.J.	11,837,826
Philadelphia, Pa.	11,797,569
Denver, Colo.	11,761,412
Detroit, Mich.	11,709,771
Marlborough, Mass.	11,708,841
Hartford, Conn.	11,667,400
Shrewsbury, Mass.	11,567,350
Dallas, Texas	11,487,115
Buffalo, N.Y.	11,494,136
Wilmington, Del.	11,446,193
Atlanta, Ga.	11,374,986
Cortland, N.Y.	11,341,011
W. Kingston, R.I.	11,336,432
Miami, Fla.	11,324,969
Charlotte, N.C.	11,294,754
Allentown/Bethlehem/Easton, Pa.	11,284,666
Cincinnati, Ohio	11,282,878
Salt Lake City, Utah	11,276,873
Camp Hill, Pa.	11,224,110
Provo, Utah	11,142,440
Tampa/St. Petersburg, Fla.	11,121,215
Delray Beach, Fla.	11,109,383
Orlando, Fla.	11,047,811
Jacksonville, Fla.	11,047,752
Yuba City/Marysville, Ca.	11,041,022
Dover, Del.	11,031,151
Raleigh/Durham, N.C.	11,030,321
Hazleton, Pa.	10,992,088
El Cajon, Ca.	10,985,316
Tucson, Ariz.	10,979,383
Omaha, Neb.	10,975,124
Ft. Lauderdale/Hollywood, Fla.	10,935,731
Bowling Green, Ohio	10,836,342
Charleston, S.C.	10,827,667
Atlantic City, N.J.	10,821,281
Grand Rapids, Mich.	10,812,594
Cape Coral, Fla.	10,762,007
Portland, Maine	10,751,735
Covington, Ky.	10,706,469
Richmond, Va.	10,687,512
Deland, Fla.	10,671,784
Norfolk/Virginia Beach, Va.	10,664,876
Columbia, S.C.	10,652,152
St. Cloud, Minn.	10,540,092
Ft. Walton Beach, Fla.	10,526,960
Savannah, Ga.	10,506,892
Knoxville, Tenn.	10,413,454
Augusta, Ga.	10,397,648
Jacksonville, N.C.	10,254,543
Mobile, Ala.	10,157,199
Nacogdoches, Texas	10,153,509
New Brunswick, Canada	7,202,080

economy. We are seeing this trend in post-NAFTA North America in the growing popularity of low-cost Canadian call center sites such as New Brunswick (see Table 1 on page 8), as well as in the emerging common market in Europe. For example, some of Boyd's clients view locations such as Spain, Northern Ireland and the Tagus Valley area of Portugal as attractive call center sites based on compelling cost savings.

■ **Price transparencies.** In the growing European call center market, the Euro's (the new currency) introduction is not only expected to stabilize the economies of the 11 countries of the European Union, but also make it much easier for the corporate site-seeker to compare operating cost structures among the different countries using the common Euro currency as a benchmark. To a lesser degree, this is also the case in North America due to NAFTA. NAFTA's harmonization of regulations and business practices and the phasing out of tariffs is also making it easier for companies to focus their site selection process on a true comparison of operating costs regardless of geographic borders.

■ **Falling teleco rates /rising teleco taxes.** Deregulation and competition have dramatically brought down the cost of interstate and overseas long distance service in recent years. The movement away from mileage-based pricing plans among the major carriers has enabled our clients to negotiate the same cost per minute rate for 800 service regardless of where in the country they locate.

Does this mean overall teleco costs are the same regardless of U.S. location? No. Sales taxes, gross receipt taxes and utility taxes levied by the states and local municipalities can vary greatly from location to location and can have a major impact on bottom-line economics. A recent client from Los Angeles (where teleco taxes have reached double-digit rates) was able to save over a quarter of a million dollars in teleco taxes per year at its new call center location. These savings alone were able to pay the annual wages of 10 of its customer service agents.

■ **Labor shortages/ inflationary wage pressures.** With labor markets as tight as they are throughout much of the U.S., inflationary wage pressures are becoming disturbing facts of life for many call centers. A judicious site selection process emphasizing cost minimization can often generate cost economies in such areas as rent, taxes and utilities that will sufficiently "write down" the cost of (excessive) wage inflation.

Putting Site Selection on the Table

Where is the most cost efficient location to operate a call center? A recent Boyd study of 60 North American sites has identified New Brunswick, Canada, as the lowest cost site. Table 1 on this page presents total annual operating costs for a 200-agent call center – occupying 27,500 sq. ft. of space – with a monthly call volume of 1.5 million minutes of billable 800 service. Costs are in U.S. dollars and include such factors as nonexempt labor, office rent, teleco charges, taxes, utilities and other typical occupancy costs.

Due to reasons such as a common language, favorable exchange rate and a plentiful supply of workers, an increasing number of call centers are establishing operations in Canada. U.S. firms with call cen-

Call Center Site Selection Checklist

I. State Legislative Climate
1. Teleco taxation policy at state (and local) levels
2. Employment at will, right-to-work and other labor policies
3. Workmen's Compensation rates and practices
4. Unemployment insurance rates and practices
5. Corporate income tax rates
6. Personal income tax rates
7. Tax rate stability/fiscal condition of state
8. Access to key state officials
9. Available incentives, including training funds, tax credits and infrastructure grants

II. Labor-Market Issues
1. Labor availability
2. Call center/service sector wage structures
3. Local fringe benefit practices
4. Education levels
5. Multi-lingual skills
6. Unemployment and labor-force participation rates
7. Underemployment recruiting potentials
8. Special sector recruiting potentials (i.e., students, seniors, military dependents, etc.)
9. Labor-force growth and geographic draw
10. Labor-management relations climate
11. Impact of competitive call centers on wages, benefits and applicant flow
12. Recruiting support, including employment agencies with call center staffing experience

III. Community Factors
1. Demographics and regional location (time zone)
2. Climate/continuity of operations/insulation from natural disaster issues
3. Telecommunications infrastructure
4. Cost and dependability of utilities services
5. Local pro-business attitudes and track record
6. Local incentives
7. Zoning and fast-track permitting factors
8. Accessibility/commercial airline service
9. Cost of living
10. Quality of life factors
11. Housing market for transferees
12. Local school system for transferees

IV. Site Factors
1. Employee access to public transportation
2. Orientation to telecommunications services, including point-of-presence and contingency/recovery factors
3. Orientation to prime residential recruiting areas
4. Highway access and visibility issues
5. Available sites (open environment) with high parking ratios
6. Competitive lease rates and practices
7. Location vis-a-vis competitive call center recruiting
8. Crime/employee safety factors

ters in New Brunswick, for example, include Xerox, Cendant, IBM, UPS and Marriott.

The same study identified the most expensive call center site is San Francisco, followed by New York and Washington, DC.

Call Center Site Selection Checklist

A thorough call center site selection process should include an independent analysis of all the geo-graphically-variable location factors listed in the box on this page.

Dollars Driving Process

Whether your company is looking to relocate its existing call center or set up a new one to help manage a rapidly growing workload, under-standing the comparative operating costs of the various sites under con-sideration is essential. Of course, careful analysis of legislative, labor, community and site-specific issues are also key to effective call center site selection, but it's hard dollars that truly drive the process in today's competitive business cli-mate.

CCMReview

John H. Boyd is president of The Boyd Company, Inc., a Princeton, N.J.-based firm that provides inde-pendent location counseling to U.S. and overseas corporations. His firm works throughout North America, Europe, Latin America and Asia. Boyd's clients include PepsiCo, Unit-ed Technologies, Time Inc., AirTouch, MCI, Pitney Bowes; Chase Manhat-tan Bank and many others. He can be reached at 609-890-0726.

Section 9

Effective Call Center Design Can Help Drive Agent Performance

by Greg Levin

When seeking to enhance agent performance, call center managers tend to focus on and make improvements in key areas, such as hiring, training, incentives and technology. Indeed each of these areas demands careful attention. The problem is that they often overshadow another key driver of agent performance – call center design.

Most call center managers know the importance of good lighting, acoustics and ergonomically sound workstations. However, effective design often takes a back seat to the "bigger" issues in today's call center, i.e., never-ending staffing challenges and ever-increasing customer e-mail and Web contacts.

The irony is that the call center industry is one field that can ill afford not to consider effective office design as one of the bigger issues. In few other fields is employee performance so dependent on the physical environment in which he or she works. Poor call center design causes costly wrist and back injuries to agents, eye strain and ear strain (which lead to expensive errors, rework and poor customer satisfaction), low morale and high turnover.

"Call centers should not be treated as traditional office environments," says Roger Kingsland, managing partner with Kingsland Scott Bauer Associates (KSBA), a Pittsburg-based firm specializing in architecture, planning, interior design and project management of call centers. "If properly designed, the resultant benefits to employees produce bottom line results."

While there hasn't been a lot of research focusing specifically on the direct link between call center design and agent performance, numerous studies do provide empirical evidence of good office design's impact on employee productivity and work quality. And much of this research can certainly be directly applied to the modern-day call center.

Michael Brill, president of the Buffalo Organization for Social and Technological Innovation (BOSTI) and a professor of architecture at University of Buffalo, has spent nearly two decades researching such office design facets as physical enclosure, aesthetics, furniture, lighting and privacy. His data suggests that the performance benefits of well-designed office spaces could equal as much as 20 percent of the annual salaries within an organization.

So what comprises good call center design? While a definitive answer to the question will depend on your center's specific requirements, following are some solid insights from call center design experts.

Look at the Overall Spatial Organization/Aesthetics

The average office worker enjoys a minimum of 11 square meters of space, compared with 4.6 meters in a typical call center, according to Christine Critchley, a consultant with Systems Concepts Ltd. and author of the white paper "Effective and Ergonomic Design of Call Centres." To keep agents from feeling cooped up and undervalued, managers need to take great care in designing the physical layout of the call center floor.

One of the most effective spatial design strategies in call centers today is the grouping or "teaming" of workstations into functional clusters of agents who work as a team, according to Rick Burkett, principal of BurkettDesign Inc. in Denver.

"We recommend organizing workstations into clusters where each member feels like a part of a cohesive, recognizable team, not just one of 500 worker bees," he says. "We also recommend having low agent-to-supervisor ratios and lots of coaching stations [located among clustered workstations] so that spontaneous training can occur in a healthy environment."

Burkett adds that organizing workstations into teams enables agents and supervisors to define their own space and to develop a strong sense of ownership, identity and control. This, in turn, helps to sustain high levels of agent enthusiasm.

In addition to arranging workstations to create a stronger sense of community among agents, call centers mustn't forget about the overall aesthetics of the workspace, advises KSBA's Kingsland. "Agents are, generally speaking, treated badly by companies with regard to environment. The aesthetics in the typical call center leaves much to be desired. And the money that companies think they are saving by not investing in office aesthetics, they lose twice over in terms of agent turnover."

Kingsland and Burkett agree that there are infinite options with regard to enhancing call center aesthetics – options that don't have to break the bank. Little things like hanging colorful art/decorations on the walls and placing plants throughout the center can go a long way toward creating positive attitudes among agents and fending off burnout. (Plants not only bring color and a more organic feeling to the call center, they also help to enhance the humidity in the air).

Painting over drab gray walls with cool bluish-green hues has been shown to have a calming affect on agents while enhancing mental alertness. And special features such as fountains and small areas with raised stone walls can have a dramatic impact on overall call center aesthetics and agent satisfaction, says Kingsland.

Ensure Individual Workstations Are Ergonomically Correct

Individual workstation design is just as, if not more, important than overall spatial organization/aesthetics in the call center. When we talk about workstation design, we're talking about ergonomics. And when talking about ergonomics, we're really talking about people, not just furniture and equipment.

Ergonomics – also called "human engineering" – is, according to *Web-*

ster's Ninth Collegiate Dictionary, "an applied science concerned with the characteristics of people that need to be considered in designing things they use so that people and things will interact most effectively."

Research has shown direct links between good ergonomics and enhanced employee performance. For example, following a comprehensive study of the impact of ergonomically designed furniture on productivity of employees who use video display terminals, Springer Associates concluded that ergonomically sound furniture contributed to a 10 percent to 15 percent performance improvement, with one-third of this improvement being attributed to enhanced seating alone.

The potential increase in productivity aside, your call center simply cannot afford not to take ergonomics seriously.

The Occupational Safety and Health Administration (OSHA) has estimated that employers spend roughly $120 billion annually on direct and indirect costs related to poor ergonomics. And according to call center furniture designer Interior Concepts, approximately one-third of workers' compensation dollars are spent on repetitive motion injuries – injuries quite common in call centers.

The good news is that such exorbitant costs can be avoided by making a relatively small investment of time and money in effective workstation design. Here's a list of the key aspects of good workstation ergonomics to guide you:

■ **Adjustable chairs.** The more adjustable the chair the better, since agents come in all shapes and sizes. Look for chairs that have seat height adjustments, back adjustments (in both height and tilt) and, preferably, some form of lumbar (lower back) support, says Critchley of Systems Concepts. She recommends that the chairs either have no arms or adjustable arms to ensure that all agents are comfortably seated close to their workstation desk.

■ **Workstation height.** The height of the workstation should be around 27 to 29 inches, says Critchley, and the underside of the workstation must be free of any bars or drawers

Ensure Lighting Systems Don't Contribute to Eye Strain

Many employee health problems are tied to eye strain caused by lighting that doesn't correspond to the unique requirements of video-display terminals (VDTs), according to KSBA's Roger Kingsland. He explains that call centers require two separate though complementary lighting systems: 1) Uniform ambient lighting for VDTs, and 2) task-lighting for hard-copy reading and writing.

"Computer terminals act as mirrors that reflect ceiling glare, causing eye strain," says Kingsland. "Therefore, a uniform light level at the ceiling is important, and because VDTs produce their own illumination, the level of illumination required for comfortable viewing is approximately half the level needed for hard-copy reading and writing."

According to Kingsland, the best ambient lighting system is indirect lighting. Such systems are usually mounted between 18 and 24 inches below the ceiling and shine upward. In addition to reducing glare, indirect lighting creates a calming level of light throughout the workspace.

The phone floor is not the only area managers should consider when focusing on lighting in the call center, says Rick Burkett of BurkettDesign Inc. Agents also spend a fair amount of time in conference and training rooms where poor lighting can cause subtle distractions during important meetings or coaching sessions, as well as in break rooms where poor lighting may interfere with the agents' ability to rejuvenate themselves before returning to the floor to handle more customer contacts.

"Conference and training rooms should be brighter than the phone floor [so that agents remain alert and ready to receive important information]," Burkett explains. "Whereas break rooms should always have lots of natural lighting and a completely different feel than the rest of the facility."

that may obstruct agents' legroom.

■ **Adjustable keyboards.** Look for keyboards that tilt and adjust enough to allow a diverse range of agents to find a comfortable typing position.

■ **Wrist rests.** The best wrist rests are those that provide some give, but not too much (such as gel-filled rests), according to Christine Jacobs of Interior Concepts. They provide a comfortable feel to wrists in a neutral position without putting undue pressure on the carpal area.

■ **Monitor position.** The angle between the monitor and the agent's line of vision should be zero degrees – or a maximum angle of 15 degrees below eye level, says Rick Benham, an ergonomic specialist with Hackley Health Systems. Agents should not have to look up at all to view the monitor, as this places unnecessary stress on the neck. Ideal are monitors with adjustable platforms that enable agents to make easy height adjustments. Benham also recommends that the monitor itself be placed 18 to 24 inches from the agent's eyes.

■ **Foot rests.** While these inexpensive products are not a necessity, many agents appreciate them during long shifts.

Merely supplying agents with ergonomically designed furniture and equipment isn't enough. Call centers need to ensure that agents are well-versed in making adjustments to their equipment for ideal comfort. One company that practices this well is Alliant Utilities. In addition to providing all agents with ample 7'x7' cubicles equipped with ergonomically advanced chairs, footrests/armrests and adjustable workstation desktops, Alliant's center in Janesville, Wis., brings in an occupational therapist to work with each new training class. The therapist shows each new-hire how to adjust the equipment and how to position his or her body to avoid costly repetitive stress injuries.

All call centers should adopt a similar program, recommends Burkett. "A good way to say you care and to back up your words with action is to provide good equipment and train people how to use it. Many benefits follow, including reduced agent injury and absenteeism, lower health insurance costs, increased productivity and higher employee morale."

Poor Acoustics Can Be Costly

There's no denying that call centers – with their open-plan workstations, the ever-present sound of agents speaking with customers, and the proximity of noise-producing office equipment (e.g., fax machines, photocopiers) – present a daunting acoustical challenge. Poor acoustics in the call center can be costly; agents who can't hear callers clearly are likely to input inaccurate data or be forced to continually ask customers to repeat information. In either case, a significant strain is placed on customer satisfaction.

While careful space layout will help minimize acoustical interference, other measures are often required. Many well-designed call centers, according to Kingsland, attain "acoustic privacy" by introducing partial height screens, highly absorptive ceilings and walls, and "noise-masking" systems.

Noise-masking is the process by which a sound – such as human speech – is masked by a slightly louder sound. "Noise-masking systems in offices employ a carefully defined spectrum of sound shaped to mask human speech," explains Kingsland. "Typically, the sound is provided by a specially designed random noise generator and a series of loud-speakers installed in the ceiling."

This "noise" thus becomes a permanent part of the call center environment. In fact, Kingsland stresses that the system mustn't be turned off while the call center is occupied or the masking effect will be lost. A typical noise-masking system costs up to $1 per square foot.

Examples of call centers that have effectively implemented noise-masking systems are AT&T's Customer Care Center in Pittsburgh and Liberty Mutual in Phoenix.

Acoustics in the call center may soon take a futuristic turn with the advent of an apparatus called a "sound dome." When an agent sits under a sound dome, which looks like a giant reading lamp, noise generated outside of the dome becomes virtually inaudible. Such technology could help to greatly increase agent concentration during a customer interaction, as well as with overall quality. And they're likely to be a hit with agents, predicts Mary Murcott, vice president of worldwide reservations for Budget RentACar in Carrollton, Texas.

Taking Call Center Design Beyond the Basics

Companies serious about enhancing agent performance and retention take call center design beyond good lighting, sound and ergonomics. Management at these centers understand the stress agents face day after day on the phones, and thus provide special amenities to help them cool down and gear up.

For example, Alliant Utilities' call center features two "quiet rooms" – each equipped with comfortable couches/recliners, books and CD players – where agents can retreat during breaks. One room has exercise machines for those who want to burn off their stress. The call center even contracts with a local massage therapist who works on tense agents during its peak season (April through October).

The company reports that its investment has more than paid off in the form of reduced agent absenteeism and turnover, as well as increased productivity.

TeleCorp (an affiliate of AT&T Wireless) has also taken innovative measures to ensure that agents remain fresh and enthusiastic. In addition to window seats for all agents, the company's Memphis call center features a full-sized fitness center and an onsite wellness program.

"We looked at every aspect of the working environment and incorporated innovative design and amenities so our employees will be prepared to provide the very best service to our customers," explains Scott Weismiller, TeleCorp's vice president of customer care.

While such amenities and services have been well-received at Alliant and TeleCorp, merely duplicating what other call centers have done may not be the best solution for your center, says KSBA's Roger Kingsland. "Things like a fitness center can end up being a big waste of money if your agents don't use it. Find out what they want before investing in what you think they want. You might put in a fitness room and then find out that agents would have been much happier with a simple barbecue pit out back."

"Agents won't have to work in crammed cubicles with high walls, and will be able to speak to customers without the physical restraints of a headset," says Murcott, who believes that sound domes will help to change the face of today's call center. The main drawback now is the price, the going rate for a single sound dome is about $600.

Removing Obstacles, Raising Performance

Your agents face enough challenges in today's rapid-fire, multi-task call center environment – don't make poor design another obstacle. Bad lighting and acoustics, endless rows of rigid and cramped workstations, and color schemes borrowed from state prisons have a slow, deteriorating affect on productivity, quality and agent motivation.

Improving call center design doesn't entail rebuilding your existing call center from the ground up. Many enhancements can be made in a relatively short period of time – enhancements that can have a dramatic impact on your center's success and

survival. Yes, these improvements require a financial investment, but the money spent will not compare to the return on investment through higher agent performance and retention, as well as decreased medical or worker's compensation costs. And with healthy, happy and thriving agents, customer satisfaction – and related revenue – will certainly increase.

Just like comprehensive training programs, alluring incentives and top technology, good call center design is an essential performance-driving – and profit-driving – tool. *CCMReview*

Greg Levin

Greg Levin is the former editor of Call Center Management Review. *Greg is a regular contributor to the publication, and also writes the "In Your Ear" call center humor column. He is currently a freelance writer based in Spain.*

Section 9

In The Center with Roger Kingsland

Create a Pleasant, Productive Environment That Will Boost Agent Retention

Call center design can have a direct effect on agent morale, productivity, customer satisfaction and, ultimately, profits.

"We like working here." What call center manager wouldn't want to hear those four words coming from more of his or her agents? What value would that bring to your operation?

The integration of online technologies with traditional voice-based customer interaction presents new challenges to get customer service representatives better trained in a wider range of support services. But as the economy stalls, call center managers are also increasingly confronted with corporate mandates to cut costs while improving

Future-Proof Your Call Center

As we move further into the multi-channel, highly networked economy, successful knowledge-based organizations must have the ability to change quickly and efficiently in order to survive. Call centers, in particular, must also have the ability to change at the "speed of business."

The best way to future-proof your call center is to allow for substantially more layout flexibility than is typical today. Components that should be considered include:

- Uniform, ceiling-mounted indirect lighting systems that are layout independent.
- Furniture on wheels or furniture systems that can be reconfigured overnight.
- Raised floors that allow ultimate cabling flexibility.

productivity and efficiency. Most are being asked to do more with less — and that's not an easy task to accomplish.

Customers, meanwhile, are ever more sophisticated in their buying patterns and expectations for fast, quality service. They want the voice on the other end of the phone line to be knowledgeable and pleasant; they want their orders placed or inquiries answered quickly — and they're not in the mood to wait.

Against that backdrop, the chronic crisis of turnover among the rank-and-file call center workers — with all the resulting increased costs of disruption, service inconsistencies and new staff training — has taken on a new sense of urgency. Savvy call center managers recognize that helping their employees more fully enjoy their time at work is not an expendable soft issue — it's a bottomline imperative.

So how can you make the work experience more pleasant and rewarding for your agents in a way that will reduce turnover, improve productivity and enhance the bottom line?

Of course, cash incentives can play a part (but only a part) of the story.

Logically enough, the process should really start at the beginning of the call center's existence — with the initial architectural design or renovation plan. Decisions made then can have lasting impact on employee morale, and thus financial performance, throughout the life of the call center.

Call Centers Are Not Typical Office Space

All too often, corporate management fails to recognize the vast differences between call centers and conventional office space. Call centers have almost double the occupation density of typical offices, and they tend to operate longer hours — many are now in oper-

ation 24-hours, seven days a week.

Workloads and staffing can vary greatly from hour to hour. Call centers also require a substantial (and potentially intrusive) technology infrastructure that can be in constant flux as new systems are developed and new processes deployed, all the while ensuring the sustainability of the technology through foolproof generation systems, uninterrupted power supplies and disaster-recovery planning.

Call center design is more than envisioning what the finished product may look like when construction is completed. It's about planning for the unknowns of call volumes and new technologies that might develop further down the road. It's about expecting the unexpected, which requires a unique approach to call center design and/or renovation — one that emphasizes flexibility and adaptability.

Consider the Agents' View (Literally)

The call center industry is rife with design decision-making that's based on expediency and short-term cost considerations — and disregards the long-range perspective that is required. For instance, cutting capital costs typically is seen as the best, if not only, way to add value to a call center project. In situations where call center workers are paid poorly and possess relatively low skill sets, management often perceives little or no justification for a thoughtful approach. In these types of call centers, the consequences of high turnover are considered an unavoidable by-product of pay and status, or of the nature of the workers who are attracted to the job.

Call center design often reflects a corporate hierarchy that is not appropriate to the realities of the situation. For example, many call centers have more private offices than are necessary. Also, those offices are generally located along the outside walls where they steal the natural light. The rank-and-file call center staff too often are relegated to noisy, stark breakrooms dominated by vending machines and trash cans.

Please don't misconstrue the point here. No one is suggesting that executives should be penalized for their positions within a call center. The argument is that executive perquisites need not be at the expense of building a pleasant, nurturing environment that gives agents a reason to more fully enjoy their jobs and stick with them.

In other words, short-term decision-making need not be the rule.

Design Issues to Consider

There is a growing body of research that proves a phenomenal performance connection between employee-centered design and improved productivity, efficiencies and return on investment. We can now accurately pinpoint how investments in areas such as ergonomics, spatial dynamics, site amenities, furniture, lighting, acoustics and heating, ventilation and air conditioning systems and others can pay off.

Following are just a few of the issues you might want to consider in the design decision-making process.

■ **Workstations.** All of us have a basic psychological need for personal space and some degree of privacy — even in a crowded, busy call center. Simple solutions include the placing of workstations in a non-fixed, varied pattern and providing each with storage space for personal belongings.

■ **Break rooms.** Typically, break rooms tend to be unpleasant places. An alternative is to create a centrally located "community center" with conference rooms, human resources offices, reading tables and other amenities. Lighting should be diffused and subtle. Some companies even include kitchen and/or daycare facilities.

■ **Color.** Use a color scheme that reduces stress and maintains suitable brightness levels, with accent colors and lighting that adds interest and variety. For instance, painting over drab gray walls with cool bluish-green hues has been shown to have a calming affect on agents while enhancing mental alertness.

■ **Exposed ceilings.** Higher ceilings can add to a person's sense of spatial freedom. You can achieve higher ceilings through exposed structural systems.

■ **Indirect lighting.** Indirect lighting shines up to the ceiling and then reflects back down onto the work surface. It is ideally suited for computer-intensive environments because it provides an appropriate contrast with the computer screen.

■ **Integrated-access floor systems.** Raised-access (computer) floors are often installed in call centers so that modular power, data and communications cables can be located in the floor cavity. A fully integrated solution would include environmental air supplied through that cavity, as well. Not only can cabling changes be made at lower cost, but the vertical flow of air from floor to ceiling improves overall air quality. Floor registers also can be installed or moved to give individuals the ability to change the air temperature in their immediate vicinity.

■ **Noise reduction.** Excessive noise is a leading cause of employee dissatisfaction with the call center work environment. The higher density of bodies in call centers, as well as the lower furniture panel heights used, compound the noise problem. Sound-masking systems reduce noise by emitting a frequency from ceiling speakers that mask the sounds of human voices.

Relatively modest investments made during a call center design process can return significant benefits during the life of the center. The challenge for call center management is to push for the right decisions, even at the risk of slightly higher upfront costs. Architectural design firms can help you to quantify the rewards and ROI those investments would generate.

After all, when it comes to your call center's bottom line, it really does matter if your employees say, "We like working here." CCMReview

Roger Kingsland

Roger Kingsland is managing partner of Kingsland Scott Bauer Associates (www.ksba.com), Pittsburgh, Pa.-based architects specializing in research-based design of call centers. He can be reached at 412-252-1500 or rkingsland@ksba.com.

Make a Business Case for Renovations

Once the components of good call center design are understood, the next step is to make a business case for incorporating them into the design solution. An excellent example is ergonomics. As most managers have become aware over the past decade, the cost to provide good ergonomic support is miniscule compared to the benefits. The example below illustrates the potential for savings. For this example, let's assume a 10 percent productivity increase for a call center using ergonomically designed furniture. (Estimate taken from a study by Springer Associates Inc. that concluded ergonomic furniture resulted in a 10-15 percent performance improvement over normal conditions.)

EQUIPMENT/FURNITURE COSTS

Chair	$550
Adjustable monitor stand	$30
Adjustable keyboard	$120
Footrest	$50
Total	$750
	(Round to $1,000)

ROI CALCULATION

a. Cost of improvements (from above) = $1,000/agent

b. Debt service to borrow cost of improvements (assume 9.5% over 5 years) = $252/agent/year

c. Average direct personnel expense (DPE*) = $20,000/agent/year

d. Productivity increase = 10%

e. DPE savings due to productivity increase [(c) x d) / 100] = $2,000/agent/year

f. Return on investment [(e)/(b)] = 793%

* Salary plus benefits

Headset Selection: Key Performance Factors to Check Out Before Buying

by P. Michael Fairweather

Average work time, service levels, hold time, speed of answer, cost per call, customer satisfaction and employee satisfaction – these metrics are a large part of the foundation of call center management. Headsets – simple communication tools that many call centers take for granted – can have a significantly positive effect on these key measures.

Technological advancements in acoustics, plastics and mechanical engineering have enabled manufacturers to make remarkable improvements in the performance and functionality of professional headsets. By understanding how these innovations affect agent performance, managers can make informed decisions about purchasing and maintaining headset systems in the call center environment.

Seen One, Haven't Seen 'em All

Headset performance, design and durability are important contributors to agent productivity. Agents who can hear and be heard clearly and feel comfortable in their headsets are able to do their jobs better because they can focus on the key customer service and sales tasks at hand.

Not all headsets are manufactured with the same set of features or the same quality. Choosing the right headset involves understanding not only how features can benefit your call center, but also how performance factors impact headset investment over time.

Key Performance Factors

Sound quality is one of the most important factors of headset performance. The fact that an agent is using a headset should be transparent to customers. Customer satisfaction is enhanced when neither agents nor customers have to repeat information. This helps the conversation move forward quickly to a successful conclusion, resulting in more accurate interactions and improving the average work time or average handle time per call. Saving just seconds per call can add up to significant cost reductions and efficiency improvement in any size call center.

One of the most important measurements of sound quality is "frequency response," or bandwidth capability – the percentage of the telephone voice signal delivered after the sound travels over a local or long-distance network. Normally, the network degrades higher frequencies, which gives voice distortion on the receiving end. Therefore, a good headset has a quality microphone that transmits the greatest frequency response, better matching the sound to the original input. The bandwidth capability that headsets can deliver ranges from as high as 96 percent with clear, natural sound to as low as 41 percent with distorted sound quality. Most manufacturers provide this "transmit and receive" test data or allow call centers to evaluate the headsets for themselves.

A second factor affecting sound quality is static electricity. As headsets move on the body, they generate static electricity. Unless the headset has static-resistant components, the static that builds with constant use creates noise on the line. To avoid this, choose headsets that use gold contacts in the quick-disconnect, as well as cords and wire de-signed to resist and eliminate static.

Microphones should have noise-canceling capability to eliminate ambient room noise and transmit only the agent's voice. Without background noise, customers can hear the agent clearly and respond quickly. An important goal of any interaction is to create, as closely as possible, the feeling of a one-on-one conversation, with the agent focused on handling the customer's request. Yet call centers are busy, active environments where supervisors may be coaching, other agents may be talking and equipment may be humming in the background. Good noise-canceling microphones can help immeasurably in blocking out extraneous noise so the customer hears only the agent. An added benefit is the reduction in overall room noise, since agents won't need to speak loudly to be heard by the customer.

But as important as this feature is, not all microphones have noise-canceling features. Clear voice tubes have omni-directional microphones that amplify the agent's voice, as well as all the noise in the call center. A microphone designed within a "housing" (a plastic casing surrounding the microphone components and connecting the microphone to the headset) gives noise-canceling microphones the ability to pick up and transmit the voice while canceling out as much as 95 percent of the background noise.

Headset wearers also have a choice of single- and dual-speaker wearing styles: "binaural," where speakers are on both ears and "monaural," with a speaker for one ear. In noisy call centers, binaural headsets help the agent to focus on the customer. But not every call center needs binaural; in some call centers, being able to hear surrounding sounds from one ear is as important.

Choose a Comfortable Design

Comfortable headsets increase productivity, improve employee morale and decrease downtime. Too often, headset purchasing decisions are made without input from the agents themselves who understand

Section 9

Checklist for Purchasing Headsets

Sound quality
- Frequency response (up to 96 percent)
- Static-resistant components
- Noise-canceling microphones

Comfort
- Ergonomic design
- Flexible booms
- Choice of wearing styles
- Pliable ear-hook

Durability
- Quick disconnect between amplifier and headset
- Number of bends in flexible boom (up to 6,000)
- Cord strength (between 47-60 pounds)
- Turret integrity (up to 50,000 boom adjustments)

Amplifiers
- Universal amplifiers for most phone systems
- Compression for audio protection (OSHA requirement)
- Mute button
- Handset/headset switch
- Representative Not Available feature

Maintenance
- Warranty (two-year minimum)
- Repair/replacement costs
- Repair turnaround time

how an uncomfortable headset can adversely affect their ability to perform their jobs at peak efficiency. Agents with comfortable headsets won't need to constantly adjust them or, worse, take them off to relieve discomfort. Being able to work without physical distractions can enhance job satisfaction and improve employee retention.

With a focus on ergonomics over the last few years, manufacturers have produced headsets designed for optimum fit and comfort. Constantly expanding databases of facial and ear measurements have improved fit. New materials have made soft, pliable ear-hooks possible, providing the first truly com-

fortable, customized fit for on-the-ear headsets. And headsets are lighter than ever, with some weighing as little as a half-ounce. Flexible microphone booms allow agents to adjust the microphone to the ideal position for their personal comfort and for optimized sound quality. Convertible headsets give agents the ability to pick their preferred wearing style or even change styles. Whenever possible, give agents an opportunity to choose their own headsets to maximize their comfort.

Review Durability Tests
Use of durable headsets reduces downtime from normal wear and tear. Agents put headsets on and

take them off, pull on their wires, stuff them in drawers – all of which can weaken parts and reduce performance. Agents who must go offline because their headsets need to be repaired or replaced can negatively affect service levels, revenue and customer satisfaction. When managing headsets as an investment, durability becomes an important part of the overall ROI calculation.

When shopping for headsets, ask suppliers for data on how individual parts of the headset performed in durability tests. Flexible booms have been tested to withstand as many as 6,000 bends – or as few as 250. Cord strength can be measured between 47 and 60 pounds of pull. And turret integrity – the ability for the boom to maintain its position – can range between 8,000 and 50,000 adjustments before succumbing to "droopy boom" syndrome. Durability cannot be discerned by visual inspection; compare suppliers and check for these statistics before purchasing a headset.

Recent Amplifier Advances
Amplifiers play an important role in determining total headset investment. By using universal amplifiers that are compatible with most phone systems, call centers that replace their telephone systems won't need to reinvest in their amplifiers – or headsets. Call centers running multiple shifts can also assign one amplifier per workstation, so only headset tops are needed for each agent.

Recent advances have also enabled amplifiers to take on multiple functions formerly available only as accessories. Some amplifiers come with an RNA (Representative Not Available) function that redirects calls to available agents; dual headset ports to eliminate the need for separate training equipment; and an under-the-desk mounting option to eliminate desktop clutter and cable tangling. Agents can use the mute feature to quiet sneezes, coughs and other distracting sounds. And a quick-disconnect feature lets agents quickly disconnect their headsets from the amplifier so they can leave their workstation without taking the headset off.

A good amplifier also offers audio protection to agents. While amplification allows users to hear the customer better, it must also protect from unexpected, loud noise bursts that come over the phone lines. Compression algorithms and protocols can identify voice and data bursts to maintain a safe acoustical level. Advanced audio protection can detect a loud fax signal and compress it down 10 decibels, making the sound safe for the ears. Look for OSHA certification from headset manufacturers; OSHA requires that all amplifiers have compression in order to receive certification – but not all amplifiers actually have it. Check this carefully!

Optimizing Headset System Investment

Equipping any call center – whether large or small – with headsets is an important and significant investment and should be managed to achieve the best ROI possible. Many factors affect the investment after the purchase.

Total cost of ownership takes into account repair, replacement, downtime and warranty. The ROI calculation needs to factor in more than just the cost of the headset and amplifier. More durable products result in fewer replacement headsets. Spare parts should also be a consideration – find out how quickly parts typically break and need to be replaced. Voice tubes, for instance, should be replaced every six months.

Check the headset warranty: a two-year guarantee is now standard. Consider the cost of the repair as well as repair turnaround time. Use all of these variables to determine which headset manufacturer will provide you with the highest quality headsets for your call center at the lowest total cost.

While some may think of headsets merely as furniture or equipment, smart call centers understand that headsets play a key role in achieving performance goals, enhancing productivity and improving agent retention – all excellent reasons to research thoroughly to find the highest quality headsets for your call center.

CCMReview

P. Michael Fairweather is president and CEO of GN Netcom, Inc. (www.gnnet com.com) – a Nashua, N.H.-based firm that designs, manufactures and markets high-quality, hands-free communications products, including telephone headsets, accessories and specialty products under the brand names GN Netcom, UNEX and ACS.

Section 9

Service Level Notes with Brad Cleveland

On Disasters, Plans and Responsibilities

Do you remember the song with the line, "How can I miss you if you never go away?" I don't recall the title, but the irony in the message has stuck with me. Unfortunately, it's a view too many managers seem to have towards their call centers. In recent months, a variety of disasters have crippled call centers for hours and, in some cases, days, and has driven home the point: You will miss your call center if it leaves!

To be blunt, some call center managers don't give a hoot about disaster recovery and planning. They view it as someone else's responsibility: "That's an area our IS and telecommunications people handle." But to be effective, it must be a collaborative effort involving the call center, the information systems and telecommunications departments, the marketing and/or communications departments, facilities, finance, suppliers, outsourcers (if applicable) and potentially others from both inside and outside the organization. When you begin to size up the diverse threats to your call center, this becomes obvious.

There are five general steps to developing a disaster recovery plan:

1. Determine the impact of being out of business for X amount of time. In revenue generating call centers, the answer to this question can be expressed in monetary terms: "We would lose $68,000 in sales in a day if our call center went down." But you can also reference customers who won't be served, information that won't be disseminated or captured, lost customers or even lives saved, depending on the services your call center provides.

The purpose of this step is twofold. First, it provides you with a benchmark against which you can assess the costs of varying levels of redundancy and backup (in some ways - not all - more protection means more money). Second, it will help position the call center within the context of the organization's priorities (e.g., which areas get restored first).

2. Identify potential threats. A disaster recovery plan, like an insurance policy, is most effective if all the risks and threats are carefully and realistically identified. While hurricanes and earthquakes do happen, most threats do not arrive in dramatic, news-making fashion.

You will need to prepare for water damage (from broken pipes, backed up drains, failed condensation pumps, roof leaks, ground or flood water, discharging fire sprinklers or the fireman's hose), fire and smoke damage, component and network failures, cable cuts, power losses from blackouts and brownouts, sabotage and lightning. Given the integrated environment, you will also need to identify how your systems will behave if a key component goes down - e.g., what happens to calls when the CTI link fails or the IVR system decides to take a break? But these threats are just the beginning. After all, a disaster is any event that causes a significant disruption in call center services. Consequently, there are a multitude of potential threats that have little to do with systems and networks (encouraging, huh?). For example:

• How do you immediately communicate critical information to your agents if your organization gets unexpected national news coverage today?

• What staffing tactics can you deploy if your marketing department runs a campaign you aren't aware of?

• What is your escalation plan if your workload far outstrips the staff you have to handle it? (Ever lost 30 percent of your agents to the flu? Did it happen at a convenient time?)

• What happens if a large number of agents can't make it to the call center (e.g., because of a storm)?

• Who changes the system announcements or reroutes calls if you must immediately evacuate the building (e.g., in the event of a bomb threat or fire)?

Developing workable answers to these questions requires a cross-functional team and a lot of thought. Tip: Don't forget to also involve several of your agents in this process.

3. Take preventative measures. As you identify potential threats, areas of vulnerability - and preventative countermeasures - will emerge. Hardware and networks are protected primarily through redundancy and diversity in equipment and services. Specific steps usually include subscribing to services from multiple carriers, deploying fire detection and suppression equipment, working with suppliers to identify critical system components you should keep on site, equipping your system for power backup and ensuring you have good wiring and adequate power line protection against lightning strikes and voltage surges.

Regular record keeping and backup is critical to prevention. Records should include information such as wiring runs, system and network reconfiguration procedures, lists of alternative systems announcements (e.g., "We are currently experiencing technical difficulties and request that you...") and home and mobile contact numbers for key people. Key information and database files should be regularly backed up and stored both onsite and offsite.

Every call center should also prepare for total relocation - yep, moving the whole shebang to an alternative site. For larger call centers, this may be as handy as rerouting calls to existing sites or to a prearranged service bureau. But small call centers should also have alternatives for rerouting calls to another department or location. Believe me, you will not appreciate the time and agony of figuring this out after a disaster strikes.

4. Develop an escalation plan. An effective escalation plan outlines appropriate responses to each potential disaster and specifies the thresholds at which they should be deployed. It should address the following:

The Five Steps in Disaster Recovery Preparation:

1) Determine the impact of being out of business
2) Identify potential threats
3) Take preventative measures
4) Develop an escalation plan
5) Practice and update the plan

• What constitutes a disaster?
• Who in the organization declares a disaster and puts the disaster recovery plan into motion? How can they be reached?
• How will key people inside and outside the organization be notified of a disaster, and what roles will they fill in the recovery effort?
• What's the appropriate escalation plan for the disaster, given its type and magnitude?

The plan should be simple to understand, easy to follow and up to date. (For sample plans and vendor references in the disaster recovery field, contact St. Louis-based Disaster Recovery Journal at 314-894-0276 or at www.drj.com.)

5. Practice and update the plan. Your carefully constructed plan will be of no value if it sits on the shelf during a disaster. Reviewing and practicing recovery plans may be reminiscent of school days, but these drills are worth a lot more than nostalgia. Many disasters happen quickly and without warning. People have to know what to do!

Rally Your Resources

Like so many other aspects of call center planning and management, effective disaster prevention and recovery requires careful planning and collaboration. Although the disaster recovery team must, by necessity, include a diverse lot of people from both inside and outside the call center, the final responsibility of ensuring that the call center is adequately prepared rests squarely on the shoulders of call center management. Why not rally some resources and begin this process today?

SLN

Section 9

Answers to Exercises

Operations Management

Answers to Exercises

Service Level/Response Time

1.

	Use Service Level	Use Response Time
Inbound calls	X	
Outbound calls		X
Email		X
Text chat	X	
Web "call me back now"	X	
Web "call me back later"		X
Web call through	X	
Fax		X
Postal Mail		X

2. a. $(201 + 5) \div (243 + 11) = 206 \div 254 = 81\%$

   b. $201 \div 243 = 83\%$

   c. $201 \div (243 + 11) = 201 \div 254 = 79\%$

   d. $201 \div (243 + 6) = 201 \div 249 = 81\%$

3. reply, response, resolution

4. scheduled, rolling

5. c, d, a, b

6. There is none.

7. T, F, F

8. 7, 9, 4, 8, 6, 5, 2, 1, 3

9. F, F

10.

	Historical	Real-time
Service level	X	
Agent status		X
Longest current wait		X
Average speed of answer	X	
Abandonment rate	X	

11. F, F

Section 10

Key Performance Indicators

1. $7,875 ÷ 225 = $35

2. 156 ÷ (225 + 28) = 62%

3. 4,495 ÷ 225 = 20 seconds

4. 19 ÷ (19 + 225) = 8%

5. $1,124 ÷ 225 = $5

6. 197 ÷ 225 = 88%

7. 185 + 39 = 224 seconds

8. (225 x 224) ÷ (35 x 1,800) = 50,400 ÷ 63,000 = 80%

9. (270 x 227) - (253 x 224) = 61,290 − 56,672 = 4,618
   4,618 ÷ 61,290 = 8%

10. 35 − 38 = -3
    -3 ÷ 38 = -8%

Forecasting and Scheduling

1. f, a, c, e, b, d

2. 650,000
   x   1.14
   741,000
   x   .07
    51,870
   ÷   31
    1,673
   x   1.5
    2,509
   x   .04
   100 calls

3. (c, d, e), a, b, d, a, c, e

4. a. 35 agents
   b. 45% in 20 seconds
   c. occupancy decreases
   d. trunk load decreases
   e. 89% (11% will be delayed)
   f. 74 seconds
   g. service level
   h. no

5. a. 18 callers
   b. 95% in 20 seconds

6. a. down
   b. diminishing
   c. larger/smaller
   d. pooled/specialized
   e. down
   f. down

7. g, s, s, g, g, g, s, s

8.

ERLANG C FOR INCOMING CALL CENTERS BY ICMI, INC.
TALK TIME IN SECONDS = **180**
AFTER-CALL WORK IN SECONDS = **30**
CALLS PER HALF-HOUR = **250**
SERVICE LEVEL OBJECTIVE IN SECONDS = **20**

Agents	COST	ASA	SL	TKLD	COST	TOTAL
30	$450	208.7	23.5%	54.0	$216.00	$666.00
31	$465	74.7	45.2%	35.4	$141.60	$606.60
32	$480	37.6	61.3%	30.2	$120.80	$600.80
33	$495	21.3	73.0%	28.0	$112.00	$607.00
34	$510	12.7	81.5%	26.8	$107.20	$617.20

   a. 61% answered in 20 seconds

9.

Routing Plan

Call Routing Hierarchy	Sales – Printers	Sales – Computers	Service – Printers	Service – Computers
Skill Choice 1	Agent Type 1	Agent Type 2	Agent Type 9	Agent Type 6 (or 8)
Skill Choice 2	Agent Type 4 (or 5)	Agent Type 4	Agent Type 5	Agent Type 8 (or 6)
Skill Choice 3	Agent Type 5 (or 4)	Agent Type 3	Agent Type 3	Agent Type 3
Skill Choice 4	Agent Type 7	Agent Type 7	Agent Type 7	Agent Type 7

10. $450 \div (420 \div 4) = 450 \div 105 = 4.3 \cong 5$ agents

11.

Rostered Staff Factor Exercise

	Base Staff Required						
	Phone	Email	Absent	Break	Training	On Schedule	RSF
8:00 - 8:30	20	4	3	0	2	29	1.21
8:30 - 9:00	22	4	3	0	2	31	1.19
9:00 - 9:30	22	4	3	0	2	31	1.19
9:30 - 10:00	28	5	3	3	0	39	1.18
10:00 - 10:30	28	5	3	4	0	40	1.21
10:30 - 11:00	34	5	3	4	0	46	1.18

12. 7.5 FTEs

13. Left to right: Flow Chart, Pareto Chart, Cause and Effect Diagram (or Fishbone), Control Chart, Scatter Diagram

Call Center Technology

1. a. TCP/IP
   b. integrated
   c. ROI
   d. value, cost
   e. browser-based
   f. media

2. g, n, k, l, h, m, c, b, h, e, a, d, a, j, e, b, f, h, j, j, f, l, i, n

3. h, g, d, e, b, f, i, c, a

Facilities and Disaster Recovery

1. a. labor
   b. Economic Development Agency
   c. 20 to 30 percent
   d. 60 percent

2. a. Telephone Consumer Protection
   b. Do Not Call (DNC), 8:00, 9:00
   c. Telemarketing Sales
   d. sales, permission (or authorization)

3. b

4. more, less

5. raised, raised, raised, conventional

6. a, b

7. a. Architectural Barriers Act
   b. Americans with Disabilities Act
   c. cumulative trauma disorders
   d. Equal Employment Opportunity Commission
   e. Occupational Safety and Health Act

8. F, F

9. T, F

CIAC Certification Handbook

Operations Management

CERTIFICATION

INFORMATION HANDBOOK

Call Center Industry Advisory Council
(CIAC)

Setting Standards of Excellence
For The Contact Center Profession

CIAC CERTIFICATION

INFORMATION HANDBOOK

This **Handbook** contains information about CIAC Certification. It explains the purposes and benefits of CIAC Certification, the CIAC Certification process, assessment requirements, and registration procedures. Adherence to the policies and procedures described in this Handbook is essential to achieve and maintain CIAC Certification. Questions about information contained in this Handbook and/or CIAC Certification should be directed to:

Call Center Industry Advisory Council, Inc. (CIAC)
330 Franklin Road
PMB 390
Brentwood, Tennessee 37027 USA

Telephone:
888-859-2422
615-373-2376

Fax:
615-515-1879
Email:
info@ciac-cert.org

Web site:
www.ciac-cert.org

Section 11

TABLE OF CONTENTS

ABOUT CIAC

CIAC is a not for profit corporation established by the contact center industry to provide standardized, competency-based professional certification for individuals who lead, manage and work in contact centers. It exists to promote the establishment of standards of competence and professionalism in the contact center industry and to recognize professionals who through successful completion of the CIAC Certification process have demonstrated mastery of industry-established, knowledge, skill, and behavioral requirements that are specific to their job role.

CIAC Mission

The mission of CIAC is twofold: 1) to raise the stature of the contact center profession; and 2) to heighten awareness of the strategic and economic value of contact centers. The ultimate goal of CIAC is to legitimize the contact center profession in order to inspire more people to purposely choose contact center careers, thereby, increasing the number of qualified professionals available for the growing number of contact center jobs.

CIAC Objectives

The primary objectives of CIAC are to:

- Promote advancement of the contact center profession and industry.

- Legitimize the contact center profession by establishing standards that define the knowledge, skills, and behaviors required for mastery-level job performance.

- Certify individuals based on their ability to demonstrate mastery of contact center role-specific competencies.

- Provide industry-recognized knowledge and skill requirements to help training providers more effectively prepare individuals for success in working in contact centers.

- Provide career pathing for the contact center career and specific guidelines for success and advancement.

- Promote a positive image of contact centers by educating the general public, government, and business community on the economic and strategic value of contact centers.

- Represent the profession on issues relating to contact centers and the individuals who lead, manage, and work in contact centers.

CIAC is not a professional association, membership organization, or training company. Its role is to serve as the vendor-neutral standards and certifying body for the contact center industry and profession.

INTRODUCTION TO CIAC CERTIFICATION

Definition of CIAC Certification

CIAC Certification is the process by which the competence of contact center professionals is assessed, validated, and formally recognized in specific areas of expertise based on the requirements of their job role as defined by the industry. It allows professionals to demonstrate an in-depth understanding of contact centers, comprehensive knowledge of the essential aspects of their job role, and to demonstrate behaviors identified as essential for success. Achievement of CIAC Certification indicates that a contact center professional (1) has demonstrated mastery of industry-established knowledge, skill, and behavioral requirements; and (2) is committed to continual learning and ongoing professional development.

CIAC Certification is an essential tool for establishing and maintaining a standard of performance excellence for contact centers. It is applicable to individuals working in all types and sizes of contact centers, across all industries. CIAC Certification is vendor-neutral and free of bias. It is focused on empowering professionals who lead, manage, and work in contact centers to enhance their job performance and advance their career through an industry-recognized credential that recognizes them to be the best in the industry. CIAC-Certified professionals enable contact center organizations to achieve and sustain best practices that exemplify performance excellence.

Purpose of CIAC Certification

The purpose of CIAC Certification is: 1) to raise the stature of the contact center profession in order to make working in contact centers a more attractive career choice; 2) to ensure professional competence and motivate the individuals who lead, manage, and work in contact centers and contact center organizations to achieve the highest standards of performance; and 3) to promote recognition that contact centers are a critical component of an enterprise's business strategy. To fulfill this purpose, CIAC:

- Worked with the industry to establish competencies based on recognized knowledge, skills, and behaviors for contact center job roles.
- Developed certification assessments that are linked to the established competencies.
- Established a certification process designed to raise the bar in order to cultivate a workforce of superior performers.
- Works with training providers to ensure the availability of quality programs that are aligned with the competencies and other required criteria necessary to effectively prepare individuals for the CIAC Certification assessments.

Benefits of CIAC Certification

CIAC Certification formally acknowledges a mastery-level command of the requirements of the job role and a commitment to maintaining high standards. The key benefits of CIAC Certification for individuals leading, managing and working in contact center include:

- Formal acknowledgement of specialized expertise.
- Achievement of a respected industry credential.
- Recognition as a role model and leader.
- Demonstration of ability to achieve business results.
- Increases an individual's current value and future marketability.
- Enhances career growth by providing motivational goals and a framework for professional development.
- Promotes continual learning through a commitment to ongoing professional development.
- Demonstrates a personal commitment to performance excellence.

CIAC Certification is important to contact centers because it:

- Provides credible criteria for making hiring decisions, evaluating performance, and/or determining training needs.
- Reduces turnover – helps to ensure "right fit" from the start.
- Increases productivity, employee morale, and commitment.
- Provides job mobility and increased career paths.
- Reduces training costs – learning is directly related to the job.
- Promotes a professional image throughout the enterprise and to customers.
- Demonstrates a commitment to performance excellence.

CIAC Certification also benefits the contact center profession and industry because it:

- Raises the stature of the profession by formally recognizing the requirement for specialized knowledge, skills, and abilities.
- Inspires career choices in contact centers by legitimizing the profession.
- Heightens awareness of advancement opportunities.
- Establishes industry-recognized competency requirements.
- Raises the bar and promotes performance excellence.

Use of CIAC Certification

CIAC Certification is voluntary in nature and intended solely for the purposes and benefits stated in this Handbook.

CIAC CERTIFICATION TRACKS

Management Track

Because job titles and descriptions tend to be narrowly defined and vary across organizations, CIAC Certification is based on "roles" rather than job titles. Roles more effectively capture the full responsibilities of a job. Role-based certification allows professionals to pursue certification in the role that best defines what they *actually* do and their *actual* scope of authority and influence; it also allows for overlap between job functions. For example, in some centers the job title contact center manager has both operational and strategic responsibility.

CIAC's first certification track is for professionals who lead and manage contact center organizations. There are also role designations for individuals who are pursuing a career in contact center management and contact center consultants. The roles represented in the CIAC Certification Management Track are:

- Strategic
- Operational
- Apprentice
- Consultant

CIAC Certification for other contact center roles (supervisors, team lead, and agents) will be provided in the future. Contact CIAC for availability.

CIAC Certification can be achieved in the following Management Track role designations:

CIAC-Certified Strategic Leader (*CCSL*) – This certification designation is for senior executives who are responsible for setting the strategic direction and vision for customer care across all channels of the organization. This role typically has bottom line responsibility for the contact center and is responsible for aligning contact center objectives with corporate business goals. Typical job titles are vice president, director, and senior-manager. In some organizations the title manager may have strategic responsibilities. CIAC Certification as a Strategic Leader requires a minimum of one year of experience specifically in a strategic management role that touches on all of the competencies required for the CCSL designation.

CIAC-Certified Operations Manager (*CCOM*) – This certification designation is for management professionals who are responsible for day-to-day contact center operations. This role typically has tactical responsibility for the center including administering the contact center budget, and management of customer care staff. The typical title for this role is manager although in some organizations supervisors may have responsibilities that overlap into operational management. CIAC Certification as an Operations Manager requires a minimum of one year of experience specifically in an operational management role that touches on all of the competencies required for the CCOM designation.

CIAC-Certified Management Apprentice (*CCMA*) – This certification designation is intended for three distinct types of professionals:

1. Individuals who are not employed in a contact center, but wish to pursue a career in contact center management.
2. Individuals working in a contact center, not in a management role, who wish to pursue a career path into contact center management.
3. Supervisors who wish to accelerate their advancement into contact center management.

Those pursuing CIAC Certification as a Management Apprentice are required to commit to a program of education, training and professional development focused on the specific competencies for the CCMA role. After one year of job experience in a contact center management role, professionals certified in the Apprentice designation may complete their CIAC Certification in the appropriate management role designation. (Apprentice certification does not require completion of a Work Product Assignment or 360° Review).

CIAC-Certified Management Consultant (*CCMC*) – This certification designation is for senior level contact center consultants, ideally who have hands-on experience in contact center management. This designation certifies that a consultant has the required knowledge in contact center management; it does not certify or verify the consultant's expertise or effectiveness in other areas of consultancy. Individuals pursuing CIAC Certification in this designation are required to successfully complete the objective assessments (knowledge assessments) based on the *strategic role* contact center management competencies. (Consultant certification does not require completion of a Work Product Assignment or 360° Review).

Through the CIAC Certification process, professionals are assessed against competency criteria that link their knowledge, skills, and behaviors with the performance requirements of a specific job role. CIAC is committed to building a strong relationship between on-the-job performance and CIAC Certification.

To accomplish this, the CIAC Certification Management Track has four domains of knowledge and skill competency requirements and a set of behavioral characteristics that cross all of the domains. The Management Track competency domains are:

- People Management
- Operations Management
- Customer Relationship Management
- Leadership & Business Management

Within each domain, there are role-specific knowledge, skill, and behavioral requirements for mastery-level contact center management. The competencies were developed by CIAC and practicing contact center executives and managers over a two-plus year period and were validated through industry surveys, focus groups, expert panel review, and secondary research. Go to the CIAC Certification web site at www.ciac-cert.org to review and/or download the Contact Center Management Competencies for each certification designation.

CIAC CERTIFICATION	CIAC CERTIFIED STRATEGIC LEADER CCSL	CIAC CERTIFIED OPERATIONS MANAGER CCOM	CIAC CERTIFIED MANAGEMENT APPRENTICE CCMA	CIAC CERTIFIED MANAGEMENT CONSULTANT CCMC
WHO	• Senior executive who is responsible for setting the strategic direction and vision for customer care across all channels of the organization`. Has a minimum of one year experience in a strategic management role that touches all areas of the CCSL competencies • Has bottom line responsibility for the contact center • Responsible for aligning contact center objectives with corporate business goals • Examples of job titles are: vice president, director, and senior-manager	• Professional who is responsible for managing day-to-day contact center operations. Has a minimum of one year of experience in an operational management role that touches all areas of the CCOM competencies • Responsible for managing customer care staff and the contact center operation • Typically administers and manages adherence to the contact center budget • Example of job title is: manager	• Individual who is pursuing a career in contact center management through training or other professional development who is presently not working in a contact center; or an • Individual who is working in a contact center but not in a management role, who wishes to pursue a career in contact center management • Supervisors who wish to accelerate their advancement into contact center management. Has a minimum of one year experience in a contact center operational management role that touches all areas of the competencies required for the CCMA designation • Testing for CCMA certification can be applied toward certification for the CCOM designation	• Senior level contact center consultants, ideally who have hands-on experience in contact center management • Certifies that a consultant has the required knowledge in contact center management; does not certify or verify the consultant's expertise or effectiveness in other areas of consultancy • Required to successfully complete knowledge assessments based on competencies for the CCMC designation
VALUE	• Proves ability to achieve business results • Validates mastery-level competence of full scope of strategic contact center management • Helps to advance the contact center profession - serves as role model for future leaders • Demonstrates a commitment to performance excellence • Attainment of a prestigious industry credential	• Recognition of specialized expertise • Increases value and marketability • Achievement of an industry-recognized credential • Facilitates continual learning • Provides a framework and goals for ongoing career development • Raises the bar for the contact center management profession	• Provides a framework and goals for ongoing career development and advancement • Increases value and marketability • Demonstrates a commitment to the contact center profession/industry • Establishes a career track and accelerates advancement into a contact center management role	• Validation of specialized knowledge • Enhances professional image • Demonstrates a commitment to the contact center profession/industry • Increases value and marketability to clients
COMPETENCY DOMAIN	• People Management • Operations Management • Customer Relationship Management • Leadership and Business Management	• People Management • Operations Management • Customer Relationship Management • Leadership and Business Management	• People Management • Operations Management • Customer Relationship Management • Leadership and Business Management	• People Management • Operations Management • Customer Relationship Management • Leadership and Business Management
ASSESSMENTS	• People Management • Operations Management • Customer Relationship Management • Leadership and Business Management • Work Product Assignment • 360°Review	• People Management • Operations Management • Customer Relationship Management • Leadership and Business Management • Work Product Assignment • 360°Review	• People Management • Operations Management • Customer Relationship Management • Leadership and Business Management • CCMA designation does not complete Work Product Assignment or 360° Review	• People Management • Operations Management • Customer Relationship Management • Leadership and Business Management • CCMC designation does not complete Work Product Assignment or 360° Review
CRITERIA	• Minimum of one year of experience in a contact center strategic management role that touches all areas of the competencies required for the CCSL designation • A minimum score of 75 percent is required on all knowledge assessments • On the 360°Review a mean score of 3.0 (on a scale of 0 - 5) is required for each competency area and a score of 3.5 is required for the overall 360°Review • Must pass all knowledge assessments in order to receive the Work Product Assignment • Testing must be completed within two years from the date the first assessment is taken	• Minimum of one year of experience in a contact center operational management role that touches all areas of the competencies required for the CCOM designation • A minimum score of 75 percent is required on all knowledge assessments • On the 360° Review a mean score of 3.0 (on a scale of 0 - 5) is required for each competency area and a score of 3.5 is required for the overall 360°Review • Must pass all knowledge assessments in order to receive the Work Product Assignment • Testing must be completed within two years from the date the first assessment is taken	• A minimum score of 70 percent is required for all knowledge assessments based on the competencies for the CCMA designation • Testing must be completed within two years from the date the first assessment is taken	• A minimum score of 75 percent is required for all knowledge assessments based on the competencies for the CCMC designation • Testing must be completed within two years from the date the first assessment is taken
SELF-ASSESSMENTS	CIAC strongly encourages candidates pursuing CIAC Certification to complete a Self-Assessment for each competency domain to assess current knowledge, skills, and experience against the required competencies. This will enable candidates to identify areas where training and/or additional job experience may be necessary before testing.			

CIAC CERTIFICATION ASSESSMENTS

Registering for CIAC Certification can be done the following ways:

- Online at www.ciac-cert.org via a link to www.ciaccertification.com.
- Online at www.ciaccertification.com.
- Call the CIAC Certification Operations Center at 888-859-2422 or 615-373-2376.

General Information

Candidates complete a knowledge assessment for each of the four (4) competency domains (four knowledge assessments in total). Candidates pursuing certification for the CIAC-Certified Strategic Leader and CIAC-Certified Operations Manager designations also complete a role-specific Work Product Assignment and a 360° Review to assess behavioral characteristics. Candidates pursuing certification as a CIAC-Certified Management Apprentice (CCMA) and Management Consultant (CCMC) do not complete the Work Product Assignment or 360° Review.

CIAC does not dictate the method by which competence necessary to achieve CIAC Certification is acquired. Candidates may prepare for the certification process by on-the-job experience, formal education, training and other means of professional development.

CIAC Certification testing is Internet-based and administered online. Knowledge assessments are administered in a proctored environment. Three hours is allowed to complete each knowledge assessment. Testing is conducted at public testing centers located in major cities and select colleges and universities. A listing of CIAC-authorized test centers can be found at www.ciaccertification.com. CIAC Certification can also be employer-sponsored in which case CIAC coordinates onsite testing through an organization's human resources or training department. For information about onsite testing contact the CIAC Certification Operations Center at 888-859-2422 or 615-373-2376 or email at info@ciac-cert.org.

The Work Product Assignment is issued upon completion of the knowledge assessments. It is completed at the candidate's work place or other location of choice. Six (6) weeks or thirty (30) workdays is allowed to complete the Work Product Assignment. Upon completion, Work Products are first reviewed and approved by the candidate's manager and then submitted to CIAC for evaluation.

The 360° Review is also completed at the work place by the candidate, his/her manager, selected peers, and direct reports. Three weeks or fifteen (15) workdays is allowed for completion of the 360° Review. The completed 360° Review is sent to CIAC for statistical compilation. A report of the results and feedback is provided to the candidate for professional development purposes. The 360° Review may be completed at any time during the CIAC Certification process.

All CIAC Certification requirements must be completed within two years from the date the first assessment is taken. Failure to complete within the allotted time will require a restart of the CIAC Certification process in full. The candidate may elect to stop the certification process at any time.

Testing Schedule

CIAC does not dictate a testing schedule. A candidate is allowed to take an assessment when ready, given that he/she has registered, received confirmation of registration, designated a testing location, and confirmed a testing date/time. It is typical that the CIAC Certification assessments are completed one at a time; however, candidates may complete the assessments one at a time or in multiples of their preference.

Assessment Scoring

CIAC understands the importance of the certification assessment results and makes every effort to ensure accurate scoring. The knowledge assessments are computer-scored and structured to have one correct answer. CIAC-trained assessors with subject matter expertise evaluate Work Products using CIAC-provided checklists with content validity. The 360° Reviews are computer-scored, providing totals and mean values for each competency area.

Communicating Assessment Results

CIAC sends assessment results directly to the candidate at the postal or email address provided on the Candidate Profile within four (4) hours after the assessment is completed. A "PASS/FAIL" notification is issued. Actual assessment scores may be accessed via the candidate's transcript. Assessment scores are maintained as confidential and released to other parties only with written authorization from the candidate. The candidate is responsible for communicating the results to his/her manager and, if applicable, for submitting a copy of the results to the human resources department for personnel record.

Assessment Results and Status

- CIAC promotes that industry certification be used for professional/career development purposes. An individual's performance on the assessments should not be used to make decisions such as demotion, transfer, termination, etc.

- In situations where CIAC Certification is employer-sponsored, CIAC provides the assessment results to the candidate in order to maintain confidentiality. It is the responsibility of the candidate and his/her manager to discuss performance on the certification assessments.

CIAC maintains a database for tracking the certification progress and status of candidates and re-certification of certified professionals. The system provides automatic status and information by candidate name and flags certified individuals who are nearing time for re-certification.

Certificates of Completion

Candidates receive a "Certificate of Completion" for each assessment that is successfully completed.

After successful completion of all certification requirements, CIAC issues the appropriate CIAC Certification credential.

PREPARING FOR CIAC CERTIFICATION TESTING

CIAC Certification testing consists of a series of assessments that are based on competencies unique to the professional's job role. The competencies are both broad and deep in breadth that cover the *full range* of knowledge, skills, and abilities related to contact center management. They are designed to be high-end in order to cultivate a workforce of master performers. CIAC Certification testing requires in-depth comprehension of the competencies. CIAC strongly encourages candidates to thoroughly review the competencies for their role designation to determine their current level of preparedness and to complete the CIAC-provided Self-Assessments to identify knowledge and skill gaps before testing.

The CIAC Contact Center Management Competencies can be viewed and/or downloaded at www.ciac-cert.org.

The number and types of assessments are determined by the candidate's certification designation (e.g., CIAC-Certified Strategic Leader, Operations Manager, etc.). All designations complete four multiple-choice knowledge assessments consisting of 60 – 100 questions each. The questions are thought-provoking and require in-depth, conceptual knowledge of the subject matter in addition to extensive hands-on experience. Those pursuing CIAC Certification as a Strategic Leader and Operations Manager also complete a Work Product Assignment and a 360° Review.

In order to establish high value around CIAC Certification, the certification process is intentionally rigorous. The process guarantees that a person who achieves CIAC Certification has mastery-level expertise and knows how to apply it on the job. CIAC strongly encourages candidates to prepare in advance of testing. The extent of preparation required is unique to each person depending on his/her current command of the required competencies, both knowledge and application. While some candidates require only refresher training, the majority of person's pursuing CIAC Certification require more extensive training in each of the competency domains.

Preparation for CIAC Certification testing is the candidate's responsibility. CIAC strongly encourages that candidates utilize the CIAC-provided Self-Assessments to compare existing knowledge, skills, and experience against the requirements in each competency domain. This enables candidates to identify specific areas where training and/or job experience is necessary before testing for CIAC Certification. Self-Assessments are available for each domain at www.ciac-cert.org.

Candidates can view and/or download the CIAC Certification 'Preparing to Test Orientation' presentation at www.ciac-cert.org.

RE-CERTIFICATION

Achieving CIAC Certification represents demonstrated mastery of the full range of required competencies for the job role. This first step demonstrates a commitment to continual learning and ongoing professional development. Re-certification is the mechanism by which a CIAC-Certified Professional demonstrates currency of expertise and maintains a competitive edge.

To maintain active CIAC Certification, the candidate completes a Master Knowledge Assessment based on current competency requirements every three (3) years from the first date of CIAC Certification issuance. To avoid a lapse in certification, the re-certification process should be completed prior to expiration of current CIAC Certification. Re-certification is available only in the current CIAC-Certified designation (e.g., CIAC-Certified Operations Manager re-certifies as same).

CIAC strongly encourages that certified professionals actively participate in industry/profession-specific professional development activities such as attending and speaking at conferences; authoring articles; active membership in industry associations; and completing related educational courses/programs.

ELIGIBILITY FOR CIAC CERTIFICATION

To qualify for CIAC Certification candidates must meet all of the requirements outlined in this Handbook.

Criteria for CIAC Certification

The criteria for CIAC Certification have been developed based on industry input as well as research of other successful certification programs.

Requirements for the Management Track designations are as follows:

- **CIAC-Certified Strategic Leader** – CIAC Certification in this designation requires a minimum of one year of experience in a contact center strategic management role. A minimum score of 75 percent is required on each of four knowledge assessments that are based on role-specific competencies; on the 360° Review a mean score of 3.0 (on a scale of 0 – 5) is required for each competency area and a 3.5 is required for the total 360° Review. Candidates must pass all knowledge assessments to receive the Work Product Assignment. All CIAC Certification testing must be completed within two years from the date the first assessment is taken.

- **CIAC-Certified Operations Manager** – CIAC Certification in this designation requires a minimum of one year of experience in a contact center operational management role. A minimum score of 75 percent is required on each of four knowledge assessments that are based on role-specific competencies; on the 360° Review a mean score of 3.0 (on a scale of 0 – 5) is required for each competency area and a 3.5 is required for the total 360° Review. Candidates must pass all knowledge assessments to receive the Work Product Assignment. All CIAC Certification testing must be completed within two years from the date the first assessment is taken.

- **CIAC-Certified Management Apprentice** – CIAC Certification in this designation requires a minimum score of 70 percent on each of four knowledge assessments that are based on role-specific competencies. This designation does not complete a Work Product Assignment or 360° Review. All CIAC Certification testing must be completed within two years from the date the first assessment is taken.

- **CIAC-Certified Management Consultant** – CIAC Certification in this designation requires a minimum score of 75 percent on each of four knowledge assessments that are based on role-specific competencies. This designation does not complete a Work Product Assignment or 360° Review. All CIAC Certification testing must be completed within two years from the date the first assessment is taken.

CIAC Certification Process

Each candidate (person) is required to complete the following process:

1. Candidate determines his/her appropriate role designation (CIAC-Certified Strategic Leader; CIAC-Certified Operations Manager, etc.).

2. Candidate completes the Self-Assessments to identify knowledge and skill gaps and to determine training need(s) before testing. Self-Assessments for each domain are available at www.ciac-cert.org.

3. Candidate acquires any necessary training or on-the-job experience. CIAC does not dictate how competence is acquired.

4. Candidate logs onto the CIAC Certification Online Registration System to initiate the CIAC Certification process. The online registration system is accessed through the CIAC Certification web site at www.ciac-cert.org by clicking **Register** on the homepage. This links the candidate to the online registration system at www.ciaccertification.com. Upon entry to the registration system, the candidate first creates a Profile following the outlined procedures:

    a) The CIAC Certification screen will appear. Click **Register**.

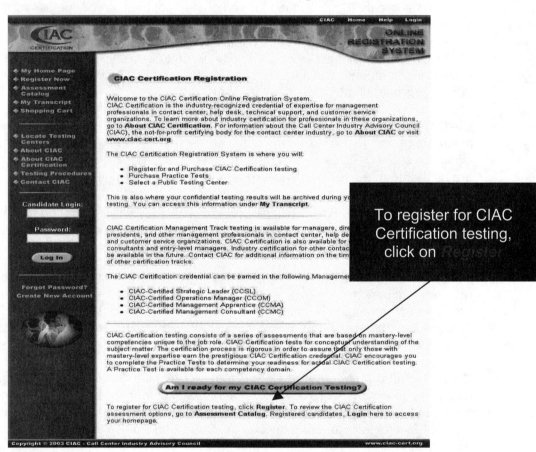

Note: The below screen will appear:

- Candidate Login: Created by candidate for login to registration system.
- First Name, Last Name, Email address.
- Secret Word: Created by candidate and used for ID purposes when contacting CIAC.
- Phone, Company Name, Title.
- Candidate selects his/her role designation.
- Tell us how you heard about CIAC Certification.

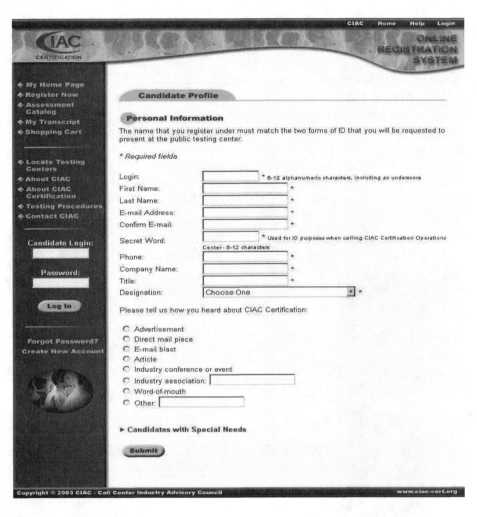

Click **Submit** to Continue

Note: A registration notification is automatically emailed to the candidate. This notification will have the candidate's login and system-generated password to be used when logging onto his/her CIAC Certification homepage at www.ciaccertification.com.

Candidates purchasing CIAC Certification testing at a price different than the Standard North American Published Price should contact the CIAC Certification Operations Center or CIAC Certification Reseller to complete the purchase transaction.

5. Candidate logs onto the Registration System using the login and password received by email to purchase certification assessment(s).

6. Candidate selects the Register-Purchase Link.

7. Candidate specifies certification track and role designation.

8. Candidate selects type of purchase. CIAC Certification can be purchased as a "package"; a single assessment; or any combination of assessments.

9. Candidate selects testing center and testing date, if applicable. If testing will be conducted at an employer site, CIAC coordinates with the appropriate contact to arrange for the required testing environment.

10. Candidate purchases CIAC Certification.

11. Candidate receives confirmation of purchase from CIAC.

> *Optional:* Candidates are encouraged to purchase the Practice Test(s) before testing in order to determine their readiness to test for CIAC Certification. A Practice Test is available for each domain and can be taken online at any time and at the candidate's choice of location. Practice Tests may be purchased at www.ciaccertification.com or by calling the CIAC Certification Operations Center at 888-859-2422 or 615-373-2376.

12. The first time a candidate logs onto his/her homepage on the CIAC Certification Online Registration System, the candidate will be requested to provide additional profile information. To do this, select **Edit Profile**. Additional information such as work and company information will be requested.

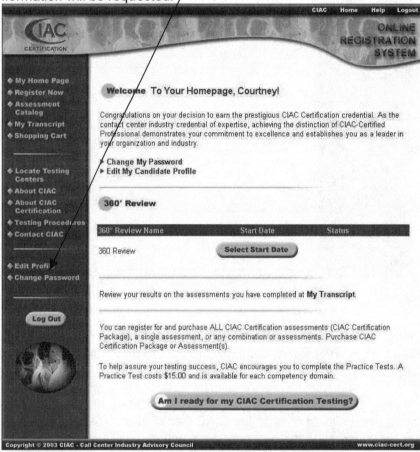

13. Candidate is responsible to contact the selected testing center to schedule date and time to take each knowledge assessment.

14. Candidate initiates 360° Review by logging onto his/her homepage and selecting a start date (the 360° Review may be completed at any time during the certification process).

15. Candidate selects 360° Review start date by clicking **Select Start Date** or selects a date in the future.

Note: A candidate will have the option to choose whether to start the 360° Review process now or designate a future start date.

16. Upon the specified start date, CIAC issues the 360° Review instrument to the candidate and the candidate's designated raters. Candidate and raters complete the 360° Review and submit it to CIAC. A mean value of 3.0 is required in each competency group and for the overall 360° Review a score of 3.5 is required (on a scale of 0 – 5). (Candidates for Management Apprentice and Management Consultant certification do not complete the 360° Review).

17. Candidate receives 360° Review Feedback Report from CIAC. If the required score is not achieved on the 360° Review, candidate completes a Professional Development Plan. Another 360° Review must be completed within twelve (12) months.

18. Candidate receives a PASS/FAIL score upon completion of each knowledge assessment with feedback indicating the scoring outcome per competency sub-category. Scoring notification is issued to the address provided in the candidate's Profile.

   a. If the minimum required score is not achieved on any assessment, the candidate refers to CIAC-provided feedback to determine additional training needs and acquires additional competence.
   b. Candidate registers to retest.
   c. Candidate retakes knowledge assessment(s).

19. Candidate receives "Certificate of Completion" by postal mail for each PASSED assessment and his/her official transcript is updated accordingly.

20. Candidate is issued a role-specific Work Product Assignment when all knowledge assessments are successfully completed. (Candidates for Management Apprentice and Management Consultant certification are not required to complete the Work Product Assignment).

21. Candidate completes the online Work Product Assignment and secures manager's review and sign-off. Manager approved Work Product is submitted to CIAC.

22. CIAC evaluates the Work Product and issues candidate a complete/incomplete status and feedback based on completeness and accuracy of outcome.

23. If the Work Product is incomplete or does not receive a PASS score, candidate utilizes CIAC provided feedback to complete the Work Product Assignment. Candidates are allowed fifteen (15) workdays to complete the Work Product Assignment.

24. After successful completion of all certification assessments, CIAC verifies the candidate has met full requirements.

25. Candidate is awarded the CIAC Certification credential for his/her role and Candidate's Official Transcript is updated.

26. Candidate must re-certify by passing a Master Knowledge Assessment every three (3) years to maintain an active CIAC Certification credential.

CIAC Certification Process
Management Track

Refer to the CIAC Certification Handbook for additional information on each step of the certification process. Go to www.ciac-cert.org to view and/or download the handbook.

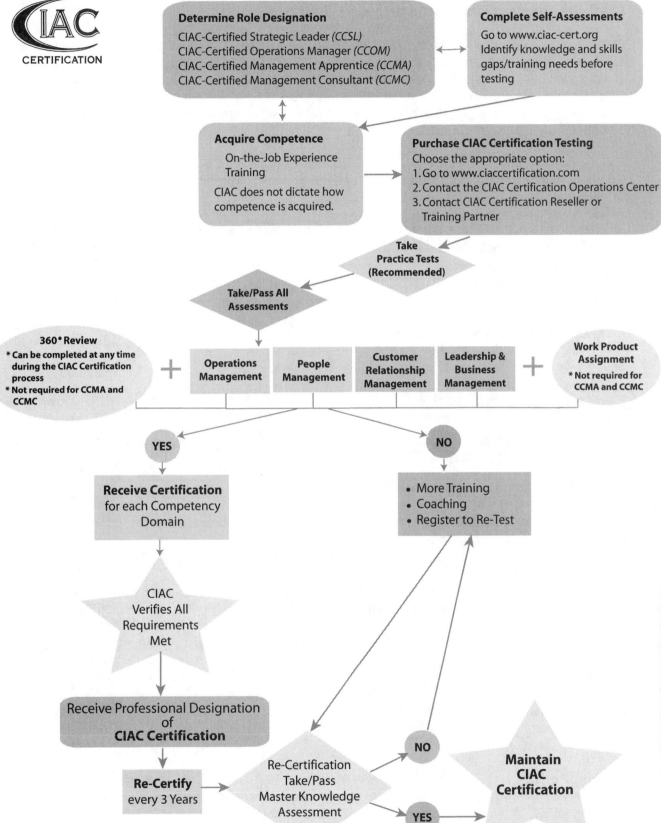

Determine Role Designation

CIAC-Certified Strategic Leader *(CCSL)*
CIAC-Certified Operations Manager *(CCOM)*
CIAC-Certified Management Apprentice *(CCMA)*
CIAC-Certified Management Consultant *(CCMC)*

Complete Self-Assessments

Go to www.ciac-cert.org
Identify knowledge and skills gaps/training needs before testing

Acquire Competence

On-the-Job Experience
Training

CIAC does not dictate how competence is acquired.

Purchase CIAC Certification Testing

Choose the appropriate option:
1. Go to www.ciaccertification.com
2. Contact the CIAC Certification Operations Center
3. Contact CIAC Certification Reseller or Training Partner

Take Practice Tests (Recommended)

Take/Pass All Assessments

360° Review
* Can be completed at any time during the CIAC Certification process
* Not required for CCMA and CCMC

+

| Operations Management | People Management | Customer Relationship Management | Leadership & Business Management |

+

Work Product Assignment
* Not required for CCMA and CCMC

YES

NO

Receive Certification for each Competency Domain

- More Training
- Coaching
- Register to Re-Test

CIAC Verifies All Requirements Met

Receive Professional Designation of CIAC Certification

Re-Certify every 3 Years

Re-Certification Take/Pass Master Knowledge Assessment

NO

YES

Maintain CIAC Certification

PRICING AND PAYMENT

CIAC Certification Management Track Pricing

The pricing shown below is *Standard Published* pricing for CIAC Certification testing for a single purchase of CIAC Certification testing for individuals in the U.S. and Canada. Volume pricing is available for the purchase of three or more CIAC Certification testing packages. Contact the CIAC Certification Operations Center at 888-859-2422 or 615-373-2376 or by email at info@ciac-cert.org for information on volume pricing and other special offers. If testing is purchased through a CIAC Certification Reseller contact this organization for information.

For pricing in countries outside the U.S. and Canada, contact the CIAC Certification Operations Center by phone at 615-373-2376 or email at info@ciac-cert.org for the name of the local CIAC Certification Reseller.

STANDARD PUBLISHED PRICING	Certified Strategic Leader & Certified Operations Manager	Certified Apprentice & Certified Consultant (no Work Product or 360°)
Knowledge Assessments (with Work Product):		
▪ People Management	$280.00	$150.00
▪ Operations Management	$280.00	$150.00
▪ Customer Relationship Management	$280.00	$150.00
▪ Leadership and Business Management	$280.00	$150.00
360° Review with Feedback Report	$ 75.00	NA
TOTAL	**$1195.00**	**$600.00**
Practice Test (for each domain)	$ 15.00 each	$ 15.00 each
Retake a Knowledge Assessment	$ 75.00 each	$ 75.00 each
Retake the 360° Review	$ 75.00 each	NA
Resubmit a Work Product Assignment	$ 75.00 each	NA
Official Transcripts	$ 15.00 each	$ 15.00 each
Master Knowledge Assessment (recertification)	$225.00	$225.00

While CIAC strives to provide high value for the fees charged, pricing is subject to change based on marketplace conditions.

Corporate Pricing

Volume pricing is available for organizations that purchase CIAC Certification for more than three candidates. The amount of discount is based on the total number of certification candidates. For more information about volume pricing contact the CIAC Certification Operations Center at 888-859-2422 or 615-373-2376 or email at info@ciac-cert.org.

Payment

Payment is due at the time of purchase. Methods of Payment are check or credit card. Purchase Orders are accepted from organizations. Contact the CIAC Certification Operations Center by phone at 888-859-2422 or 615-373-2376 or email at info@ciac-cert.org for questions concerning payment.

Refund Policy

CIAC will honor a request for refund due to cancellation of an assessment based on the following policy. A refund request must be submitted in writing by postal mail to the address provided in the front of this Handbook or by email to info@ciac-cert.org. For questions about obtaining a refund or to discuss a refund contact the CIAC Certification Operations Center at 888-859-2422 or 615-373-2376.

- CIAC's General Policy for cancellation of an assessment less than sixty-one (61) days from date of purchase:

   CIAC's first choice for a request to cancel an assessment within sixty (60) days of its original purchase is to grant full credit toward a future purchase on an open account basis. If requested, the full payment amount will be refunded. A credit or payment refund will be issued to the organization. In the event of a full refund, if payment was by check, CIAC's refund will be by check. If payment was by credit card, the card of origin will be credited.

- CIAC's General Policy for cancellation of assessments greater than sixty-one (61) days but less than one (1) year from date of purchase:

   CIAC will issue full credit toward a future purchase on an open account basis per the above crediting procedures. Requests for a payment refund will be charged a 25% processing fee per assessment.

- CIAC's General Policy for cancellations of assessments greater than one year from date of purchase:

   Outside of extenuating circumstances, CIAC will not grant credit for or issue a payment refund for cancellation of an assessment purchased more than one year ago.

- CIAC's General Policy for cancellations of an assessment purchased as part of "a package" regardless of date of purchase:

   CIAC will honor a request to cancel one or a portion of assessments purchased as "a package" by issuing a pro-rated credit on the basis that each of the assessments not cancelled will be calculated at the then prevailing full retail price of a stand-alone assessment. These stand-alone amounts will be deducted from the package price and the difference will be refunded to the originating purchaser less 25% processing fee.

Ineligibility of Refund

In some instances, CIAC will not refund registration fees. These situations include:

- Refund requests made by telephone. Refund requests must be made in writing (email is acceptable).
- Failure to take a scheduled assessment (no show).
- For the 360° Review, after the review instrument has been distributed.
- Transcripts once processed.

REVIEW AND NOTIFICATIONS

Denial and Revocation of CIAC Certification
CIAC Certification will be denied or revoked for any of the following reasons:

- Failure to pass required certification assessments.
- Violation of certification assessment procedures and/or policies.
- Falsification of information.
- Not completing certification requirements within the allowed time (two years from the date the first assessment is taken).
- Failure to meet re-certification requirements.

A candidate may appeal for reconsideration by submitting a written appeal to the CIAC President stating the reason(s) for the request. CIAC will review the appeal and notify the candidate of the resulting decision.

Address Change
All correspondence and assessment scores will be sent to the postal or email address specified in the Candidate Profile. In the event of a change in this information, the candidate can revise his/her contact information by following the instructions to "Edit Profile" in the online registration system. The candidate may also contact the CIAC Certification Operations Center at 888-859-2422 or 615-373-2376 to request a change of mailing or email address. CIAC will issue a confirmation to verify the change of information.

Assessment Date Change (Reschedule)
To change a confirmed assessment date and time, the candidate is required to contact the test center where he/she is registered to test. To change from one test center to another, it will be necessary for the candidate to notify the CIAC Certification Operations Center.

Accommodations for Candidates with Disabilities
CIAC complies with all laws and regulations pertaining to persons with disabilities and makes every reasonable effort to accommodate the needs of disabled or impaired candidates. In order to accommodate the special needs of disabled or impaired candidates, CIAC requests these candidates contact the CIAC Certification Operations Center at 888-859-2422 or 616-373-2376 to discuss the needed accommodations.

Below are a few examples of special needs:
- Candidate requires the services of a test reader because of vision impairment.
- Candidate needs someone to operate the keyboard due to a physical handicap.
- Candidate needs a time extension because of a learning disability.

Candidates with special needs are required to submit a form identifying the type of accommodation requested. In some cases, a physician's name may be required. When approved, CIAC will contact the test center to arrange for the necessary accommodations and/or assistance. CIAC will make every effort to expedite requirements to accommodate disabled candidates. Please note that this process can take up to thirty (30) days after notification to complete.

CIAC Certification Testing

Public Testing Centers

Testing for CIAC Certification is offered at authorized public testing centers. A listing of authorized public testing centers by location is available at www.ciaccertification.com or by calling the CIAC Certification Operations Center at 888-859-2422 or 615-373-2376 or local CIAC Certification Reseller.

Onsite Testing

As an alternative to public testing centers, organizations with multiple candidates can administer CIAC Certification testing onsite. A proctor is required for onsite testing and certain other conditions must be met to ensure a high integrity-testing environment. CIAC will work with the organization's human resources or training department to arrange for onsite testing. Contact the CIAC Certification Operations Center at 888-859-2422 or 615-373-2376 for information about onsite testing.

Testing Center Policies

Test Area Admission - General Policies

- Only individuals actively engaged in CIAC Certification testing are permitted in the testing room. Any other persons accompanying the candidate must wait in the lobby area of the testing center. Unaccompanied children are not allowed at the Test Center.

- Personal items may not be taken into the testing room. This includes bags, purses, hats, briefcases, books, beepers, cell phones, calculators, palm pilots and watches. All personal items will be placed in a secure storage compartment provided by the test center and the candidate will retain the key during the test session. All electrical equipment must be turned off before the item is placed in the storage compartment so as not to disrupt the testing environment. Items too large to be stored in the compartment must be stored off the premises. Candidates must keep their identification with them at all times.

- Tobacco products, food, drink, and chewing gum are not allowed in the testing room.

Before the Test Session

- A proctor will escort the candidate to the testing room.
- The candidate's assessment will be loaded at the designated workstation.
- Study materials or scratch paper cannot be brought into the testing area. The proctor can provide scratch paper if needed.
- Any papers used by the candidate while testing will be collected at the end of the test, including scrap paper.
- If needed, the proctor will provide a calculator upon request.

During the Test Session

- Do not attempt to browse outside of the "testing window" or access the Internet. This will cause automatic submittal of the assessment for scoring.
- Do not click the 'Submit' button until the assessment is completed and ready to be submitted for scoring.
- Three hours is allowed to complete each knowledge assessment. Break time is not built into the time allotted for testing. If a break is necessary, the clock will continue to run, decreasing the amount of time remaining to complete the assessment. If a break is

taken the candidate must sign out/in using the "Sign-in/Sign-out Log". The assessment will be terminated if the candidate leaves the testing room without notifying the proctor. Personal belongings may not be accessed during a break.

Candidate Misconduct

If a candidate engages in misconduct the proctor will request the behavior to cease. If the behavior persists, the candidate will be requested to leave the testing room and the assessment will be terminated. The following behaviors are considered misconduct:

- Giving or receiving assistance of any kind during the assessment.
- Using prohibited aids.
- Attempting to take the test for someone else.
- Attempting to remove scratch paper from the testing room.
- Talking with other candidates during testing.
- Tampering with the operation of the computer or attempting to use it for any function other than taking the test.
- Distracting any other candidate in any way from taking their assessment.

Reasons to Notify the Proctor
- Loss of Internet connection.
- Technical problems with the testing software.
- Need to leave the testing room.
- Disruptive behavior from other test candidates.
- Uncomfortable testing environment.

The proctor cannot answer any questions concerning the assessments.

After Submittal of CIAC Certification Assessment
- Candidate will be prompted to inform the proctor to end the testing session.
- Changes are not allowed once the assessment has been submitted.
- Assessment results will be emailed to candidate's registered email address. The proctor or any other employee of the test center does not have access to test results.
- Test Center computers are for assessment purposes only.

Refer to the CIAC Certification web site www.ciac-cert.org for Frequently Asked Questions and Answers.

About Incoming Calls Management Institute

Incoming Calls Management Institute (ICMI), based in Annapolis, Maryland, offers the most comprehensive educational resources available for call center (contact center, interaction center, help desk) management professionals. ICMI's focus is helping individuals and organizations understand the dynamics of today's customer contact environment in order to improve performance and achieve superior business results. From the world's first seminar on incoming call center management, to the first conference on call center/Internet integration and subsequent research on multichannel integration, ICMI is a recognized global leader. Quality, usability and value have become trademarks of ICMI's award-winning services. ICMI is independent and is not associated with, owned or subsidized by any industry supplier; ICMI's only source of funding is from those who use its services.

ICMI's services include:

- Public and onsite (private) seminars

- Web seminars and e-learning courses

- Certification review seminars and study guides

- Industry studies and research papers

- Consulting services

- Software tools for scheduling and analysis

- Books (including the industry's best-selling book, *Call Center Management on Fast Forward*)

- *QueueTips*, the popular (and free) monthly e-newsletter

- Membership in Incoming Calls Management Institute

- *Call Center Management Review*, the authoritative monthly journal for ICMI members

For more information and to join a network of call center leaders, see www.incoming.com

Incoming Calls Management Institute
Post Office Box 6177
Annapolis, Maryland 21401
410-267-0700 • 800-672-6177
icmi@incoming.com
www.incoming.com

Section 12

Bring This Content to Life in Your Own Organization!

Want to instill the most important principles from this series into the culture and operational dynamics of your organization? What would it be worth to have your entire management team truly working in sync to create services that generate loyalty and create exceptional value?

ICMI's powerful educational seminars provide you with real-world solutions to help you improve performance and achieve better business results. Benefits of bringing one of ICMI's seminars into your organization include:

• Content is based on the experiences and practices of the world's leading call centers.

• Programs are delivered by the industry's top facilitators.

• Content is tailored to your specific environment.

• Courses build a common understanding throughout your organization.

• ICMI's first-hand knowledge of the call center environment eliminates misconceptions and fads from the seminar content.

• You are guaranteed an objective, educational experience, since ICMI is independent and is not associated with, owned or subsidized by any industry supplier.

• Learning occurs in a stimulating atmosphere that is both productive and fun!

Visit www.incoming.com for a current listing of Web-based, public and in-house seminars. Or contact ICMI at 410-267-0700, or icmi@incoming.com

ICMI's Mission

Incoming Calls Management Institute (ICMI) exists solely to advance the call center profession by promoting managerial excellence. We are dedicated to fostering the development of a new breed of call center management professionals – individuals with the vision, expertise, and commitment necessary to enable their respective organizations to thrive in an era of fast-changing, networked economies, global competition and heightened customer expectations.

Section 12

Order Form

QTY.	Item	Price	Total
	ICMI Handbook and Study Guide Series		
	Module 1: People Management***	$199.00	
	Module 2: Operations Management***	$199.00	
	Module 3: Customer Relationship Management***	$199.00	
	Module 4: Leadership and Business Management***	$199.00	
	Call Center Management On Fast Forward: Succeeding In Today's Dynamic Inbound Environment		
	Book**	$34.95	
	Cassette set, 6 tapes**	$49.95	
	Book and Cassette tape set bundle***	$69.95	
	Call Center Technology Demystified: The No-Nonsense Guide to Bridging Customer Contact Technology, Operations and Strategy**	$39.95	
	Topical Books: The Best of *Call Center Management Review*		
	Call Center Recruiting and New Hire Training*	$16.95	
	Call Center Forecasting and Scheduling*	$16.95	
	Call Center Agent Motivation and Compensation*	$16.95	
	Call Center Agent Retention and Turnover*	$16.95	
	Industry Studies		
	Monitoring Study Final Report II (published 2002)*	$99.00	
	Multichannel Call Center Study (published 2001)*	$99.00	
	Agent Staffing and Retention Study (published 2000)*	$79.00	
	Forms Books		
	Call Center Sample Monitoring Forms*	$49.95	
	Call Center Sample Customer Satisfaction Forms Book*	$49.95	
	Software		
	QueueView: A Staffing Calculator – CD ROM*	$49.00	
	Easy Start™ Call Center Scheduler Software – CD-ROM*	$299.00	
	Call Center Manager's Jump-Start Toolkit****	$279.00	
	Call Center Humor: The Best of *Call Center Management Review* Volume 3*	$9.95	
	The Call Centertainment Book*	$8.95	
	Shipping & Handling @ $5.00 per US shipment, plus .50¢ per* item, $1.00 per** item, $2.00 per*** item and $3.00 per**** item. Additional charges apply to shipments outside the US.		
	Tax (5% MD residents, 7% GST Canadian residents)		
	TOTAL (US dollars)		

Please contact us for quantity discounts

For more information on our products, please visit **www.incoming.com**

Order Form

❏ Please send me a free issue of *Call Center Management Review* (ICMI's journal for members) and information on ICMI's publications, services and membership.

Please ship my order and/or information to:

Name _____

Title _____

Industry _____

Company _____

Address _____

City _____ State _____ Postal Code _____

Telephone (   ) _____

Fax (   ) _____

Email _____

Method of Payment (if applicable)

❏ Check enclosed (Make payable to ICMI Inc.; U.S. Dollars only)

❏ Charge to: ❏ American Express   ❏ MasterCard   ❏ Visa

Account No. _____

Expiration Date _____

Name on Card _____

Fax order to:	410-267-0962
call us at:	800-672-6177
	410-267-0700
order online at:	www.incoming.com
or mail order to:	ICMI Inc.
	P.O. Box 6177, Annapolis, MD 21401

About the Authors

Brad Cleveland is President and CEO of Annapolis, Maryland based Incoming Calls Management Institute. Recognized for his pioneering work in call center management, he has advised organizations ranging from small start-ups to national governments and multinational corporations, and has delivered keynotes and seminars in over 25 countries. Brad has appeared in a wide range of media, including *The Washington Post, Wall Street Journal,* and on PBS, CNBC and Knowledge TV. His critically-acclaimed book, *Call Center Management on Fast Forward: Succeeding in Today's Dynamic Inbound Environment,* co-authored with journalist Julia Mayben, is used by call center managers around the world.

Debbie Harne is Director of Educational Services for ICMI, and spearheaded the launch of ICMI Membership, a network of management professionals from over 40 countries. With a background in training and education, Debbie has been instrumental in developing ICMI's technology-based educational services, and has responsibilities for the quality and direction of ICMI's instructor-led and Web-based management seminars. She is proficient in instructional design and ensuring the transfer of training to the job, and has customized ICMI educational services for innovative, in-house study programs in a variety of companies.

How to Contact the Authors

Do you have suggestions for future editions? Comments? Feedback? Please contact us!

Incoming Calls Management Institute
Post Office Box 6177
Annapolis, Maryland 21401
410-267-0700 • 800-672-6177
icmi@incoming.com
www.incoming.com
Brad Cleveland, direct: bradc@incoming.com
Debbie Harne, direct: debbieh@incoming.com

Section 12